FEDERAL

TAX RESEARCH

GUIDE TO

MATERIALS AND TECHNIQUES

By

GAIL LEVIN RICHMOND

Professor and Associate Dean
Nova Southeastern University Shepard Broad Law Center

SIXTH EDITION

UNIVERSITY TEXTBOOK SERIES

New York, New York

FOUNDATION PRESS

2002

COPYRIGHT © 1990, 1997 FOUNDATION PRESS
COPYRIGHT © 2002 By FOUNDATION PRESS
        395 Hudson Street
        New York, NY 10014
        Phone Toll Free 1–877–888–1330
        Fax (212) 367–6799
        fdpress.com

ISBN 1–58778–378–9

 TEXT IS PRINTED ON 10% POST CONSUMER RECYCLED PAPER

To

Henry and Amy Richmond

and

Herbert and Sylvia Levin

PREFACE

In 1975 I first offered a Tax Practice Seminar involving current issues in taxation. Students selected issues and presented their findings as ruling requests, audit protest memoranda, and statements before congressional committees. After being deluged with requests for library tours, I consulted the standard legal research texts to compile readings describing the available materials. Much to my surprise, I discovered those texts devoted little, if any, space to materials commonly used for tax research. This text is an outgrowth of my 1975 library tours.

Research techniques are highly personalized. While the format of this text reflects my own preferences, it can be adapted to almost any variation the user may devise. Although I use it most frequently as an instructional guide for students, I know of many practitioners who have used it as an aid to finding materials.

The problems included at the end of most chapters cover both historical materials and fairly recent items. Both types have value as teaching tools. Most problems involving recent law can be solved using electronic sources; those problems enhance or introduce online and CD-ROM research skills. Historical materials appear for a different reason. Because many electronic databases omit coverage of older materials, those problems force users to consult print or microform materials. Because electronic searches may involve usage fees, users who have access to print materials should be able to use them in situations where such use is cost effective.

Every new edition benefits from suggestions made by numerous tax professors, practitioners, and librarians. Library staff members at my own institution are particularly generous with their time and with their budget allocations. I could not describe so many items were they not committed to maintaining an excellent tax collection.

I wish to acknowledge the assistance of Catherine Antonakos and Deborah Brown, who deterred visitors to my office during this revision's final weeks. My assistant, Bernadette Baugh, and a student assistant, Eva Ugarte, assisted with the Table of Contents and Index. My research assistant, Janet Buchanan, provided invaluable assistance at various stages in this revision.

GAIL LEVIN RICHMOND

Fort Lauderdale, Florida
July 2002

Summary of Contents

Page

Preface v

Part One. Introduction to Tax Research 1
Chapter 1. Overview 2
Chapter 2. Sources of Law 7
Chapter 3. Research Process 11

Part Two. Primary Sources: Legislative 29
Chapter 4. Constitution 30
Chapter 5. Statutes 36
Chapter 6. Legislative Histories 61
Chapter 7. Treaties and Other International Material 84

Part Three. Primary Sources: Administrative 106
Chapter 8. Treasury Regulations 107
Chapter 9. Internal Revenue Service Documents 135

Part Four. Primary Sources: Judicial 172
Chapter 10. Judicial Reports 173

Part Five. Secondary Sources 195
Chapter 11. Citators 196
Chapter 12. Looseleaf Services, Encyclopedias, and Treatises 220
Chapter 13. Legal Periodicals 240
Chapter 14. Form Books and Model Language 255
Chapter 15. Newsletters 259

Part Six. Collections of Primary Source Materials 267
Chapter 16. Print Materials 268
Chapter 17. Microforms 284
Chapter 18. CD-ROM 286
Chapter 19. Online Legal Research 302

Part Seven. Appendixes 332
Appendix A. Commonly Used Abbreviations 333
Appendix B. Alternate Citation Forms 340
Appendix C. Potential Research Errors 342
Appendix D. Bibliography 344
Appendix E. Publishers of Publications Discussed in Text 350
Appendix F. Commonly Owned Publishers 356

Index 357

TABLE OF CONTENTS

Page

Preface V

PART ONE. INTRODUCTION TO TAX RESEARCH 1

Chapter 1. Overview 2
  A. Introduction 2
  B. External Factors Affecting Research 3
  C. Format of This Text 3
    1. Listing and Describing Sources 3
    2. Problem Assignments 4
    3. Illustrations and Tables 4
    4. Bold Face and Arrows 4
    5. Citation Format 5
    6. Appendixes 5

Chapter 2. Sources of Law 7
  A. Primary and Secondary Sources 7
  B. Hierarchy of Authority 7
    1. Precedential and Persuasive Authority 8
    2. Substantial Authority 8
  C. Problems 10

Chapter 3. Research Process 11
  A. Research Goals 11
  B. Research Methodology 12
  C. Print Versus Electronic Research 13
    1. Availability of Materials 13
    2. Updating Frequency 14
    3. Type of Search 14
    4. Cost 16
    5. Need for Original Page Citations 17
  D. Summary 17
  E. Illustrative Problem 17
  F. Additional Problems 27

PART TWO. PRIMARY SOURCES: LEGISLATIVE 29

Chapter 4. Constitution 30
  A. Taxing Power 30
  B. Constitutional Litigation 31
    1. Items Challenged 31
    2. Supreme Court Litigation Versus Constitutional Litigation 31
  C. Research Process 33
  D. Problems 33

Page

Chapter 5. Statutes 36
  A. Introduction 36
  B. Functions of Statutes 36
  C. Statutory Scheme 36
    1. Internal Revenue Code 36
    2. Other Statutes 38
    3. "Legislative" Pronouncements from the Executive Branch 39
  D. Terminology 39
    1. Bills and Acts 39
    2. Public Law Names and Numbers 40
    3. Revenue Acts and Other Relevant Acts 40
    4. Codified and Uncodified Provisions 41
    5. Section Numbers 43
    6. Enactment Date, Effective Date, and Sunset Date 43
  E. Scope and Definitions 45
    1. Scope of Provisions 45
    2. Definitions 45
  F. Locating Current, Repealed, and Pending Legislation 46
    1. Current Code—Codifications 47
    2. Individual Acts 48
    3. Previous Law 49
    4. Pending Legislation 49
    5. Potential Legislation 51
  G. Citators for Statutes 51
  H. Interpreting Statutory Language 52
    1. Sources for Interpreting Statutes 52
    2. Using Statutory Language 52
    3. Selected Maxims of Construction 54
  I. Problems 56

Chapter 6. Legislative Histories 61
  A. Introduction 61
  B. Groups Involved in Legislation 61
    1. Congressional Committees 61
    2. Congressional Support Entities 62
    3. The Executive Branch 62
    4. Other Groups 63
  C. Legislative Process 63
    1. Introduction of Bill 64
    2. Referral to Committee and Committee Action 64
    3. House and Senate Floor Debate 64
    4. Conference Committee Action 65
    5. Floor Action on Conference Report 65
    6. Correcting Drafting Errors 65
    7. Presidential Action 66
  D. Locating Legislative History Documents: Citations and Text 67
    1. Statements on the Floor of Congress 67
    2. Committee Hearings 69

Page

    3. Tax-Writing Committee Reports 70
    4. Other Congressional Reports 72
    5. Executive Branch Documents 72
  E. Unenacted Bills 73
  F. Using Legislative History in Statutory Interpretation 73
    1. In Lieu of Administrative Interpretations 73
    2. Tracing Changes in Statutory Language 74
  G. Judicial Deference 76
  H. Problems 78

Chapter 7. Treaties and Other International Material 84
  A. Introduction 84
  B. Functions of Treaties 84
  C. Relationship of Treaties and Statutes 85
    1. Authority for Treaties 85
    2. Conflict Between Treaties and Statutes 85
  D. Treaty Terminology 86
  E. Treaty Numbering Systems 86
  F. Treaty History Documents 87
  G. Locating Treaties and Their Histories 95
    1. United States Government Sources 95
    2. Online Subscription Services 96
    3. Other Print and Electronic Sources 96
  H. Pending Treaties 99
  I. Citators for Treaties 99
  J. Interpreting Treaties 99
    1. Administrative Interpretations 99
    2. Judicial Interpretations 100
  K. OECD and WTO 101
    1. OECD 101
    2. WTO 101
  L. Other International Material 102
    1. General Information 102
    2. Material in Other Languages 102
    3. Treaties with Native American Tribes 102
  M. Problems 102

PART THREE. PRIMARY SOURCES: ADMINISTRATIVE 106

Chapter 8. Treasury Regulations 107
  A. Introduction 107
  B. Functions of Regulations 107
  C. Regulatory Scheme 107
    1. Treasury Regulations 107
    2. Other Regulations 108
  D. Regulations Numbering System 108
    1. Regulations Subdivisions 108
    2. Regulations Numbering Scheme 108

Page

3. Importance of Regulations Prefixes 110
4. Relationship of Code Subdivisions to Regulations Subdivisions .. 110
5. Letters in Section Numbering 111
E. Regulatory Authority 111
1. Entities Involved 111
2. Limitations on Authority 112
F. Terminology 115
1. Proposed, Temporary, and Final Regulations 115
2. Interpretive and Legislative Regulations 116
3. Project Numbers and Notices of Proposed Rulemaking 116
4. Treasury Decisions 117
5. Preambles and Texts of Regulations 118
6. Filing Date, Effective Date, and Sunset Date 118
7. Semiannual Agenda and Priority Guidance Plan 119
G. Scope and Definitions 119
1. Scope of Provisions 119
2. Definitions 119
H. Regulatory Process 119
1. IRS and Treasury 119
2. Congress 120
I. Locating Regulations Documents 121
1. Semiannual Agenda and Priority Guidance Plan 121
2. Proposed Regulations 123
3. Temporary and Final Regulations 124
4. Earlier Versions of Regulations 126
5. Preambles 128
6. Hearings Transcripts and Other Taxpayer Comments 128
J. Citators for Regulations 129
K. Judicial Deference 130
L. Problems 132

Chapter 9. Internal Revenue Service Documents 135
A. Introduction 135
B. Types of IRS Documents 135
1. Means of Publication 135
2. Initial Audience 136
3. Status as Precedent or Substantial Authority 136
C. Officially Published IRS Documents 136
1. Revenue Rulings 136
2. Revenue Procedures and Procedural Rules 138
3. Notices 139
4. Announcements 140
5. Other Documents Published in the Internal Revenue Bulletin ... 141
6. Other IRS Document 142
D. Publicly Released IRS Documents 142
1. Disclosure Legislation and Litigation 142
2. Numbering System 143

	Page
3. Private Letter Rulings	144
4. Determination Letters	144
5. Technical Advice Memoranda	144
6. Actions on Decisions	145
7. General Counsel Memoranda	146
8. Field Service Advice; Strategic Advice Memoranda	146
9. Technical Expedited Advice Memoranda	146
10. Service Center Advice	147
11. IRS Legal Memoranda	147
12. Chief Counsel Bulletins	147
13. Litigation Guideline Memoranda	148
14. Industry Specialization Program; Market Segment Specialization Papers; Market Segment Understandings	148
15. Chief Counsel Notices	149
16. IRS Information Letters	149
17. IRS Compliance Officer Memoranda	149
18. IRS Technical Assistance	150
19. Internal Revenue Manual	150
20. Other Documents	150
E. Unreleased Documents	152
1. Advance Pricing Agreements	152
2. Closing Agreements	152
3. Technical Assistance	152
F. Locating IRS Documents	152
1. Officially Published Documents in Internal Revenue Bulletin	152
2. Other Officially Published Documents	157
3. Publicly Released Documents	157
G. Uniform Issue List	159
H. Citators for IRS Documents	159
I. Judicial Deference	162
1. Officially Published Documents	162
2. Other IRS Documents	163
3. IRS Litigating Positions	164
J. Problems	165
PART FOUR. PRIMARY SOURCES: JUDICIAL	172
Chapter 10. Judicial Reports	173
A. Introduction	173
B. Court Organization	173
1. Trial Courts	173
2. Courts of Appeals	176
3. Supreme Court	178
C. Locating Decisions	178
1. Finding Lists	178
2. Locating Citations	178
3. Digests of Decisions	180
4. Texts of Decisions	180

Page

5. Tax-Oriented Case Reporter Services 182
6. Parallel Citations 184
D. Pending Litigation, Briefs, and Petitions 184
E. Citators for Decisions 185
F. Evaluating Decisions 186
  1. In General 186
  2. Unpublished Opinions 187
  3. Statements Regarding Deference 187
G. Problems 188

PART FIVE. SECONDARY SOURCES 195

Chapter 11. Citators 196
A. Introduction 196
B. Terminology 196
C. Citator Format and Coverage 196
  1. Arrangement 197
  2. Syllabus Number and Judicial Commentary 198
  3. Miscellaneous Differences 198
D. Shepard's Citations; Federal Tax Citator 198
  1. Constitution, Statutes, and Treaties 199
  2. Regulations and IRS Documents 200
  3. Judicial Decisions 201
E. RIA Citator 202
  1. Constitution, Statutes, and Treaties 203
  2. Regulations and IRS Documents 203
  3. Judicial Decisions 203
F. CCH Standard Federal Tax Reporter—Citator 204
  1. Constitution, Statutes, and Treaties 204
  2. Regulations and IRS Documents 205
  3. Judicial Decisions 205
G. West's KeyCite 206
  1. Constitution, Statutes, and Treaties 206
  2. Regulations and IRS Documents 207
  3. Judicial Decisions 207
H. Illustrations 207
I. Updating Services in Lieu of Citators 218
J. Problems 219

Chapter 12. Looseleaf Services, Encyclopedias, and Treatises 220
A. Code Section Arrangement 220
  1. Standard Federal Tax Reporter 221
  2. United States Tax Reporter—Income Taxes 227
B. Subject Arrangement: Multiple Topics 230
  1. Federal Tax Coordinator 2d 231
  2. Tax Management Portfolios 233
  3. Mertens, Law of Federal Income Taxation 234
  4. Rabkin & Johnson, Federal Income, Gift and Estate Taxation ... 236

Page

   C. Subject Arrangement: Limited Scope 238
   D. Problems 239

Chapter 13. Legal Periodicals 240
   A. Introduction 240
   B. Categorizing Periodicals 240
   C. Citations to Periodicals 241
      1. General Legal Periodicals Indexes 242
      2. Tax-Oriented Periodicals Indexes 244
      3. Other Periodicals Indexes 245
      4. Looseleaf Services 246
      5. Newsletters 246
      6. Citators 246
      7. Miscellaneous Sources 247
      8. Digests 247
   D. Texts of Periodicals 248
      1. Print 248
      2. Online 248
      3. CD-ROM 249
      4. Microform 249
   E. Citators for Articles 250
   F. Problems 250

Chapter 14. Form Books and Model Language 255
   A. Using Forms, Checklists, and Model Language 255
   B. Form Books Available 256
   C. Finding Forms and Other Documents 256
   D. Publication Format for Forms 257
   E. Problems 258

Chapter 15. Newsletters 259
   A. Introduction 259
   B. Categorizing Newsletters 259
      1. Frequency of Publication 259
      2. Subject Matter 260
      3. Relation to Looseleaf Services 260
      4. Publication Format 260
   C. Descriptions of Newsletters 260
      1. Daily Tax Report; Tax Management Weekly Report 261
      2. Daily Tax Highlights & Documents; Tax Notes 262
      3. Federal Tax Day News and Documents; Federal Tax Weekly 264
      4. Daily Tax Bulletin; Federal Tax Bulletin 265

PART SIX. COLLECTIONS OF PRIMARY SOURCE MATERIALS 267

Chapter 16. Print Materials 268
   A. Treasury and IRS Materials 268

Page

1. Internal Revenue Bulletin; Cumulative Bulletin;
   Bulletin Index-Digest System 268
2. U.S. Code Congressional & Administrative
   News—Federal Tax Regulations 273
3. Cumulative Changes 273
B. Legislative and Administrative History Materials 273
1. Internal Revenue Acts—Text and Legislative History;
   U.S. Code Congressional & Administrative News—Internal
   Revenue Code 273
2. Primary Sources 274
3. Cumulative Changes 274
4. Barton's Federal Tax Laws Correlated 276
5. Seidman's Legislative History of Federal Income
   and Excess Profits Tax Laws 279
6. The Internal Revenue Acts of the United States:
   1909-1950; 1950-1972; 1973- 280
7. Legislative History of the Internal Revenue Code of 1954 281
8. Eldridge, The United States Internal Revenue System 283
9. Cumulative Bulletin 283

Chapter 17. Microforms 284
A. Advantages and Disadvantages 284
B. Format 285
C. Available Materials 285

Chapter 18. CD-ROM 286
A. Advantages and Disadvantages 286
B. Search Strategies 287
1. Similarity to Searching Print Materials 287
2. Search Strategies Unique to Electronic Materials 287
3. Differences Between CD-ROM and Online Services 288
C. Representative Materials 288
1. Tax Analysts 288
2. Research Institute of America 292
3. Bureau of National Affairs 295
4. Commerce Clearing House 298
5. Kleinrock 299
6. LexisNexis 300
7. Warren, Gorham & Lamont 300
8. Clark Boardman Callahan 301
9. Other Publishers 301
D. Problems 301

Chapter 19. Online Legal Research 302
A. Introduction 302
B. Advantages and Disadvantages 302
C. Available Materials 303
D. Online Subscription Services—General Focus 303

Page

    1. LexisNexis 304
    2. Westlaw 308
    3. Loislaw 311
    4. Versuslaw 314
  E. Online Subscription Services—Tax Focus 317
    1. Tax Research NetWork 317
    2. TaxExpert Online 320
    3. Checkpoint 322
    4. TaxBase 322
    5. TaxCore 322
  F. Other Online Services 323
    1. Government Sites 323
    2. Other Sites 327
  G. Using Search Engines 327
    1. Search Engines, Directories, and Portals 328
    2. Sample Search 329
  H. Problems 331

PART SEVEN. APPENDIXES 332

Appendix A. Commonly Used Abbreviations 333
Appendix B. Alternate Citation Forms 340
Appendix C. Potential Research Errors 342
Appendix D. Bibliography 344
Appendix E. Publishers of Publications Discussed in Text 350
Appendix F. Commonly Owned Publishers 356

INDEX 357

FEDERAL

TAX RESEARCH

GUIDE TO

MATERIALS AND TECHNIQUES

SIXTH EDITION

PART ONE

INTRODUCTION TO TAX RESEARCH

Chapter 1. Overview

Chapter 2. Sources of Law

Chapter 3. Research Process

CHAPTER 1. OVERVIEW

SECTION A. INTRODUCTION

This text describes primary and secondary sources of federal tax law and presents information about services containing these sources. It also discusses evaluating and updating the results of your research.

Many attorneys believe federal tax research has nothing in common with traditional legal research methods,[1] but that belief is erroneous. You can solve federal tax research problems using techniques mastered in a basic legal research course, and you can often use traditional materials.[2]

Even if you can use traditional methods and sources, you will probably prefer using materials that focus on taxation. Most library collections contain such materials but differ in how they shelve them. Many libraries shelve them together in a "tax alcove." Other libraries group some tax-oriented materials (e.g., looseleaf services, treatises, and legislative histories) together and shelve others (e.g., tax-oriented periodicals) in the general collection. Even if dispersed throughout the collection, these materials are no more difficult to locate or use than are traditional research tools.

Electronic research follows a similar pattern. You can select from general services (e.g., Westlaw) that include tax libraries, or you can use services (e.g., Tax Research NetWork and OnPoint) that focus on tax materials.

Because so many research tools are available, a library or database may lack a source discussed in this text or may contain materials omitted here.

---

[1] Gail Levin Richmond, *Research Tools for Federal Taxation*, 2 LEGAL REFERENCE SERVICES Q., Spring 1982, at 25, discusses this phenomenon. See also Carol A. Roehrenbeck & Gail Levin Richmond, *Three Researchers in Search of an Alcove: A Play in Six Acts*, 84 LAW LIBR. J. 13 (1992).

[2] Because I assume users have at least minimal familiarity with traditional legal research tools, this text devotes relatively little space to such items. In some instances, particularly if a library lacks a tax-oriented tool, you may need to consult traditional materials. To assist you in locating nontax materials, I include references to the appropriate chapters in J. MYRON JACOBSTEIN, ROY M. MERSKY & DONALD J. DUNN, FUNDAMENTALS OF LEGAL RESEARCH (8th ed. 2002) [cited throughout as Fundamentals of Legal Research].

Because it focuses on the types of materials available, this text should help you conduct successful tax research in virtually any law library or electronic resource.[3]

SECTION B. EXTERNAL FACTORS AFFECTING RESEARCH

Three phenomena affect the research process: the proliferation of available sources; technological change; and publishing industry consolidation.

The number of available materials continually expands. Since this text's last edition, for example, the Internal Revenue Service began issuing additional types of guidance. Litigation resulted in the release of other, previously unavailable, items. In addition, the Tax Court began public release of Summary Opinions.

Technology, particularly CD-ROM materials and online sites, enhances the research process by covering numerous sources and allowing for easy database searching. Online sites provide both subscription and free access to materials. The federal government has been quite active in providing free online access to primary source materials.

Finally, the publishing industry continues to consolidate. Several once-independent companies are now commonly owned.[4] Some publications described in prior editions have been renamed, eliminated, or limited to electronic format. Because I do not know when this process will end, I focus on general tax research principles. You can adapt your research strategy to the appearance of new materials and the disappearance of old ones.

SECTION C. FORMAT OF THIS TEXT

1. Listing and Describing Sources

Because several research tools contain more than one type of authority, I could discuss them in multiple sections of this text. In most instances, I

---

[3] See Gail Levin Richmond, *Federal Tax Locator: Basic Tax Library*, COMMUNITY TAX L. REP., Fall/Winter 2001, at 11; Katherine T. Pratt, *Federal Tax Sources Recommended for Law School Libraries*, 87 LAW LIBR. J. 387 (1995); Louis F. Lobenhofer, *Tax Law Libraries for Small and Medium-Sized Firms*, PRAC. TAX LAW., Fall 1988, at 17, and Winter 1989, at 31.

[4] Appendix F lists commonly owned publishers.

opted to describe each tool once, generally in Parts Five and Six.[5] Parts Two through Four discuss the available primary sources, list research tools containing these sources, and provide cross-references to descriptions in Parts Five and Six. This format avoids unnecessary repetition and allows you to gain familiarity with all the features of a particular tool in one place.

A caveat is in order. Neither my descriptions nor the illustrations can substitute for the information contained in the user's guide to each service. This is particularly important for online and CD-ROM services, which vary in their search command structures and continually change both coverage dates and sources included. Pathfinders and similar library-prepared reference materials are also useful guides.

2. Problem Assignments

Most chapters include a series of short problems. Locating the primary source materials you need for solving problems in Parts One through Four generally requires using materials described in Parts Five and Six. You should consult those descriptions on an as-needed basis. Although you can easily solve many of the problems using electronic sources, you may need to use print and microform materials when you search for older items.

3. Illustrations and Tables

Illustrations appear throughout this text. Because I obtained many of them through scanning or using the print screen function, the font or text size may differ slightly from a publisher's original version. The final product is close to the original and should not inconvenience or confuse researchers.

Illustrations are designed to show primary and secondary source material as it appears in the source from which it is excerpted. Tables compile useful information about particular topics.

Because I refer to some illustrations and tables in more than one chapter, I numbered them by chapter (e.g., Illustration 3-1; Table 5-3) to make them easier to locate.

4. Bold Face and Arrows

To call your attention to terms discussed in this text, I put them in bold face type. Arrows (➔) indicate discussion relating to an illustration or table.

---

[5] I describe a source in Parts Two through Four if it used for a single purpose. American Federal Tax Reports, for example, is discussed in Chapter 10.

5. Citation Format

Legal citation format is prescribed in a variety of sources, including TaxCite, The Bluebook, and the ALWD Citation Manual.[6] These sources differ in their treatment of various items, and their citation format often differs from that used by the material's original publisher. Differences are particularly notable for IRS material. For example, TaxCite uses P.L.R. to cite private letter rulings (e.g., P.L.R. 2001-50-019); The Bluebook uses Priv. Ltr. Rul. (e.g., Priv. Ltr. Rul. 2001-50-019). Although both hyphenate the ruling numbers, the IRS itself does not use hyphens and is likely to use PLR rather than the other identifiers. If you search for 200150019, you can easily find it online; if you search for 2001-50-019, you are less likely to be successful.

Because citation manuals, law reviews, and courts use different citation formats, Appendix B includes several variations for selected primary sources. Before submitting your research, remember to format each citation in the style your recipient mandates.

Note that I did not italicize signals (such as "see" and "compare") or Latin terms (such as "i.e." and "e.g.") in text or footnotes. Unless they are part of a footnote citation, I also eliminated italicization for the names of primary and secondary source materials and other research tools (such as United States Code, OneDisc, and Westlaw). I made this decision primarily to enhance readability. It does not reflect a preference for a particular citation system.

6. Appendixes

Part Seven contains six Appendixes:

- Appendix A   Commonly Used Abbreviations

- Appendix B   Alternate Citation Forms

---

[6] TAXCITE: A FEDERAL TAX CITATION AND REFERENCE MANUAL (1995) (compiled by The Virginia Tax Review, Tax Law Review, and the ABA Section of Taxation; the ABA group was assisted by student editors of The Tax Lawyer); THE BLUEBOOK: A UNIFORM SYSTEM OF CITATION (17th ed. 2000) (compiled by the editors of the Columbia Law Review, Harvard Law Review, University of Pennsylvania Law Review, and The Yale Law Journal); ALWD CITATION MANUAL: A PROFESSIONAL SYSTEM OF CITATION (2000) (compiled by the Association of Legal Writing Directors and Darby Dickerson). Although the initial ALWD Citation Manual did not cover taxation, the compilers announced plans to add tax citations in future editions and on their online site (http://www.alwd.org). The second edition is planned for 2003.

- Appendix C   Potential Research Errors

- Appendix D   Bibliography

- Appendix E   Publishers of Publications Described in Text

- Appendix F   Commonly Owned Publishers

CHAPTER 2. SOURCES OF LAW

The appropriate starting place for tax research depends on the nature of the problem and your familiarity with the subject matter. While many research efforts begin with the relevant statutory provisions, others start with explanatory materials. The appropriate ending place depends on the type of problem and the number of sources you need to consult before resolving the issues raised.

At various points between the start and finish, most research efforts involve several types of authority. These types can be described as primary or secondary; within a category such as primary authority, some sources carry more weight than do others. Sections A and B discuss these concepts.

SECTION A. PRIMARY AND SECONDARY SOURCES

Research tools include primary and secondary sources of law. **Primary sources** emanate from a branch of government: legislative; executive (including administrative); or judicial. Primary sources include the Constitution, statutes, treaties, legislative histories,[7] Treasury regulations, Internal Revenue Service (IRS) documents, and judicial decisions. **Secondary sources**—including treatises, looseleaf services, and articles—explain (and sometimes criticize) these primary authorities. Primary sources are discussed in Parts Two through Four; Parts Five and Six cover secondary sources and collections of primary source documents.

SECTION B. HIERARCHY OF AUTHORITY

Primary sources of law are more authoritative than are secondary sources, and some primary authorities carry more weight than do others. The value of a particular authority varies depending upon the body reviewing it and

---

[7] This text describes legislative histories in the materials on primary sources for several reasons: they emanate from a branch of government; the IRS considers them authority for avoiding the substantial understatement penalty described later in this chapter; and you would consult them immediately after reading statutory text in many research efforts. Nevertheless, many legislative history documents are considered secondary sources.

the purpose for which it is being submitted. The following subsections, covering precedential authority and substantial authority, illustrate these distinctions.

1. Precedential and Persuasive Authority

The Treasury Department and IRS recognize a hierarchy of sources. Courts also value some authorities more than others. Certain holdings constitute **binding precedent**, which must be followed. Others are considered merely **persuasive** and receive little, if any, deference. Secondary sources fall into the latter category, but so do many primary sources. For example, the IRS will follow a Supreme Court decision in its dealings with other taxpayers. It may, however, choose to ignore an adverse lower court opinion and continue litigating a particular issue.[8]

An authority's status as precedential requires more than its being issued by a particular court or agency. The form of issuance is also relevant. In some instances, for example, the IRS is not bound by its own pronouncements. Although it issues both officially published revenue rulings and privately published letter rulings, third parties with comparable facts may rely only on the revenue rulings. In like manner, a court may refuse to treat as precedential an opinion issued under a "no publication" rule. These limitations are discussed further in Parts Three and Four, which cover administrative and judicial sources.

2. Substantial Authority

An authority may have value even if the IRS rejects it. First, the Service might be incorrect. A court (perhaps even the Supreme Court) may rely on the particular authority in rendering its decision. Second, the item relied upon may shield the taxpayer from the Code section 6662(b)(2) penalty for substantial understatement of income tax liability.

Section 6662(d)(2)(B)(i) waives this 20 percent penalty if the taxpayer has **substantial authority** for a position. This determination requires that the taxpayer's position be backed by recognized authority and that the authority be substantial.[9]

---

[8] See, e.g., Rev. Rul. 95-16, 1995-1 C.B. 9, in which the IRS announced it would stop litigating an issue it had lost in four appellate courts and the Tax Court. IRS announcements concerning its litigation plans are discussed in Chapters 9 and 10.

[9] The question of whether authority is substantial might arise in a tax ethics or tax practice and procedure course.

Treasury regulations list the following items as authority:[10]

• applicable provisions of the Internal Revenue Code and other statutory provisions;

• proposed, temporary and final regulations construing such statutes;

• revenue rulings and revenue procedures;

• tax treaties and regulations thereunder, and Treasury Department and other official explanations of such treaties;

• court cases;

• congressional intent as reflected in committee reports, joint explanatory statements of managers included in conference committee reports, and floor statements made prior to enactment by one of a bill's managers;

• General Explanations of tax legislation prepared by the Joint Committee on Taxation (the Blue Book);

• private letter rulings and technical advice memoranda issued after October 31, 1976;

• actions on decisions and general counsel memoranda issued after March 12, 1981 (as well as general counsel memoranda published in pre-1955 volumes of the Cumulative Bulletin);

• Internal Revenue Service information or press releases; and

• notices, announcements and other administrative pronouncements published by the Service in the Internal Revenue Bulletin.

Conclusions reached in treatises or other legal periodicals and opinions rendered by tax professionals do not constitute authority for avoiding this penalty. In addition, the regulation provides rules by which overruled and reversed items lose their status as authority.

---

[10] Treas. Reg. § 1.6662-4(d)(3)(iii). Taxpayers can also avoid this penalty by adequately disclosing the relevant facts if there is a reasonable basis for the tax treatment claimed. I.R.C. § 6662(d)(2)(B)(ii). The section 6662 regulations also constitute authority for avoiding the penalty imposed on tax return preparers for taking a position that does not have a realistic possibility of being sustained on the merits. See I.R.C. § 6694(a); Treas. Reg. § 1.6694-2(b).

SECTION C. PROBLEMS

Researchers who are unfamiliar with specialized court reporters or IRS documents can find these materials online. Westlaw citations are provided for the IRS documents in problem 3; you can also locate them on LexisNexis and other online services. IRS documents are discussed in Chapter 9.[11]

1. Did the taxpayer establish substantial authority? If there was an appeal, did the result change?

    a. Misle v. Commissioner, 80 T.C.M. (CCH) 518 (2000)

    b. Martens v. Commissioner, 79 T.C.M. (CCH) 1483 (2000)

    c. In re CM Holdings, Inc. (Internal Revenue Service v. CM Holdings, Inc.), 254 B.R. 578 (D. Del. 2000)

2. What type of pronouncement constituted substantial authority?

    a. Burditt v. Commissioner, 77 T.C.M. (CCH) 1767 (1999)

    b. Estate of Kluener v. Commissioner, 154 F.3d 630 (6th Cir. 1998)

    c. Booth v. Commissioner, 108 T.C. 524 (1997)

3. What type of pronouncement constituted substantial authority?

    a. Field Service Advice 199907004 (Nov. 9, 1998; released Feb. 19, 1999) (1999 WL 77932) (FTX-FSA)

    b. Field Service Advice (Nov. 17, 1994) (1994 WL 1725562) (FTX-FSA)

    c. Field Service Advice (Mar. 25, 1992; released Nov. 20, 1998) (1992 WL 1354714) (FTX-FSA)

    d. Technical Advice Memorandum 9022001 (Sept. 11, 1989; released June 1, 1990) (1990 WL 699510) (FTX-TAM)

---

[11] Chapter 9 also discusses release dates for publicly released IRS documents.

CHAPTER 3. RESEARCH PROCESS

SECTION A. RESEARCH GOALS

Your goals may influence the course your research takes and the product you produce. Are you structuring a new transaction? Are you litigating the effects of a transaction your clients already completed? Are you testifying before Congress or the Treasury Department to advocate a statutory or administrative change?

In the first situation, future legislation and regulations may be as important as existing law. Because retroactive effective dates are a fact of life, you must be able to locate pending legislation and proposed regulations. In addition, you may consider requesting a letter ruling to provide comfort that the IRS agrees with your tax analysis.

After a transaction closes, future legislation is less important.[12] Your interest may shift to judicial opinions and to cases currently being litigated. If your client's substantive position fails, you may need to locate sufficient authority to avoid the substantial understatement penalty described in Chapter 2.[13] If the client prevails, you may look for authority to justify charging part of your legal fees to the government.[14]

In testifying at congressional or Treasury Department hearings, you may want to include detailed history supporting your position. You can find previous legislative and regulatory changes and their effects by tracing rules back to their inception and reading cases and commentary about prior versions.

The above list is not exclusive. You may be researching sources for an article, bibliography, CLE presentation, or class assignment. Your assignment may be narrow in scope (e.g., go to the Tax Court website and find all

---

[12] But technical corrections bills may affect transactions that took place several years earlier.

[13] I.R.C. § 6662(b). In addition, you may need to avoid I.R.C. § 6694(a) preparer penalties. See also Treas. Dept. Circular 230, § 10.34 (31 C.F.R. § 10.34).

[14] I.R.C. § 7430 provides for recovery of attorneys' fees if the government's position was not substantially justified and the taxpayer meets certain other requirements.

opinions authored by Judge Vasquez in 2002), or it may require you to consult a variety of primary and secondary sources (e.g., research and write an article arguing for the reinstatement of income averaging). No matter what your goal is, successful research requires an ability to locate relevant sources.

SECTION B. RESEARCH METHODOLOGY

Tax research begins much the same way as do other types of legal research. Using a set of facts presented in a problem, you must determine the issues raised and ascertain any additional facts that might be relevant. Because a project may be completed over a period of weeks or months, you must regularly update your research.

To resolve the issues you isolate, you must locate any governing statutory language. Legislative history or administrative pronouncements would be the next step if you desire guidance in interpreting the statute. If there are administrative pronouncements, courts may have ruled on their validity, so you must locate judicial decisions.[15] In some instances, you may consider constitutional challenges to the statute itself or to an administrative interpretation. If your problem involves non-U.S. source income or citizens of other countries, the research expands to include applicable treaties.

If you are familiar with the subject matter involved, you could often locate all of the above items without resort to any secondary materials other than a citator. When you lack such familiarity, you might conduct the research effort in an entirely different manner. Before reading the applicable statute, you could use secondary materials to determine which Code section is involved and to learn about the underlying issues. Looseleaf services, treatises, and periodical articles will be particularly useful for this purpose.

Various factors influence the amount of time spent using explanatory material. Clearly written statutes require less explanation than do complex ones. The amount of explanatory material available for a statute increases over the time since its enactment. If materials discussing a statutory amendment are limited, secondary materials criticizing the original provision may be useful guides to the change. If the change involves a completely new Code section, the explanatory material is initially limited to congressional reports.

---

[15] Chapters 8 and 9 discuss the Supreme Court's decisions in Chevron U.S.A. Inc. v. Natural Resources Defense Council, Inc., 467 U.S. 837 (1984), and United States v. Mead Corp., 533 U.S. 218 (2001). Both involve the appropriate deference courts must pay to administrative determinations.

Section C discusses a related topic, selecting between print and electronic research sources.

Section E includes a hypothetical fact pattern and isolates several issues for research. This problem should assist you in approaching the variety of research tools and levels of authority involved in a tax problem.

The problem in Section E appears in a separate text section to facilitate using it as both an introduction to the research process and as a reference tool for subsequent material. Research problems in other chapters cover particular types of authority relevant to those chapters. Section F includes additional problems that integrate a variety of authorities. You may wish to answer those problems after you have read more of this text.

SECTION C. PRINT VERSUS ELECTRONIC RESEARCH

Given the large number of materials available in both print (bound and looseleaf), microform, and electronic (CD-ROM and online) formats, how do you decide which format to select? Although that question has no single correct answer, factors discussed in the following paragraphs and in Chapters 18 and 19 will influence your choice.[16]

1. Availability of Materials

What is available in your library? Older materials, for example, may be available only in print or in microform.[17] This is particularly true for legislative history materials. In other situations, the library may not carry print subscriptions to materials available in electronic format. Decisions not to carry can be based on shelf space and filing costs,[18] availability of similar services from another publisher, or relative lack of use by library patrons.

If you subscribe to an electronic service, to which of its files do you have access? Many CD-ROM and subscription online services have pricing options that allow access to different databases.

---

[16] The discussion in this section largely ignores microforms. See Chapter 17 for a discussion of their advantages and disadvantages.

[17] The definition of "older" varies by source. Because online services do expand retrospective coverage, you may find an electronic source that includes the material you seek.

[18] For example, IRS letter ruling services require extensive shelf space.

2. Updating Frequency

How often is each source updated? Some print materials are updated weekly; others receive less-frequent supplementation. CD-ROM materials are not updated more frequently than monthly; some receive only quarterly or annual updating.[19] Online databases should be updated at least as often as print sources and often are updated more frequently. Primary source materials posted by the government body that produces them may be available immediately after being issued. This is particularly true for judicial opinions available at a court's website.

3. Type of Search

Is the research best conducted based on indexes or by searching for words or concepts? Research that is best done by searching for particular words or concepts is probably better served by electronic media than by print sources. Electronic searching is more efficient if, for example, you are searching for a "common law" or Code section phrase or for items associated with a particular judge or attorney. It may be more efficient if you are searching for articles by author or topic. It is always more efficient for updating recent judicial decisions or administrative rulings using citators.

Before you begin researching, do you need to familiarize yourself with the topic? If so, cost constraints may cause you to start with print materials, a topic that is discussed in Subsection C.4.

a. Words and Concepts

Judicially declared concepts such as "step-transaction doctrine" and "form over substance" are not specifically covered in citators if they are neither case names nor Code sections. You can find materials relevant to these concepts using a print source's index; you can often find them more quickly by searching for those terms in an electronic service.[20] The same is true for concepts that do appear in the Code (e.g., "effectively connected"). Electronic searches also indicate far more quickly than do print versions which Code sections cite other sections. Their databases are updated more frequently than are print Code cross-reference tables and editorial omissions are less likely.

---

[19] Some CD-ROM services provide a link to more recent materials available online.

[20] Using a print index is advisable if you don't know all the relevant words or concepts.

b. Names of Judges or Attorneys

Searches involving particular judges or attorneys are at best difficult to accomplish using print materials. Finding every case in which Judge L. Paige Marvel appeared before the Tax Court when she was in practice or in which she authored an opinion after joining the court would require reading numerous volumes of regular and memorandum decisions.[21] These searches can be easily accomplished online using field or segment searches such as those shown below.[22]

Westlaw: JU(MARVEL) AT(PAIGE /2 MARVEL) in the Tax Court database (FTX-TCT).

LexisNexis: WRITTENBY(MARVEL) OR COUNSEL(PAIGE W/2 MARVEL) in the US Tax Court Cases, Memorandum Decs., & Board of Tax Appeals Decisions file (TCTCM).

A search run May 4, 2002, yielded 50 documents in Westlaw and 55 in LexisNexis. LexisNexis included two Summary Opinions; Westlaw included none. LexisNexis included a Memorandum Opinion omitted from Westlaw. LexisNexis also included two cases in which Judge Marvel dissented or concurred but did not write a separate opinion. In other words, neither service provided completely accurate results.

c. Articles

Searches for articles on particular topics or by particular authors are also more conveniently done in electronic media. Print articles indexes are not cumulative; each volume covers one or more years, necessitating a lengthy search. The process is further complicated because each index covers slightly different publications; at least one index imposes minimum page requirements for articles. Although their electronic versions have the same coverage limitations, you can search electronic databases far more quickly.

Two important limitations apply in selecting between print and electronic articles indexes. The first relates to availability; the second, to coverage

---

[21] The search would be impossible to conduct using print sources if it included Summary Opinions, which are not compiled in bound volumes. CD-ROM services can be used for this type of search only if they include the attorneys' names.

[22] The illustrative searches assume that the Tax Court has had only one Judge Marvel, and that you aren't sure how many attorneys with that last name have appeared before the court. If you are also unsure how many Judge Marvels have served on the court, you could add the judge's first name in the first search segment.

dates. Neither Index to Federal Tax Articles, which has the most extensive retrospective coverage, nor Federal Tax Articles is currently available in any electronic format. Although both Index to Legal Periodicals and Current Law Index are available in electronic formats, pre-1980 materials are not currently included in the electronic databases. Articles indexes are discussed further in Chapter 13.

d. Citators

There are at least two advantages to using a citator online. First, you can accomplish the search more quickly because you won't have to consult several volumes of print materials. Second, the online citators provide easy access to the citing material. You can print out a list of citations or jump to them directly using online hyperlinks. Citators are discussed further in Chapter 11.

Electronic services can also quickly perform citator-like searches. Even if, for example, a CD-ROM case service lacks a citator, you can still use the initial case name as a search term and find all later cases or other material citing it.

4. Cost

Research tools are not free. Both your time and the cost of materials must be factored into a decision between competing sources. As noted in Subsection C.1, your library may have limited your choice by deciding which materials it carries. Cost may determine which materials you select from those to which you have access.

You do not pay separately to use print and CD-ROM materials; the subscription price is a fixed cost. You pay nothing to use nonsubscription online materials, such as those available at government websites. On the other hand, pricing for subscription services such as Westlaw or LexisNexis may include time charges. You should consider both the time savings in speed (your "hourly rate" as a practitioner) and the incremental cost (fee for use) associated with subscription services.

If you are trying to familiarize yourself with a topic, print services may be preferable to electronic sources. The less you know about the topic, the more likely you are to spend significant amounts of time reading explanatory material. Although you can reduce online time by downloading text, your lack of familiarity with the topic may result in your downloading too much or too little. If you have difficulty reading large amounts of text from a computer screen, you must factor in physical "costs" when deciding between print sources and CD-ROM or online versions.

5. Need for Original Page Citations

If you must cite to the original volume and page numbers, the original print source obviously provides that information. Many online services also include original pagination; CD-ROM sources are less likely to do so. If you need to cite more than one publication (e.g., official and unofficial citations), online services are more likely to include parallel citations than are print materials.

When using electronic sources, you take a slight risk that citations or pagination will be incorrect. Many websites, particularly those of government entities, avoid this problem by providing documents in PDF format. This format doesn't merely add pagination at appropriate breaks; it actually reproduces the original document. With the appropriate software, you can perform word searches in these PDF documents.

SECTION D. SUMMARY

Research generally involves using both primary and secondary sources. Various factors influence the order in which you consult them and the format in which you conduct your research. These factors include:

(1) how complicated the problem is in relation to your knowledge of the subject matter;

(2) the specific tools available in your library;

(3) the frequency with which services are updated;

(4) the cost-effectiveness of each service for the particular task;

(5) your need for correct page citations; and

(6) personal preferences you develop as you gain research expertise.

Remember that your research is not complete until you use appropriate updating tools to check your authorities.

SECTION E. ILLUSTRATIVE PROBLEM

The following example illustrates strategies you can employ and sources you can consult in doing tax research.

1. Fact Pattern

Your clients recently refinanced their mortgage to take advantage of declining interest rates. When they purchased their home last year, interest rates were quite high. They made a down payment of $20,000 and borrowed $130,000 at 11.5 percent interest; their home was secured by a mortgage to Friendly Bank. The agreement with Friendly required them to refinance the loan or repay its full balance within five years.

Interest rates dropped to six percent last month. Generous Bank loaned your clients $129,500 and charged only one point ($1,295). They repaid Friendly the $129,500 principal remaining due on the original loan. They paid the point charged by Generous with funds in their checking account at Country Bank.

2. Goals for Research

Your clients wonder how much of this year's interest they can deduct and how to handle the point, which represents prepaid interest.

Because they approached you after completing this transaction, your goals include assessing the tax consequences and advising on the appropriate tax return treatment. If they had approached you before refinancing, you might have advised them to pay a higher interest rate instead of paying the point. That advice would involve the interplay of tax consequences and their estimate of how long they plan to own the home.[23]

Note that I excluded several potential issues from consideration. For example, because I stipulated that the point is prepaid interest, you need not research the difference between deductible and nondeductible loan fees. Because I stated that the $1,295 was on deposit with a third bank rather than added to the new loan, you can avoid researching the question of when interest is actually paid.

3. Initial Research Strategy

Because federal tax rules are grounded in statutory provisions, locating relevant statutory text is critical. The method you use to locate that text is affected by your degree of familiarity with the subject matter.

If you were familiar with the Internal Revenue Code, you could go directly

---

[23] No matter how favorable the tax consequences are, a transaction must make sense financially. Tax consequences are but one factor to consider in judging the financial aspects. Intrafamily transactions must also meet clients' personal goals.

to Code section 163, which provides the rules for deducting interest, and section 461, which applies to prepayments. If you did not remember the section numbers, you could obtain that information from the subject index accompanying the Code. [See Illustrations 3-1 and 3-2.]

If you had no knowledge of the area, you might consult one of the treatises or looseleaf services described in Chapter 12, using its topical index to locate discussions of interest and points paid as an interest substitute. Those discussions would refer you to sections 163 and 461.

Illustration 3-1. Excerpt from RIA Code Topic Index

Interest—Cont'd	CODE SEC.	Interest—Cont'd	CODE SEC.
. market discount bonds—Cont'd		. paid	
.. deferred interest deduction	1277	.. information returns	6049
.. net direct interest expense	1277	.. purchase or carry, to	
. mortgage credit certificates	163	... market discount bonds	1277
. mortgages		... short-term obligations issued at a discount	1282
.. residential property	25; 163	.. taxable year of deduction	461
. nonpayment of tax	6601; 6621	. penalties	6601
. notice requirement	6631	. personal holding companies	543
. obligations, tax-exempt	265	. personal interest	
. original issue discount	163	.. disallowance of deductions	163
.. current reporting	1272	. points, deduction	461
.. ratable daily portion	1272	. prepaid, taxable year of deduction	461
. overpayments, on		. rates, undiscounted losses	846
.. payment of estimated tax	6611		
.. rates, determination of	6621		

Illustration 3-2. Excerpt from CCH Code Topical Index

Interest paid		Interest paid—continued	
. cooperative housing tenant stockholders		. investment indebtedness, limitation	163(d)
	216	. loans to pay insurance premiums	264
. corporations		. loans with below-market interest rates	
.. disqualified debt instruments	163(l)		7872
. debt-financed acquisitions—see		. mortgage	25
Debt-financed acquisitions		. original issue discount	163(e)
. deduction	163	.. high yield obligations	163(e)(5); 163(i)
.. registered obligations	163(f)	. overpayments, IRS paid	6611
. deferred payment	483	. personal interest	163(h)
. educational loans	221	. prepaid, method of accounting	461(g)
. financial institutions	265	. pro rata interest disallowance	264(f)
. information returns	6049	. related person, limitation	163(j)
. insurance purchased with borrowed funds		. related taxpayers, transactions between	
	264		267

➡️ Each publisher decides how extensive its index will be and how topics will be divided. The RIA Index includes only a few items under the subheading "Paid" in its heading for "Interest" but provides a more extensive index for "Interest" than does the CCH Index. The CCH Index indicates subsections.

a. Code Section 163

Your research indicates that Code section 163 is an appropriate place to begin your research. [See Illustration 3-3.]

Illustration 3-3. Excerpt from Code Section 163

SEC. 163. INTEREST

(a) General rule.—There shall be allowed as a deduction all interest paid or accrued within the taxable year on indebtedness.

....

(h) Disallowance of deduction for personal interest.—

(1) In general.—In the case of a taxpayer other than a corporation, no deduction shall be allowed under this chapter for personal interest paid or accrued during the taxable year.

(2) Personal interest.—For purposes of this subsection, the term "personal interest" means any interest allowable as a deduction under this chapter other than—

....

(D) any qualified residence interest (within the meaning of paragraph (3)), and

....

(3) Qualified residence interest.—For purposes of this subsection—

(A) In general.—The term "qualified residence interest" means any interest which is paid or accrued during the taxable year on—

(i) acquisition indebtedness with respect to any qualified residence of the taxpayer, or

....

(B) Acquisition indebtedness.—

(i) In general.—The term "acquisition indebtedness" means any indebtedness which—

(I) is incurred in acquiring, constructing, or substantially improving any qualified residence of the taxpayer, and

....

Such term also includes any indebtedness secured by such residence resulting from the refinancing of indebtedness meeting the requirements of the preceding sentence (or this sentence) ....

→Relevant provisions are found in several places in this section. That is a common characteristic of tax statutes. See Chapter 5 for a discussion of terminology used in discussing statutory material.

Illustration 3-3 reproduces relevant rules found in Code section 163(a) & (h). First, the general rule provides a deduction for interest paid or accrued during the taxable year. Second, "personal interest" is not deductible. Third, qualified residence interest is not considered personal interest, a conclusion that is not intuitively obvious. If you had ended your reading with section 163(h)(1), you would have given your clients erroneous advice.

Section 163 answers some of our questions. "Qualified residence interest" includes amounts paid to purchase or to substantially improve a qualified residence. Because amounts spent to refinance a loan also qualify, the new loan is considered an amount borrowed for the purchase of the residence.[24]

Section 163 does not answer all our questions. Further research is necessary because it does not specifically address points.

b. Code Section 461

Code section 461(g) applies to prepaid interest. That section generally disallows a current deduction for prepaid interest. Instead, the interest is allocated to the period "with respect to which the interest represents a charge for the use or forbearance of money." In other words, your clients would prorate their deduction of the $1,295 over the life of the loan. However, they may qualify for a current deduction under section 461(g)(2), which provides:

> This subsection shall not apply to points paid in respect of any indebtedness incurred in connection with the purchase or improvement of, and secured by, the principal residence of the taxpayer to the extent that, under regulations prescribed by the Secretary, such payment of points is an established business practice in the area in which such indebtedness is incurred, and the amount of such payment does not exceed the amount generally charged in such area.

Section 461 uses the term "in connection with the purchase" rather than the term "to purchase." It provides no rules for determining if points are paid in connection with a purchase. Because your clients had a loan with onerous terms, including a five-year window for refinancing or paying in full, you want to argue that they meet the "in connection with" test.

4. Finding Additional Authority

If you research the "in connection with" issue, your initial question involves statutory interpretation. When does indebtedness incurred "in con-

---

[24] Section 163 may have other requirements that we are not researching here.

nection with" a purchase or improvement differ from indebtedness incurred "to" purchase or improve?

Normally, your first step would be taken in the Code itself. Many sections include definition provisions designed to limit the meaning of a particular word or phrase.[25] In other instances, definitions are provided elsewhere in the Code. For example, section 7701 includes an extensive list of definitions.

Neither Code section 461 nor section 7701 defines "in connection with" in this context. Because the Code contains no definition, you must focus your research on authorities interpreting the statutory language. You might start with congressional reports and progress to Treasury regulations, IRS rulings, and judicial opinions. You would consult treatises and other secondary sources as necessary throughout this process.[26] Illustrations 3-4 through 3-9 present selected materials relevant to our issue.

I locate IRS materials and judicial opinions using citators (Chapter 11) and reference materials that provide citations to particular Code sections, Treasury regulations, and IRS rulings. Looseleaf service supplement sections (Chapter 12) and newsletters (Chapter 15) are useful for locating recent changes. CD-ROM (Chapter 18) and online services (Chapter 19) are another means of locating relevant materials; online services are particularly useful for updating your research.

5. Updating Your Research

In a field that changes as rapidly as taxation, constant updating is critical. The relative frequency of supplementation will influence your choice between tools providing the same information. Remember to record the date each time you update your research. If you are using a looseleaf service or other source that is updated periodically, you should also note the date of the last release included in the service. You need not use that source for later material until the library receives its next updating release.

In addition to updating, you must always check the relative time span covered by new statutes and other material. Statutory changes that occurred

---

[25] See, e.g., I.R.C. § 71(a), which includes amounts received as alimony in gross income. Alimony is specifically defined in § 71(b). The recipient avoids being taxed on amounts received as "alimony" under the terms of a state court decree if those amounts fail to satisfy the § 71(b) requirements.

[26] Don't ignore dictionaries. Many courts use both general and law-related dictionaries in statutory interpretation. You can also consult a tax-oriented dictionary for explanations of terms you may encounter. See, e.g., RICHARD A. WESTIN, WG&L TAX DICTIONARY (2002).

this year, for example, may overrule or otherwise weaken the authority of regulations or rulings issued in an earlier year.

6. A Note on Print Versus Electronic Sources

With the exception of the AOD in Illustration 3-9, I completed this problem using print resources. I could instead have used electronic sources for the various steps.

The Code and Treasury regulations are available through subscription-based CD-ROM and online services and through government and other free websites. As explained in Chapter 8, the numbering system for most regulations is based on the underlying Code section. Once you know the Code section, you know which final, temporary, and proposed regulations you seek.

If I needed to familiarize myself with the area before going to the primary sources, I could have read treatises or looseleaf services on CD-ROM or online. Using the print versions is likely to reduce both cost and potential eyestrain.

I probably could have located both Revenue Ruling 87-22 and the *Huntsman* decision more quickly using either a CD-ROM or an online service such as Westlaw or LexisNexis. I could have searched for rulings and cases using the relevant Code sections and various phrases, such as "in connection with," as search terms rather than using a Code-rulings table or print citator to find these materials.

7. Illustrations

The solution to this problem involved a variety of sources, including those illustrated in this subsection:

- Illustration 3-4. Temporary Treasury Regulation § 1.163-10T

- Illustration 3-5. Mertens Code-Rulings Table

- Illustration 3-6. Revenue Ruling 87-22

- Illustration 3-7. RIA Citator 2nd

- Illustration 3-8. Huntsman v. Commissioner (8th Circuit opinion)

- Illustration 3-9. Action on Decision 1991-02

Illustration 3-4. Excerpt from Temporary Treasury Regulation Section 1.163-10T

Section 1.163-10T Qualified residence interest (temporary).

   (a) *Table of contents.* This paragraph (a) lists the major paragraphs that appear in this § 1.163-10T.

          ....

   (j) *Determination of interest paid or accrued during the taxable year.*—(1) *In general.* For purposes of determining the amount of qualified residence interest with respect to a secured debt, the amount of interest paid or accrued during the taxable year includes only interest paid or accrued while the debt is secured by a qualified residence.

   (2) *Special rules for cash-basis taxpayers.*—(i) *Points deductible in year paid under section 461(g)(2).* If points described in section 461(g)(2) (certain points paid in respect of debt incurred in connection with the purchase or improvement of a principal residence) are paid with respect to a debt, the amount of such points is qualified residence interest.

➜The above provision fails to answer our question. It repeats the statute without further explanation.

➜This provision was issued as a proposed regulation (Project LR-137-86) and as a temporary regulation (T.D. 8168). These terms are discussed in Chapter 8.

Illustration 3-5. Excerpt from Mertens Code-Rulings Table

Code Sec.	Rev. Rul.
461(f)(3)	89–6
461(f)(4)	89–6
461(g)	83–84, 87–22
461(g)(1)	87–22

➜Mertens provides references from Code sections to IRS revenue rulings and procedures. Citators also provide this information. Citators are discussed in Chapter 11.

➜The Mertens Code-Rulings Table has a current supplement for more recent material. Mertens also has a Rulings Status Table, which you can check to see if the IRS has revoked or modified Revenue Ruling 87-22. As of May 1, 2002, the tables showed no IRS action on this ruling.

Illustration 3-6. Excerpt from Rev. Rul. 87-22, 1987-1 C.B. 146

ISSUE

(1) If a taxpayer pays points on the refinancing of a mortgage loan secured by the principal residence of the taxpayer, is the payment deductible in full, under section 461(g)(2) of the Internal Revenue Code, for the taxable year in which the points are paid?

....

FACTS

Situation 1. In 1981, *A* obtained a 16-percent mortgage loan (old mortgage loan) exclusively for the purchase of a principal residence. On August 20, 1986, *A* refinanced the old mortgage loan, which had an outstanding principal balance of $100,000, with a $100,000, 30-year, 10-percent mortgage loan (new mortgage loan) from *L*, a lending institution. The new loan was secured by a mortgage on *A*'s principal residence. Principal and interest payments were due monthly, with the first payment due October 1, 1986, and the last payment due September 1, 2016. In order to refinance, *A* paid 3.6 points ($3,600) to *L* at the loan closing.

....

LAW AND ANALYSIS

....

An exception to the general rule of section 461(g)(1) of the Code is set forth in section 461(g)(2). Section 461(g)(2) provides that section 461(g)(1) shall not apply to points paid in respect of any indebtedness incurred in connection with the purchase or improvement of, and secured by, the principal residence of the taxpayer to the extent that such payment of points is an established business practice in the area in which such indebtedness is incurred and the amount of such payment does not exceed the amount generally charged in such area. Therefore, unlike the rule applicable to other instances of prepaid interest, if the requirements of section 461(g)(2) of the Code are satisfied, the taxpayer is not limited to deducting the points over the period of the indebtedness. *Schubel v. Commissioner*, 77 T.C. at 703-04.

In *Situation 1*, the proceeds of the new mortgage loan were used solely to repay an existing indebtedness. The legislative history of section 461(g)(2) of the Code states that a loan does "not qualify under [the] exception [in section 461(g)(2)] . . . if the loan proceeds are used for purposes other than purchasing or improving the taxpayer's principal residence. . . ." H.R. Rep. No. 94-658, 94th Cong., 1st Sess. 101 (1975), 1976-3 (Vol. 2) C.B. 695, 793. Although the indebtedness secured by the new mortgage was incurred in connection with *A*'s continued ownership of *A*'s principal residence, the loan proceeds were used for purposes other than purchasing or improving the residence, and thus the indebtedness was not "incurred in connection with the purchase or improvement of" that residence, as that language is used in section 461(g)(2). Accordingly, the points paid by *A* with respect to *A*'s new mortgage loan do not meet the requirements of section 461(g)(2) of the Code.

➔This ruling is adverse to our clients' position.

Illustration 3-7. Excerpt from RIA Citator 2nd (vol. 2, 1978-89)

Rev Rul 87-22, 1987-1 CB 146
     s—IR-87-34, 1987 PH ¶ 54,743
     k—Huntsman, James Richard and Zenith Annette, 91 TC
       919, 91 PH TC 458
     n—Huntsman, James Richard and Zenith Annette, 91 TC
       922, 91 PH TC 459
     e—Rev Proc 87-15, 1987-1 CB 625

➔At the time *Huntsman* was decided, Prentice-Hall (PH; P-H)) published what is now the RIA Citator. Note that the illustration above does not include a citation to the appellate court opinion [Illustration 3-8]. Although the Tax Court cited Revenue Ruling 87-22, the appellate court did not. Using a citator to trace the Tax Court opinion, you would have found the appellate opinion.

➔You might use the other citators described in Chapter 11 to see what results you get (both items found and use of symbols to indicate the type of action).

Illustration 3-8. Excerpt from Huntsman v. Commissioner,
905 F.2d 1182, 1184 (8th Cir. 1990)

Before LAY, Chief Judge, BEAM, Circuit Judge, and HANSON,* District Judge.

LAY, Chief Judge.   ....
[2] In determining the scope of section 461(g)(2), we first look to the language of the statute. *United States v. James*, 478 U.S. 597, 604 ... (1986) (citing *Blue Chip Stamps v. Manor Drug Stores*, 421 U.S. 723, 756 ... (1975) (Powell, J., concurring)). The statute merely requires a taxpayer's indebtedness to be "in connection with" the purchase or improvement of the taxpayer's residence. Thus, we find a fair reading of the statute requires that the indebtedness need only have an "association" or "relation" with the purchase of the taxpayer's residence.[5] The statute does not require all indebtedness to be "*directly related* to the actual acquisition of the principal residence." *Huntsman*, 91 T.C. at 921 (emphasis added).

➔The Eighth Circuit Court of Appeals reversed the Tax Court. The Huntsmans' facts are not identical to your clients' (although they are close).

➔In addition to checking for precedent in your particular jurisdiction (discussed in Chapter 10), you should check to see if the IRS accepts this result. [See Illustration 3-9.]

Illustration 3-9. Excerpt from IRS Action on Decision 1991-02

The test that the Eighth Circuit has created requires examination of the facts of each case to determine if the refinancing is sufficiently connected with the purchase or improvement of the taxpayer's residence. The Service believes that Congress enacted section 461(g)(2) to eliminate the case-by-case approach to deductibility of points. Moreover, the legislative history indicates that Congress intended to limit the exception to points paid on indebtedness incurred to purchase or improve the taxpayer's principal residence. Accordingly, the Service maintains its position that points paid for a loan to refinance a mortgage on a taxpayer's principal residence are not deductible under I.R.C. § 461(g)(2). Thus it will not follow the court's holding with respect to this type of refinancing agreement outside of the Eighth Circuit. However, in the absence of an intercircuit conflict, the Service is of the opinion that the issue lacks sufficient demonstrable administrative importance to warrant a petition for certiorari.

RECOMMENDATION:

No certiorari

→In addition to using a citator to determine if other courts followed *Huntsman*, you should determine if the IRS plans to continue litigating this issue. AOD 1991-02 indicates that the IRS chief counsel's office did not recommend petitioning for certiorari in *Huntsman* but that the IRS would not follow *Huntsman* in other circuits. See Chapter 9 for information on researching IRS positions and for a less traditional AOD [Illustration 9-2].

SECTION F. ADDITIONAL PROBLEMS

1. Points

Assume a slightly different fact pattern from the one in Section E. Your clients own a home that is not subject to any debt. They must replace their leaky roof; patching it is inadequate. To get the funds they need, they will borrow from a bank and use the home as security. They will pay points in the amount of $200.

You must research two questions regarding Code section 461(g). The first relates to the term "improvement." Does replacing a roof constitute an improvement if it does not extend the home's life?

If it is an improvement, you must then determine if taking a current deduction for points is mandatory. This question is important because your clients have few potential itemized deductions. Even if they pay the $200, they will be unable to itemize their deductions this year. They hope to begin itemizing next year. Taking the standard deduction means forgoing any tax deduction for the points unless they can amortize them over the loan term. Obviously, that is impossible if section 461(g)(2) mandates a current deduction. Unfortunately, the roof can't wait until next year.

2. Personal Injury

Husband was injured in an automobile accident. He sued for pain and suffering, lost wages, medical costs, and punitive damages. He settled with the other driver's insurance company for $300,000. The settlement did not specifically allocate amounts to any elements of his claim. Wife was not involved in the accident but sued and received a $25,000 settlement for loss of consortium. Their attorney received 25 percent of each settlement.

Using the year and jurisdiction your instructor assigns, answer the following questions. What portion of the settlement can Husband exclude from gross income? Can he deduct accident-related medical bills when he receives care next year? Although she was not involved in the accident, can Wife exclude her settlement?

3. Divorce

Husband and Wife own all the stock of a corporation. They are divorcing, and Wife will become the sole shareholder. The corporate stock each owns is valued at $250,000.

The corporation could redeem Husband's shares and pay him $250,000. Alternatively, Wife could give him a promissory note for his shares and take title to them. The corporation could redeem these shares from Wife for $250,000. After Wife transferred the $250,000 to Husband, he would cancel her note. Wife would become the sole shareholder under either scenario.

Discuss the tax consequences for both spouses from either method. Use the law in effect for the year and jurisdiction your instructor specifies.

4. Rental Income

Your client was approached by a movie producer, who wants to film her home. He is interested only in the home's facade; he will film interior shots at the production company's studio. The producer offered your client rent for "camping out" on her lawn. Although he believes he will need only two days, he has offered $7,000 for ten days or $12,000 for twenty days.

Find any tax provisions concerning the short-term rental of a home. Discuss how these apply to the time periods involved and to renting the facade only. What advice do you give your client?

PART TWO

PRIMARY SOURCES: LEGISLATIVE

Chapter 4. Constitution

Chapter 5. Statutes

Chapter 6. Legislative Histories

Chapter 7. Treaties and Other International Material

Chapter 4. Constitution

Section A. Taxing Power

Congress's power to impose taxes emanates from the United States Constitution. That document includes several taxation provisions.

Table 4-1. Constitutional Provisions Regarding Taxation

Art. I, § 2, cl. 3: Representatives and direct Taxes shall be apportioned among the several States which may be included within this Union, according to their respective Numbers .... (Before amendment)

Art. I, § 7, cl. 1: All Bills for raising Revenue shall originate in the House of Representatives; but the Senate may propose or concur with Amendments as on other Bills.

Art. I, § 8, cl. 1: The Congress shall have Power To lay and collect Taxes, Duties, Imposts and Excises, to pay the Debts and provide for the common Defence and general Welfare of the United States; but all Duties, Imposts and Excises shall be uniform throughout the United States;

Art. I, § 9, cl. 4: No Capitation, or other direct, Tax shall be laid, unless in Proportion to the Census or Enumeration herein before directed to be taken.

Art. I, § 9, cl. 5: No Tax or Duty shall be laid on Articles exported from any State.

Art. I, § 10, cl. 2: No State shall, without the Consent of the Congress, lay any Imposts or Duties on Imports or Exports, except what may be absolutely necessary for executing it's inspection Laws: and the net Produce of all Duties and Imposts, laid by any State on Imports or Exports, shall be for the Use of the Treasury of the United States; and all such Laws shall be subject to the Revision and Controul of the Congress.

Amend. XVI: The Congress shall have power to lay and collect taxes on incomes, from whatever source derived, without apportionment among the several States, and without regard to any census or enumeration.

Because the income tax is specifically authorized by the Constitution's sixteenth amendment, it avoids an earlier holding that it was a direct tax subject to apportionment based on population.[27] The estate and gift taxes, on the other hand, are indirect taxes subject only to the requirement that they be uniform throughout the United States.

SECTION B. CONSTITUTIONAL LITIGATION

1. Items Challenged

Because several constitutional provisions explicitly mention taxation [Table 4-1], courts must occasionally determine whether a taxing statute or administrative interpretation complies with these rules. Examples appear in Table 4-2.

Table 4-2. Litigation Involving the Constitution's Tax Provisions

Mobley v. United States, 8 Cl. Ct. 767 (1985) (the apportionment clause of art. I, § 2, cl. 3)

Moore v. United States House of Representatives, 733 F.2d 946 (D.C. Cir. 1984) (the origination clause of art. I, § 7, cl. 1)

United States v. Ptasynski, 462 U.S. 74 (1983) (the uniformity clause of art. I, § 8, cl. 1)

United States v. International Business Machines Corp., 517 U.S. 843 (1996) (the export clause of art. I, § 9, cl. 5)

Most cases raising constitutional claims involve provisions that do not mention taxation. Table 4-3 lists several cases involving these provisions. Neither group of provisions generates a substantial body of important tax litigation in any given year.

2. Supreme Court Litigation Versus Constitutional Litigation

Keep two facts in mind. First, many constitutional claims are dismissed by lower courts and never reach the United States Supreme Court. Second, most substantive tax litigation involves interpreting statutes or other rules rather than constitutional claims. If Congress disagrees with a Supreme Court decision regarding interpretation, it can "overrule" the Court by amending the statute.

---

[27] Pollock v. Farmers' Loan & Trust Co., 158 U.S. 601 (1895); cf. Springer v. United States, 102 U.S. 586 (1881), concluding the Civil War income tax was indirect.

Table 4-3. Litigation Involving the Constitution's Nontax Provisions

Demko v. United States, 216 F.3d 1049 (Fed. Cir. 2000) (nondelegation doctrine–judicially derived from art. I, § 1)

NationsBank of Texas, N.A. v. United States, 269 F.3d 1332 (Fed. Cir. 2001) (separation of powers doctrine–art. I, § 7, cl. 2)

Clinton v. City of New York, 524 U.S. 417 (1998) (the presentment clause–art. I, § 7, cl. 2)

United States v. Rosengarten, 857 F.2d 76 (2d Cir. 1988) (ex post facto laws–art. I, § 9, cl. 3)

Freytag v. Commissioner, 501 U.S. 868 (1991) (the appointments clause–art. II, § 2, cl. 2)

United States v. Hatter, 532 U.S. 557 (2001) (the compensation clause–art. III, § 1)

Hernandez v. Commissioner, 490 U.S. 680 (1989) (establishment of religion and free exercise of religion–amend. I)

Regan v. Taxation with Representation, 461 U.S. 540 (1983) (freedom of speech and association–amend. I; equal protection–amend. V)

United States v. Carlton, 512 U.S. 26 (1994) (retroactivity as a denial of due process–amend. V)

Manufacturers Hanover Trust Co. v. United States, 775 F.2d 459 (2d Cir. 1985) (equal protection/sex discrimination–amend. V)

Ianniello v. Commissioner, 98 T.C. 165 (1992) (double jeopardy–amend. V; excessive fines and cruel and unusual punishments–amend. VIII)

South Carolina v. Baker, 485 U.S. 505 (1988) (infringement on powers reserved to states–amend. X)

Shapiro v. Baker, 646 F. Supp. 1127 (D.N.J. 1986) (judicial doctrine of intergovernmental tax immunity)

➡️Because these decisions don't involve the Constitution's taxation provisions, it is easiest to find them using treatises and looseleaf services.

SECTION C. RESEARCH PROCESS

If you want to know if a court has ruled on the constitutionality of a statute or administrative interpretation, use the citator materials discussed in Chapters 5 (Statutes) and 8 (Treasury Regulations).

If you seek judicial decisions that cite to constitutional provisions, you can use Shepard's Federal Statute Citations to compile a list of cases. Unfortunately, it does not cover IRS material or Tax Court Memorandum decisions; its coverage of Tax Court Regular decisions in the 1996 volume is rather limited. None of the tax-oriented print citators discussed in Chapter 11 provides citations to the Constitution.

Because substantive tax research rarely involves the Constitution, you may decide to perform your research using traditional nontax materials.[28] You can also search CD-ROM and online tax services for specific constitutional provisions or common terms (e.g., due process). Standard Federal Tax Reporter volume 1 includes materials on litigation involving constitutional claims.

SECTION D. PROBLEMS

1. Indicate the constitutional challenge made and whether the taxpayer succeeded at the court indicated or on appeal.

a. Estate of Koester v. Commissioner, 83 T.C.M. (CCH) 1429 (2002)

b. Mueller v. Commissioner, 79 T.C.M. (CCH) 1887 (2000)

c. Miller v. Commissioner, 114 T.C. 511 (2000)

d. United States v. Gresham, 118 F.3d 258 (5th Cir. 1997)

e. Byrd v. Raines, 956 F. Supp. 25 (D.D.C. 1997)

f. Skaggs v. Carle, 898 F. Supp. 1 (D.D.C. 1995)

g. Nationalist Movement v. Commissioner, 102 T.C. 558 (1994)

---

[28] The most useful materials are annotated Constitutions, such as those included in United States Code Annotated and United States Code Service, and digests. See Fundamentals of Legal Research chs. 6 and 8. 1 BORIS I. BITTKER & LAWRENCE LOKKEN, FEDERAL TAXATION OF INCOME, ESTATES AND GIFTS ch. 1 (3d ed. 1999 & 2002 Cum. Supp.), discusses tax litigation involving constitutional claims.

h. Democratic Party v. National Conservative Political Action Committee, 578 F. Supp. 797 (E.D. Pa. 1983)

i. Big Mama Rag, Inc. v. United States, 631 F.2d 1030 (D.C. Cir. 1980)

j. Mapes v. United States, 217 Ct. Cl. 115 (1978)

2. Mobley v. United States, 8 Cl. Ct. 767 (1985), held that the minimum tax was not a direct tax subject to apportionment among the states based on population. The cases below also involve claims regarding apportionment. Indicate which tax was challenged and the outcome at the highest court to issue an opinion.

a. United States v. Thomas, 115 F. 207 (C.C.S.D.N.Y. 1902)

b. Mt. Tivy Winery, Inc. v. Lewis, 42 F. Supp. 636 (N.D. Cal. 1942)

c. Egtvedt v. United States, 112 Ct. Cl. 80 (1948)

d. Jourdain v. Commissioner, 71 T.C. 980 (1979)

e. Carver v. United States, 54 A.F.T.R.2d 84-5089, 84-2 U.S.T.C. ¶ 9565 (E.D. Mich. 1983)

3. United States v. United States Shoe Corp., 523 U.S. 360 (1998), involved the Harbor Maintenance Tax. Provide a citation to the following decisions involving that tax. Indicate the constitutional argument raised and the outcome at the highest court to issue an opinion.

a. a challenge by Thomson Consumer Electronics Inc.

b. a challenge by Swisher International Inc.

c. a challenge by Sony Electronics Inc.

d. a challenge by Amoco Oil Co.

e. a challenge by Florida Sugar Marketing and Terminal Association, Inc.

4. Cite to the judicial decision that involved the constitutionality of the provision listed. Give the holding and any appellate action.

a. a 2000 decision by the Court of Federal Claims discussing whether a retroactive tax increase violated the Eighth Amendment's excessive fines clause

b. a 1999 decision discussing the constitutionality of I.R.C. § 162(e) as amended in 1993

c. a 1998 decision discussing the export clause and I.R.C. § 4121

d. a 1999 published opinion discussing I.R.C. § 6653(b) and double jeopardy and also involving claims under the fifth and sixth amendments

e. a 2002 circuit court ruling discussing an Establishment Clause challenge to the disallowance of a deduction for religious school tuition

f. a 1997 district court ruling discussing the amendment made by Pub. L. No. 103-66, § 13208, 107 Stat. 312, 469 (1993)

5. Locate the petition or brief filed in the case described below and determine the constitutional challenge. If a judicial opinion was issued, what was the outcome?

a. A taxpayer petition, challenging Public Law No. 106-230, filed in the Southern District of Alabama in 2000

b. A Department of Justice brief, arguing that the alternative minimum tax does not place a substantial burden on the free exercise of religion, filed in the Tenth Circuit in 1999

6. On what Code section's constitutionality did the Ninth Circuit ask Professor Erwin Chemerinsky to submit a brief in 2002? In what case did it make this request?

7. What constitutional challenge was rejected in the following IRS documents?

a. Technical Advice Memorandum 200045009

b. Private Letter Ruling 8952003

Chapter 5. Statutes

Section A. Introduction

This chapter discusses statutes passed by Congress and authorized by the United States Constitution. It covers terminology used to describe statutes, lists sources in which you can locate current, repealed, and pending statutes, and introduces rules of interpretation.

In interpreting statutes, judges and administrative agencies may look to legislative history, a topic covered in Chapter 6. If a taxpayer has ties to another country, treaties may also be relevant. Treaties and their relationship to statutes are discussed in Chapter 7.

Your goals for Chapters 5 and 6 include locating all relevant documents, determining their relative importance, and updating your research to encompass pending items. In accomplishing these goals, you should become familiar with the process by which statutes are enacted and the terminology used to describe statutory and legislative history documents.

Section B. Functions of Statutes

Although the Constitution authorizes taxes, it does not provide specific rules for measuring income, allowing deductions, or determining rates. That task is accomplished by Congress, which has enacted statutes imposing a variety of taxes.

Statutes define the tax base and penalties for noncompliance, provide effective dates, authorize administrative agencies to interpret the laws, and direct those same agencies to make reports to Congress. Your research may require you to locate statutes serving these purposes.

Section C. Statutory Scheme

1. Internal Revenue Code

United States Code (U.S.C.) Title 26, more commonly referred to as the Internal Revenue Code of 1986, contains the vast majority of statutes covering income, estate and gift, excise, and employment taxes. The 1986 Code replaced the 1954 Code, which had replaced the 1939 Code. I refer to the 1986 statutory materials as the Code throughout this text. References to the two previous Codes–1939 and 1954–will include the year.[29]

a. Code Subdivisions

The Code is divided into eleven subtitles.

Table 5-1. Internal Revenue Code Subtitles

Subtitle	Subject
A	Income Taxes
B	Estate and Gift Taxes
C	Employment Taxes
D	Miscellaneous Excise Taxes
E	Alcohol, Tobacco, and Certain Other Excise Taxes
F	Procedure and Administration
G	The Joint Committee on Taxation
H	Financing of Presidential Election Campaigns
I	Trust Fund Code
J	Coal Industry Health Benefits
K	Group Health Plan Requirements

Each subtitle is further subdivided into smaller units. These subdivisions include chapter; subchapter; part; subpart; section; subsection; paragraph; subparagraph; clause; and subclause. [See Table 5-2.] Subdivisions may also be divided into sentences.

b. Code Subdivision Numbering System

Titles, chapters, parts, and sections are identified by number. Subtitles, subchapters, and subparts are identified by letter. Although subsections usually are identified by letter (e.g., subsection 163(d)), a few are designated by number (e.g., subsection 212(1)). Successive subdivisions bear letters or numbers, as appropriate. The Code uses both upper and lower case letters and both Roman and Arabic numerals.

---

[29] Before 1939, tax statutes were reenacted in their entirety, or with necessary changes, on a regular basis. Because many current provisions can be traced back to the 1939 Code or even earlier—I.R.C. § 263, for example, contains language taken almost verbatim from § 117 of the 1864 Act—cross-references to these earlier materials are extremely useful. See Act of June 30, 1864, ch. 173, 13 Stat. 223, 281-82. Chapter 6 covers materials used to trace statutory language.

Table 5-2. Code Subdivisions: Section 45F(c)(1)(A)(i)(I)

Title 26	Internal Revenue
Subtitle A	Income taxes
Chapter 1	Normal taxes and surtaxes
Subchapter A	Determination of tax liability
Part IV	Credits against tax
Subpart D	Business related credits
Section 45F	Employer-provided child care credit
Subsection (c)	Definitions
Paragraph (1)	Qualified child care expenditure
Subparagraph (A)	In general
Clause (i)	[text of clause]
Subclause (I)	[text of subclause]

→Although clause (i) and subclause (I) include only text, many subdivisions include both the headings shown above and text.

→In using the Code's numbering system, be careful to note the correct section or subdivision. Several sections have a capital letter as part of the section number. Thus, section 2056(a) is not the same as section 2056A.

c. Unique and Repeated Code Subdivisions

Title, subtitle, chapter, and section numbers and letters are used only once. Other subdivision classifications are used multiple times. For example, although there are several Subchapter As, there is only one Chapter 1 (which appears in Subtitle A). The first chapter in Subtitle B is Chapter 11.

Although subchapter, part, and subpart classifications are used multiple times, subchapters are the most likely to cause a problem if you aren't careful. Practitioners frequently refer to four groups of sections in Subtitle A by their subchapter designation—Subchapter C, Subchapter J, Subchapter K, and Subchapter S.[30] If given an assignment to research a particular subchapter, make sure you ascertain the correct one before you begin.

2. Other Statutes

Several tax-related provisions appear outside the Internal Revenue Code. These include provisions codified elsewhere and uncodified provisions. These provisions are discussed in Subsection D.4.

---

[30] These subchapters cover, respectively, corporations, trusts and estates, partnerships, and "small business" corporations. Although Subtitle A has several Subpart Fs, international practitioners often refer to Subpart F as a shorthand for the controlled foreign corporation Code sections in Chapter 1, Subchapter N, Part III.

3. "Legislative" Pronouncements from the Executive Branch

The Treasury Department makes "legislative" pronouncements by issuing legislative regulations pursuant to an express statutory grant of authority. Regulations are discussed in Chapter 8.

The President also has limited "legislative" powers. For example, Code section 112(c) provides:

> For purposes of this section—
>
> (2) The term "combat zone" means any area which the President of the United States by Executive Order designates, for purposes of this section or corresponding provisions of prior income tax laws, as an area in which Armed Forces of the United States are or have (after June 24, 1950) engaged in combat.

Presidential declarations of this nature can be found in the Weekly Compilation of Presidential Documents,[31] the Federal Register,[32] and the Internal Revenue Bulletin.[33] Although all are available from government websites, you may find it easier to search across multiple years in commercial services such as Westlaw and LexisNexis.

SECTION D. TERMINOLOGY

The following paragraphs introduce terms used in discussing tax legislation. Additional information is found in Chapter 6, Legislative Histories.

1. Bills and Acts

When proposed legislation is introduced in the Senate or House of Representatives, it is assigned a **bill** number. Each chamber numbers its bills separately in chronological order. A House bill is referred to as H.R. (e.g., H.R. 3838); a Senate bill is identified as S. Senators introduce bills involving taxation despite the constitutional requirement that bills for raising revenue originate in the House.

After a bill passes either chamber, it can be called an **act**. Because many

---

[31] See http://www.access.gpo.gov/nara/nara003.html.

[32] See http://www.access.gpo.gov/su_docs/aces/aces140.html.

[33] See http://www.irs.gov.

bills pass only one chamber before dying, this terminology might confuse anyone who thinks the term act is reserved for actual statutes.[34] If you have access to the H.R. or S. number, you can find the bill in the Congressional Record whether or not it was enacted. Statutes at Large includes bill numbers for enacted legislation.

2. Public Law Names and Numbers

Although they carry Public Law numbers, acts are frequently referred to by a **popular name**;[35] Congress often designates that name in the act's text. If the popular name includes a year, you can easily locate the act's text in Statutes at Large or The Internal Revenue Acts of the United States (Chapter 16). If the year is not part of the name, use Shepard's Acts and Cases by Popular Names to obtain a citation. You can also obtain citations using an online service (Chapter 19) or in the Popular Names tables in U.S.C., U.S.C.A., or U.S.C.S.

When a bill does become law, it receives a **Public Law number** (Pub. L. No.). These numbers are chronological by Congress.[36] They bear no relation to the original bill number and provide no information about the session of that Congress.[37]

3. Revenue Acts and Other Relevant Acts

Acts that have "Revenue" or "Tax" in their popular names clearly announce their relevance to taxation. Other acts that are likely to include substantive tax law include those with "Deficit Reduction," "Income," "Trade," or "Investment" in their titles.

Even if an act has a name, that name may contain no hint that it includes tax provisions. Other acts that include tax provisions may lack popular names altogether. For example, the Ricky Ray Hemophilia Relief Fund Act of 1998 treats certain payments as damages for purposes of Code section

---

[34] The bill's original title may include the word Act. Unless a bill is enacted by the time a particular Congress ends, it dies. Its supporters must reintroduce it in a subsequent Congress and start the legislative process over. This rule does not apply to treaties (Chapter 7), which remain alive for action by a subsequent Congress.

[35] Different parts of an act may have their own "popular names."

[36] Statutes enacted before 1957 have chapter numbers instead of Pub. L. numbers.

[37] The Tax Reform Act of 1986 is Pub. L. No. 99-514, 100 Stat. 2085. The Public Law number indicates that it was passed in the 99th Congress; it does not indicate in which of the two sessions. It was introduced in the 99th Congress as H.R. 3838.

104(a)(2).[38] Public Law Number 107-22, which changed the name of Education IRAs to Coverdell Education Savings Accounts, is an example of an act to which Congress assigned no popular name.[39]

4. Codified and Uncodified Provisions

a. Codification in the I.R.C. and Elsewhere

Although most substantive tax provisions are included in the Internal Revenue Code, other titles of United States Code may include provisions relevant to your research. A provision may be codified in another title of United States Code because an agency other than the Treasury Department has primary responsibility for the area of law involved. For example, many rules affecting retirement benefits appear in the Internal Revenue Code, but others appear in 29 U.S.C., the title that covers Labor.[40]

You can locate provisions in other titles using a subject matter index to U.S.C. The Related Statutes materials in Standard Federal Tax Reporter Code volume II includes texts of many of these statutes. A CD-ROM (Chapter 18) version of U.S.C. or an online research tool (Chapter 19) may be superior for this type of research.

b. Uncodified Provisions

Many revenue act provisions are never added to the Code or to any other title of U.S.C. Most uncodified provisions involve effective dates for particular sections of the act. Others, however, may direct the Treasury Department or IRS to do (or refrain from doing[41]) something. [See Illustration 5-1.] A third group involves substantive law provisions. [See Illustration 5-2.]

Because we expect Congress to establish effective dates for legislation, it is second nature to look for this material in the act or in a Code publication that includes effective date annotations. The other types of information are less common, however, and may well escape notice by someone who has not

[38] Pub. L. No. 105-369, § 103(h), 112 Stat. 3368, 3371 (1998).

[39] 115 Stat. 196 (2001). Pub. L. No. 107-22 began as a Senate bill. S. 1190, 107th Cong., 1st. Sess. (2001). Although it amended the Code, it had no revenue implications and thus did not violate the origination clause. U.S. CONST. art. I, § 7, cl. 1.

[40] See also 37 U.S.C. § 558, providing tax deferments for military personnel while they are missing in action.

[41] See, e.g., Pub. L. No. 95-427, § 1, 92 Stat. 996 (1978), imposing a temporary moratorium on the issuance of fringe benefit regulations.

followed the progress of the particular legislation. They may also be traps for the unwary. Rules providing guidance in the employee/independent contractor area that are not codified anywhere are often referred to by their act section number.[42]

Illustration 5-1. Material Omitted from Code

SEC. 1012. REPEAL OF TAX-EXEMPT STATUS FOR CERTAIN ORGANIZA-TIONS PROVIDING COMMERCIAL-TYPE INSURANCE.

....

(c) Effective Date.—   ....

(2) STUDY OF FRATERNAL BENEFICIARY ASSOCIATIONS.—The Secretary of the Treasury or his delegate shall conduct a study of organizations described in section 501(c)(8) of the Internal Revenue Code of 1986 and which received gross annual insurance premiums in excess of $25,000,000 for the taxable years of such organizations which ended during 1984. Not later than January 1, 1988, the Secretary of the Treasury shall submit to the Committee on Ways and Means of the House of Representatives, the Committee on Finance of the Senate, and the Joint Committee on Taxation the results of such study, together with such recommendations as he determines to be appropriate. The Secretary of the Treasury shall have authority to require the furnishing of such information as may be necessary to carry out the purposes of this paragraph.

→This excerpt is from is Pub. L. No. 99-514, § 1012, 100 Stat. 2085, 2392 (1986). Studies such as this may lead to future legislation.

Illustration 5-2. Material Omitted from Code

SEC. 803. NO FEDERAL INCOME TAX ON RESTITUTION RECEIVED BY VICTIMS OF THE NAZI REGIME OR THEIR HEIRS OR ESTATES.

(a) IN GENERAL.—For purposes of the Internal Revenue Code of 1986, any excludable restitution payments received by an eligible individual (or the individual's heirs or estate) and any excludable interest—

(1) shall not be included in gross income; and

(2) shall not be taken into account for purposes of applying any provision of such Code which takes into account excludable income in computing adjusted gross income, including section 86 of such Code (relating to taxation of Social Security benefits).

For purposes of such Code, the basis of any property received by an eligible individual (or the individual's heirs or estate) as part of an excludable restitution payment shall be the fair market value of such property as of the time of the receipt.

→This excerpt is from Pub. L. No. 107-16, § 803,115 Stat. 38, 149 (2001). Although these provisions affect tax consequences, they are not codified.

---

[42] Revenue Act of 1978, Pub. L. No. 95-600, § 530, 92 Stat. 2763, 2885, extended indefinitely by the Tax Equity and Fiscal Responsibility Act of 1982, Pub. L. No. 97-248, § 269(c), 96 Stat. 324, 552, and amended by the Small Business Job Protection Act of 1996, Pub. L. No. 104-188, § 1122, 110 Stat. 1755, 1766.

5. Section Numbers

The Code, the Public Laws amending it or otherwise affecting taxation, and the bills that may become Public Laws all divide their provisions into sections. These section numbering systems bear no relationship to each other.[43] Take for example, Code section 1202(a), which reads as follows:

(1) In general.—In the case of a taxpayer other than a corporation, gross income shall not include 50 percent of any gain from the sale or exchange of qualified small business stock held for more than 5 years.

Congress added the original version of that section to the Code in 1993, including it as section 13113(a) of the Revenue Reconciliation Act of 1993. The provision began as section 14113(a) of H.R. 2264, the Omnibus Budget Reconciliation Act of 1993, a subtitle of which was the Revenue Reconciliation Act of 1993.

The section is the basic unit used in finding the law. As discussed in Section C, the Code contains only one section 1, not one for each part, chapter, or other unit. Although sections are numbered sequentially, breaks in the sequence provide room for Congress to insert new sections as needed.

6. Enactment Date, Effective Date, and Sunset Date

a. Enactment and Effective Dates

Most acts have two relevant dates. The **enactment date** is the date the President signs the act (or allows it to become law without his signature) or Congress overrides a presidential veto. The **effective date**, on which the act's provisions apply to particular transactions, may coincide with, follow, or even precede the enactment date.

Tax legislation frequently involves several effective dates for individual sections of an act. It is risky to assume that the enactment date is the effective date or that the effective date of one section applies to all parts of a new act. [See Illustration 5-3.] Because effective dates rarely become part of the Code, you must usually locate them in the act itself.[44] The items listed in Subsection F.2. are useful for this purpose.

---

[43] When researching an act or Code provision, remember to match the appropriate section number to the document being used.

[44] Effective dates do appear in the Code for provisions that phase in over time. For example, the dollar limits for expensing depreciable property in I.R.C. § 179(b)(1) vary based on the year the property is placed in service.

Illustration 5-3. Effective Date Provisions in Economic Growth and Tax Relief Reconciliation Act of 2001, Section 303

(i) EFFECTIVE DATES.—

(1) IN GENERAL.—Except as provided in paragraph (2), the amendments made by this section shall apply to taxable years beginning after December 31, 2001.

(2) SUBSECTION (g).—The amendment made by subsection (g) shall take effect on January 1, 2004.

➔Although this act became law on June 7, 2001, several of its provisions had different effective dates. The act section can be found in Pub. L. No. 107-16, 115 Stat. 38, 57.

The exact language Congress uses is critical for determining an effective date. Table 5-3 indicates effective date formats with quite different meanings.

Table 5-3. Effective Date Formats

Effective for transactions occurring in taxable years beginning after December 31, 2001

Effective for transactions occurring after December 31, 2001

Effective for transactions occurring in taxable years ending after December 31, 2001

➔Do not assume that all taxable years begin on January 1. Some taxpayers have fiscal years that begin in months other than January.

➔If a taxpayer has a calendar year, the three effective dates above might yield the same results. If a taxpayer instead has a fiscal year that ends January 31, a transaction that occurs January 15, 2002, will be covered by the second and third effective dates but not by the first.

b. Sunset Date

As a general rule, Code provisions remain in effect until amended, repealed, or declared unconstitutional. Congress may provide a specific **sunset date** for an individual Code provision. Unlike effective dates, sunset dates generally do appear in the Code.

**Illustration 5-4. Sunset Date for Code Section 30:
Credit for Qualified Electric Vehicles**

(e) Termination.—

This section shall not apply to any property placed in service after December 31, 2006.

➜Note: sunset dates are frequently extended by subsequent legislation. The term **extenders** is commonly used for tax bill provisions postponing sunset dates. Section 30 has already been extended once.

SECTION E. SCOPE AND DEFINITIONS

1. Scope of Provisions

Some provisions apply to the entire Code; others affect only a particular subtitle or smaller unit. The latter groups indicate their scope by using language such as "for purposes of this paragraph." If you fail to note the scope of a particular provision, you risk drawing erroneous conclusions. Illustration 5-5 shows varying scope limitations within a single Code subsection.

Sections appearing in one subtitle or other subdivision of the Code may apply to other subdivisions. Provisions affecting more than one type of tax (separate subtitles) may appear in neither subtitle. Instead, they can be found in Subtitle F, Chapter 80, Subchapter C (Code sections 7871-7873).

Although tax research requires access to rules found in varying parts of the Code, the Code lacks a comprehensive cross-referencing system.[45] Because they include textual discussion, looseleaf services and treatises (Chapter 12) are useful in locating various provisions applicable to the problem being researched.

2. Definitions

Many terms appear in the Code without definition. "Gross income" is one example. Others are defined within a section solely for purposes of that

---

[45] Use of statutory language, including scope limitations and cross-references between sections of one Code, is discussed in this chapter. Cross-referencing section numbers from one Code to an earlier or later Code is discussed in Chapter 6, Legislative Histories.

section. For example, section 1202(c) defines "qualified small business stock" for purposes of section 1202.

Some definitions apply to more than one Code section. Chapter 79 of the Code includes several definition provisions, most of which apply to the entire Code. If you cannot locate a definition in an individual section, be sure to check the definitions in Subtitle F, Chapter 79 (Code sections 7701-7704).

Illustration 5-5. Excerpt from Code Section 165(g) Illustrating Scope

---

(g) Worthless Securities.—

(1) General rule.—If any security which is a capital asset becomes worthless during the taxable year, the loss resulting therefrom shall, **for purposes of this subtitle**, be treated as a loss from the sale or exchange, on the last day of the taxable year, of a capital asset.

(2) Security defined.—**For purposes of this subsection**, the term "security" means—

(A) a share of stock in a corporation;

(B) a right to subscribe for, or to receive, a share of stock in a corporation; or

(C) a bond, debenture, note, or certificate, or other evidence of indebtedness, issued by a corporation or by a government or political subdivision thereof, with interest coupons or in registered form.

(3) Securities in affiliated corporation.—**For purposes of paragraph (1)**, any security in a corporation affiliated with a taxpayer which is a domestic corporation shall not be treated as a capital asset. **For purposes of the preceding sentence**, a corporation shall be treated as affiliated with the taxpayer only if— ....

→The general rule applies for purposes of all income tax provisions ("this subtitle"). Specific limitations and definitions have narrower application ("this subsection," "paragraph (1)," "the preceding sentence").

SECTION F. LOCATING CURRENT, REPEALED, AND PENDING LEGISLATION

In researching a tax problem, the time frame involved is quite important. If, for example, the research involves a proposed transaction, current law is certainly important. However, if that law is of recent vintage, the repealed statute it replaced may assist you in interpreting what the revised statute means. Moreover, if you ignore pending legislation, you do so at your peril. A bill changing the tax consequences of a proposed transaction could be enacted before your client negotiates a binding contract.[46]

If you are researching the law that is currently in effect, you should consult a codification rather than the most recent amending act. Codifications reflect the original statute as amended by all subsequent changes. Individual acts, on the other hand, reflect only amendments. Remember, however, that individual acts include effective dates, instructions to administrative agencies, and other material that is never codified.

1. Current Code—Codifications

Several publishers produce annual versions of the Internal Revenue Code.[47] Those publishing in a looseleaf format regularly integrate new material into the codification volumes. Publishers using bound volumes use supplements for new matter. CD-ROM (Chapter 18) and online services (Chapter 19) insert new material directly into the relevant database.[48]

• U.S. Code Congressional & Administrative News—Internal Revenue Code (Chapter 16) (hardbound)

• Mertens, Internal Revenue Code (softbound)

• Standard Federal Tax Reporter[49] (Chapter 12) (looseleaf)

---

[46] Effective dates for new legislation frequently precede the actual enactment date. See, e.g., the original version of I.R.C. § 163(h)(3)(C), allowing interest deductions with respect to debt exceeding a taxpayer's cost of purchasing and improving a residence if the excess debt was incurred by August 16, 1986 (over two months before the 1986 Act was enacted). Transactions subject to binding contracts on the effective date are often exempted. Notice 90-6, 1990-1 C.B. 304, provides guidance with respect to the existence of a binding contract for purposes of the Revenue Reconciliation Act of 1989. Major changes often include transition rules that benefit specific taxpayers. See, e.g., Pub. L. No. 99-514, § 204, 100 Stat. 2085, 2146 (1986).

[47] Nontax-oriented codifications include United States Code, United States Code Annotated, and United States Code Service. See Fundamentals of Legal Research ch. 9. These codifications include statutes that are codified outside 26 U.S.C.

[48] The GPO website offers online access to U.S.C. and its supplements.

[49] SFTR includes all federal taxes in its two Code volumes but covers only income and employment taxes in the remainder of the set. CCH also publishes Federal Estate and Gift Tax Reporter and Federal Excise Tax Reporter. Because their formats resemble that of SFTR, this text includes few separate references to those services. The Code also appears in each looseleaf service's compilation volumes.

• United States Tax Reporter[50] (Chapter 12) (looseleaf)

If you are unsure which Code section applies, use the publisher's topical index to assist you. [See Illustrations 3-1 and 3-2.]

2. Individual Acts

Looseleaf services integrate the text of recent statutes into their codifications, but separate versions of an act are still valuable. These versions may be available more quickly than the pages needing insertion into a codification. In addition, when the entire act is printed as a unit, it will include effective dates and congressional instructions to the IRS. [See Illustrations 5-1 and 5-3.] This information is omitted from the codifications or reproduced in relatively small print.

Acts are first published as slip laws and then bound in Public Law number order into the appropriate volume of United States Statutes at Large.[51] The U.S. Government Printing Office website, GPO Access, provides text with Statutes at Large pagination for laws enacted in the 104th and subsequent Congresses.[52] Westlaw and LexisNexis also provide full text but do not include the pagination.

You can also locate these acts in nontax services[53] and in the tax-oriented materials listed below.

• Internal Revenue Bulletin; Cumulative Bulletin (Chapter 16)

• Internal Revenue Acts—Text and Legislative History (Chapter 16)

Mertens, Law of Federal Income Taxation—Code volumes (Chapter 12)

---

[50] All federal taxes are covered in the USTR Code volumes. Code provisions also appear in the related looseleaf services' compilation volumes. USTR has three components, USTR—Income Taxes (income and employment taxes), USTR—Estate & Gift Taxes, and USTR—Excise Taxes. Because all are similar in format, references to USTR in this text are based on the income tax service.

[51] Statutes at Large is available in CD-ROM and online from Potomac Publishing Company; coverage begins in 1789.

[52] See Public and Private Laws at http://www.access.gpo.gov/nara/nara005.html. The site includes PDF and text versions.

[53] U.S. Code Congressional and Administrative News (USCCAN) and United States Code Service Advance are two such sources. See Fundamentals of Legal Research ch. 9.

included the text of new acts for the 1954 Code. Mertens remains useful for 1954 Code historical research.

3. Previous Law

The materials listed in subsection 1 contain the current law. Those listed below provide the previous versions of amended sections as well as the text of legislation that has been repealed altogether. Periods covered by each are indicated. To determine the Code section number used in an earlier Code, use the cross-reference tables discussed in Chapter 6, Legislative Histories.

• Cumulative Changes (Chapter 16) (separate services for each Code)

• Barton's Federal Tax Laws Correlated (Chapter 16) (1913-52)

• Seidman's Legislative History of Federal Income and Excess Profits Tax Laws (Chapter 16) (1861-1953)

• Legislative History of the Internal Revenue Code (Chapter 16) (1954-65)

• Mertens, Law of Federal Income Taxation—Code (Chapter 12) (1954-85)

• Internal Revenue Acts—Text and Legislative History; U.S. Code Congressional & Administrative News—Internal Revenue Code (Chapter 16) (prior years' volumes; these two sets are best used together for this purpose) (1954 to date)

• Tax Management Primary Sources (Chapter 16) (1969 to date)

• The Internal Revenue Acts of the United States: 1909-1950; 1950-1972; 1973- (Chapter 16)

All of them allow you to trace the language of particular Code and act sections through their various permutations. The process is easier in the first four sources, which use fewer volumes.

If Seidman's is unavailable, you can use Eldridge, The United States Internal Revenue System (Chapter 16). It provides annotated text for revenue acts prior to 1894 but does not provide as much information as does Seidman's.

4. Pending Legislation

The weekly Congressional Index is an excellent print source for locating and tracking pending items. This service provides a brief digest of pending bills. It also indicates a bill's progress, listing hearings and other pertinent information. [See Illustrations 5-6 and 5-7.] Bills are indexed by subject matter as well as by author and bill number. Useful tables provide information about enactments by Public Law number; enactments by bill or resolution number; names of laws amended or enacted; and vetoes.[54] You can track bills at the Library of Congress THOMAS website, http://thomas.loc.gov.

Illustration 5-6. Excerpt from Congressional Index

H 2511—Energy—income tax—energy production, encouragement

By McCrery.

To amend the Internal Revenue Code of 1986 to provide tax incentives to encourage energy conservation, energy reliability, and energy production. (To Ways and Means.)

→ H.R. 2511 was introduced by Representative McCrery in the 107th Congress, 1st Session.

Illustration 5-7. Excerpt from Congressional Index

2511	
Introduced	7/17/01
Ref to H Ways & Means Com	7/17/01
Ordered reptd w/amdts by Ways & Means Com	7/18/01
Reptd w/amdts, H Rept 107-157, by Ways & Means Com	7/24/01

→As of May 2, 2002, Congressional Index reported no further action. The THOMAS website lists H.R. 4 as a related bill. As of May 2, the Senate had asked the House for a conference on that bill (See Chapter 6).

Although tax-oriented looseleaf services may cover pending legislation, only Daily Tax Report and Tax Notes list a significant number of bills introduced in the current Congress; their descriptions of most items are cursory. Both are discussed in Chapter 15.

Online services (Chapter 19) are often the best means for following pending bills. Tax Notes and Daily Tax Report are available online through general services such as Westlaw or LexisNexis and through their publishers' separate online service. You should try using government's THOMAS site, particularly for recent bills, or a commercial service such as Congressional Universe.

---

[54] Other useful tools include those published by Congressional Information Service (CIS), which follow a bill's progress through Congress, and the Weekly Compilation of Presidential Documents. See Fundamentals of Legal Research ch. 10.

5. Potential Legislation

Long before a bill is introduced, taxpayers may receive hints that it is on the horizon. In presidential election years, for example, party platforms include potential legislative agendas. Presidential budget messages may also serve this function. Items of this nature appear in newsletters (Chapter 15) as well as in many general interest newspapers.[55] You can also find presidential documents at the President's website, http://www.whitehouse.gov. Political parties have their own sites.

Prior congressional action is another source of potential legislation. Treasury Department studies mandated in one act [Illustration 5-1] may lead to provisions enacted in a later year.[56] In addition, unenacted legislation from one Congress is often reintroduced in a subsequent one. Legislators often issue press releases announcing they are working on bills.

Although Treasury regulations usually follow (and interpret) statutes, there are occasional role reversals. Legislation may be enacted to codify positions taken in regulations.[57] Unpopular court decisions may also trigger legislative activity.[58]

SECTION G. CITATORS FOR STATUTES

After Congress passes an act, litigation may ensue over the constitutionality or interpretation of individual Code sections. Constitutional litigation is discussed in Chapter 4, which includes several examples of such claims. Litigation is more likely to involve disputes between the IRS and taxpayers over conflicting interpretations of statutory provisions.

Both Shepard's Federal Tax Citator and Shepard's Federal Statute

---

[55] American Law Institute proposals can be harbingers of future bill proposals. See, e.g., H.R. 6261, 98th Cong., 2d Sess. (1984), incorporating ALI proposals on generation-skipping taxes. FEDERAL ESTATE AND GIFT TAX PROJECT—STUDY ON GENERATION-SKIPPING TRANSFERS UNDER THE FEDERAL ESTATE TAX (Discussion Draft No. 1, Mar. 28, 1984).

[56] These and other government studies are discussed in Chapter 6.

[57] This occurred in 1996 for life insurance benefits paid before death during a terminal illness (I.R.C. § 101(g)), in 1984 for certain fringe benefits (I.R.C. § 132), and in 1971 for asset depreciation range (ADR) depreciation (1954 I.R.C. § 167(m)).

[58] See, e.g., I.R.C. § 108(d)(7)(A), a response to Gitlitz v. Commissioner, 531 U.S. 206 (2001).

Citations indicate if a federal court has determined a statute's constitutionality or if it has interpreted a statute.[59] Federal Statute Citations does not include Tax Court Memorandum decisions; Federal Tax Citator omitted all Tax Court decisions until the 1996-1998 Supplement volume. If you need earlier Tax Court coverage of statutes, try searching electronically in a database that includes the Tax Court. Citators are discussed in Chapter 11.

SECTION H. INTERPRETING STATUTORY LANGUAGE

1. Sources for Interpreting Statutes

When litigation arises involving the meaning of a statute, someone must interpret it. Although Congress has delegated the authority to issue interpretive rules to the Treasury Department (Chapter 8),[60] regulations rarely follow on the heels of a law's enactment.

In addition to administrative interpretations, or in their absence when none are available, courts may turn to legislative history documents (Chapter 6) as expressions of congressional intent. Legislative history materials take on particular significance if administrative rules are alleged to be unreasonable and the statute's "plain meaning" is in doubt.[61]

2. Using Statutory Language

As noted in Chapter 3, careful reading of Code provisions is a critical part of the research process. If the Code provides its own definition for a term, you must locate that definition. If a term is specifically defined for purposes of a particular Code subdivision (e.g., Code section 165(g)(2) in Illustration 5-5), you cannot automatically use that definition for another subdivision.

a. Intra-Code Cross-References

Because a single Code section rarely governs a transaction, your research must include a search for other operative sections. Congress frequently

---

[59] Citators used to determine the validity of administrative interpretations are described in that chapter and discussed further in Chapters 8 and 9, which cover Treasury Department and IRS interpretations.

[60] I.R.C. § 7805.

[61] Chevron U.S.A. Inc. v. Natural Resources Defense Council, Inc., 467 U.S. 837 (1984), and United States v. Mead Corp., 533 U.S. 218 (2001), are discussed in Chapters 8 and 9.

offers guidance in accomplishing this task by providing cross-references between Code sections that govern the same transaction.[62] Unfortunately, cross-references may appear in only one of the sections.[63] An intra-Code cross-reference table may provide the information you need.

Cross-reference tables showing Code sections citing to a particular section appear in Standard Federal Tax Reporter (Chapter 12). Although CD-ROM (Chapter 18) and online (Chapter 19) services lack tables, they may have other finding aids you can use to find cross-references. The OneDisc, for example, provides cross-references in the Background Notes for most Code sections. Services such as TaxExpert Online also include cross-references.

As Illustrations 5-8 through 5-10 indicate, different sources may yield different results. There is no substitute for reading the Code sections.

Illustration 5-8. Excerpt from Standard Federal Tax Reporter Code Volume I Cross Reference Table III

Section	Referred to in
707	42, 121, 144, 147, 163, 170, 179, 179A, 197, 213, 221, 267, 304, 351, 355, 453, 465, 469, 475, 514, 613A, 631, 643, 685, 706, 736, 860L, 871, 936, 988, 1031, 1033, 1060, 1202, 1235, 1259, 1397, 1400B, 1400C, 1402, 2701, 5881, 6038A, 6111, 7519, 7612

➔The SFTR table covers only cross-references within the Internal Revenue Code. Other services include additional titles of United States Code.

➔As of May 2002, this table is several years old.

Illustration 5-9. OneDisc Background Notes for Section 707

Section Referred to in Other Sections

This section is referred to in sections 42, 48, 144, 147, 170, 179, 267, 453, 465, 469, 514, 613A, 631, 706, 736, 936, 988, 1235, 1402, 5881, 6038A, 7519 of this title; title 42 section 411.

➔Background Notes covers additional titles of U.S.C.

➔A simple word search using OneDisc yields additional Code sections.

---

[62] I.R.C. §§ 267 and 707(b) specifically refer to each other.

[63] I.R.C. § 104 refers to I.R.C. § 213, but § 213 fails to mention § 104.

Illustration 5-10. Excerpt from TaxExpert Online

SECTION REFERRED TO IN OTHER SECTIONS

This section is referred to in sections 42, 144, 147, 163, 170, 179, 267, 355, 453, 465, 469, 514, 613A, 631, 706, 736, 936, 988, 1031, 1060, 1235, 1402, 2701, 5881, 6038A, 7519 of this title; title 42 section 411.

→Although OneDisc and TaxExpert Online are both electronic services, they give different results; both results differ from the SFTR table in Illustration 5-8. Tables compiled based on editorial judgment can yield inaccurate results for both print and electronic sources.

b. Limitations of Cross-Reference Tables and Similar Tools

These sources are worthless if Code sections interact but don't explicitly refer to each other.[64] Even if sections do refer to each other, an infrequently updated cross-reference table or other tool may not reflect the most recent statutory changes. Using a term search in a CD-ROM or online service presents much less risk that your source will not be current.

Reliance on these tools may induce a dangerous sense of security. If you are an experienced practitioner, you know which types of provisions affect others. In approaching a deductibility problem, for example, you would consider sections allowing the deduction as well as potential disallowance sections and timing provisions. You may locate these by glancing through the Code itself or by using a subject matter Code section index. [See Illustrations 3-1 and 3-2.] Alternatively, you might use a subject-oriented looseleaf service (Chapter 12) to obtain this information. Less-experienced researchers should follow this technique.

c. Limitations on Cross-References as Interpretive Aids

While cross-references are useful in locating relevant statutory material, they lack independent interpretive significance. Code section 7806(a) provides that "[t]he cross references in this title to other portions of the title, or other provisions of law, where the word 'see' is used, are made only for convenience, and shall be given no legal effect."

3. Selected Maxims of Construction

Judges cite various rules of statutory construction in the course of inter-

---

[64] Before its 1986 revision, I.R.C. § 336 failed to mention § 1245 and vice versa. Section 1245 clearly governed transactions affected by each section.

preting statutes. The decisions listed below state or repeat several of these rules.[65] To appreciate their effect, you should read the opinions cited for each proposition. The weight given legislative history is discussed in Chapter 6; that given administrative interpretations is discussed in Chapters 8 and 9.

• The fundamental principle of statutory construction, *expressio unius est exclusio alterius*, applies. There is a firm presumption that everything in the I.R.C. was intentionally included for a reason and everything not in the code was likewise excluded for a reason—the expression of one thing is the exclusion of another. Speers v. United States, 38 Fed. Cl. 197, 202 (1997).

• "Under the principle of *ejusdem generis*, when a general term follows a specific one, the general term should be understood as a reference to subjects akin to the one with specific enumeration." .... In the usual instance, the doctrine of *ejusdem generis* applies where a "catch-all" term precedes, or more often follows, an enumeration of specific terms in order to expand the list without identifying every situation covered by the statute. Host Marriott Corp. v. United States, 113 F. Supp.2d 790, 793 (D. Md. 2000).

• [T]he presumption is against interpreting a statute in a way which renders it ineffective or futile. Matut v. Commissioner, 86 T.C. 686, 690 (1986).

• [T]he courts have some leeway in interpreting a statute if the adoption of a literal or usual meaning of its words "would lead to absurd results *** or would thwart the obvious purpose of the statute." .... Or, to put it another way, we should not adopt a construction which would reflect a conclusion that Congress had "legislate[d] eccentrically." Edna Louise Dunn Trust v. Commissioner, 86 T.C. 745, 755 (1986).

• We should avoid an interpretation of a statute that renders any part of it superfluous and does not give effect to all of the words used by Congress. Beisler v. Commissioner, 814 F.2d 1304, 1307 (9th Cir. 1987).

• [T]he whole of [the section's] various subparts should be harmonized if possible. Water Quality Association Employees' Benefit Corp. v. United States, 795 F.2d 1303, 1307 (7th Cir. 1986).

[65] The Code also includes rules of construction: "No inference, implication, or presumption of legislative construction shall be drawn or made by reason of the location or grouping of any particular section or provision or portion of this title, nor shall any table of contents, table of cross references, or similar outline, analysis, or descriptive matter relating to the contents of this title be given any legal effect." I.R.C. § 7806(b).

• In terms of statutory construction, the *context* from which the meaning of a word is drawn must of necessity be the words of the statute itself. Strogoff v. United States, 10 Cl. Ct. 584, 588 (1986).

• [H]eadings and titles are not meant to take the place of the detailed provisions of the text. Nor are they necessarily designed to be a reference guide or a synopsis. Where the text is complicated and prolific, headings and titles can do no more than indicate the provisions in a most general manner;.... Factors of this type have led to the wise rule that the title of a statute and the heading of a section cannot limit the plain meaning of the text. Stanley Works v. Commissioner, 87 T.C. 389, 419 (1986).

• When a statute does not define a term, we generally interpret that term by employing the ordinary, contemporary, and common meaning of the words that Congress used. Merkel v. Commissioner, 192 F.3d 844, 848 (9th Cir. 1999).

• As a matter of statutory construction, identical words used in different parts of the Internal Revenue Code are normally given the same meaning. Disabled American Veterans v. Commissioner, 94 T.C. 60, 71 (1990).

• Stated another way, Congress must make a clear statement that a double benefit is intended before we will construe a provision to allow this result. Transco Exploration Co. v. Commissioner, 949 F.2d 837, 841 (5th Cir. 1992).

SECTION I. PROBLEMS

1. Indicate the subtitle, chapter, subchapter, part, and subpart for section

    a. 453   c. 2056   e. 6671

    b. 857   d. 4461   f. 7872

2. Indicate the function the President is authorized to exercise by Code section

    a. 168(g)(6)(A)   c. 2014(h)

    b. 891   d. 5708

3. Give the bill number for Pub. L. No.

    a. 106-230   b. 95-618   c. 89-809   d. 86-69

4. Indicate the popular name for

    a. Pub. L. No. 98-397   c. Pub. L. No. 88-563

    b. Pub. L. No. 94-452   d. Pub. L. No. 85-866

5. Indicate the full Statutes at Large citation, including Public Law or chapter number, for

    a. Bankruptcy Tax Act of 1980   c. Public Salary Tax Act of 1939

    b. Excess Profits Tax Act of 1950   d. Revenue Act of 1924

6. Indicate which tax provision appears in

    a. No Child Left Behind Act, Pub. L. No. 107-110, § 1076(t)

    b. Wendell H. Ford Aviation Investment and Reform Act for the 21st Century, Pub. L. No. 106-181, § 1001(a)

    c. ICC Termination Act of 1995, Pub. L. No. 104-88, § 304(a)

    d. Energy Policy Act of 1992, Pub. L. No. 102-486, § 1938

7. List the Treasury Department study mandated in

    a. Tax Treatment Extension Act of 1980, § 6

    b. Technical and Miscellaneous Revenue Act of 1988, § 6056

    c. Taxpayer Bill of Rights 2 Act, § 401

    d. Tax and Trade Relief Extension Act of 1998, § 2022

8. Indicate which act Congress required of the executive branch in

    a. Pub. L. No. 94-455, § 1064(a)   b. Pub. L. No. 97-34, § 201(a)

9. List the Code section added by

    a. Pub. L. No. 95-600, § 134(a)   c. Pub. L. No. 97-248, § 351(a)

    b. Pub. L. No. 101-508, § 11602(a)   d. Pub. L. No. 85-866, § 204(a)

10. Give the enactment date for

   a. Revenue Act of 1921

   b. Current Tax Payment Act of 1943

   c. Individual Income Tax Act of 1944

   d. Revenue Act of 1951

11. Give the enactment date for

   a. Federal Tax Lien Act of 1966

   b. Tax Reduction Act of 1975

   c. Pub. L. No. 98-601

   d. Financial Institutions Reform, Recovery, and Enforcement Act of 1989

   e. FSC Repeal and Extraterritorial Income Exclusion Act of 2000

12. List the effective date of the act provision listed below. Indicate if it precedes, coincides with, or follows the enactment date.

   a. Surface Transportation Revenue Act of 1998, § 9010(a)(1)

   b. Small Business Job Protection Act of 1996, § 1704(f)(2)(A)

   c. Pub. L. No. 100-647, § 1018(l)(3)

   d. Pub. L. No. 95-502, § 301(a)

13. Give the sunset date for Code section

   a. 40   c. 198

   b. 168(j)   d. 4041(b)(2)A)

14. The Code sections listed below have been repealed. Provide the following information relating to that repeal: Public Law number (or chapter), act section number, and effective date of repeal. (A section added in the 1954 Code might have been repealed in that Code or in the 1986 Code.)

   a. 1954 Code § 128

b. 1954 Code § 214

c. 1954 Code § 5115

d. 1986 Code § 956A

e. 1986 Code § 4283

f. 1986 Code § 4978A

15. List the Code subtitles affected by Code section 7873.

16. Indicate the scope limitations (e.g., subtitle, section, clause) for Code section

    a. 103(c)   b. 412(c)(7)(B)   c. 419A(a)   d. 464(e)

17. Indicate which Code section defines

    a. Educational services   c. Highly erodible cropland

    b. Enrolled actuary   d. School bus

18. Congress occasionally defines Code section terms by citing to other federal statutes. Find a Code section that takes its definition from

    a. Americans With Disabilities Act of 1990

    b. Communications Satellite Act of 1962

    c. Community Development Banking and Financial Institutions Act of 1994

    d. Investment Company Act of 1940

19. List all Code sections that refer to Code section

    a. 79   b. 1033   c. 2513   d. 7871

20. Indicate which principle(s) of statutory interpretation the court enunciated or reiterated in the listed case. (Ignore discussions of deference.)

    a. Hillman v. Commissioner, 263 F.3d 338 (4th Cir. 2001)

    b. Marsh & McLennan Companies, Inc. v. United States, 50 Fed. Cl. 140

(2001)

    c. Mellon Bank, N.A. v. United States, 47 Fed. Cl. 186 (2000)

    d. True Oil Company v. Commissioner, 170 F.3d 1294 (10th Cir. 1999)

    e. Dobra v. Commissioner, 111 T.C. 339 (1998)

    f. Goeden v. Commissioner, 75 T.C.M. (CCH) 1581 (1998)

21. Do an online or CD-ROM search to find a more recent judicial decision citing a principle of interpretation listed in Section H. Your instructor may assign a particular principle for you to research.

22. Print out the tax planks from the Democratic and Republican platforms from the most recent presidential campaign.

23. Print out the tax proposals from the President's most recent State of the Union Address and Budget Message.

Problems dealing with constitutional challenges appear in Chapter 4.

Chapter 6. Legislative Histories

Section A. Introduction

This chapter continues the discussion of statutes begun in Chapter 5 by describing legislative history materials and indicating where they can be found. In addition to hearings, reports by tax-writing committees, and congressional floor debate, it includes reports by other committees and by entities such as the General Accounting Office. This chapter also explains the process for tracing current statutes back to earlier versions. Legislative history documents for treaties are covered in Chapter 7.

Section B. Groups Involved in Legislation[66]

1. Congressional Committees

The **House Committee on Ways and Means** and the **Senate Committee on Finance** have primary jurisdiction over revenue bills. Other relevant committees include each chamber's **Budget Committee** and committees with jurisdiction over other areas with tax implications.[67] Each of these committees has subcommittees. If the House and Senate pass different versions of a bill, a **Conference Committee** meets to resolve these differences.

Five members each from Ways and Means and Finance sit on the **Joint Committee on Taxation** (JCT).[68] While the JCT may issue proposals and reports, it is not charged with drafting legislation and its reports lack the interpretive significance of those issued by the tax-writing committees.

The **Joint Economic Committee**, which is also staffed by members of

---

[66] Table 6-1 provides website information for entities described in this section.

[67] E.g., the Subcommittee on Tax, Finance and Exports of the House Small Business Committee.

[68] I.R.C. §§ 8001-8023. The JCT is charged with investigating the operation and effects of the tax system, its administration, and means of simplifying it. Id. § 8022. It also reviews tax refunds exceeding $2,000,000. Id. § 6405.

each chamber, reviews the economy and recommends improvements in economic policy. Areas on which it issues reports include taxation.

2. Congressional Support Entities

Three entities are organized as nonpartisan support services. Each issues reports on various tax administration and policy issues.

The **General Accounting Office** is the investigative arm of Congress. "GAO examines the use of public funds, evaluates federal programs and activities, and provides analyses, options, recommendations, and other assistance to help the Congress make effective oversight, policy, and funding decisions."[69] The GAO issues numerous reports on tax administration and on substantive tax topics. It is headed by the Comptroller of the Currency.

The **Congressional Budget Office** supports congressional legislative efforts by providing economic forecasts, analyzing presidential budgets, and providing cost estimates for pending legislation.[70]

The **Congressional Research Service** (known as the Legislative Reference Service between 1914 and 1970) performs research on public policy matters for Congress. Although its work is confidential, several of its reports are available. The CRS Director is appointed by the Librarian of Congress with the consent of the Joint Committee on the Library.[71]

3. The Executive Branch

The **President** may initiate legislation, which a member of Congress will introduce, in messages to Congress (e.g., the State of the Union Address) or in other speeches. The **Office of Management and Budget** assists the President in formulating a budget and works with administrative agencies to ensure that their reports and testimony are consistent with the President's goals. The **Council of Economic Advisors** provides analysis and advice on developing and implementing economic policy.

Several other executive branch entities issue reports with respect to taxation. As discussed in Chapter 5, Congress frequently asks the **Treasury Department** to study and report on issues. The **IRS National Taxpayer**

---

[69] GAO Website (http://www.gao.gov) (visited May 4, 2002).

[70] CBO Website (http://www.cbo.gov/respon.shtml) (visited May 4, 2002).

[71] CRS reports are not available on the CRS website. These reports are available through services such as Tax Notes Today.

Advocate issues two reports to Congress each year. The first outlines goals and activities planned for the next year. The second discusses serious issues facing taxpayers and recommendations for solving them.[72]

Table 6-1. Websites for Various Government Entities

Congressional Budget Office	www.cbo.gov
Congressional Research Service	www.lcweb.loc.gov/crsinfo/
Council of Economic Advisors	www.whitehouse.gov/cea/
General Accounting Office	www.gao.gov
Government Printing Office	www.gpo.gov
House of Representatives	www.house.gov
Budget	budget.house.gov
Ways & Means	waysandmeans.house.gov
IRS National Taxpayer Advocate	www.irs.gov/advocate
Joint Economic Committee	www.house.gov/jec/
Joint Committee on Taxation	www.house.gov/jct/
Library of Congress/THOMAS	thomas.loc.gov/
Office of Management and Budget	www.whitehouse.gov/omb/
President	www.whitehouse.gov
Senate	www.senate.gov
Budget	budget.senate.gov/
Finance	finance.senate.gov/
Treasury Department	www.treas.gov
Office of Tax Analysis	www.treas.gov/ota/
Office of Tax Policy	www.treas.gov/taxpolicy/

➔If you lack a web address, you can access government sites at FirstGov (http://www.firstgov.gov). It lists all branches of government under Agencies.

4. Other Groups

Members of Congress regularly receive written input from constituents, committees of the American Bar Association and the American Institute of Certified Public Accountants, trade associations, and lobbyists. These groups also testify at hearings on proposed legislation.

SECTION C. LEGISLATIVE PROCESS

The process for enacting tax legislation is virtually identical to that used for other federal laws. The major difference relates to the constitutional limitation discussed in Chapter 4, that revenue-raising bills must originate

---

[72] See TAX NOTES TODAY, 2002 TNT 41-1 (Mar. 1, 2002) for a report on possible legislative initiatives in response to the Advocate's December 2001 report.

in the House of Representatives.[73]

1. Introduction of Bill

The sponsoring legislator may present remarks for inclusion in the Congressional Record at the bill's introduction. If the administration is proposing an item, a presidential message may accompany the bill transmitted to Congress.

The bill receives a bill number when it is introduced. Similar bills may be introduced in the same chamber; each will have a separate bill number. The bill may be simultaneously introduced in each chamber and receive separate bill numbers in each. Bill numbers are sequential for each term of Congress (e.g., H.R. 1; S. 1); there is not a separate numbering system for each session within the two-year term.

2. Referral to Committee and Committee Action

After its introduction, the bill is referred to the appropriate committee, generally the House Ways and Means Committee or the Senate Finance Committee. The committee (or a subcommittee thereof) may hold hearings, which will be published, and issue a committee report to accompany the bill that is reported out of committee. These reports are numbered by Congress (e.g., H.R. Rep. No. 107-251, 107th Cong., 1st Sess. (2001)).

The version of the bill that the committee chair initially issues is referred to as the "chairman's mark."[74] After committee deliberation, which may include input from committee, IRS, and Treasury staffs and from other groups described in Section B, the marked-up bill may differ significantly from its initial version.

The bill, or a similar version, may have been simultaneously considered in the other chamber or considered after being passed in the first chamber. The process in the second chamber, generally the Senate, is comparable to that described above.

---

[73] See James V. Saturno, Blue-Slipping: The Origination Clause in the House of Representatives (Congressional Research Service Report, 2002), available on LexisNexis at 2002 TNT 114-16.

During the 104th Congress, the House adopted a three-fifths "super-majority" vote to pass a tax rate increase. H.R. Res. 6, 104th Cong., 1st Sess. (1995) (House Rule XXI, cl. 5).

[74] As of this writing, all tax-writing committee chairs have been male.

3. House and Senate Floor Debate

A bill sent to the floor by committee can die in one chamber, pass intact, or pass with amendments. Each chamber separately deliberates on the bill before voting. Although Senate rules permit more extensive debate and floor amendments than do House procedures, each chamber can change the bill. A bill sent from one chamber to the other is called an **engrossed bill**.

Questions and answers and other statements made during floor debate can illuminate the meaning of legislation.[75] Be aware, however, that statements can be made to an empty chamber or added as text but not spoken.

If both chambers pass the bill with identical terms, it can be sent to the President. If the versions differ, a Conference Committee is appointed.

4. Conference Committee Action

The Conference Committee meets to resolve House and Senate differences. It generates a third report, which is usually numbered as a House report. That report explains the resolution of House-Senate differences. [See Illustration 6-1.]

5. Floor Action on Conference Report

Unlike the pre-conference bills, a bill that emerges from the Conference Committee cannot be further amended during floor debate. Each chamber must pass it or reject it as written. That "final" version (the **enrolled version**) is then prepared for submission to the President.

6. Correcting Drafting Errors

Unlike treaties, bills die when a Congress's second session ends.[76] Members work under extreme time pressure to pass pending legislation by that date. As a result, a conference report's version may contain errors, which Congress passes along with the rest of the bill. If both chambers agree, Congress can adopt a concurrent resolution making necessary changes

---

[75] In Ashburn v. United States, 740 F.2d 843 (11th Cir. 1984), the court referred to committee reports and congressional debates as evidence of the meaning of a phrase in the Equal Access to Justice Act. See also Commissioner v. Engle, 464 U.S. 206 (1984), in which the Court's opinion on the meaning of I.R.C. § 613A cited to testimony at hearings, floor debate, and committee reports. Be aware that the Supreme Court has become less receptive to using legislative history materials in construing statutes.

[76] Chapter 7 discusses other differences between statutes and treaties.

before the act is enrolled for submission to the President. If they do not agree, or find the errors too late, a technical corrections bill is inevitable.[77]

Illustration 6-1. Excerpt from H. Rep. No. 107-84, 107th Cong., 1st Sess. (2001), at 158

a skill required in a trade or business currently engaged in by the taxpayer, or (2) meets the express requirements of the taxpayer's employer, applicable law or regulations imposed as a condition of continued employment. However, education expenses are generally not deductible if they relate to certain minimum educational requirements or to education or training that enables a taxpayer to begin working in a new trade or business.[31]

HOUSE BILL

No provision.

SENATE AMENDMENT

The provision extends the exclusion for employer-provided educational assistance to graduate education and makes the exclusion (as applied to both undergraduate and graduate education) permanent.

Effective date.—The provision is effective with respect to courses beginning after December 31, 2001.

CONFERENCE AGREEMENT

The conference agreement follows the Senate Amendment.

→The conference report explains current law in addition to reporting on each chamber's proposals and resolution of House-Senate differences.

7. Presidential Action

The President has four options. The bill becomes law if the President signs it within ten days of its presentment. It also becomes law if the President does nothing so long as Congress remains in session during that period. Alternatively, the President can veto the bill; Congress can override a veto only by a two-thirds vote in each chamber.[78] If the President does nothing

---

[77] See, e.g., H.R. Con. Res. 328, 98th Cong., 2d Sess. (1984), 98 Stat. 3454 (1984), making technical changes to the Tax Reform Act of 1984. Compare H.R. Con. Res. 395, 99th Cong., 2d Sess. (1986), which failed to pass, leaving flaws in the 1986 Act. When using the THOMAS website, search for these as H. rather than H.R.

[78] For example, Congress overrode President Franklin Roosevelt's veto of the Revenue Act of 1943, ch. 63, 58 Stat. 21 (1944).

and the congressional session ends during the ten-day period, the bill is "pocket-vetoed." The President may issue a statement when signing or vetoing a bill.

SECTION D. LOCATING LEGISLATIVE HISTORY DOCUMENTS: CITATIONS AND TEXT

The process used for locating legislative history documents varies depending on whether you are using print materials or electronic services. If you are using print materials, your research may involve two steps. First you must obtain the appropriate citations for the documents needed. Then you must locate those documents. When researching online or in a CD-ROM database, you may be able to find your documents using word and Code section searches even if you lack their citations.[79]

1. Statements on the Floor of Congress

The Congressional Record prints statements made when a bill is introduced, presidential messages accompanying an administration bill, and statements, questions, and answers made during floor debate. Make sure you check the Congressional Record pages for each chamber. The numbering system indicates which chamber (H for House and S for Senate).

Congressional Record can be accessed through its indexes, but it is easier to search online. You can refine your search to a limited number of dates by using Congressional Index, which provides the dates various events occurred with respect to a bill. [See Illustration 5-7.]

Congressional Record can be searched online through commercial services such as Westlaw, LexisNexis, and CIS Congressional Universe. [See Illustration 6-2.] The government makes it available online through GPO Access, beginning with 1994.[80]

Several tax-oriented sources print excerpts from Congressional Record:

- Tax Management Primary Sources (Chapter 16) (since 1969)

---

[79] Beginning in 1975, Statutes at Large includes citations to committee reports, Congressional Record items, and presidential messages immediately following the text of each act.

[80] Http://www.access.gpo.gov/su_docs/aces/aces150.html. The Library of Congress THOMAS site provides limited access to Congressional Record; it frequently sends you to the GPO site for full text. See http://thomas.loc.gov.

• Internal Revenue Acts—Texts and Legislative History (Chapter 16) (since 1954)

• Seidman's Legislative History of Federal Income and Excess Profits Tax Laws (Chapter 16) (1863-1953)

Although it does not contain Congressional Record text, Barton's Federal Tax Laws Correlated (Chapter 16) provides page citations for the period from 1953 through 1969.

Illustration 6-2. Excerpt from Congressional Universe Showing Congressional Floor Action on H.R. 2922, 102d Congress

Legislative Chronology:

1st Session Activity:
07/17/91 137 Cong Rec H 5594
                 Referred to the House Energy and Commerce
                 Committee
07/17/91 137 Cong Rec H 5594
                 Referred to the House Ways and Means
                 Committee
07/18/91 137 Cong Rec E 2586
                 Remarks by Rep. Cardin
09/12/91 137 Cong Rec H 6539
                 Cosponsors added
10/08/91 137 Cong Rec H 7648
                 Cosponsors added
11/26/91 137 Cong Rec H 11891
                 Cosponsors added

2nd Session Activity:
05/13/92 138 Cong Rec H 3240
                 Cosponsors added
06/09/92 138 Cong Rec H 4447
                 Cosponsors added
07/01/92 138 Cong Rec D 839
                 House Subcommittee on Select Revenue
                 Measures held a hearing

2. Committee Hearings

Transcripts of hearings can be located in the library's government documents section or in its microform collection. Online versions are available through services as Westlaw, LexisNexis, and Congressional Universe; dates of coverage vary. For example, hearings since the late 1980s are included in the Tax Analysts database on LexisNexis. [See Illustration 6-3.]

Beginning with the 105th Congress, transcripts of hearings (including written submissions) can be found using the Government Printing Office website. Congressional websites also include some transcripts.

Illustration 6-3. Excerpt from H.R. 2922 Hearing Transcript

Release date: 01 JUL 92
SUBCOMMITTEE ON SELECT REVENUE MEASURES
COMMITTEE ON WAYS AND MEANS

July 1, 1992

CHAIR RANGEL: The subcommittee will come to order.

Today, the Subcommittee on Select Revenue Measures will receive testimony on H.R.2922, the Lead-Based Paint Hazard Abatement Act, and the issue of taxing the lead industry to fund the cleanup of lead-based paint in our nation's homes.

H.R.2922 introduced by Congressmen Cardin, Stark, McDermott, Moody, Donnelly, Ford of Tennessee, Matsui, Guarini, myself and others, would establish a new lead abatement trust fund. The fund would be financed by an excise tax on lead produced in or imported into the United States.

Expenditures from the fund would be authorized for grants to state and local governments for the abatement of hazards associated with lead-based paint in low-income housing and day care centers.

Unfortunately, our nation's children all too often are innocent victims of lead poisoning. Poor children, in particular, cannot protect themselves from high-dose exposure in their homes and in day care centers. It is truly tragic to see our children — our nation's most valuable resource — needlessly suffer from this health risk.

Therefore, it is important for this subcommittee to examine whether there is a role for tax legislation in addressing this serious problem.

Today, we will hear more about the scope of the problem. Further, we will hear about whether or not it is appropriate to tax the lead industry to pay for the cleanup of paint in homes.

➔Tax Notes Today also covers administrative hearings (Chapter 8).

3. Tax-Writing Committee Reports

You can find committee reports in the library's government documents or microform collections if you have the appropriate citation. Reports are numbered sequentially by Congress, not by committee. The numbering does not restart when a term of Congress goes into its second session. Reports use initials to indicate which chamber issued them; the citation also indicates the number and session of Congress.[81]

a. Citations

Online sources provide immediate access to reports even if you lack citations. Unfortunately, they rarely cover pre-1954 Code material. If you need a citation to a report, several services provide that information.[82]

• Bulletin Index-Digest System (Chapter 16) (1954-1994)

• Barton's Federal Tax Laws Correlated (Chapter 16) (through 1969)

• Standard Federal Tax Reporter—Citator (Chapter 12) (Cumulative Bulletin rather than report number citations for amendments to 1954 and 1986 Codes; listed in Code section order)

• TaxCite (citations to reports printed in the Cumulative Bulletin for commonly cited statutes enacted between 1913 and 1993)

• Legislative History of the Internal Revenue Code of 1954 (Chapter 16) (1954 through 1969)

b. Text in Print

Once you have a citation, you can find full or partial text of committee reports in several publications. Print sources include the following:

---

[81] The House Budget Committee report for the Taxpayer Relief Act of 1997, Pub. L. No. 105-34, 111 Stat. 788, is H.R. REP. NO. 105-148, 105TH CONG., 1ST SESS. (1997). The Senate Finance report for the same act is S. REP. NO. 105-33, 105TH CONG., 1ST SESS. (1997). The Conference report is H.R. REP. NO. 105-220, 105TH CONG., 1ST SESS. (1997). Note that the House report did not emanate from the Ways and Means Committee.

[82] The government occasionally prepares citations to legislative history materials. See, e.g., Joint Committee on Taxation, Listing of Selected Federal Tax Legislation Reprinted in the IRS Cumulative Bulletin, 1913-1990 (JCS-19-91) (Dec. 19, 1991). This study appeared as a supplement to Daily Tax Report and can be accessed in the Tax Notes Today (TAXANA; TNT) file in LexisNexis at 91 TNT 258-17.

• Standard Federal Tax Reporter (Chapter 12) (limited coverage)

• United States Tax Reporter (Chapter 12) (limited coverage)

• Rabkin & Johnson, Federal Income, Gift and Estate Taxation (Chapter 12) (1954 Code only)

• Cumulative Bulletin (Chapter 16) (since 1913)[83]

• Internal Revenue Acts—Text and Legislative History (Chapter 16) (since 1954)

• Tax Management Primary Sources (Chapter 16) (since 1969)

• Seidman's Legislative History of Federal Income and Excess Profits Tax Laws (Chapter 16) (1863-1953)

• The Internal Revenue Acts of the United States: 1909-1950; 1950-1972; 1973- (Chapter 16)

Each service has limitations. These include providing only partial texts, printing only one committee report rather than all reports for an act, or omitting original pagination. Seidman's omits estate and gift taxes altogether. Updating for Primary Sources is relatively slow; its publisher no longer lists this service in its brochures or on its website.

The Internal Revenue Acts of the United States: 1909-1950 (and later series) provides full text with original pagination for all materials. Because it omits pre-1909 material, you should consult Seidman's, which includes partial texts, for earlier reports. [See Illustration 16-4.] The Internal Revenue Acts would be much easier to use if it had a comprehensive index.

c. Text in Electronic Format

If you need reports published in the last ten to fifteen years, online and

---

[83] Committee reports for 1913 through 1938 appear in 1939-1 (pt. 2) C.B. With the exception of the 1954 Code, for which none are included, reports for most acts appeared in the Cumulative Bulletin. It is unclear to what extent post-1998 reports will appear in the Bulletin since the IRS adopted its current format.

William S. Hein & Co., Inc., issued a one-volume work, Internal Revenue Code of 1954: Congressional Committee Reports, covering the 1954 Code's history. In addition, Professor Bernard Reams compiled a multivolume work containing texts of committee reports, hearings, and debates. This set is available from Hein as part of The Internal Revenue Acts of the United States series (Chapter 16).

CD-ROM services provide the most comprehensive coverage and may be the easiest to search. Tax Analysts publishes a Legislative History CD-ROM, which prints committee reports since 1986. The Westlaw Federal Tax Legislative History database (FTX-LH) begins in 1948 with selective coverage and provides full coverage since 1990. LexisNexis and Congressional Universe also include committee reports.

The government makes committee reports for the 104th and later Congresses available online through the Government Printing Office website. Those published in PDF format retain original pagination.

4. Other Congressional Reports

One of the most important reports issued by the Joint Committee on Taxation's staff is the General Explanation ("Blue Book") of tax legislation.[84] Because the Joint Committee is not an official tax-writing committee, the Blue Book is not an official committee report and is not covered by many of the services that cover committee reports.[85] The same is true for other Joint Committee staff reports and for reports of legislative subcommittees.

You may also want access to reports issued to Congress by supporting entities such as the Congressional Budget Office, Congressional Research Service, and General Accounting Office.

You can find these items online, in microform collections (Chapter 17), and in library government documents collections. Government websites are particularly likely to include documents generated since 1993.[86] An important advantage of locating these documents online, whether through government websites or subscription services, is your ability to search for them based on concept rather than by document number.

5. Executive Branch Documents

Presidential messages appear in the Weekly Compilation of Presidential

---

[84] The General Explanation issued by the Joint Committee staff is not the only "Blue Book." Other government entities also issue so-called Blue Books. See, e.g., Department of the Treasury, General Explanations of the Administration's Fiscal Year 2003 Revenue Proposals (Blue Book) (Feb. 4, 2002), available at the Office of Tax Policy website (http://www.treas.gov/taxpolicy/).

[85] Tax Analysts' Legislative History CD-ROM includes several JCT staff reports.

[86] See Government Printing Office Electronic Information Access Enhancement Act of 1993, Pub. L. No. 103-40, 107 Stat. 112, codified at 44 U.S.C. § 4101.

Documents, which can be located online at the Government Printing Office website through its GPO Access Executive page. You can also locate presidential documents at the White House website. Reports issued by the Office of Management and Budget, the Council of Economic Advisors, and the National Taxpayer Advocate can be found at their websites. Subscription-based online services also carry many of these documents.

SECTION E. UNENACTED BILLS

Services such as Congressional Universe don't limit their coverage to enacted legislation. You can locate "legislative history" documents such as those described in Section D even for bills that do not become law. [See Illustration 6-3.] The GPO Access and THOMAS websites also cover unenacted legislation. Their coverage does not extend as far back as does that of Congressional Universe and similar commercial services.

SECTION F. USING LEGISLATIVE HISTORY IN STATUTORY INTERPRETATION

After a bill becomes law, the interpretive process begins. Whether you are researching to determine the best way to structure a transaction, or because litigation is already in process, you must locate authoritative interpretations of the law. In addition to locating legislative history materials issued for a current act, you may need to trace a Code section back to its original version.

1. In Lieu of Administrative Interpretations

Because Congress authorizes the Treasury Department to issue rules and regulations, you might start searching for interpretations in Treasury regulations (Chapter 8) or IRS documents (Chapter 9). Because these agencies cannot issue guidance as quickly as Congress enacts major legislation, they invariably have a backlog of regulations and rulings projects.[87]

If no regulations are available, you can consult legislative history materials to ascertain congressional intent. Even after regulations appear, you can

---

[87] In a worst case scenario, regulations lag several years behind statutes. For example, Congress enacted I.R.C. § 385 in 1969; regulations adopted in 1980, and subsequently amended, were ultimately withdrawn. Regulations interpreting I.R.C. § 501(c)(9) were issued in 1980; Congress enacted that section's predecessor in 1928.

use legislative history to challenge their validity.[88] As discussed in Section G, courts vary in the degree of weight they grant legislative history.[89] Do not overlook this fact in doing your research.

2. Tracing Changes in Statutory Language

Legislative history necessarily includes the process by which a section evolved from its original version. Most 1986 Code provisions were continued from the 1954 Code using the same section numbering scheme. Although the 1939 Code's number system is quite different, you can easily trace current provisions to that Code or to earlier revenue acts.

Chapter 5 lists sources publishing the texts of prior laws. The materials below aid you in determining which sections of those laws are relevant.

a. 1986-1954-1939 Code Cross-Reference Tables

Code cross-reference tables provide cross-references between the 1939 and 1954 Codes. Although cross-references directly from the 1986 Code would also be helpful, the 1954 Code tables will suffice so long as the 1954 and 1986 section numbering systems remain substantially identical.

Certain limitations affect your use of cross-reference tables. First, Congress changed section numbers (adding new items and deleting or moving old ones) after enacting the 1954 Code and again in the 1986 Code. Cross-reference tables may not reflect these changes.[90] You must determine when each provision received its current section number. If the table has not been amended since then, use the previous section number in your tracing effort.

A second limitation is also worth noting. These tables reflect their compilers' opinions as to the appropriate cross-references. Different publishers' tables may yield different results. Illustrations 6-4 and 6-5 reflect this phenomenon for 1954 Code section 443 and 1939 Code section 47.

---

[88] See, e.g., United States v. Nesline, 590 F. Supp. 884 (D. Md. 1984), holding invalid a regulation that varied from the plain language of the statute and had no support in the committee reports; cf. Tutor-Saliba Corp. v. Commissioner, 115 T.C. 1 (2000), holding that a regulation comported with congressional intent.

[89] The Treasury Department and IRS cite to legislative history in administrative documents. See, e.g., T.D. 8810, 64 Fed. Reg. 3398 (1999) (conference report); Rev. Rul. 88-64, 1988-2 C.B. 10 (statement during floor debate).

[90] For example, the table in Illustration 6-5 lists 1939 Code § 23(aa)(1) as the predecessor of 1954 Code § 141. However, 1986 Code § 141 deals with an entirely different topic. 1954 Code § 141 corresponds to 1986 Code § 63(c).

These services provide tables cross-referencing the 1954 and 1939 Codes:

• United States Statutes at Large (Appendix in volume 68A following text of 1954 Code)

• Standard Federal Tax Reporter (Chapter 12) (Code volume I)

• Rabkin & Johnson, Federal Income, Gift and Estate Taxation (Chapter 12) (volume 7B)

• Mertens, Law of Federal Income Taxation—Code (Chapter 12) (1954-58 Code volume) (1954 to 1939 only)

• Cumulative Changes (Chapter 16) (1954 Code volume I)

• Barton's Federal Tax Laws Correlated (Chapter 16) (looseleaf volume)

• Seidman's Legislative History of Federal Income and Excess Profits Tax Laws (Chapter 16) (1953-1939 volume II)

• Legislative History of the Internal Revenue Code of 1954 (Chapter 16)

• Joint Committee on Taxation, Derivations of Code Sections of the Internal Revenue Codes of 1939 and 1954 (JCS-1-92) (Jan. 21, 1992), reprinted in Daily Tax Report, Jan. 23, 1992 (Special Supplement).

b. Tracing Pre-1939 Statutes

You can trace back provisions that predate the 1939 Code using the following tools.

• United States Statutes at Large (Appendix in volume 53 (pt. 1) following text of 1939 Code) (separate tables trace sections predating the Revised Statutes of 1875 back to their original enactment)

• Barton's Federal Tax Laws Correlated (Chapter 16)

• Seidman's Legislative History of Federal Income and Excess Profits Tax Laws (Chapter 16)

• Joint Committee on Taxation, Derivations of Code Sections of the Internal Revenue Codes of 1939 and 1954 (JCS-1-92), Jan. 21, 1992, reprinted in Daily Tax Report, Jan. 23, 1992 (Special Supplement) (citations to Statutes at Large but no text)

Illustration 6-4. Excerpt from Seidman's 1953-1954 Code Reference Table I

1953 CODE SEC.	1954 CODE SEC.	1953 CODE SEC.	1954 CODE SEC.	1953 CODE SEC.	1954 CODE SEC.
13(a)	—	23(n)	167	44	453, 7101
15(a)	11	23(o)(1)-(5)	170	45	482
15(c)	1551	23(p)	404	46	442
21	63	23(q)(1)-(3)	170	47(b)-(c)	443, 6011(a)
22(a)	61	23(r)(1)	591	48	441, 7701

→Seidman's ceased publication when the 1954 Code was adopted. Its 1953-1954 table reflects the initial version of the 1954 Code. It does not reflect any section renumbered in a later year.

Illustration 6-5. Excerpt from 1954-1939 Cross Reference Table in Standard Federal Tax Reporter Code Volume I

101 . . . . 22(b)(1)	265 . . . . 23(b), 24(a)(5)	443 47(a),(c),(e),(g),146(a)
102 . . . . 22(b)(3)	266 . . . . 24(a)(7)	446 41
103 . . . . 22(b)(4)	267 . . . . 24(b), (c)	451 . . . . 42(a)
104 . . . . 22(b)(5)	268 . . . . 24(f)	453 44
105, 106	269 129	454 . . . . . . 42(b), (c), (d)
107 . . . . 22(b)(6)	270 130	455 . . . .
108 . . . . 22(b)(9), (10)	271 . . . . 23(k)(6)	456 . . . .
109 . . . . 22(b)(11)	272	461 43
110	273 . . . . 24(d)	471 . . . . 22(c)
111 . . . . 22(b)(12)	274-279	472 . . . . 22(d)(1)-(5)
112 . . . . 22(b)(13)	281	481 . . . .
113 . . . . 22(b)(14)	301 . . 22(e), 115(a), (b),	482 45
114 . . . . 22(b)(16)	(d), (e), (j)	483 . . . .
115 . . . . 116(d), (e)	302 . . . . . . 115(c), (g)(1)	501 . 101 except (12) and
116-119	303 . . . . 115(g)(3)	last par. and 165(a), 421
121-123	304 . . . . 115(g)(2)	502 . . . . . . Last par. 101
141 . . . . 23(aa)(1)	305 . . . . . . 115(f)(1), (2)	503 3813

SECTION G. JUDICIAL DEFERENCE

Although judicial opinions cite legislative history documents in deciding between conflicting statutory interpretations, many judges prefer to resolve cases based on the so-called "plain meaning" of the statute. Those judges may give more deference to Treasury regulations than to legislative history if the statute is deemed ambiguous.[91]

The following items illustrate judicial statements regarding the deference courts give legislative history. Several of these statements reiterate statements made in earlier cases.

• Delving into the legislative history is unnecessary because the statutes' language is unambiguous. United States v. Farley, 202 F.3d 198, 210 (3d Cir. 2000).

• While the court makes its holding under the plain meaning rule of statutory construction, the court's conclusion is supported by the predecessor to § 402(a) which was § 165(b) of the IRC of 1939 which had its beginnings in § 219(f) of the Internal Revenue Act of 1921. Shimota v. United States, 21 Cl. Ct. 510, 518 (1990).

• The language of the statute leaves us with uncertainty .... The Secretary has not issued any regulations under section 613(e)(3), that might have provided guidance. We look to the legislative history behind the statute for assistance. Newborn v. Commissioner, 94 T.C. 610, 627 (1990).

• Indications of congressional intent contained in a conference committee report deserve great deference by courts because "the conference report represents the final statement of terms agreed to by both houses, [and] next to the statute itself it is the most persuasive evidence of congressional intent." RJR Nabisco, Inc. v. United States, 955 F.2d 1457, 1462 (11th Cir. 1992).

• [The Bluebook] is not part of the legislative history although it is entitled to respect.... Where there is no corroboration in the actual legislative history, we shall not hesitate to disregard the General Explanation as far as congressional intent is concerned. Redlark v. Commissioner, 106 T.C. 31, 45 (1996).

• [The Blue Book] of course does not rise to the level of legislative history, because it was authored by Congressional staff and not by Congress. Nevertheless, such explanations are highly indicative of what Congress did, in fact, intend. Estate of Hutchinson v. Commissioner, 765 F.2d 665, 669-70 (7th Cir. 1985).

---

[91] Deference to administrative interpretations is discussed in Chapters 8 and 9. Even if not accorded deference for purposes of resolving an issue, committee reports, managers' statements in the conference report, pre-enactment floor statements by one of a bill's managers, and the Blue Book all constitute authority for purposes of avoiding the substantial understatement penalty discussed in Chapter 2.

• Congress conveys its directions in the Statutes at Large, not in excerpts from the Congressional Record, much less in excerpts from the Congressional Record that do not clarify the text of any pending legislative proposal. Begier v. Internal Revenue Service, 496 U.S. 53, 68 (1990) (Scalia, J., concurring).

• While Congress's later view as to the meaning of pre-existing law does not seal the outcome when addressing a question of statutory interpretation, it should not be discounted when relevant. Sorrell v. Commissioner, 882 F.2d 484, 489 (11th Cir. 1989).

• While headings are not compelling evidence of meaning in themselves, the corresponding section of the Senate report clarifies and reinforces this analysis. That section is headed "Production, acquisition, and *carrying* costs" (emphasis added) and expresses the intent that "a single, comprehensive set of rules should govern the capitalization of costs of producing, acquiring, and *holding* property" (emphasis added). Reichel v. Commissioner, 112 T.C. 14, 18 (1999).

• Surrounding sentences are context for interpreting a sentence, but so is the history behind the sentence—where the sentence came from, what problem it was written to solve, who drafted it, who opposed its inclusion in the statute. Sundstrand Corp. v. Commissioner, 17 F.3d 965, 967 (7th Cir. 1994).

• We also find the Government's reading more faithful to the history of the statutory provision as well as the basic tax-related purpose that the history reveals. O'Gilvie v. United States, 519 U.S. 79, 84 (1996).

• Legislative history that is inconclusive, however, should not be relied upon to supply a provision not enacted by Congress. St. Laurent v. Commissioner, 71 T.C.M. (CCH) 2566, 2570 (1996).

SECTION H. PROBLEMS

1. Who introduced the following bill? What Code section would it add?

a. H.R. 205, 107th Congress	d. H.R. 124, 104th Congress
b. S. 664, 106th Congress	e. H.R. 60, 103d Congress
c. S. 89, 105th Congress	f. S. 2639, 102d Congress

2. Indicate the bill number and all action for the bill described below.

a. 106th Congress (Archer, House): To amend the Internal Revenue Code of 1986 to reduce individual income tax rates, to provide marriage penalty relief, to reduce taxes on savings and investments, to provide estate and gift tax relief, to provide incentives for education savings and health care, and for other purposes

b. 104th Congress (Hutchinson, Senate): A bill to amend the Internal Revenue Code of 1986 to allow homemakers to get a full IRA deduction

c. 99th Congress (Rostenkowski, House): A bill to repeal the contemporaneous recordkeeping requirements added by the Tax Reform Act of 1984, and for other purposes

d. 96th Congress (Anderson, House): A bill to amend the Internal Revenue Code of 1954 to impose a 50 cent excise tax on gasoline and special motor fuels, to provide that revenues from the tax shall be used for a reduction in social security taxes, and for other purposes

3. On March 21, 2002, Senator Charles Grassley announced he was working on legislation to "go after not only the corporate expatriation abuse, but also the abusers who seek big government contracts while skirting their U.S. tax obligations." Did Senator Grassley introduce such legislation in 2002? If so, provide the bill number and any subsequent congressional action.

4. What was the purpose of H.R. Con. Res. 138, 105th Cong.? Did it pass?

5. What definition of "potato storage facility" appears in the introduced version of H.R. 4718, 107th Cong., 2d Sess.?

6. Provide the following information regarding the congressional hearing indicated

a. Witness list for July 10, 2001, Senate Finance Committee hearing on The Role of Tax Incentives in Energy Policy

b. Witness list for December 7, 1995, Senate Governmental Affairs Committee hearing on S. 94.

c. Name of entity represented by John Chapoton at the House Ways & Means Committee Oversight Subcommittee hearing on tax shelters, September 20, 1985

7. Provide House, Senate (and Conference, if one exists) report numbers for

    a. Pub. L. No. 106-519

    b. Miscellaneous Revenue Act of 1982

    c. Revenue Act of 1962

    d. Pub. L. No. 86-89

    e. Revenue Act of 1941

    f. Revenue Act of 1921

8. Provide a citation (report number and pages containing the discussion) to the congressional report described below.

    a. Conference Committee report explaining the provisions concerning the tax credit for electricity produced by wind and closed-loop biomass facilities in the Ticket to Work and Work Incentives Improvement Act of 1999

    b. Conference Committee report explaining the provisions concerning depreciation period for retail motor fuels outlet stores in the Small Business Job Protection Act of 1996

    c. Senate Finance Committee report explaining amendments to the optional valuation rule for the estate tax in the Revenue Act of 1984.

    d. Discussion of the telephone excise tax in both the House Ways & Means Committee and Senate Finance Committee reports for Pub. L. No. 86-564.

    e. Conference Committee report indicating where in the legislative process Section 225 of the Tax Equity and Fiscal Responsibility Act of 1982 originated.

9. Print the first page of the report requested.

    a. Conference Committee report on the Act of October 22, 1914

    b. Senate Finance Committee report for the Revenue Act of 1928

    c. House Ways & Means Committee report for the Act of August 8, 1947

    d. Senate Finance Committee report on Pub. L. No. 88-4

e. Conference Committee report for the Surface Transportation Revenue Act of 1998

10. With respect to the document listed, provide the information requested by your instructor (author, month of issue, portion of text, etc.).

a. a 1997 Congressional Budget Office report: For Better or for Worse: Marriage and the Federal Income Tax

b. a 1992 Congressional Budget Office report: Effects of Adopting a Value-Added Tax

c. a 1987 Congressional Budget Office report: Tax Policy for Pensions and Other Retirement Saving

d. a 2001 Congressional Research Service report: Saving for College Through Qualified Tuition (Section 529) Programs

e. a 1999 Congressional Research Service memo: Effectiveness of the Proposed Tax Credits for Vaccine Research in H.R. 1274

f. a 1997 Congressional Research Service report: Should Credit Unions Be Taxed?

g. a 2002 General Accounting Office report: IRS's Efforts to Improve Compliance with Employment Tax Requirements Should Be Evaluated

h. a 2000 General Accounting Office report: Alternative Minimum Tax, An Overview of Its Rationale and Impact on Individual Taxpayers

i. a 1990 General Accounting Office report: Low-Income Housing Tax Credit Utilization and Syndication

j. a 2002 Joint Economic Committee study: The Effects of the Duration of Federal Tax Reductions: Examining the Empirical Evidence

k. a 1997 Joint Economic Committee study: Reforming K-12 Education Through Saving Incentives

l. a 1991 Joint Economic Committee study: Taxes and Deficits: New Evidence ("The $1.59 Study")

m. a 2002 Joint Committee on Taxation document: Present Law and Background Relating to Executive Compensation

n. a 1998 Joint Committee on Taxation pamphlet: Tax Amnesty

o. a 1995 Joint Committee on Taxation report: Issues Presented by Proposals to Modify the Tax Treatment of Expatriation

p. a 2001 Treasury Department Office of Tax Analysis paper: Regional Differences in the Utilization of the Mortgage Interest Deduction

q. a 1998 Treasury Department Office of Tax Analysis paper: Tax Evasion by Small Business

r. a 2000 Treasury Department document: Report to The Congress on Tax Benefits for Adoption

s. the most recent semiannual report of the National Taxpayer Advocate

11. Provide a Congressional Record citation for a

a. statement by Representative Hoyer during debate on the conference report for H.R. 1836, 107th Congress, 1st Sess.: "Mr. Speaker, I was here in 1981. The gentleman from Texas ... was not. He was then an economist, perhaps not so successfully because he came to Congress."

b. statement by Representative Johnson (Connecticut) during debate on H.R. 4579, 105th Congress, 2d Sess.: "Mr. Speaker, I say to the gentleman from Pennsylvania ... I will take it. If this bill directs benefits to the 'narrow base of the Republican party,' absolutely. You bet it does, because it directs itself to the interests of all the working people of America. The great middle-class that has made this economic boom possible."

c. statement by Representative Dorgan on October 16, 1990, during debate on the measure that became Pub. L. No. 101-508: "Mr. Speaker, today we will hear another verse of the same old song. Once again the country faces a budget crisis, and once again the President's jet leaves Andrews Air Force Base ...."

d. discussion by Senator Millikin of the reason for enacting section 204 of the Technical Changes Act of 1953.

e. statement by Representative Treadway regarding the provision that became section 612 of the Revenue Act of 1928, ch. 852, 45 Stat. 791: "Though the result does not simplify particularly the wording of the statute, it does clarify a very muddled situation."

12. When did the current 1986 Code section number change, and what was the previous number in the 1954 Code?

    a. 22   b. 27

13. What was the subject of the now-repealed 1954 Code section with the same section number as the 1986 Code section listed below?

    a. 221   b. 1301   c. 2057

14. Which 1939 Code section corresponds to the 1954 Code section listed?

    a. 262   c. 911   e. 2042

    b. 331   d. 1501   f. 3111

15. Which 1954 Code section corresponds to the 1939 Code section listed?

    a. 2   c. 1003   e. 3791(b)

    b. 206   d. 2650   f. 4013(a)

16. What is the pre-1939 Code origin of the 1939 Code section listed?

    a. 55(c)   c. 937   e. 2657

    b. 321   d. 2300   f. 3916

17. What did the decision below say about using legislative history to interpret a statute?

    a. Copeland v. Commissioner, 2002 WL 742058 (5th Cir. 2002)

    b. Frontier Chevrolet Co. v. Commissioner, 116 T.C. 289 (2001)

    c. Tax and Accounting Software Corp. v. United States, 111 F. Supp. 2d 1153 (N.D. Okla. 2000)

    d. Cramer v. Commissioner, 64 F.3d 1406 (9th Cir. 1995)

CHAPTER 7. TREATIES AND OTHER INTERNATIONAL MATERIAL

SECTION A. INTRODUCTION

This chapter discusses treaties and other documents you can consult when researching the treatment of taxpayers with ties to both the United States and another country.

Treaties are agreements between two (bilateral) or more (multilateral) countries. Other relevant materials include statutes; congressional, State Department, and presidential documents; regulations; rulings; and judicial opinions. Documents issued by organizations to which the United States belongs, such as the World Trade Organization, may also be relevant to your research effort.

Your goals include locating all relevant documents, determining their relative hierarchy and validity, and updating your research to encompass pending items. In accomplishing these goals, you should become familiar with the process by which treaties come into force and the terminology used to describe documents. You must also take into account changes in sovereignty. Newly independent or merged countries are not always covered by a treaty between the United States and the country with which they were formerly (or are currently) affiliated.

SECTION B. FUNCTIONS OF TREATIES

Although United States citizens residing abroad pay United States income tax on both domestic and foreign-source income, they may also be taxed in the foreign country of residence. Similar problems may arise with regard to property and transfer taxes. Several statutory mechanisms exist to reduce the burden of taxation by more than one country. These include foreign income and death tax credits, an income tax deduction for foreign income and real property taxes, and an exclusion for certain foreign source income.[92] Treaties between the United States and the other country are another means to limit harsh tax consequences.

---

[92] I.R.C. §§ 27, 164(a), 911, 912 & 2014.

Treaties serve other tax-related purposes. These include promoting trade by reducing tariffs and reducing tax evasion through exchanges of information with other countries. Although the United States may have separate income, estate, gift, and other treaties with a given country, in many instances the only tax treaty will be that covering income.

SECTION C. RELATIONSHIP OF TREATIES AND STATUTES

1. Authority for Treaties

Treaties are authorized by the Constitution. Article II, section 2, clause 2, provides that the President "shall have Power, by and with the Advice and Consent of the Senate, to make Treaties, provided two thirds of the Senators present concur ...." Article VI, clause 2, includes both statutes and treaties as the "supreme Law of the Land."

2. Conflict Between Treaties and Statutes

In determining which governs a transaction, neither a treaty nor a statute automatically receives preferential treatment by virtue of its status. As noted, the Constitution includes both statutes and treaties as the "supreme Law of the Land." While normally the "last in time" rule applies to reconcile conflicts between a treaty and a statute, that rule does not always apply.

In enacting Code sections, Congress can decide that treaty provisions will override statutory rules governing income earned (or property transferred) abroad by a United States citizen or resident or transactions undertaken in this country by a foreign national.[93] Congress can also provide that statutory rules will apply instead of treaty language. In addition, treaties can be overruled by a later statute, by a later treaty, or by treaty termination. Statutory repeal is an extraordinary step, taken in the 1986 Act for cases of treaty shopping.[94] Section J, Interpreting Treaties, includes several judicial

---

[93] See I.R.C. §§ 894(a) & 7852(d). Disclosure requirements apply to taxpayers who claim that a tax treaty overrules or modifies an internal revenue law. I.R.C. § 6114; Treas. Reg. § 301.6114-1; IRS Form 8833. See also I.R.C. § 7701(b); Treas. Reg. § 301.7701(b)-7.

[94] Pub. L. No. 99-514, § 1241(a), 100 Stat. 2085, 2576 (1986), modified for income tax treaties in 1988 by Pub. Law. No. 100-647, § 1012(q)(2)(A), 102 Stat. 3342, 3523. I.R.C. § 884(e)(1) currently reads: "No treaty between the United States and a foreign country shall exempt any foreign corporation from the tax imposed by subsection (a) . . . unless— (A) such treaty is an income tax treaty, and (B) such foreign corporation is a qualified resident of such foreign country."

decisions discussing the interplay between statutes and treaties.[95]

SECTION D. TREATY TERMINOLOGY

Treaties are often referred to as **conventions**. Because there may be a long delay between initial treaty negotiations and ultimate ratification, a pending treaty may be amended several times before it goes into force. A treaty may also be amended after it enters into force. Amending documents, referred to as **protocols**, may be considered by Congress along with the original treaty or at a later date.

The Senate can consent to the treaty as signed by the parties or it can express **reservations**. If the countries involved accept these reservations, the treaty process goes forward. If they do not, the treaty may be renegotiated or it may effectively die. A **ratified** treaty goes **into force** only after the governments exchange **instruments of ratification**.

As was true for statutes, you must take note of **effective dates**. A treaty can become effective on the date it goes into force, at a later date, or even at an earlier date. Different treaty provisions may become effective at different dates. If a treaty is later amended by a protocol, the protocol is subject to the ratification process that applied to the original treaty.

SECTION E. TREATY NUMBERING SYSTEMS

Treaties are numbered in a variety of ways, depending on which source is involved. Relevant numbering systems are those used by the State Department, the Senate, and the United Nations.

The State Department assigns each treaty a Treaties and Other International Acts Series (T.I.A.S.) number. T.I.A.S. began in 1945. The government previously published treaties in Treaty Series (T.S.) (1-994) and in Executive Agreement Series (E.A.S.) (1-506). T.I.A.S. numbering begins at 1501 to reflect that it continues the other series.

A treaty will also receive a Senate Executive Document number or a Senate Treaty Document number. The Senate Executive Document system assigned each treaty a letter and a number based on the Congress that

---

[95] S. Rep. No. 100-445, 100th Cong., 2d Sess. 316 (1988), discusses the relationship of statutes and treaties and the amendment of I.R.C. § 7852 by the Technical and Miscellaneous Revenue Act of 1988, Pub. L. No. 100-647, § 1012(aa), 102 Stat. 3342, 3531 (1988).

received the treaty for ratification. The Senate Treaty Document nomenclature began in the 97th Congress; this system gives each treaty a number and also indicates in which Congress the Senate Foreign Relations Committee published its recommendation to the full Senate.

The United Nations numbering system applies to treaties registered with that body (United Nations Treaty Series; UNTS). The United States is party to some, but not all, of these treaties.

You will rarely need to know the treaty numbers if your goal is limited to finding a treaty. The sources noted in Section G allow you to locate treaties by country. The T.I.A.S. number is important for using Shepard's Federal Statute Citations to find decisions interpreting treaties through 1995.

Table 7-1. Treaty Numbers for the 1975 Income and Capital Tax Convention Between the United States and Iceland

Numbering System	Number
State Department	T.I.A.S. 8151
Senate	S. Exec. E, 94-1
United Nations	Reg. No. 14972, 1020 UNTS 211

Table 7-2. Treaty Numbers for the 1989 Income and Capital Tax Convention Between the United States and Germany

Numbering System	Number
State Department	T.I.A.S. not yet assigned
Senate	S. Treaty Doc. 101-10
United Nations	Reg. No. 29534, 1708 UNTS 3

SECTION F. TREATY HISTORY DOCUMENTS

The treaty history discussed in this section is illustrated by excerpts from documents for the income tax treaty between the United States and Denmark.

Treaties, in common with statutes, involve both legislative and executive branches of government. However, the order in which each group acts is reversed. Treaties begin with the executive branch and are negotiated by representatives of each government. Unlike acts, pending treaties do not expire at the end of a Congress.

Although State Department representatives are consulted, the Treasury Office of Tax Policy has primary responsibility for tax treaty negotiations. The treaty signing process has two steps. After a treaty is **initialed**, it can still be changed; once it is **signed**, the Treasury Department releases it and sends it to the Senate for its consent. The House is not involved in the treaty process.

The Treasury Department issues a press release alerting tax practitioners that a treaty has been signed and transmitted to the Senate. The Department release bears a number, in this case LS-64.

Illustration 7-1. Press Release Announcing Treaty Signing

TREASURY NEWS

FROM THE OFFICE OF PUBLIC AFFAIRS

FOR IMMEDIATE RELEASE
August 19, 1999
LS-64

UNITED STATES AND DENMARK SIGN NEW INCOME TAX TREATY

The Treasury Department announced Thursday that Assistant Secretary for Tax Policy Donald C. Lubick and Danish Chargé daffaires Lars Møller signed a new income tax Treaty between the United States and Denmark at the State Department in Washington. This tax Treaty, if ratified, will replace the current Treaty that entered into force on December 1, 1948, and will represent an important step toward achieving Treasurys goal of updating the United States existing tax treaty network.

➔This screen capture was taken from the Treasury Department website, http://www.treas.gov/press/releases/ps64.htm.

In addition to the treaty text, the Senate Foreign Relations Committee receives the State Department's **letter of submittal** to the President and the President's **letter of transmittal** to the Senate. The Foreign Relations Committee issues a Senate Treaty Document, which contains these letters and the text of the treaty. [See Illustrations 7-2 and 7-3.]

The Treasury Department prepares a Technical Explanation for use by the Senate Foreign Relations Committee. The Joint Committee on Taxation also issues reports. The Foreign Relations Committee will hold hearings before issuing a Senate Executive Report transmitting the treaty to the full Senate for ratification. Debate by the full Senate will appear in the Congressional Record. [See Illustrations 7-4 through 7–9.]

After the treaty is ratified by the appropriate government entities in each country, the countries exchange instruments of ratification and announce that the treaty has gone into effect. The Treasury Department will issue a press release announcing this information.

Illustration 7-2. Excerpt from Letter of Submittal

LETTER OF SUBMITTAL

DEPARTMENT OF STATE,
Washington, September 7, 1999.

The PRESIDENT,
The White House.

THE PRESIDENT: I have the honor to submit to you, with a view to its transmission to the Senate for advice and consent to ratification, the Convention Between the United States of America and the Government of the Kingdom of Denmark for the Avoidance of Double Taxation and the Prevention of Fiscal Evasion with Respect to Taxes on Income, signed at Washington on August 19, 1999 ("the Convention"), together with a Protocol.

This Convention replaces the current convention between the United States of America and the Government of the Kingdom of Denmark signed at Washington on May 6, 1948. This proposed Convention generally follows the pattern of the U.S. Model Tax Treaty while incorporating some features of the OECD Model Tax Treaty and recent U.S. tax treaties with developed countries. The proposed Convention provides for maximum rates of tax to be applied to various types of income, protection from double taxation of income and exchange of information. It also contains rules making its benefits unavailable to persons that are engaged in treaty shopping....

The rules for the taxation of pension income under Article 18 of the proposed Convention vary from the rules found in the current treaty and the U.S. Model. The proposed Convention provides for taxation of private pensions only in the source State, subject to an exception for persons currently receiving pensions, who will continue to be taxed only in the country of residence.

➜This treaty provides tax rules for pension income that differ from rules found in the United States Model Income Tax Convention. The Model Convention can be found online at the Treasury Department Office of Tax Policy website (http://www.treas.gov/taxpolicy/).

Illustration 7-3. Excerpt from President's Letter of Transmittal

LETTER OF TRANSMITTAL

THE WHITE HOUSE, September 21, 1999.

To the Senate of the United States:

I transmit herewith for Senate advice and consent to ratification the Convention Between the Government of the United States of America and the Government of the Kingdom of Denmark for the Avoidance of Double Taxation and the Prevention of Fiscal Evasion with Respect to Taxes of Income, signed at Washington on August 19, 1999, together with a Protocol. Also transmitted for the information of the Senate is the report of the Department of State with respect to the Convention.

It is my desire that the Convention and Protocol transmitted herewith be considered in place of the Convention for the Avoidance of Double Taxation, signed at Washington on June 17, 1980, and the Protocol Amending the Convention, signed at Washington on August 23, 1983, which were transmitted to the Senate with messages dated September 4, 1980 (S. Ex. Q, 96th Cong., 2d Sess.) and November 16, 1983 (T. Doc. No. 98-12, 98th Cong., 1st Sess.), and which are pending in the Committee on Foreign Relations. I desire, therefore, to withdraw from the Senate the Convention and Protocol signed in 1980 and 1983.

➔Note how long the prior proposed treaty was pending.

Illustration 7-4. Excerpt from Treasury Technical Explanation

INTRODUCTION

This is a Technical Explanation of the Convention and Protocol between the United States and Denmark signed at Washington on August 19, 1999 (the "Convention" and "Protocol"). References are made to the Convention between the United States and Denmark for the Avoidance of Double Taxation and the Prevention of Fiscal Evasion with Respect to Taxes on Income signed at Washington, D.C., on May 6, 1948 (the "prior Convention"). The Convention replaces the prior Convention.

Negotiations took into account the U.S. Treasury Department's current tax treaty policy, as reflected in the U.S. Treasury Department's Model Income Tax Convention of September 20, 1996 (the "U.S. Model") and its recently negotiated tax treaties, the Model Income Tax Convention on Income and on Capital, published by the OECD in 1992 and amended in 1994, 1995 and 1997 (the "OECD Model"), and recent tax treaties concluded by Denmark.

The Technical Explanation is an official guide to the Convention and Protocol. It reflects the policies behind particular Convention provisions, as well as understandings reached with respect to the application and interpretation of the Convention and Protocol. In the discussions of each Article in this explanation, the relevant portions of the Protocol are discussed. This Technical Explanation has been provided to Denmark. References in the Technical Explanation to "he" or "his" should be read to mean "he or she" and "his or her."

Illustration 7-5. Excerpt from Joint Committee on Taxation Explanation (JCS-8-99)

EXPLANATION OF PROPOSED INCOME TAX TREATY AND PROPOSED PROTOCOL BETWEEN THE UNITED STATES AND THE KINGDOM OF DENMARK

SCHEDULED FOR A HEARING
BEFORE THE
COMMITTEE ON FOREIGN RELATIONS
UNITED STATES SENATE
ON OCTOBER 13, 1999

PREPARED BY THE STAFF
OF THE
JOINT COMMITTEE ON TAXATION

OCTOBER 8, 1999

....

INTRODUCTION

This pamphlet, prepared by the staff of the Joint Committee on Taxation, describes the proposed income tax treaty, as supplemented by the proposed protocol, between the United States of America and the Kingdom of Denmark ("Denmark"). The proposed treaty and proposed protocol were both signed on August 19, 1999. The Senate Committee on Foreign Relations has scheduled a public hearing on the proposed treaty and proposed protocol on October 13, 1999.

Part I of the pamphlet provides a summary with respect to the proposed treaty and proposed protocol. Part II provides a brief overview of U.S. tax laws relating to international trade and investment and of U.S. income tax treaties in general. Part III contains an article-by-article explanation of the proposed treaty and proposed protocol. Part IV contains a discussion of issues with respect to the proposed treaty and proposed protocol.

I. SUMMARY

The principal purposes of the proposed income tax treaty between the United States and Denmark are to reduce or eliminate double taxation of income earned by residents of either country from sources within the other country and to prevent avoidance or evasion of the taxes of the two countries. The proposed treaty also is intended to promote close economic cooperation between the two countries and to eliminate possible barriers to trade and investment caused by overlapping taxing jurisdictions of the two countries.

→Note the reference to discussion of issues regarding this treaty in Part IV.

Illustration 7-6. Excerpt from Hearings (S. HRG. 106-356)

BILATERAL TAX TREATIES AND PROTOCOL: ESTONIA, TREATY DOC. 105-55; LATVIA, TREATY DOC. 105-57; VENEZUELA, TREATY DOC. 106-3; DENMARK, TREATY DOC. 106-12; LITHUANIA, TREATY DOC. 105-56; SLOVENIA, TREATY DOC. 106-9; ITALY, TREATY DOC. 106-11; GERMANY, TREATY DOC. 106-13

HEARING
BEFORE THE
COMMITTEE ON FOREIGN RELATIONS
UNITED STATES SENATE

ONE HUNDRED SIXTH CONGRESS
FIRST SESSION

OCTOBER 27, 1999

....

The committee met, pursuant to notice, at 3:05 p.m. in room SD-419, Dirksen Senate Office Building, Hon. Chuck Hagel presiding.

Present: Senators Hagel and Sarbanes.

Senator HAGEL. Good afternoon.

The committee meets today to consider bilateral income tax treaties between the United States and Estonia, Latvia, Lithuania, Venezuela, Denmark, Italy, and Slovenia as well as an estate tax protocol with Germany.

....

The treaties prevent international double taxation by setting down rules to determine what country will have the primary right to tax income and at what rates. These bilateral international tax treaties are important for America's economic growth.

....

The treaties with Denmark and Italy would modernize existing treaty relationships. These treaties generally track with the U.S. tax treaty model, although some deviate to various degrees from the U.S. model.

....

A variety of other issues has been raised by the Joint Committee on Taxation. I know our witnesses are fully aware of these issues and will be prepared to discuss them. As usual, the Joint Committee staff has prepared careful analysis of each of the treaties.

Illustration 7-7. Excerpt from Senate Foreign Relations Committee Report

TAX CONVENTION WITH DENMARK

NOVEMBER 3, 1999.—Ordered to be printed

Mr. HELMS, from the Committee on Foreign Relations,
submitted the following

R E P O R T

[To accompany Treaty Doc. 106-12]

The Committee on Foreign Relations, to which was referred the Convention between the Government of the United States of America and the Government of the Kingdom of Denmark for the Avoidance of Double Taxation and the Prevention of Fiscal Evasion with Respect to Taxes on Income, signed at Washington on August 19, 1999, together with a Protocol, having considered the same, reports favorably thereon, with one declaration and one proviso, and recommends that the Senate give its advice and consent to ratification thereof, as set forth in this report and the accompanying resolution of ratification....

VI. COMMITTEE COMMENTS

On balance, the Committee on Foreign Relations believes that the proposed treaty with Denmark is in the interest of the United States and urges that the Senate act promptly to give advice and consent to ratification. The Committee has taken note of certain issues raised by the proposed treaty, and believes that the following comments may be useful to the Treasury Department officials in providing guidance on these matters should they arise in the course of future treaty negotiations....

A. CREDITABILITY OF DANISH HYDROCARBON TAX.

....

The Congressional tax-writing committees and this Committee have made it clear in the past that treaties are not the appropriate vehicle for granting credits for taxes that might not otherwise be creditable under the Code or Treasury regulations. The Committee believes that it would be more appropriate for the United States to address unilaterally problems of the sort raised by special oil and gas taxes imposed by foreign countries. The Committee believes that treaties should not be used in the future to handle foreign tax credit issues which are more appropriately addressed either legislatively or administratively. Nevertheless, the Committee believes that given the circumstances surrounding the Danish hydrocarbon tax, it is justifiable to provide a credit for such tax in this case.

➔Note the discussion in A. of using treaties to grant tax credits.

Illustration 7-8. Excerpt from Congressional Record

Mr. DOMENICI. Mr. President, I ask unanimous consent that the Senate proceed to consider the following treaties on today's Executive Calendar: Nos 4 through 14. I further ask unanimous consent that the treaties be considered as having passed through their various parliamentary stages, up to and including the presentation of the resolutions of ratification; all committee provisos, reservations, understandings, and declarations be considered agreed to; any statements be printed in the RECORD; and the Senate take one vote on the resolutions of ratification to be considered as separate votes. Further, that when the resolutions of ratification are voted upon, the motions to reconsider be laid upon the table, the President be notified of the Senate's action, and the Senate return to legislative session.

The PRESIDING OFFICER. Without objection, it is so ordered.

....

TAX CONVENTION WITH DENMARK

The resolution of ratification is as follows:

Resolved, (two-thirds of the Senators present concurring therein), That the Senate advise and consent to the ratification of the Convention between the Government of the United States of America and the Government of the Kingdom of Denmark for the Avoidance of Double Taxation and the Prevention of Fiscal Evasion with Respect to Taxes on Income, signed at Washington on August 19, 1999, together with a Protocol (Treaty Doc. 106-12), subject to the declaration of subsection (a) and the proviso of subsection (b).

(a) Declaration.—The Senate's advice and consent is subject to the following declaration, which shall be binding on the President:

(1) Treaty interpretation.—The Senate affirms the applicability to all treaties of the constitutionally based principles of treaty interpretation set forth in Condition (1) of the resolution of ratification of the INF Treaty, approved by the Senate on May 27, 1988, and Condition (8) of the resolution of ratification of the Document Agreed Among the States Parties to the Treaty on Conventional Armed Forces in Europe, approved by the Senate on May 14, 1997.

(b) Proviso.—The resolution of ratification is subject to the following proviso, which shall be binding on the President:

(1) Supremacy of constitution.—Nothing in the Convention requires or authorizes legislation or other action by the United States of America that is prohibited by the Constitution of the United States as interpreted by the United States.

➔Note the limitations on the President in the Declaration and Proviso.

Illustration 7-9. Excerpt from Treaty

CONVENTION BETWEEN THE GOVERNMENT OF THE UNITED STATES OF AMERICA AND THE GOVERNMENT OF THE KINGDOM OF DENMARK FOR THE AVOIDANCE OF DOUBLE TAXATION AND THE PREVENTION OF FISCAL EVASION WITH RESPECT TO TAXES ON INCOME

The Government of the United States of America and the Government of the Kingdom of Denmark, desiring to conclude a Convention for the avoidance of double taxation and the prevention of fiscal evasion with respect to taxes on income, have agreed as follows:

Article 1
General Scope

1. Except as otherwise provided in this Convention, this Convention shall apply to persons who are residents of one or both of the Contracting States.

2. This Convention shall not restrict in any manner any benefit now or hereafter accorded:

➔When this treaty went into force, the Treasury Department issued a press release (LS-521) to announce the effective date.

➔The treaty went into force on March 31, 2000. The effective dates were payments on or after May 1, 2000 (withholding taxes) and taxable years beginning on or after January 1, 2001 (all other taxes).

SECTION G. LOCATING TREATIES AND THEIR HISTORIES

Once a treaty goes into force, it is added to the State Department's Treaties and Other International Acts Series (T.I.A.S.). T.I.A.S. is the treaty equivalent of Statutes at Large; the treaty document equivalent of United States Code is United States Treaties and Other International Agreements (U.S.T.). Because official treaty publications are not updated nearly as quickly as their statutory counterparts, you should use other sources to obtain the text of recent treaties.

Tax treaties and their revising protocols are published in various places, several of which are limited to tax treaties. Many sources also provide access to at least some treaty history documents. Unfortunately, few sources provide access to all relevant information.

The sources below illustrate the formats in which you can locate treaties and other documents. Your library may also carry them in microform.

1. United States Government Sources

The Internal Revenue Service website includes PDF versions of treaty texts other than the most recently ratified treaties. The site also includes Treasury Technical Explanations for many of the treaties and Publication 901, which lists the most current treaties and provides information about how each treaty affects specific categories of taxpayers. It does not include congressional action, Joint Committee explanations, or press releases.

The Treasury Department Office of Tax Policy website provides access to proposed treaties, press releases, Joint Committee on Taxation explanations, and Treasury Technical Explanations. It does not include all these items for every treaty, and it does not include congressional action. In addition, it does not cover documents issued before October 1996. Many of its documents are available in both PDF and word processing formats.

The weekly Internal Revenue Bulletin contains the most recent material, which is reprinted in the Cumulative Bulletin at six month intervals.[96] Because of their arrangement, these publications are more useful for finding IRS material relating to treaties than for finding the treaties themselves. In addition to treaty texts, these services include the Senate Executive Reports and the Treasury Technical Explanations. The I.R.B. is available in print, online at the IRS website, and through subscription online services.[97]

2. Online Subscription Services

Tax treaties are available on both LexisNexis and Westlaw. Other online databases include Tax Treaties Online (Oceana) and U.S. Bilateral Tax Treaties Database (RIA Checkpoint). The publishers listed below make treaties available in the formats indicated.

3. Other Print and Electronic Sources

a. Tax Analysts Publications (CD-ROM and online)

Tax Analysts covers treaty documents in CD-ROM and online publications. Its CD-ROM offerings are U.S. Tax Treaties and Worldwide Tax Treaties (annual and quarterly); its online service is TaxBase. Some libraries

---

[96] These services are discussed in greater detail in Chapter 16. IRS Publication 901 contains selected information about treaties, including tax rates and exempt compensation.

[97] See Joint Committee on Taxation, Listing of Selected International Tax Conventions and Other Agreements Reprinted in the IRS Cumulative Bulletin, 1913-1990 (JCS-20-91), Dec. 31, 1991, for citations to both treaty documents and administrative guidance. This document is available in the Tax Notes Today file on LexisNexis at 92 TNT 2-8.

also own the publisher's microfiche collection.[98] Treaty documents include full texts of treaties and all documents comprising each treaty's legislative history. The service covers income, transfer tax, shipping and air transport, information exchange, and social security treaties. It also includes model treaties, administrative documents (such as revenue rulings and field service advice), and judicial interpretations.

b. CCH Publications (looseleaf, CD-ROM, and online)

The CCH Tax Treaties service reproduces texts of United States income and estate tax treaties. In a separate volume, it covers exchange of information agreements, shipping and air transport treaties, and social security treaties.[99] It reproduces selected treaty documents, including letters of submittal and transmittal, letters of understanding, and Treasury and congressional reports. CCH includes editorial comments and annotations, and it reproduces IRS publications providing withholding rate tables and Cumulative Bulletin citations for each treaty and protocol. It also includes texts of model treaties. Supplementation is monthly; new developments are in the last volume.

CCH publishes a monthly Tax Treaties CD-ROM and offers treaty coverage in its online Tax Research NetWork service. The electronic services include hyperlinks to full text treaty history documents, administrative documents (such as revenue procedures and letter rulings), and judicial decisions.

c. RIA Publications (looseleaf, CD-ROM, and online)

Chapter 20 of the Federal Tax Coordinator 2d[100] looseleaf service contains the text of United States income and estate and gift tax treaties. There is also explanatory material. Supplementation is weekly. RIA includes treaties in its monthly OnPoint CD-ROM and in its online Checkpoint service.

---

[98] Tax Analysts initially published an extensive microfiche database, which is useful for historical research. Coverage included bilateral, multilateral, and model tax treaties worldwide and United States tax-related treaties and agreements. Coverage for United States treaties included those currently in force, not yet in force, and superseded or terminated. A print index provided appropriate citations to the treaties and treaty documents covered. Treaty documents added before 1996 appeared in the Tax Notes International Microfiche Database; those added after 1995 appeared in the Tax Analysts Microfiche Database.

[99] The volume spines indicate that social security treaties are found in the same volumes as income and estate tax treaties. This was not the case in May 2002.

[100] There is a comprehensive discussion of this service in Chapter 12.

d. BNA Publications (looseleaf, CD-ROM, and online)

Tax Management Portfolios—Foreign Income[101] covers many countries but does not yet publish a Portfolio for each treaty country. The Detailed Analysis sections contain explanations, significant cases, and other annotations. The Working Papers sections print treaty texts as Worksheets. BNA includes treaties in its monthly Portfolios Plus Library CD-ROM and in its online TaxCore and BNATAX Management Library services.

e. Rhoades & Langer, U.S. International Taxation and Tax Treaties (looseleaf, CD-ROM, and online)

This treatise covers the treaty and non-treaty aspects of both inbound and outbound transactions. Following the topical discussion in the main text sections, Appendix A prints the text of current, proposed, and prior income tax treaties. It also prints estate and gift tax treaties, information exchange agreements, transportation agreements, social security totalization agreements, and other relevant agreements. Appendix B includes model treaties: OECD; United States; and United Nations.

In addition to its T.I.A.S. citation, a brief legislative history accompanies each treaty. If a treaty no longer applies, the service still covers that country and indicates when the treaty went out of force.

Cross-references to any pertinent regulations, revenue rulings and letter rulings follow each treaty article. Although the other treaties had annotations, estate and gift tax treaties were not annotated as of May 2002.

f. Legislative History of United States Tax Conventions (Roberts & Holland Collection) (looseleaf)

This looseleaf service, introduced in 1986, updates and expands a four-volume 1962 version prepared by the Joint Committee on Taxation staff. The sixteen volumes contain the full text of treaties and legislative history documents, including presidential messages, Senate Executive Reports, floor debate, Joint Committee staff explanations, and hearings. Official pagination is retained. This service focuses on the history of the treaty rather than on subsequent judicial and administrative interpretations.

Supplementation is relatively infrequent; as of early 2002, the most recent supplement carried a 1998 date.

---

[101] A more extensive discussion of the Tax Management Portfolios appears in Chapter 12.

SECTION H. PENDING TREATIES

The government regularly announces the status of treaty negotiations. This information is carried in newsletters, looseleaf services, and on government websites.

If you want to determine if a tax treaty has been signed and is pending before the Senate, you can locate this information in the CCH Congressional Index, Senate volume (Treaties–Nominations tab). Looseleaf services are a good source of information about treaties that are being negotiated.

SECTION I. CITATORS FOR TREATIES

Two sources that formerly provided citations to judicial and administrative decisions regarding treaties are now of limited use for recent events. Shepard's Federal Statute Citations, discussed in Chapter 11, provides citations to court decisions involving treaties through 1995; you need the U.S.T. and T.I.A.S. citations to use this volume. Citations to IRS pronouncements (1954-1993/94) can be found in the Service's Bulletin Index-Digest System, discussed in Chapter 16.

In the absence of a formal citator, you can locate judicial and administrative rulings involving the application of a treaty in looseleaf, CD-ROM, and online services that focus on treaties or that have extensive treaty coverage.

SECTION J. INTERPRETING TREATIES

1. Administrative Interpretations

In many instances, the executive branch must issue regulations and other rulings to implement or interpret treaty provisions. For example, Title 26, Chapter I, Subchapter G of the Code of Federal Regulations provides regulations regarding tax treaties. These regulations do not follow the regulations numbering system described in Chapter 8, and they do not cover all treaty countries.[102]

The Internal Revenue Service issues revenue rulings and other guidance

---

[102] See, e.g., Treas. Reg. § 513.2: "The fact that the payee of the dividend is not required to pay Irish tax on such dividend because of the application of reliefs or exemptions under Irish revenue laws does not prevent the application of the reduction in rate of United States tax with respect to such dividend."

interpreting treaty provisions. You can locate these documents by using the treaty country as a search term instead of using a Code section. Chapter 9 discusses locating IRS documents.

2. Judicial Interpretations

Because treaties and statutes are both approved by Congress, many of the rules of interpretation applied to statutes apply to treaties. The list below illustrates interpretation rules applied to treaties and to situations involving a conflict between a treaty and a statute.

• [W]hen a treaty and an act of Congress conflict "the last expression of the sovereign will must control". Lindsey v. Commissioner, 98 T.C. 672, 676 (1992).

• Unless the treaty terms are unclear on their face, or unclear as applied to the situation that has arisen, it should rarely be necessary to rely on extrinsic evidence in order to construe a treaty, for it is rarely possible to reconstruct all of the considerations and compromises that led the signatories to the final document. However, extrinsic material is often helpful in understanding the treaty and its purposes, thus providing an enlightened framework for reviewing its terms. Xerox Corp. v. United States, 41 F.3d 647, 652 (Fed. Cir. 1994).

• Even where a provision of a treaty fairly admits of two constructions, one restricting, the other enlarging, rights which may be claimed under it, the more liberal interpretation is to be preferred. North West Life Assurance Co. of Canada v. Commissioner, 107 T.C. 363, 378 (1996).

• We construe a treaty like a contract. Amaral v. Commissioner, 90 T.C. 802, 813 (1988).

• It does appear, however, that in the case of treaties, courts have sometimes been more willing to resort to extra-textual, preparatory material to determine meaning, and also to allow for more liberal interpretation of the words of a treaty. In such instances the decision of the courts to resort to sources beyond the treaty language and/or to a more liberal interpretation of the written word often has occurred because the treaty language is not completely clear and requires further explanation. Snap-On Tools, Inc. v. United States, 26 Cl. Ct. 1045, 1065 (1992).

• Thus, to the extent that a treaty can reasonably be interpreted to avoid conflict with a subsequent enactment, such an interpretation is to be preferred. Norstar Bank of Upstate New York v. United States, 644 F. Supp 1112, 1116 (N.D.N.Y. 1986).

SECTION K. OECD AND WTO

The United States belongs to several international organizations whose activities may affect U.S. tax legislation and administration. The OECD and WTO are two of the most important.

1. OECD

The Organisation for Economic Co-operation and Development was formed in December 1960 as a continuation of the Organisation for European Economic Co-operation. The OECD issues "internationally agreed instruments, decisions and recommendations to promote rules of the game in areas where multilateral agreement is necessary for individual countries to make progress in a globalised economy."[103]

The United States is a signatory to the OECD Mutual Administrative Assistance in Tax Matters Convention, which entered into force in 1995. The OECD has published several model treaties, such as the OECD Model Tax Convention on Income and on Capital, which the United States takes into account in negotiating tax treaties. Treaty explanations indicate variances from the OECD Model Treaty. [See Illustration 7-2.] A recent OECD project concerns harmful tax competition. That project led to a list of so-called Uncooperative Tax Havens.[104]

2. WTO

The World Trade Organization was formed in 1995 to deal with the global rules of trade between nations. It succeeded the General Agreement on Tariffs and Trade (GATT). Trade disputes resolved by WTO panels extend beyond such traditional measures as tariffs. The WTO has held that Internal Revenue Code provisions favoring foreign sales corporations are invalid export subsidies.[105]

---

[103] OECD website (http://www.oecd.org) (visited June 4, 2002). This site includes OECD Model Treaty information.

[104] The list, issued April 18, 2002, and available at the OECD website, covers countries that have not made a commitment to transparency and effective exchange of information. The OECD site also discusses so-called Harmful Tax Practices.

[105] World Trade Organization Appellate Body ruling (WT/DS108/AB/RW) (Jan. 14, 2002) on appeal from Panel Report, United States - Tax Treatment for "Foreign Sales Corporations" - Recourse to Article 21.5. of the DSU by the European Communities (the "Panel Report"). The WTO Dispute Settlement Body adopted the Appellate Body ruling on January 29, 2002 (WT/DS/108/25). These documents are available at the WTO website, http://www.wto.org.

Section L. Other International Material

1. General Information

If a transaction will take place in another country, you may need information about that country's tax laws and general business climate. Pamphlets published by major accounting firms and other organizations provide useful background information. Individual country websites are easy to access.[106] Background material appears in sources such as the Tax Management Portfolios (Chapter 12) and the PricewaterhouseCoopers Guide Series.

Although background materials provide an introduction, they cannot substitute for primary source materials. Many United States law libraries have collections of materials from other countries, particularly countries that use English as their primary language.

2. Material in Other Languages

Although not limited to international taxation, a practitioner may need access to materials in a language other than English. Treaties to which the United States is a signatory are published in both English and the official language of the other country. A limited number of United States tax forms are available from the IRS website in Spanish. The IRS also publishes Publication 850, an English-Spanish glossary of words and phrases.

3. Treaties with Native American Tribes

Treaties the United States entered into with Native Americans are beyond the scope of this text. You should be aware that tax rules applied to Native Americans may involve claims of treaty-based exemptions.[107]

Section M. Problems

1. Which tax treaties are in force between the U.S. and

a. Brazil	c. Finland	e. Luxembourg
b. Ethiopia	d. Japan	f. United Kingdom

---

[106] See, e.g., http://www.inlandrevenue.gov.uk (United Kingdom Inland Revenue); Business Guide to Denmark, Business Lounge page, at http://www.denmark.dk.

[107] See, e.g., Cook v. United States, 86 F.3d 1095 (Fed. Cir. 1996).

2. List any U.S. tax treaties that

   a. currently await Senate consent

   b. currently are being renegotiated

   c. were signed this year

3. When were the following U.S.-(Country Listed) treaties signed?

   a. Austria estate, inheritance and gift tax

   b. Sri Lanka income tax and protocol

   c. Tunisia income tax and protocol

4. Locate an announcement of the notification to Malta that the U.S. was terminating their 1980 income tax treaty; indicate the effective date of termination.

5. What is the T.I.A.S. number for the following treaties, and when did they enter into force?

   a. 1988 U.S.-Indonesia Income Tax Convention

   b. 1984 U.S.-Barbados Income Tax Convention

   c. 1989 U.S.-Isle of Man Shipping Agreement

6. What is the Senate Treaty Document number for the U.S.-Bermuda Income Tax Treaty?

7. When was the most recent protocol signed for the 1997 U.S.-Ireland Income and Capital Gains Tax Treaty?

8. What is the report number for the Senate Foreign Relations Committee Report on the U.S. treaty with

   a. Canada—1997 income tax protocol

   b. Cyprus—1984 income tax

   c. Greece—1964 Protocol to estate and gift tax

   d. South Africa—1997 income and capital gains tax

9. After completing Chapter 9, provide a citation for and holding of

a. a 1997 IRS announcement regarding the exemption from U.S. income tax on pensions that U.S. permanent residents receive from the French government

b. a 1996 IRS letter ruling regarding the exemption from tax under Code section 4371 of premiums received by a Swedish insurer

c. a 2001 IRS field service advice memorandum regarding the U.S. income tax treaty with Canada and Code section 59(a)(2)

d. a 2001 IRS technical assistance memorandum discussing whether the U.S.-Japan income tax treaty exempts Japanese flight attendants flying for U.S. airlines from F.I.C.A. tax

e. a 1999 IRS service center advice concerning the savings clause of the U.S.-Canada income tax treaty and social security benefits

f. a 1995 IRS action on decision concerning a Tax Court case involving the U.S-Japan income tax treaty

g. a 1999 IRS technical advice memorandum involving the U.S.-Canada income tax treaty and Treas. Reg. § 1.882-4(a)

h. a 1997 IRS notice regarding whether it will treat Hong Kong and China as separate countries for treaty purposes

i. a 1999 IRS field service advice regarding whether denying a standard deduction violated the U.S.-Greece income tax treaty

10. After completing Chapter 10, locate the following court filings and then determine if the case was litigated and the outcome of any litigation.

a. a 1995 petition by a Scottish woman that lump-sum pension payments are exempt from U.S. tax under the U.S.-United Kingdom income tax treaty

b. a 1999 petition by an Israeli citizen that California lottery winnings are exempt from U.S. tax under the U.S.-Israel income tax treaty

11. After completing Chapter 10, locate and give the holding and any appeals action for

a. a Tax Court decision involving both the U.S.-United Kingdom and U.S.-Germany income tax treaties and the alternative minimum tax.

b. a Court of Federal Claims decision involving a distribution from an employee stock ownership plan and the U.S.-Canada income tax treaty

c. a Court of Federal Claims decision involving withholding of tax from a research stipend and the U.S.-Russian Federation income tax treaty

12. For which treaty countries do Treasury regulations exist? (See Chapter 8)

13. Is Azerbaijan covered by either the 1973 U.S.-U.S.S.R. or 1992 U.S.-Russia income tax treaty?

14. When did the 1945 U.S.-U.K. income tax treaty apply to Aden? When was the termination of coverage announced?

15. Print out tax information from a country-specific website.

16. Locate the OECD list of "Unco-operative Tax Havens." Does the United States have any tax treaties with any of these countries?

17. Print out the first page of the following 2002 Congressional Research Service report: Global Taxation and the United Nations: A Review of Proposals.

PART THREE

PRIMARY SOURCES: ADMINISTRATIVE

Chapter 8. Treasury Regulations

Chapter 9. Internal Revenue Service Documents

CHAPTER 8. TREASURY REGULATIONS

SECTION A. INTRODUCTION

This chapter discusses regulations, which Congress authorizes in the Internal Revenue Code and in other statutes. It explains the different types of regulations—proposed, temporary, and final—and the difference between legislative and interpretive regulations. It also covers other terms used to describe regulations, judicial deference to administrative positions, and sources in which you can find relevant documents.

Your goals for this chapter include locating all relevant documents, determining their relative importance, and updating your research to include projects that may result in proposed regulations.

SECTION B. FUNCTIONS OF REGULATIONS

As discussed in Chapters 5 and 6, Congress enacted the Internal Revenue Code and other statutes governing income, transfer, and excise taxes. Taxpayers interpret those statutes in determining their liability for these taxes. Courts become involved when there is a controversy between the government and a taxpayer. In interpreting statutes, both taxpayers and courts must consider administrative interpretations.

The Treasury Department and Internal Revenue Service (IRS) interpret and enforce internal revenue laws. In some areas, such as employee benefits, they share their authority with other administrative agencies. This chapter focuses on one form of administrative guidance, regulations, primarily those issued as Treasury regulations. Chapter 9 focuses on IRS pronouncements.

SECTION C. REGULATORY SCHEME

1. Treasury Regulations

Title 26 of the Code of Federal Regulations (C.F.R.) contains most of the regulations you will need for resolving tax problems; this is the Internal Revenue title of C.F.R. Instead of citing these regulations as 26 C.F.R. sections, you can cite them as Treasury Regulations (Treas. Reg.). Regulations in 31 C.F.R. (Money and Finance: Treasury) cover other Treasury Department functions, including Practice Before the Internal Revenue Service.[108]

Regulations issued for 1954 Code sections also apply to the 1986 Code to the extent Code sections remained unchanged. Regulations interpreting the 1939 Code followed a different numbering system. Unless I indicate otherwise, you can assume that references cover regulations interpreting the current statutory provisions.

2. Other Regulations

If another agency has authority for provisions affecting tax law, its regulations are also relevant. For example, the Labor Department issues regulations in the employee benefit area that appear in 29 C.F.R. Several Code sections defer to other agency interpretations.[109]

SECTION D. REGULATIONS NUMBERING SYSTEM

1. Regulations Subdivisions

Title 26 C.F.R. has no subtitles and only one chapter (Chapter I – Internal Revenue Service, Department of the Treasury). Chapter I is divided into seven subchapters and numerous parts. [Table 8-1.]

There are subdivisions within each part, but they are not separately numbered and often lack formal titles (e.g., subpart). For example, one subdivision of Subchapter A, Part 1, is Normal Taxes and Surtaxes. Two of its subdivisions are Determination of Tax Liability and Computation of Taxable Income. Those units are themselves further subdivided.

The authority information (Code section 7805 or another section) appears immediately after a listing of sections in a particular group.

2. Regulations Numbering Scheme

Most regulations section numbers have two segments, which are separated by a decimal point, and a third segment, which follows a hyphen. The

---

[108] This group of sections begins at 31 C.F.R. § 10.0.

[109] See, e.g., I.R.C. § 4064(b)(1)(B): "The term 'automobile' does not include any vehicle which is treated as a nonpassenger automobile under the rules which were prescribed by the Secretary of Transportation ...."

first segment, often called the prefix, indicates where the regulation appears; the prefixes use the part numbers illustrated in Table 8-1.

The segment that follows the decimal point generally indicates the Code section being interpreted. Thus, Treas. Reg. § 1.106-1 interprets Code section 106. The third segment, which follows the hyphen, is similar to the subdivisions used for Code subsections and is discussed in Subsection 4.

Each regulations section is further subdivided into

- paragraphs (e.g., Treas. Reg. § 1.61-2(d));

- subparagraphs (e.g., Treas. Reg. § 1.61-2(d)(2)); and

- subdivisions (e.g., Treas. Reg. § 1.61-2(d)(2)(i)).

Smaller units exist but do not receive formal names. For example, Treas. Reg. § 1.274-2(b)(1)(iii)(a) says: "Except as otherwise provided in (b) or (c) of this subdivision ...." The subdivision referred to is (iii); (a), (b), and (c) are smaller units of (iii).

Regulations frequently contain examples. These may appear in a separate Examples subdivision (e.g., Treas. Reg. § 1.119-1(f)) or as part of a subdivision to which the example applies (e.g., Treas. Reg. § 1.162-5(b)(3)(ii)).

Table 8-1. List of Subchapters and Partial List of Parts

Subchapter A	Income Tax
Part 1	Income taxes
Part 2	Maritime construction reserve fund
Part 3	Capital construction fund
Part 4	Temporary income tax regulations under section 954 of the Internal Revenue Code
Part 5	Temporary income tax regulations under the Revenue Act of 1978
Subchapter B	Estate and Gift Taxes
Subchapter C	Employment Taxes and Collection of Income Tax at Source
Subchapter D	Miscellaneous Excise Taxes
Subchapter F	Procedure and Administration
Subchapter G	Regulations Under Tax Conventions
Subchapter H	Internal Revenue Practice
Part 601	Statement of procedural rules
Part 602	OMB control numbers under the Paperwork Reduction Act
Part 701	Presidential election campaign fund

→Subchapter E (Parts 170-299) is currently Reserved.

3. Importance of Regulations Prefixes

Including the prefix in the regulation is critical for finding the correct regulation. First, regulations in different parts interpret the same Code section. For example, Treas. Reg. §§ 1.7520-1, 20.7520-1, and 25.7520-1 all interpret Code section 7520. Differences in their texts reflect their application to different taxes.

Second, regulations in some parts don't interpret a Code section but their number is a Code section number. For example, Treas. Reg. § 1.1-1 is an income tax regulation for Code section 1. Treas. Reg. § 2.1-1 is a definition section dealing with the maritime construction reserve fund; it has nothing to do with Code section 1.[110]

4. Relationship of Code Subdivisions to Regulations Subdivisions

The portion of the regulation that follows the hyphen does not indicate the Code subsection involved. In fact, there may be significantly more regulations sections than Code subsections. Table 8-2 illustrates the relationship of Code and regulations sections for Code section 61(a).

Table 8-2. Relationship of Code and Regulations Subdivisions

Code Section	Regulations Section
61(a)	1.61-1, 1.61-14
61(a)(1)	1.61-2, 1.61-15, 1.61-21
61(a)(2)	1.61-3, 1.61-4, 1.61-5
61(a)(3)	1.61-6
61(a)(4)	1.61-7
61(a)(5)	1.61-8
61(a)(6)	1.61-8
61(a)(7)	1.61-9
61(a)(8)	1.61-10
61(a)(9)	1.61-10
61(a)(10)	1.61-10
61(a)(11)	1.61-11
61(a)(12)	1.61-12
61(a)(13)	1.61-13
61(a)(14)	1.61-13
61(a)(15)	1.61-13

➔Some Code sections have more than one regulations section; others share a regulations section.

---

[110] Regulations in Part 601 follow this pattern. For example, Treas. Reg. § 601.101 has nothing to do with I.R.C. § 101.

5. Letters in Section Numbering

Most section numbers follow this format: Treas. Reg. § 1.61-1. Two other formats involve the use of letters. The first involves capital letters. Capitals must be used for regulations whose Code section includes a capital letter. For example, Treas. Reg. § 1.263A-1 is a regulation for Code section 263A. Other regulations, such as Treas. Reg. § 1.170A-1, interpret Code sections that do not include a capital letter.[111] Treas. Reg. § 1.672(a)-1 illustrates the second format, involving lower case letters. The letter in parentheses may indicate the relevant Code subsection but does not necessarily do so.

If the regulations section includes a letter, it follows all regulations for the Code section that don't include a letter. If more than one letter is used, those regulations appear in alphabetical order. For example, the regulations for Code section 142 appear in the following order in C.F.R.:[112]

1.142-1	Exempt facility bonds.
1.142-2	Remedial actions.
1.143-3	Refunding issues (Reserved).
1.142-4	Use of proceeds to provide a facility.
1.142(a)(5)-1	Exempt facility bonds: Sewage facilities.
1.142(f)(4)-1	Manner of making election to terminate tax-exempt bond financing.

Temporary regulations appear in the normal order. Thus, regulations for Code section 25 appear in the following order:

1.25-1T	Credit for interest paid on certain home mortgages.
1.25-2T	Amount of credit.
1.25-3	Qualified mortgage credit certificate.

SECTION E. REGULATORY AUTHORITY

1. Entities Involved

The two most important entities involved in promulgating regulations are

---

[111] The section 170 regulations that lack the A (e.g., Treas. Reg. § 1.170-1) interpret the statute before its 1969 amendment.

[112] Looseleaf services (Chapter 12) don't necessarily follow the C.F.R. order. Their editors may insert other regulations that relate to the particular Code section. See, e.g., the 2002 edition of Standard Federal Tax Reporter, which inserts Treas. Reg. §§ 1.103-7, 1.103-8, 17.1, and 1.103-9 in its coverage of I.R.C. § 142.

the Internal Revenue Service and the Treasury Department. Regulations are drafted by the Internal Revenue Service but they are issued under the authority of the Secretary of the Treasury.

Code section 7805(a) authorizes the Secretary to "prescribe all needful rules and regulations for the enforcement" of the tax statutes. Other Code sections that refer to regulations also use the term "the Secretary." That term is defined in Code section 7701(a)(11)(B) as "the Secretary of the Treasury or his delegate." The Secretary has delegated the drafting function to the Commissioner of Internal Revenue.[113] That function involves several steps, which are outlined in Section H.

2. Limitations on Authority

There are several limitations on the IRS's authority to issue regulations. These relate to retroactivity and taxpayer burden. The government describes its compliance with these rules in the preambles that accompany regulations. [See Illustration 8-1.]

a. Code Section 7805(b) and Retroactivity

In addition to section 7805(a), which authorizes issuing regulations, Code section 7805(b) limits the Treasury Department's authority to issue regulations with retroactive effect. Beginning with statutes enacted on July 30, 1996, a proposed, temporary, or final regulation cannot apply to any taxable period before the earliest of its filing with the Federal Register[114] or the date on which a notice substantially describing its expected contents is issued to the public. This rule does not apply to regulations filed or issued within 18 months of the statute's enactment, necessary to prevent abuse, or issued to correct procedural defects in previously issued regulations.[115]

b. Code Section 7805(f) and Small Business

Section 7805(f) requires the Treasury Department to submit proposed and temporary regulations to the Small Business Administration's Chief Counsel for Advocacy. The Chief Advocate is required to comment on the regulation's impact on small business. The preamble accompanying the final regulations

---

[113] Treas. Reg. § 301.7805-1(a).

[114] A final regulation can be retroactive to the date its proposed or temporary version was filed.

[115] Congress can legislatively waive Section 7805(b), and the IRS can authorize taxpayers to elect retroactive application.

must discuss these comments.[116]

c. Executive Order 12866

In 1993, President Clinton issued an order setting forth a statement of regulatory philosophy and principles and providing a regulatory planning and review process for proposed and existing regulations. The Office of Management and Budget is charged with ensuring that regulations follow the stated philosophy and principles. The order also requires that agencies submit their regulatory plans for the year for OMB review.

d. Administrative Procedure Act

Agencies must publish notices of proposed rulemaking in the Federal Register.[117] These notices must include information about the time and place for a public rulemaking procedure, indicate the agency's legal authority for promulgating the regulation, and indicate the terms or substance of the proposed rule. Publication generally must precede the effective date by at least 30 days. Although interpretative rules are exempt from these requirements, tax regulations generally follow the act's requirements.[118]

e. Regulatory Flexibility Act

Federal agencies that are required to publish notices of proposed rulemaking must prepare and publish for comment an initial regulatory flexibility analysis. This requirement also applies to notices of proposed rulemaking for interpretive rules involving the internal revenue laws that impose information collection requirements on small business.[119] The analysis includes information about the agency's objectives, the small entities affected, and the type of compliance requirements that will be involved.

f. Paperwork Reduction Act

An agency that wants to require information submissions from the private

---

[116] Comparable requirements apply to final regulations that are not based on proposed regulations, but the submission must occur before the regulation is filed.

[117] 5 U.S.C. § 553.

[118] The legislative-interpretive distinction is also important when a court is deciding how much deference the rule merits. Deference is discussed in Section K.

[119] See 5 U.S.C. § 603. A final regulatory flexibility analysis, including a description of public comments and the agency's response, accompanies the final regulation. Id. § 604.

sector must obtain OMB approval. Illustration 8-1 includes a section discussing information collections.

Illustration 8-1. Preamble Discussion of Regulatory Constraints

---

Paperwork Reduction Act

The collections of information in this final rule have been reviewed and, pending receipt and evaluation of public comments, approved by the Office of Management and Budget (OMB) under 44 U.S.C. 3507 and assigned control number 1545-1767. The collections of information in this regulation are in §1.472-8(e)(3)(iii)(B)(3) and (e)(3)(iv). To elect the IPIC method, a taxpayer must file Form 970, "Application to Use LIFO Inventory Method." This information is required to inform the Commissioner regarding the taxpayer's elections under the IPIC method. This information will be used to determine whether the taxpayer is properly accounting for its dollar-value pools under the IPIC method. The collections of information are required if the taxpayer wants to obtain the tax benefits of the LIFO method. The likely respondents are business or other for-profit institutions, and/or small businesses or organizations.

....

Special Analyses

It has been determined that this Treasury decision is not a significant regulatory action as defined in Executive Order 12866. Therefore, a regulatory assessment is not required. It also has been determined that section 553(b) of the Administrative Procedure Act (5 U.S.C. chapter 5) does not apply to these regulations. Pursuant to section 7805(f) of the Code, the proposed regulations preceding this Treasury decision was submitted to the Chief Counsel for Advocacy of the Small Business Administration for comment on their impact on small business. It is hereby certified that the collections of information in this Treasury decision will not have a significant economic impact on a substantial number of small entities. First, only taxpayers that adopt, or change to, the IPIC method will be affected by the collections of information. Second, relatively few small entities are expected to adopt, or change to, the IPIC method. Third, the burden of the collections of information is not significant. Therefore, a Regulatory Flexibility Analysis under the Regulatory Flexibility Act (5 U.S.C. chapter 6) is not required.

➔The excerpts above appear in T.D. 8976, 67 Fed. Reg. 1075 (Jan. 9, 2002).

➔T.D. 8976 also appears in 2002-5 I.R.B. 421 (Feb. 4, 2002).

SECTION F. TERMINOLOGY

This section introduces relevant terminology used for regulations and related documents.

1. Proposed, Temporary, and Final Regulations

You should expect to encounter regulations in three different stages. The citation format clearly indicates whether the item is a Proposed Regulation (e.g., Prop. Treas. Reg. § 1.801-4); a Temporary Regulation (e.g., Temp. Treas. Reg. § 1.71-1T); or a Final Regulation (e.g., Treas. Reg. § 1.106-1). Assuming the citation is correct, a regulation that does not include either a "Prop." or a "T" is a final regulation. Each type can be cited as authority for avoiding the substantial understatement penalty discussed in Chapter 2.

a. Proposed Regulations

Proposed regulations offer guidance for taxpayers seeking to comply with statutory rules. Taxpayers receive an opportunity to submit written comments or testify at hearings before proposed regulations become final.

b. Temporary Regulations

The IRS can simultaneously issue a proposed regulation as a **temporary regulation**. Unlike a proposed regulation, a temporary regulation is effective when it is published in the Federal Register. It provides immediate, binding guidance, and receives more deference than a proposed regulation. It becomes operative without the benefit of public comment.

Code section 7805(e) mandates that temporary regulations issued after November 20, 1988, also be issued as proposed regulations; this ensures that there will be a notice and comment procedure.[120] The section also requires that temporary regulations expire no more than three years after they are issued. This limitation does not apply to temporary regulations issued before that date, and several older temporary regulations are still in effect.

c. Final Regulations

Regulations issued after any necessary notice and comment period are referred to as **final regulations**. The final regulations may differ from the proposed or temporary regulations they replace for various reasons, including government response to taxpayer comments or judicial decisions. In

---

[120] Proposed regulations need not be issued as temporary regulations.

addition to regulatory analysis information [Illustration 8-1], the preamble accompanying the Treasury Decision will indicate comments received and any resulting changes.

2. Interpretive and Legislative Regulations

Regulations issued pursuant to the Code section 7805(a) general mandate are referred to as **interpretive** (or interpretative). These contrast to **legislative** regulations, issued for Code sections in which Congress included a specific grant of authority. The specific grant of authority allows IRS experts to write rules for technical areas.

The information accompanying each regulation indicates Treasury's authority for issuing the regulation, either a specific Code section (legislative) or Code section 7805(a) (interpretive), or both. If the regulation is a final or temporary regulation, this information is added to the appropriate part of 26 C.F.R. As illustrated in Section K, courts give legislative regulations more deference than they accord interpretive regulations.

Note that interpretive and legislative relate to the authority for a particular regulation; proposed, temporary, and final relate to steps in the process for issuing regulations.

3. Project Numbers and Notices of Proposed Rulemaking

a. Project Numbers

When the IRS opens a regulations project, it assigns it a **project number**. It then uses those project numbers for its proposed regulations. Although the project numbering system has changed several times, certain parts have remained constant.

Before the 1988 reorganization, most projects were drafted in the IRS Legislation and Regulations Division and began with the letters LR. Employee benefits and exempt organization projects were designated EE; international projects, INTL. Projects begun under this system received new letter designations but not new numbers after 1988.

Between 1988 and August 1996, project numbers indicated the IRS division with responsibility for the project. [See Table 8-3.] The current numbering system began in August 1996. All project numbers begin with REG, followed by a series of numbers, followed by the project's year. There is no indication of which IRS division has authority for the regulations project. A recent example of this numbering system is REG-107100-00, covering proposed regulations for Code sections 874 and 882. The -00 indicates a 2000 project.[121]

Although the numbering system no longer indicates which division produced the regulation,[122] that information does appear in the Drafting Information section included in the regulation's preamble.

Table 8-3. IRS Project Designations, 1988-1996

CO	Corporate
EE	Employee Benefits and Exempt Organizations
FI	Financial Institutions and Products
GL	General Litigation
IA	Income Tax and Accounting
INTL	International
PS	Passthroughs and Special Industries

b. Notices of Proposed Rulemaking

The IRS publishes the text of a proposed regulation and its accompanying preamble as a **Notice of Proposed Rulemaking (NPRM)**. Notices include the project number and the Regulation Identification Number (RIN) (discussed in Section I). Neither number reflects the underlying Code section number or the year the proposal is filed with the Federal Register.

The Service may publish an **Advance Notice of Proposed Rulemaking (ANPRM)**. Advance notices indicate rules the Service expects to propose and request public comment that may influence the resulting NPRM. The ANPRM also includes the project number and the RIN.

4. Treasury Decisions

Final and proposed regulations are issued as Treasury Decisions (T.D.). Treasury Decisions are numbered sequentially; the current numbering system began in 1900. It does not indicate the year of issue or the Code section involved. Because the regulation text is added to the C.F.R., the most important information in the T.D. is the preamble. [See Illustration 8-1.]

---

[121] 67 Fed. Reg. 4217 (2002).

[122] The IRS operating divisions that followed the Internal Revenue Service Restructuring and Reform Act of 1998, Pub. L. No. 105-206, 112 Stat. 685, don't replace the chief counsel units. The operating divisions (Wage & Investment; Small Business/Self-Employed; Large & Mid-Size Business; and Tax Exempt/Government Entities) are not part of the chief counsel's office. The chief counsel division for exempt organizations is now called tax exempt and government entities; general litigation has become part of procedure and administration.

5. Preambles and Texts of Regulations

Preambles to T.D.s and NPRMs discuss the regulation and provide other useful information, much of which is discussed elsewhere in this chapter.

Table 8-4. Preamble Segments

Paperwork Reduction Act
Background
Explanation of Provisions
Effective Date
Special Analyses
Comments and Public Hearing
Drafting Information
List of Subjects

Two items follow the preamble. The first is the amendment to the affected C.F.R. subdivision. This amendment indicates the Code section authorizing each regulation, a concept discussed in Subsection F.2. The second item is the **text** of the regulation. That language will be added to the Code of Federal Regulations if it is a temporary or final regulation. If it is a proposed regulation, it appears in the Federal Register but not the C.F.R.

6. Filing Date, Effective Date, and Sunset Date

Because they are not statutes, regulations are not enacted. Instead they are issued to the public by being filed with the Federal Register. The **filing date** generally precedes the publication date by a day or two. The T.D. information following each temporary and final regulation includes the Federal Register date. That date is also listed before preambles to proposed, temporary, and final regulations. The date is important because of the rules concerning retroactivity discussed in Subsection E.2.

The preamble to the T.D. or NPRM includes the regulation's **effective date**, which can vary from its filing date and publication dates. The effective date for a proposed regulation is likely to read as follows: "These regulations are applicable to taxable years ending after the date final regulations are published in the Federal Register."

Final regulations generally continue in effect indefinitely. Temporary regulations issued after November 20, 1988, **sunset** no later than three years after they are issued. Although a final regulation continues in effect until it is withdrawn, its validity may be seriously compromised if the Code section it interprets is amended or if a judicial opinion rejects its reasoning. Use the T.D. date to determine when a regulation was promulgated or amended. If a regulation contradicts its Code section, it probably has not been amended to reflect the most recent statutory change.[123] If it varies from a judicial holding, the IRS may have decided to continue litigating its position rather than withdraw the regulation.

7. Semiannual Agenda and Priority Guidance Plan

Administrative agencies announce their regulatory plans twice a year in the **Semiannual Agenda of Regulations**. In addition, the Treasury and IRS issue an annual **Priority Guidance Plan (Business Plan)** for guidance they hope to issue during the next twelve months. These documents are discussed further in Section I.

SECTION G. SCOPE AND DEFINITIONS

1. Scope of Provisions

As is the case for the Code, rules appearing in a regulation section may apply only to that section, or a subdivision thereof, or they may apply to several sections. See, for example, Treas. Reg. § 1.48-12(b)(3)(iii):

Definition of internal structural framework. For purposes of this section, the term "internal structural framework" includes all load-bearing internal walls and any other internal structural supports, including the columns, girders, beams, trusses, spandrels, and all other members that are essential to the stability of the building.

2. Definitions

As was true for the Code itself, the regulations frequently define terms within individual sections. In addition, several regulations sections enlarge upon definitions found in Internal Revenue Code Subtitle F, Chapter 79.[124]

SECTION H. REGULATORY PROCESS

1. IRS and Treasury

Regulations begin as projects assigned to drafters in the relevant IRS division of the chief counsel's office. [See Table 8-3.] The Semiannual Agenda

---

[123] Looseleaf services that print regulations often indicate that a regulation does not reflect a statutory change.

[124] See, e.g., Treas. Reg. § 301.7701-1.

of Regulations or Priority Guidance Plan will generally list these items. The Semiannual Agenda lists the Code section and Project Number and indicates a target date by which action, such as publishing the proposed regulations, will occur. The Priority Guidance Plan lists topics (e.g., Exempt Organizations, Financial Issues and Products) alphabetically. Within each topic, it lists both regulations and other guidance it hopes to issue; Code sections are included for most items. For example, the 2001 Plan includes as an item within the Excise Taxes group "Proposed regulations under section 4081 relating to the revision of definition of diesel fuel."

Because the IRS may issue advance notices regarding its proposals,[125] researchers interested in future regulations must also check IRS documents discussed in Chapter 9.

After a notice and comment period, the IRS has several options. These include finalizing the regulation without modifications, finalizing it with modifications, modifying the proposed regulation and asking for additional comments, or withdrawing the proposed regulation and starting the drafting process over again. Because proposed regulations, unlike temporary regulations, do not sunset after three years, the IRS can also retain the proposal in its original form without further action.

2. Congress

In March 1996, Congress added a congressional review procedure for agency rules. This procedure allows Congress to disapprove a "major" rule by a **joint resolution of disapproval**. A disapproved rule does not become effective unless the President vetoes the disapproval and Congress fails to override the veto.

Major rules are suspended for up to 60 days for the congressional review and for additional time if needed for the override process.[126] Section E discusses other limitations applicable to regulations.

---

[125] See, e.g., Notice 2002-8, 2002-4 I.R.B. 398.

[126] 5 U.S.C. §§ 801-808. A major rule is "any rule that the Administrator of the Office of Information and Regulatory Affairs of the Office of Management and Budget finds has resulted in or is likely to result in–(A) an annual effect on the economy of $100,000,000 or more; (B) a major increase in costs or prices for consumers, individual industries, Federal, State, or local government agencies, or geographic regions; or (C) significant adverse effects on competition, employment, investment, productivity, innovation, or on the ability of United States-based enterprises to compete with foreign-based enterprises in domestic and export markets." Id. § 804(2).

SECTION I. LOCATING REGULATIONS DOCUMENTS

The first step in locating administrative documents is determining which items you need. The following paragraphs divide documents by type rather than by where they can be found.

1. Semiannual Agenda and Priority Guidance Plan

a. Semiannual Agenda

The Semiannual Agenda is issued twice a year and published in the Federal Register. It is required by the Regulatory Flexibility Act and Executive Order 12866. Its format conforms to the Regulatory Information Service Center (RISC) Unified Agenda Format.[127]

In addition to the IRS, the Treasury Department is responsible for the Bureau of Alcohol, Tobacco, and Firearms, the Comptroller of the Currency, the United States Customs Service, and the Office of Thrift Supervision. As a result, its Agenda is quite lengthy. Because it is not arranged in Code section order, it is difficult to search manually.

The Agenda is divided into two parts. In the first part, items are grouped by agency. Within that grouping, they are subdivided into the following categories: Prerule Stage; Proposed Rule Stage; Final Rule Stage; Long-Term Actions; and Completed Actions. The items in each category appear in **Sequence Number** order and also carry a **Regulation Identification Number (RIN)**. The sequence number changes from one Agenda to another; the project's RIN never changes. If you know a project's RIN but not the actual project number, you can find it using an online search in the Agenda.

Neither the Sequence Number nor the RIN indicates the relevant Code section or the regulations Project Number.[128] Part II provides this information for each item in Part I. Part II is arranged by Sequence Number. [See Illustrations 8-2 and 8-3.]

Although the Agenda is issued semiannually, a Regulatory Plan is required only in the second Agenda of the year. That plan indicates the most

---

[127] The Regulatory Information Service Center is part of the General Services Administration (www.gsa.gov). The form used in preparing Agenda items can be found at http://reginfo.gov/ridf.htm.

[128] The project illustrated in Illustrations 8-2 and 8-3 is RIN 1545-AV01; its Project Number is REG-101520-97; it involves Code section 6343.

important items that should be issued within the year.[129]

Several publishers include the Agenda in their services. For example, Tax Analysts includes it in the OneDisc CD-ROM. Services covering the Federal Register, such as LexisNexis and Westlaw, include the Agenda in their databases.[130] You can also access it through the Government Printing Office site, GPO Access.

Illustration 8-2. Excerpt from Semiannual Agenda Part I

Internal Revenue Service---
Proposed Rule Stage

Sequence Number	Title	Regulation Identification Number
2872	Reporting Requirements for Widely Held Fixed Investment Trusts	1545-AU15
2873	Special Rules Applicable to Sales of Debt Instrument Between Record Dates and the End of Accrual Periods	1545-AU95
2874	Return of Levied Property in Certain Cases	1545-AV01

➔ Part I indicates Sequence Numbers, a general description of the subject, and the RIN number. Part II, shown in Illustration 8-3, is also arranged by Sequence Number.

b. Priority Guidance Plan

The Priority Guidance Plan, which is also referred to as the Business Plan and the Guidance Priority Plan, includes both regulations and other forms of guidance that Treasury and IRS plan to issue during the year. Until 2002, the Plan covered a calendar year. Beginning with the plan issued in 2002, it covers a fiscal year ending June 30. It appears on the OneDisc CD-ROM, is covered by newsletters such as Daily Tax Report and Tax Notes, and can be found online at the IRS website.

---

[129] The Agendas are scheduled for April and October but may appear later.

[130] See, e.g., Department of the Treasury, Semiannual Agenda and Fiscal Year 2002 Regulatory Plan, 66 Fed. Reg. 62076 (Dec. 3, 2001). If you don't have a citation, you can find it by searching for either Semiannual Agenda or Unified Agenda.

Illustration 8-3. Excerpt from Semiannual Agenda Part II

2874. RETURN OF LEVIED PROPERTY IN CERTAIN CASES

Priority: Substantive, Nonsignificant

Legal Authority: 26 USC 7805

CFR Citation: 26 CFR 301

Legal Deadline: None

Abstract: Section 501(b) of the Taxpayer Bill of Rights 2 amended section 6343 of the Internal Revenue Code to authorize the Secretary to return levied property in four enumerated circumstances. Section 1102(d)(1)(B) of RRA 98 changed "Taxpayer Advocate" to "National Taxpayer Advocate" as a person who determines what is in the best interest of the taxpayer. The **regulations** set forth the circumstances in which the Secretary may return property and procedures to implement these sections.

	Timetable:		
	Action	Date	FR Cite
NPRM		12/00/01	

Regulatory Flexibility Analysis Required: No

Small Entities Affected: No

Government Levels Affected None

Additional Information: REG-101520-97

→Illustration 8-3 covers Sequence Number 2874 from Illustration 8-2. The portion shown above indicates the project's priority and legal authority (Code section 7805 in this case); in which part of 26 C.F.R. the regulation will be placed (part 301); a timetable for various actions (in this case the NPRM is the only action for which a timetable had been set); whether the project requires a regulatory flexibility analysis, affects small entities, or affects any government levels; and the regulation's project number. The Abstract provides relevant Code section and background information.

→Illustration 8-3 omits the names of the IRS and Treasury drafting and reviewing attorneys and the IRS attorney to contact for information. This information does appear in the Agenda listing.

2. Proposed Regulations

Proposed regulations are not included in the Code of Federal Regulations, but they do appear in the Federal Register, which can be searched in print and electronically. Several services provide access to proposed regulations, which they arrange in order of their publication. The steps you use to locate proposed regulations vary based on which of three features you know: the project number; the Federal Register date; or the underlying Code section number.[131]

If you know the project number but not the underlying Code section or the Federal Register date, you can locate the proposed regulation electronically by searching on the project number. You can do likewise if you know either of the other two items. [See Illustration 8-4.]

---

[131] You can also search the Federal Register online using the RIN number.

Looseleaf services that include proposed regulations in a separate volume may arrange them by Federal Register date. Those services generally include a table that cross-references from the underlying Code or regulations section to the appropriate page, paragraph, or section in the looseleaf service. They are unlikely to have tables cross-referencing project numbers.

3. Temporary and Final Regulations

a. C.F.R. and Federal Register

Temporary and final regulations are relatively easy to find. These items appear in both the Federal Register (as Treasury Decisions) and the Code of Federal Regulations (as "codified" regulations). Use the method for finding the Federal Register version that you would use to find a proposed regulation. Because the C.F.R. section numbers generally correspond to Code section numbers, it is easier to find temporary and final regulations in the C.F.R. than in the Federal Register.[132] You might choose to search in the Federal Register because it includes the preambles and C.F.R. doesn't.

Keep one limitation in mind if you use the print version of the C.F.R. The government does not replace C.F.R. volumes every time an agency promulgates a new regulation. Instead it republishes C.F.R. titles on an annual basis; several titles are replaced each calendar quarter. The annual reissue of Title 26 includes regulations issued as of April 1. Searching C.F.R. print updates for later material is a tedious process.[133] It is easier to find regulations using a tax-oriented looseleaf service (print or electronic) or to search C.F.R. online.

b. Looseleaf Services

Standard Federal Tax Reporter and United States Tax Reporter incorporate temporary and final regulations into their compilation volumes, which are arranged in Code section order. Each is available in print and in electronic versions.

Other tax-oriented services provide print versions of tax regulations. These include Mertens, Federal Tax Regulations, published in annual

---

[132] The method for issuing regulations in the Federal Register makes that publication analogous to Statutes at Large for revenue acts. Each T.D. is listed separately by publication date rather than by Code section. The Code of Federal Regulations, which is in section number order, is analogous to United States Code for statutes.

[133] See Fundamentals of Legal Research ch. 13 for information about using the Federal Register to find regulations issued after the annual C.F.R. compilation.

softbound volumes with updating throughout the year in a looseleaf Current Developments binder.

If you want the most recent items, don't use a print source such as U.S. Code Congressional & Administrative News—Federal Tax Regulations (Chapter 16). It is published annually and not updated during the year.

Looseleaf services are discussed further in Chapter 12. The USCCAN materials are described in Chapter 16.

c. Electronic Services

Several electronic sources print the text of regulations. Tax-oriented CD-ROM services include OneDisc, OnPoint, TaxExpert, Portfolios Plus Library, and Tax Practice Series. These and other CD-ROM services are discussed further in Chapter 18. Depending on the subscription option you select, the CD-ROM may be updated monthly, quarterly, or annually. You can search for more recent regulations using a weekly print updating service or a newsletter. You are most likely to find the most recent changes by using an online service for updating your results.

Illustration 8-4. OneDisc Search Options

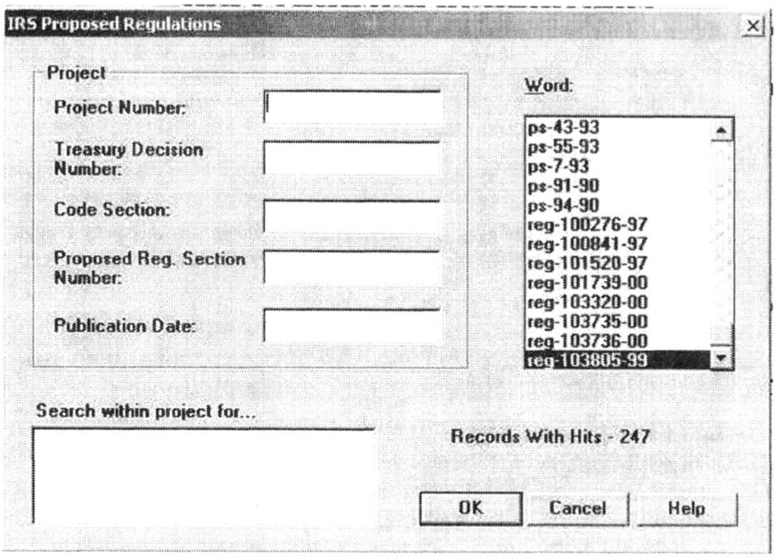

➔The <u>W</u>ord wheel lists project numbers. You can also search on the other fields or by words you insert in the "Search within project for..." field.

➔ The Treasury Decision field is useful if there actually is a T.D. (e.g., when a temporary regulation is issued simultaneously).

Online subscription sources for regulations include general services such as LexisNexis, Westlaw, Loislaw, and VersusLaw. You can also search for regulations online in tax-oriented subscription services. These include Tax Research NetWork, Checkpoint, TaxBase, TaxExpert Online, and TaxCore. Online services are discussed in Chapter 19.

You can also access regulations online at government sites. The National Archives and Records Administration publishes online when new C.F.R. volumes appear (www.access.gpo.gov/nara/cfr/). If you use this site, you must update your research for Treasury regulations appearing after April 1. You can do so using the site's links to online versions of List of CFR Sections Affected (LSA).

The Cornell Law School Legal Information Institute is another nonsubscription source for regulations (http://cfr.law.cornell.edu/cfr/). It pulls from the C.F.R. materials and offers both text and PDF versions. It also links to the Federal Register for updating material.

Illustration 8-5. Excerpt from Cornell LII C.F.R. Site

- Title 26 -- Internal Revenue
    - o CHAPTER I -- INTERNAL REVENUE SERVICE, DEPARTMENT OF THE TREASURY
        - PART 1 -- INCOME TAXES

Section

- 1.0-1 Internal Revenue Code of 1954 and regulations. [PDF]
- 1.1-1 Income tax on individuals. [PDF]
- 1.1-2 Limitation on tax. [PDF]
- 1.1-3 Change in rates applicable to taxable year. [PDF]

➔The Cornell site offers both regular text and PDF access to regulations. The PDF version reproduces appropriate pages from C.F.R.

4. Earlier Versions of Regulations

a. 1954 and 1986 Codes

Prior language may be important if you are evaluating recent changes in a regulation or if your research involves a completed transaction. If you need the language of a 1954 or 1986 Code regulation, you can find that regulation's language in United States Code Congressional & Administrative News—Federal Tax Regulations (Chapter 16). This service has separate volumes for each year since 1954 and prints regulations in effect on January 1 of the particular year.

If you don't have access to that service, or if you need a regulation that was both issued and withdrawn within a single calendar year and thus would not have been included, two other services may be of assistance. Cumulative Changes (Chapter 16) prints each version of a regulation. It has separate volumes for each Code. Until the mid-1990s, Mertens, Law of Federal Income Taxation (Chapter 12), published a Regulations series. That series published all income tax regulations issued or amended within a given time span (two or more years per volume).

If you lack access to the services listed above, make a list of T.D. numbers for the regulation you are tracing. Those numbers appear immediately after the particular regulation in C.F.R. and in most other versions of the regulations. The T.D.s are published in the Cumulative Bulletins, which your library is likely to carry.[134] The C.B.s are discussed in Chapter 16.

Note one limitation in using T.D. numbers to find older versions of regulations. If a 1954 Code regulation was originally published before 1960, the IRS republished it that year in T.D. 6498, 6500, or 6516. The USCCAN service ignores the pre-1960 publication in its history notes; Cumulative Changes omits the 1960 T.D. numbers but includes the pre-1960 T.D.s. If you use any service to find T.D. numbers, be sure you know how that service treats those early items.

b. 1939 Code and Earlier

Early regulations don't follow the regulations format used elsewhere in this text. Initially they were issued with respect to individual revenue acts and were divided into articles rather than section numbers. The first named set of regulations was referred to as Regulations Number 33 and was issued in 1914.[135] The article numbers did not correspond to act section numbers.

The Federal Register became available online in 1994 and in print in 1936. As a result, it is not a good source for finding early regulations. Even for years it covers, it is tedious to search in print. In many libraries, the best source for 1939 Code and earlier regulations will be the Cumulative Bulletin. It began publication in 1919; the first Treasury Decision it includes is T.D. 2836.

---

[134] Finding Lists in the CCH and RIA citators indicate which volume of the Internal Revenue Bulletin or Cumulative Bulletin contains each T.D. For recent items, RIA is more likely to refer to the paragraph in United States Tax Reporter.

[135] See Henry Campbell Black, A Treatise on the Law of Income Taxes (2d ed. 1915).

The Government Printing Office published a Treasury Decisions–Internal Revenue service from 1899 until 1942. It covers 1898 through July 9, 1942. The current T.D. numbering system began in 1900 with the third volume of that series. Those volumes have subject indexes.

Be aware that many of the early Treasury Decisions look less like regulations and more like "public" private letter rulings.[136] Letter rulings are discussed in Chapter 9.

5. Preambles

The Federal Register includes the preambles for each proposed, temporary, and final regulation with the regulation text. Excerpts or full text also appear in the Internal Revenue Bulletin and Cumulative Bulletin.[137]

Tax-oriented looseleaf services separate preambles from the regulations text. If they print the preambles, they do so in separate volumes.[138] Mertens, Federal Tax Regulations, publishes preambles for tax regulations in looseleaf volumes. Coverage begins in 1985. Standard Federal Tax Reporter (Chapter 12) prints preambles for proposed regulations in its U.S. Tax Cases Advance Sheets volume; it includes current year preambles for T.D.s in the Regulations Status Table in its New Matters volume. United States Tax Reporter (Chapter 12) prints preambles to proposed regulations in a separate volume for preambles (volume 18); it prints current year preambles for T.D.s in the IRS Rulings section of its Recent Developments volume.

Electronic services may include preambles as a separate database (CD-ROM services) or in their Federal Register coverage.

6. Hearings Transcripts and Other Taxpayer Comments

Newsletters such as Daily Tax Report and Tax Notes report on testimony at hearings and taxpayer written comments. The Tax Notes Today file in LexisNexis includes texts of unofficial hearings transcripts and other tax-

---

[136] "SIR: In reply to a letter of inquiry addressed to this office on the 29th ultimo by Frederick D. Howe, treasurer and manager of the Warren Specialty Company, Auburn, N.Y., will you please inform him that the beverage (liqueur) called creme de menthe being, as it is understood, a compound of distilled spirits with other materials, any person manufacturing it for sale must be required to pay special tax as a rectifier ...." T.D. 33, 3 Treasury Decisions–Internal Revenue 32 (1900).

[137] Preambles for proposed regulations were added to the C.B. in 1981.

[138] If a regulation was issued in both proposed and temporary format, a looseleaf service may carry only the preamble to the temporary regulation.

payer comments. You can also find these items online using services such as TaxCore. The preamble to final regulations summarizes taxpayer comments made in response to the NPRM.

SECTION J. CITATORS FOR REGULATIONS

Regulations rarely keep pace with congressional activity. Whenever a Code section changes, researchers must review existing regulations. They may no longer be relevant. They may even be totally invalid. If a temporary or final regulation appears to contradict statutory language, check the date of its most recent T.D. to see if it predates the statutory change.

When an existing regulation affects a transaction, that regulation's success or failure in litigation is certainly relevant. The government is bound nationally by adverse decisions in the Supreme Court. It is effectively bound within a particular circuit by an adverse circuit court decision because trial courts follow the law of their circuit. The IRS is not bound in its dealings with taxpayers in circuits that have not addressed the regulation. Because the Supreme Court hears relatively few tax cases, the government may decide not to withdraw a regulation merely because the Tax Court or a single circuit court invalidates it.[139]

A citator indicating judicial action on regulations is extremely useful for determining how courts ruled on challenges to particular regulations. The citators listed below, and described further in Chapter 11, serve that purpose. These citators follow two basic arrangement patterns—regulations section order or Treasury Decision number order. Because Treasury Decisions often involve more than one regulations section, citators based on section numbers are more likely to provide the desired information.

• Shepard's Code of Federal Regulations Citations (C.F.R. section); Shepard's Federal Tax Citator (C.F.R. section and T.D. number) (print and online)[140]

• RIA Citator (T.D. number) (print, CD-ROM, and online)

---

[139] Compare Western Nat. Mut. Ins. Co. v. Commissioner, 65 F.3d 90 (8th Cir. 1995), invalidating Treas. Reg. § 1.846-3(c), with Atlantic Mut. Ins. Co. v. Commissioner, 111 F.3d 1056 (3d Cir. 1997), holding the regulation valid. The Supreme Court upheld the Third Circuit. See 523 U.S. 382 (1998).

[140] Although the general Shepard's service is limited to C.F.R. citations, the online version does provide citations to T.D.s.

• CCH Standard Federal Tax Reporter—Citator (T.D. number) (print and online)

• West's KeyCite (C.F.R. section)[141] (online)

It is usually easier to locate this information using a citator's electronic version.[142] You can also search both CD-ROM and online services without using a citator by using the regulations section number and a variant of valid (or invalid) as your search terms. For example, I have two options for researching Treas. Reg. § 1.469-2 in Westlaw. I could enter the following in the Westlaw FTX-CS (Federal Taxation–Cases) database: 1.469-2 & valid invalid.[143] I could also go directly to the regulation and then use the KeyCite function. If I used a service that lacked a citator, my search would resemble the first option (modified to reflect that service's command structure).

SECTION K. JUDICIAL DEFERENCE

In determining the degree of deference they should give regulations, courts are guided by several Supreme Court decisions, the most important of which is *Chevron*.[144] The *Chevron* Court held[145]

---

[141] KC History does provide information about corrections of errors in the T.D.

[142] The Shepard's and CCH citators are available on LexisNexis; the CCH citator is also available on Tax Research NetWork. The RIA citator is available on Westlaw and Checkpoint. KeyCite is available on Westlaw.

[143] Unlike LexisNexis, Westlaw does not require an "or" in this search. If I wanted to find decisions that used the term "validity," I could have refined my search by adding root expanders. Remember to check search terminology options when you use an electronic service. See Chapter 19 for information about search terms.

[144] Chevron U.S.A. Inc. v. Natural Resources Defense Council, Inc., 467 U.S. 837 (1984).

[145] Id. at 842-43 (footnotes omitted). The Court added: "If Congress has explicitly left a gap for the agency to fill, there is an express delegation of authority to the agency to elucidate a specific provision of the statute by regulation. Such legislative regulations are given controlling weight unless they are arbitrary, capricious, or manifestly contrary to the statute.[12] Sometimes the legislative delegation to an agency on a particular question is implicit rather than explicit. In such a case, a court may not substitute its own construction of a statutory provision for a reasonable interpretation made by the administrator of an agency.[13]" Id. at 843-44 (footnotes omitted).

When a court reviews an agency's construction of the statute which it administers, it is confronted with two questions. First, always, is the question whether Congress has directly spoken to the precise question at issue. If the intent of Congress is clear, that is the end of the matter; for the court, as well as the agency, must give effect to the unambiguously expressed intent of Congress.[9] If, however, the court determines Congress has not directly addressed the precise question at issue, the court does not simply impose its own construction on the statute,[10] as would be necessary in the absence of an administrative interpretation. Rather, if the statute is silent or ambiguous with respect to the specific issue, the question for the court is whether the agency's answer is based on a permissible construction of the statute.[11]

Although *Chevron* is not a tax decision, it is cited in many tax cases and therefore appears if you enter *Chevron* into an electronic service. There are also tax cases involving the same company. Examples in Chapter 19 illustrate the risks of searching by case name alone in electronic services.

The excerpts below illustrate judicial approaches to deference. Two statements apply irrespective of the approach taken. First, the degree of deference accorded legislative regulations is higher than that accorded interpretive regulations. Second, proposed regulations receive much less deference than do temporary or final regulations.

• To invoke these passages from our decisions for the general proposition that regulations may not add rules not found in the statute and not precluded by the statute is to misread them. Indeed, supplementation of a statute is a necessary and proper part of the Secretary's role in the administration of our tax laws. Hachette USA, Inc. v. Commissioner, 105 T.C. 234, 251 (1995).

• Although the difference between these two approaches [*Chevron* and *National Muffler*] is negligible at best—any regulation which is "based upon a permissible construction" of an ambiguous statute will almost always "implement the congressional mandate in some reasonable manner" and vice versa, the Ninth Circuit is correct to rely upon the more narrowly tailored holding of *National Muffler*. Bell Federal Savings & Loan Association v. Commissioner, 40 F.3d 224, 227 (7th Cir. 1994).

• If the regulations constituted a reasonable interpretation of [the statute], we would be compelled to uphold them even if [the taxpayer's] interpretation were more reasonable. Estate of Bullard v. Commissioner, 87 T.C. 261, 281 (1986).

• The reasonableness of each possible interpretation of the statute can also be measured against the legislative process by which [it] was enacted. Commissioner v. Engle, 464 U.S. 206, 220 (1984).

• "[L]egislative" regulations ... are entitled to even greater weight than regulations issued pursuant to the general authority granted by Congress under section 7805(a). Fife v. Commissioner, 82 T.C. 1, 15 (1984).

• Where the Commissioner acts under specific authority, our primary inquiry is whether the interpretation or method is within the delegation of authority. Rowan Cos., Inc. v. United States, 452 U.S. 247, 253 (1981).

• A regulation may have particular force if it is a substantially contemporaneous construction of the statute by those presumed to have been aware of congressional intent.... Other relevant considerations are the length of time the regulation has been in effect, the reliance placed on it, the consistency of the Commissioner's interpretation, and the degree of scrutiny Congress has devoted to the regulation during subsequent re-enactments of the statute.[146] National Muffler Dealers Ass'n, Inc. v. United States, 440 U.S. 472, 477 (1979) (footnotes omitted).

• [Proposed regulations] carry no more weight than a position advanced on brief.... F.W. Woolworth Co. v. Commissioner, 54 T.C. 1233, 1265 (1970).

SECTION L. PROBLEMS

1. What legislative regulation was authorized by the listed Code section?

    a. 617   b. 679   c. 956   d. 1234B

2. What agency's interpretation must the IRS follow for the Code section listed below?

    a. 42   b. 1393

3. List all T.D.s issued for the regulation listed below.

    a. 1.61-4   c. 1.502-1

    b. 1.163-13   d. 20.2055-1

---

[146] At one time courts invoked a "re-enactment doctrine" if a regulation had been in effect through several revenue acts and Congress did not override it. Now that Congress amends specific provisions rather than re-enacting the entire Code, this doctrine is of questionable value.

4. Does the IRS consider the regulation listed legislative or interpretive?

  a. 1.101-7   c. 4.954-1

  b. 1.302-1   d. 7.48-1

5. What agency's action led to a 1990 change in Treas. Reg. § 1.163-5(c)?

6. What impact on small business did the IRS indicate the regulations promulgated in T.D. 8940 would have?

7. Locate a 1997 preamble to a regulation the IRS classified as a "major rule."

8. Provide the List of Subjects from the T.D. listed below. (A single T.D. may involve multiple subjects and multiple Code sections.)

  a. 7850   b. 7962   c. 8341   d. 8900

9. Who drafted the T.D. listed below?

  a. 8400   b. 8500   c. 8600   d. 8700

10. An attorney from which chief counsel division drafted the T.D. listed below?

  a. 8450   b. 8550   c. 8650   d. 8750

11. Who drafted the most recent version (original or amended) of Treasury regulation section

  a. 1.179-1   c. 25.2503-2

  b. 1.902-1   d. 801.1

12. Who drafted the proposed regulations covered by Project Number

  a. EE-113-82   c. REG-114998-99

  b. PS-217-84   d. REG-125626-01

13. List any items in the most recent Priority Guidance Plan relating to guidance for a topic selected by your instructor.

14. Go to the most recent Priority Guidance Plan. Your instructor will select a regulations project. Find that project in the most recent Semiannual Agenda and indicate all relevant dates for guidance.

15. Locate the court decision described and any subsequent appeals. Indicate the outcome.

a. a 1997 District Court decision involving Temp. Treas. Reg. § 1.163-9T(b)(2)(i)(A) and a general contractor

b. a 1998 District Court decision brought by the Kentucky Commissioner of Insurance and involving Treas. Reg. § 1.1502-47(a)(2)(ii)

c. a 2000 Tax Court decision involving both Treas. Reg. § 1.469-2(f)(6) and the definition of a binding contract under Wisconsin law

d. a 2000 Tax Court decision involving Treas. Reg. § 25.2702-3(e) and Wal-Mart stock

e. a 2001 Tax Court decision involving Temp. Treas. Reg. § 301.6245-1T and a football team

f. a 2002 Tax Court decision involving Treas. Reg. § 1.267(a)-3 and the 1967 U.S.-France income tax treaty

16. Which group did the person giving testimony represent at the hearing indicated?

a. Mark McConaghy at a 1993 hearing on proposed regulations defining research and experimental expenditures under I.R.C. § 174

b. Stefan Tucker at a 1996 hearing on proposed check-the-box regulations.

c. Martin Rosenstein at a 2000 hearing on proposed regulations regarding construction allowances for lessees under I.R.C. § 110

d. Peter Scott at a 2001 hearing on proposed regulations regarding the I.R.C. § 121 exclusion

17. Draft comments on a proposed regulation selected by your instructor.

Chapter 9. Internal Revenue Service Documents

Section A. Introduction

This chapter discusses guidance, other than regulations, issued by the Internal Revenue Service. These documents can be issued more quickly than regulations, in part because they are not subject to notice and comment procedures. In addition to describing the different types of guidance, this chapter indicates which can be cited as precedential and which constitute "substantial authority," concepts discussed in Chapter 2. It also discusses sources in which you can find these documents, the role of the Freedom of Information Act and other statutes affecting the release of IRS documents, and judicial deference to various IRS pronouncements.

Your goals for this chapter include learning which documents are available and where they can be found, determining their relative importance, and locating IRS and judicial action with respect to items you've located.

Section B. Types of IRS Documents

There are several methods for categorizing IRS documents. Three such methods are their means of publication, their initial audience, and their status as precedent or as substantial authority.

1. Means of Publication

The IRS publishes several documents in the weekly Internal Revenue Bulletin. The most important of these are revenue rulings, revenue procedures, notices, and announcements. Items currently included in the I.R.B. are cumulated every six months and appear in the Cumulative Bulletin. Chapter 16 discusses changes in the C.B. format over time.

The IRS issues other types of guidance, such as private letter rulings and actions on decisions, that it does not publish in the I.R.B. Many of these items were released to the public following Freedom of Information Act (FOIA) litigation; others have been exempted from release by statute.

The materials in Sections C through E categorize IRS documents by their

135

publication status: officially published in the I.R.B. or in other IRS publications; available because of FOIA litigation; or exempted from release by statute.[147]

2. Initial Audience

Documents published in the Internal Revenue Bulletin are directed to all taxpayers and their representatives. Private letter rulings, on the other hand, are directed to a specific taxpayer; the IRS makes them available to other readers after deleting identifying material. Still other documents are written for government personnel. Many of them, such as field service advice, are publicly available.

3. Status as Precedent or Substantial Authority

Items printed in the Internal Revenue Bulletin constitute authority for avoiding the substantial understatement penalty discussed in Chapter 2. These documents can be cited as precedent, and the IRS considers itself bound by them in its dealings with taxpayers whose facts are the same as those discussed in the documents. As discussed in Section I, the degree of deference they receive from courts is mixed.

Items that are not published in the I.R.B. fall into two categories. A few of them are not precedential but nevertheless constitute authority for avoiding the substantial understatement penalty. Others are neither precedential nor authority for avoiding the penalty. Even though these documents are not precedential, courts occasionally cite them.

SECTION C. OFFICIALLY PUBLISHED IRS DOCUMENTS

1. Revenue Rulings (Rev. Rul.)

a. Background

The IRS issues rulings designed to apply the law to particular factual situations. Unlike regulations, rulings do not first appear in proposed form for public comment.

Rulings fall into two categories—revenue rulings and letter rulings. If the IRS determines a ruling is of general interest, it publishes it in the Internal Revenue Bulletin and Cumulative Bulletin as a **revenue ruling**.

---

[147] As new items come to light, they may initially be placed in a fourth category—subject to FOIA litigation.

Although a revenue ruling is not as authoritative as a Treasury regulation, any taxpayer whose circumstances are substantially the same as those described in the ruling can rely upon it.[148] Revenue rulings also constitute authority for avoiding the substantial understatement penalty. Subject to the limitations in Code section 7805(b), revenue rulings can apply retroactively unless their text indicates otherwise. [See Illustration 3-6 for an excerpt from a revenue ruling.]

Although the number varies from year to year, there have been relatively few revenue rulings issued in recent years.[149] Many of those actually issued represent regularly scheduled guidance rather than rulings on new topics.

b. Numbering System

The IRS numbers revenue rulings chronologically.[150] The ruling number has two segments separated by a hyphen; the first indicates the year and the second indicates the ruling number for that year.[151] The ruling number does not indicate which Code section is involved.

The IRS began issuing numbered revenue rulings in 1953 and adopted the current numbering system in 1954. Earlier rulings, with different names, appeared in pre-1953 Cumulative Bulletins. [See Table 9-1.]

c. Format

Revenue rulings begin by indicating the regulations section involved; the Code section number also appears.

Most recent revenue rulings contain five segments: Issue; Facts; Law; Analysis; and Holding. A sixth section, Effect on Other Documents, appears if the current ruling revokes, modifies, obsoletes, or otherwise affects a prior holding. Rulings also indicate the IRS employee who drafted them or who can be contacted if the taxpayer has questions; Cumulative Bulletins issued

---

[148] Although it happens rarely, the IRS has issued adverse rulings based on a set of facts encountered in an audit and then asserted the ruling as authority when the taxpayer litigated. See Rev. Rul. 79-427, 1979-2 C.B. 120, discussed in Niles v. United States, 710 F.2d 1391, 1393 (9th Cir. 1983).

[149] The IRS issued over 700 revenue rulings in 1955; it released 66 in 2001.

[150] The first ruling issued in 2002 is Rev. Rul. 2002-1. Each week's rulings are numbered sequentially, often in Code section order.

[151] The Service began using four digits for years in 2000. Before that it used two digits.

before 1998 omit drafting information.

Table 9-1. Pre-1953 Titles of Published Rulings

A.R.M.	Committee on Appeals and Review Memorandum
A.R.R.	Committee on Appeals and Review Recommendation
A.T.	Alcohol Tax Unit; Alcohol and Tobacco Tax Division
C.L.T.	Child-Labor Tax Division
C.S.T.	Capital-Stock Tax Division
C.T.	Carriers Taxing Act of 1937; Taxes on Employment by Carriers
D.C.	Treasury Department Circular
Dept. Cir.	Treasury Department Circular
E.P.C.	Excess Profits Tax Council Ruling or Memorandum
E.T.	Estate and Gift Tax Division or Ruling
Em.T.	Employment Taxes
G.C.M.	Chief Counsel's Memorandum; General Counsel's Memorandum; Assistant General Counsel's Memorandum
I.T.	Income Tax Unit or Division
L.O.	Solicitor's Law Opinion
MS.	Miscellaneous Unit or Division or Branch
M.T.	Miscellaneous Division or Branch
Mim.	Mimeographed Letter; Mimeograph
Mim.	Solicitor's Law Opinion
O.	Office Decision
Op. A.G.	Opinion of Attorney General
P.T.	Processing Tax Decision or Division
S.	Solicitor's Memorandum
S.M.	Solicitor's Memorandum
S.R.	Solicitor's Recommendation
S.S.T.	Social Security Tax and Carriers' Tax; Social Security Tax; Taxes on Employment by Other than Carriers
S.T.	Sales Tax Unit or Division or Branch
Sil.	Silver Tax Division
Sol. Op.	Solicitor's Opinion
T.	Tobacco Division
T.B.M.	Advisory Tax Board Memorandum
T.B.R.	Advisory Tax Board Recommendation
Tob.	Tobacco Branch

2. Revenue Procedures (Rev. Proc.) and Procedural Rules

a. Background

Revenue procedures are published statements of IRS practices and procedures. These documents are published in the Internal Revenue Bulletin and Cumulative Bulletin. Procedures of general applicability may also be added to the IRS Statement of Procedural Rules and published in the Code of Federal Regulations.

Several revenue procedures are issued each year to provide guidance on how to obtain rulings and other IRS advice. [See Table 9-2.] For example, the first procedure each year (e.g., Rev. Proc. 2002-1) provides procedures for obtaining rulings, determination letters, and closing agreements. It also includes a sample ruling request format and a schedule of user fees.

Revenue procedures constitute authority for avoiding the substantial understatement penalty.

b. Numbering System

Revenue procedures have been numbered chronologically since 1955. Beginning in 2000, the Service began using all four digits to indicate the year. The procedure number does not indicate the Code or regulations section involved.

Items included in the IRS Statement of Procedural Rules are part of 26 C.F.R. and are numbered as Treasury regulations (Chapter 8). Their prefix is 601.

c. Format

Revenue procedures include several subdivisions, the exact number of which are determined by the procedure's scope and complexity. The following subdivisions are commonly used: Purpose; Background; Scope; Effective Date; Effect on Other Documents; and Drafting Information. In appropriate cases, the procedure will also include sections such as Record Keeping, Request for Comments, and Paperwork Reduction Act.

3. Notices

The IRS issues **notices** to provide guidance before revenue rulings and regulations are available. As noted in Chapter 8, notices can describe future regulations in a manner that will pass muster under the Code section 7805(b) rules on retroactivity.[152]

Notices are numbered by year; the number does not indicate the Code or

---

[152] In some cases, the Service has used announcements to provide information and elicit comments about regulations it is drafting. See, e.g., Ann. 2002-9, 2002-7 I.R.B. 536 (deductibility and capitalization of costs associated with intangible assets).

regulations section involved. Notices constitute authority for avoiding the substantial understatement penalty.

Notices may be subdivided into parts similar to those used for revenue rulings and procedures. Shorter notices have few if any formal subdivisions.

Table 9-2. Regularly Issued Revenue Procedures Regarding Guidance

Procedure	Subject
Year-1	Obtaining revenue rulings, determination letters, and closing agreements; user fees
Year-2	Requesting technical advice
Year-3	Areas for which the IRS will not issue a ruling
Year-4	Obtaining rulings for exempt organizations and employee plans
Year-5	Technical advice for exempt organizations and employee plans
Year-6	Obtaining determination letters regarding the qualification of employee plans
Year-7	Areas for which the IRS will not issue a ruling (international)
Year-8	User fees for employee plans and exempt organization rulings

➔These procedures, particularly the third item, may be updated during the year.

4. Announcements (Ann.)

Announcements alert taxpayers to a variety of information but are somewhat less formal than revenue rulings, revenue procedures, and notices. Information provided in announcements includes corrections to previously published regulations, lists of organizations classified as private foundations, and extensions of time to file forms.[153] They are numbered by year; the numbering does not indicate the underlying Code section. Announcements constitute authority for avoiding the substantial understatement penalty. These I.R.B. documents were added to the Cumulative Bulletin in 1998.

---

[153] For example, Ann. 2002-24, 2002-9 I.R.B. 606, announced a change in a date for a hearing on proposed regulations.

Illustration 9-1. Notice 2002-16, 2002-9 I.R.B. 567

Weighted Average Interest Rate Update	range of interest rates used to calculate current liability for the purpose of the full funding limitation of § 412(c)(7) of the Internal Revenue Code as amended by the Omnibus Budget Reconciliation Act of 1987 and as further amended by the Uruguay Round Agreements Act, Pub. L. 103-465 (GATT).	The average yield on the 30-year Treasury Constant Maturities for January 2002 is 5.45 percent. The following rates were determined for the plan years beginning in the month shown below.

Notice 2002-16

Notice 88-73 provides guidelines for determining the weighted average interest rate and the resulting permissible

Month	Year	Weighted Average	90% to 105% Permissible Range	90% to 110% Permissible Range
February	2002	5.70	5.13 to 5.98	5.13 to 6.27

Drafting Information

The principal author of this notice is Todd Newman of the Employee Plans, Tax Exempt and Government Entities Division. For further information regarding this notice, please call Mr. Newman at (202) 283-9888 (not a toll-free number).

5. Other Documents Published in the Internal Revenue Bulletin

The weekly Bulletins contain other information, much of which is issued by the IRS. Information from the IRS includes disbarment notices, delegation orders (Del. Order) announcing delegations of authority to various IRS offices, and **notices of acquiescence and nonacquiescence (acq.; nonacq.).**[154] The acquiescence notices are important because they indicate if the IRS will continue to litigate an issue it has lost in a judicial proceeding. IRS litigation plans are discussed further in Subsection D.6.

Non-IRS material includes Executive Orders issued by the President; Treasury regulations; new legislation and treaty documents; and Supreme Court decisions. These materials are discussed in other chapters.

[154] Most, but not all, I.R.B. items were cumulated every six months in the Cumulative Bulletin. Since 1998, the C.B. reprints all I.R.B. items. See Chapter 16 for a discussion of the C.B.

6. Other IRS Documents

The IRS publishes numerous tax return forms, accompanying instructions, and explanatory booklets. These documents contain few, if any, citations to authority, and they do not indicate if the IRS position has been disputed. Even if they are misleading, taxpayers who rely on them cannot cite them as authority against a contrary IRS position.[155] These documents are not authority for avoiding the substantial understatement penalty.

The numbering system for tax return forms and explanatory booklets does not indicate the underlying Code section number. In addition, the numbering systems for forms and booklets are not coordinated. For example, Code section 280A provides the rules governing deductions for an office in the taxpayer's home. IRS Form 8829 is used for computing that deduction. Publication Number 587 explains the deduction rules to the public.

SECTION D. PUBLICLY RELEASED IRS DOCUMENTS

The documents discussed in this section are useful for determining the IRS position on relevant issues. None of them can be cited as precedent,[156] but several constitute authority for avoiding the substantial underpayment penalty discussed in Chapter 2. Litigation resulted in their release and in the enactment of statutes requiring or restricting taxpayer access. You can find most of these documents on the IRS website.

1. Disclosure Legislation and Litigation

The lawsuit that first resulted in disclosure of unpublished documents involved private letter rulings and was brought under the Freedom of Information Act (FOIA).[157] That lawsuit resulted in the disclosure of rulings issued after October 31, 1976, and led to the enactment of Code section 6110, an IRS-specific disclosure statute.

---

[155] See Osborne v. Commissioner, 97-2 U.S.T.C. ¶ 50,524, 79 A.F.T.R.2d 97-3011 (6th Cir. 1997). See also TAM 8350008, involving an IRS refusal to allow a taxpayer to claim reliance on a portion of the Internal Revenue Manual or on the 1982 version of IRS Publication 544. But see Gehl Co. v. Commissioner, 795 F.2d 1324 (7th Cir. 1986); the decision not to seek certiorari is explained in AOD 1988-002.

[156] I.R.C. § 6110(k)(3).

[157] Tax Analysts and Advocates v. Internal Revenue Service, 405 F. Supp. 1065 (D.D.C. 1975) (brought under 5 U.S.C. § 552).

Section 6110, which has been amended several times since its 1976 enactment, requires the release of written determinations and of background file documents related to those written determinations. Written determinations are defined as rulings, determination letters, technical advice memoranda, and chief counsel advice.[158]

The term **chief counsel advice (CCA; C.C.A.)** covers:[159]

> written advice or instruction, under whatever name or designation, prepared by any national office component of the Office of Chief Counsel which–
> (i) is issued to field or service center employees of the Service or regional or district employees of the Office of Chief Counsel; and
> (ii) conveys–
> (I) any legal interpretation of a revenue provision;
> (II) any Internal Revenue Service or Office of Chief Counsel position or policy concerning a revenue provision; or
> (III) any legal interpretation of State law, foreign law, or other Federal law relating to the assessment or collection of any liability under a revenue provision.

Revenue provisions include statutes, regulations, revenue rulings and procedures, tax treaties, and other published or unpublished guidance.[160]

Section 6110 provides timetables for disclosure by the Service. The disclosure date is later than the document's actual issue date to allow time for notifying taxpayers that rulings they have requested are being made public and purging taxpayer-identifying information.

2. Numbering System

Unless a different system is indicated, the publicly released documents

---

[158] I.R.C. § 6110(a) & (b). Background file documents are "the request for that written determination, any written material submitted in support of the request, and any communication (written or otherwise) between the Internal Revenue Service and persons outside the Internal Revenue Service in connection with such written determination ... received before issuance of the written determination."

The IRS makes written determinations available in its FOIA Reading Room and on its website. It releases background documents only on written request; there are fees for finding these items, deleting confidential information, and duplicating them. Id. § 6110(e) & (k); Rev. Proc. 95-15, 1995-1 C.B. 523.

[159] CC-2002-026 (May 16, 2002) discusses obtaining and processing chief counsel advice. This document will be added to IRM 35.8.12.7.1.

[160] I.R.C. § 6110(i).

discussed in Section D use a common numbering system. The system is based on a multi-digit number (e.g., 84-37-084 or 200203010). Although citation manuals use the hyphens, the IRS does not use them for these documents on its website. Letters preceding the numbers indicate the type of document (e.g., private letter ruling, technical advice memorandum).

The hyphens are useful because they call attention to what the number means. The digits preceding the first hyphen reflect the year the document was released; the next two digits indicate the week of release; the final digits are the document number for that week.

Although the document number does not reflect the underlying Code section, many documents also include Uniform Issue List (UIL) numbers. UIL numbers, which do reflect the underlying Code section, are discussed in Section G. The IRS website lets you sort documents by UIL number.

3. Private Letter Rulings (PLR; P.L.R.; Ltr. Rul.; Priv. Ltr. Rul.)

Private letter rulings are written in response to taxpayer requests for guidance as to a proposed transaction's tax consequence. In addition to the underlying facts, issues raised, and legal analysis, these rulings indicate which chief counsel's office division produced them.

Some private letter rulings are formally published as revenue rulings, but most are available to the public only through the section 6110 disclosure procedure. Although the IRS is not bound by them in its dealings with other taxpayers,[161] letter rulings issued after October 31, 1976, constitute authority for avoiding the substantial understatement penalty.

4. Determination Letters

Determination letters are similar to letter rulings but emanate from IRS district offices rather than the national office. District office personnel issue them only if they can be based on well-established rules that apply to the issues presented. Otherwise, the matter is appropriately handled by the national office.

5. Technical Advice Memoranda (TAM; T.A.M.; Tech. Adv. Mem.)

Technical advice memoranda are issued by the national office in response

---

[161] But see Ogiony v. Commissioner, 617 F.2d 14, 17-18 (2d Cir. 1980) (Oakes, J., concurring). Although commenting that they had no precedential force, the Supreme Court has cited private letter rulings as evidence of IRS inconsistent interpretation. See Rowan Cos., Inc. v. United States, 452 U.S. 247, 261 n.17 (1981).

to IRS requests arising out of tax return examinations. Unlike letter rulings, which focus on proposed transactions, technical advice memoranda cover completed transactions. In contrast to field service advice, discussed in Subsection D.8, technical advice requests involve both the taxpayer and the IRS, but both parties must agree on the underlying facts. Memoranda issued after October 31, 1976, constitute authority for avoiding the substantial understatement penalty.

6. Actions on Decisions (AOD; A.O.D.; Action on Dec.; Action on Decision)

The IRS uses several means for announcing future litigation information. One mechanism is the notice of acquiescence or nonacquiescence in cases it has lost. Those notices appear in the Internal Revenue Bulletin. Until early 1993, the Service issued those notices only for Tax Court Regular decisions. It now issues them for all trial and circuit courts.[162]

An **action on decision** indicates *why* the Service recommends (1) appealing or not appealing an adverse decision and (2) acquiescing or not acquiescing in that decision. These are separate recommendations. The Service may recommend not acquiescing and continuing to litigate an issue even though it decides not to appeal the particular case it lost. For example, AOD 1984-022, reproduced as Illustration 9-2, involved a question of fact. The appellate court would be unlikely to reverse for this reason, but the IRS was not willing to concede the underlying issue in future litigation. [See Illustration 3-9 for a more traditional AOD.]

Unlike notices of acquiescence, AODs were never limited to Tax Court decisions. As is true for acquiescence notices, the IRS does not issue an AOD for every case it loses. Taxpayers can use AODs issued after March 12, 1981, as authority for avoiding the substantial understatement penalty.

AODs are numbered sequentially by year. The numbering system provides no information about the underlying case name or issue involved. In 2001 the IRS began including CC (Chief Counsel) in the AOD number (e.g., AOD CC-2002-02) on its website.[163] Although the IRS refers to these docu-

---

[162] Although these notices should be the primary means of publishing this information in the Bulletin, the IRS occasionally uses other guidance for this purpose See, e.g., Rev. Rul. 94-47, 1994-2 C.B. 18; Notice 96-39, 1996-2 C.B. 309; Notice 95-57, 1995-2 C.B. 337.

[163] The website is not consistent in its use of digits. In some years, it has used three digits (e.g., -001) and in others two digits (e.g., -01) for the AOD number. Be prepared to search both ways for a document if you lack the case name.

ments as AOD without periods, citation systems use other formats. For example, The Bluebook uses *action on dec.*; Tax Cite uses *action on decision*.

7. General Counsel Memoranda (GCM; G.C.M.; Gen. Couns. Mem.)

Just as actions on decisions provide the reasoning behind litigation decisions, **general counsel memoranda** indicate the reasoning and authority used in revenue rulings, private letter rulings, and technical advice memoranda. IRS personnel used them in formulating positions.[164] Taxpayers can use GCMs issued after March 12, 1981, as authority for avoiding the substantial understatement penalty.

GCMs are numbered sequentially (e.g., GCM 39278). The numbering system does not indicate the year of issue, the Code section, or the document about which they supply information. The number of GCMs declined markedly during the 1990s; none has been issued since 1997 (GCM 39891).

8. Field Service Advice (FSA; F.S.A.); Strategic Advice Memoranda (SAM; S.A.M.)

IRS field attorneys, revenue agents, and appeals officers may request national office advice if a case presents a significant legal question of first impression and no guidance exists as to the chief counsel's legal position or policy.[165] The auditor may seek **field service advice** instead of a technical advice memorandum and may do so without the taxpayer's knowledge. Field service advice does not constitute authority for avoiding the substantial understatement penalty.

If the technical expedited advice memorandum pilot program proves successful, the IRS may limit FSAs to the function they were originally supposed to have, providing field personnel with case-specific legal development strategies and assessment of litigation hazards. They may be renamed **strategic advice memoranda**.

9. Technical Expedited Advice Memoranda (TEAM; T.E.A.M.)

In mid-2002, the IRS announced a pilot project for a new form of guidance. **Technical expedited advice memoranda**, which would initially be available only for matters under the jurisdiction of the associate chief counsel (Income Tax & Accounting), would result in a streamlined process

---

[164] Do not confuse these GCMs with revenue rulings issued before 1953, many of which were also called general counsel memoranda. [See Table 9-1.]

[165] IRM 35.19.4.1 (Apr. 8, 1992).

for technical advice. Both the taxpayer and IRS would be involved in the process, as is currently the case for TAMs. If the two sides disagree on the facts, the national office could provide answers based on both sets of facts.[166] That is not currently allowed for TAMs.

10. Service Center Advice (SCA; S.C.A.)

The national office issues **service center advice** with regard to tax administration responsibilities. The Service began using the common numbering system for these documents in 1999. It used a separate numbering system in 1997 and 1998. SCAs do not constitute authority for avoiding the substantial understatement penalty.

11. IRS Legal Memoranda (ILM; I.L.M.)

Legal memoranda provide information about taxpayers to IRS field or service center personnel. These documents may respond to a field office query or they may provide information to the field (e.g., notice that a taxpayer's request to change accounting method has been denied). These documents do not constitute authority for avoiding the substantial understatement penalty. Although these documents use the common numbering system, different services call them by different names. Searching by number yields the same results irrespective of system; searching by title may not.[167]

12. Chief Counsel Bulletins

There are several types of chief counsel bulletins. These documents provide information to IRS employees about litigation in a variety of areas. None of them constitutes authority for avoiding the substantial understatement penalty.

Collection, Bankruptcy and Summonses Bulletins (CBS; C.B.S.) summarize recent court decisions. These documents were called General Litigation Bulletins through June 2000. Although numbered in a separate series, these bulletins also share the common numbering system. For example, Bulletin No. 490 is also CBS 200139029.

---

[166] Rev. Proc. 2002-30, 2002-24 I.R.B. 1184. See Tax Notes, June 3, 2002, at 1419, for a discussion of TEAM and SAM announcements by IRS Chief Counsel B. John Williams.

[167] At the time this book went to press, the IRS website, Westlaw, and LexisNexis called these documents chief counsel advice or chief counsel advisories. OneDisc called them IRS legal memoranda (ILM).

Criminal Tax Bulletins (CTB; C.T.B.) compile cases pertaining to criminal tax matters. They use the common numbering system.

Disclosure Litigation Bulletins (DLB; D.L.B.) discuss litigation and other developments concerning FOIA and related litigation. They do not use the common numbering system. Their numbering is by year (e.g., DLB 2000-3).

Tax Litigation Bulletins (TLB; T.L.B.) summarize recent court decisions and briefs. They also include recommendations for appellate action. These bulletins are numbered by year (e.g., TLB 96-5).

13. Litigation Guideline Memoranda (LGM; L.G.M.)

Litigation guideline memoranda discuss variations on fact patterns and tactical approaches that IRS field personnel might use in litigation. In mid-1999, the Service released memoranda issued between January 1, 1986, and October 20, 1998. LGMs are now released using the timetable set forth in Section 6110. The numbering system initially reflected the IRS division involved (e.g., INTL-1 involved the foreign tax credit). Later items use the common numbering system (e.g., LGM 200018050).

14. Industry Specialization Program (ISP; I.S.P.); Market Segment Specialization Papers (MSSP; M.S.S.P.); Market Segment Understandings (MSU; M.S.U.)

These documents provide guidance to agents auditing returns in various types of businesses (**industry specialization program**); describe how the IRS reviews tax returns for various types of business (**market segment specialization papers**); and discuss employer/independent contractor issues in various industries (**market segment understandings**). They do not constitute authority for avoiding the substantial understatement penalty.

Examples of these documents include an ISP issued in 2000 that discussed the useful life of slot machines in the gaming industry; an MSSP issued in 2001 designed to assist IRS auditors in identifying and developing issues that are unique or frequent to business consultants (e.g., travel, employee/independent contractor, meals and entertainment, and claiming a not-for-profit activity as a business); and an MSU issued in 1998 for the moving industry.

These documents include numerous citations to authority. ISPs include UIL numbers. MSSPs include glossaries of terms a researcher can use to become familiar with a particular industry before meeting with a client.[168]

These documents are identified by type, date, and industry; they do not carry separate numbers.

15. Chief Counsel Notices (CCN; C.C.N.)

The IRS uses **chief counsel notices** to notify personnel of policies, procedures, instructions, and delegations of authority. They do not constitute authority for avoiding the substantial understatement penalty.

Since fiscal 2001, these documents are numbered by year with CC as a prefix. Some include UIL numbers. For example, CC-2002-021 notified staff that the national office had changed its litigating position regarding capitalization of transaction costs related to the acquisition, creation, or enhancement of intangible assets or benefits. This document's cancellation date was set as the date on which the item announced was incorporated into the CCDM.[169] The UIL number this document related to was 263.00-00.

16. IRS Information Letters (IIL; I.I.L.)

The national office and key district directors issue **information letters** to taxpayers to call their attention to well-established principles of tax law. For example, IIL 200003007 was issued to a taxpayer who had requested a second extension of time to sell stock in a subsidiary. The letter discussed the applicable Code section 332 rules. These documents do not constitute authority for avoiding the substantial understatement penalty.

17. IRS Compliance Officer Memoranda (ICM; I.C.M.)

Compliance officer memoranda are issued to regional compliance and appeals personnel. They provide information on issues involving compliance and taxpayers' rights. They do not constitute authority for avoiding the substantial understatement penalty. The IRS does not number them; OneDisc includes six of them (1996 through 1999), numbered by year.

---

[168] For example, a 1997 MSSP for artists and art galleries includes brief explanations of painting styles (e.g., abstract, pop art, realism), painting techniques (e.g., oil, pastel) and print types (e.g., artist proof, lithograph, serigraph).

[169] CC-2002-021 was issued March 15, 2002. It noted that the Service had issued an Advance Notice of Proposed Rulemaking (ANPRM) regarding capitalization on January 24, 2002. The chief counsel notice did not provide a citation to that ANPRM (REG-125638-01). CCDM is the Chief Counsel Directives Manual, part of the IRM.

18. IRS Technical Assistance (ITA; I.T.A.)

The national office provides **technical assistance** to other IRS offices. Technical assistance issued to district and regional offices, chief counsel field offices, and service centers is disclosable. These documents are not authority for avoiding the substantial understatement penalty.

These documents use the common numbering system (e.g., 200211042 dealt with whether the recipient of a transferable state remediation tax credit had gross income). Although Tax Analysts indexes these documents as ITAs, LexisNexis, Westlaw, and the IRS website classify them as chief counsel advice or advisory.

19. Internal Revenue Manual (IRM; I.R.M.)

Your research may involve IRS operating policies. For example, you may want to determine IRS procedures for appeals or for dealing with rewards to informants. The **Internal Revenue Manual** is an excellent source of information about Service policies. It does not constitute authority for avoiding the substantial understatement penalty.

The Manual has numerous subdivisions; its numbering system is based on topics. For example, IRM 120.1.5 covers return related penalties; IRM 120.1.5.8 covers the substantial understatement penalty.[170] IRM Parts 30 through 42 constitutes the Chief Counsel Directives Manual. It is easier to search the IRM online using a commercial service than using the IRS website, which includes only those parts of the IRM that have been revised.

20. Other Documents

Technical Memoranda (TM; T.M.; Tech. Mem.) provided background information on regulations. Much of their content is reflected in the preambles to T.D.s and NPRMs. Westlaw carries so-called Non Docketed Service Advice Reviews (NSAR; coverage from 1992 through 1999); these are memoranda to field personnel who raised questions regarding particular transactions (e.g., 1999 IRS NSAR 5242 concerned whether to let a taxpayer amend a return to reflect a subsequent year's purchase price reduction). Don't be surprised if electronic research yields a handful of documents in a category you have not yet encountered. They may reflect no more than early responses to disclosure litigation. None of these documents constitutes authority for avoiding the substantial understatement penalty.

---

[170] IRM 20.1.5.8.4.1 (Aug. 20, 1998) covers items that constitute substantial authority. This IRM section does not add significantly to the information contained in Treas. Reg. § 1.6662-4(d)(3), but its arrangement makes it easier to read.

Illustration 9-2. AOD 1984-022

ACTION ON DECISION CC-1984-022

CC:TL
Br2:DCFegan

Re: Harold L. and Temple M. Jenkins v.
Commissioner
Venue: C.A. 6th
Dkt. No.: 3354-79
Dec. November 3, 1983
Opinion: T.C. Memo 1983-667

Issue: Whether Conway Twitty is allowed
a business expense deduction for payments to
reimburse the losses of investors in a defunct
restaurant known as Twitty Burger, Inc.
0162.01-17; 0162.29-00.

Discussion: The Tax Court summarized its
opinion in this case with the following "Ode to
Conway Twitty":

"Twitty Burger went belly up
But Conway remained true
He repaid his investors, one and all
It was the moral thing to do.

"His fans would not have liked it
It could have hurt his fame
Had any investors sued him
Like Merle Haggard or Sonny James.

"When it was time to file taxes
Conway thought what he would do
Was deduct those payments as a
business expense
Under section one-sixty-two.

"In order to allow these deductions
Goes the argument of the Commissioner
The payments must be ordinary and necessary
To a business of the petitioner.

"Had Conway not repaid the investors
His career would have been under cloud
Under the unique facts of this case
Held: The deductions are allowed."

Our reaction to the Court's opinion is
reflected in the following "Ode to
Conway Twitty: A Reprise":

Harold Jenkins and Conway Twitty
They are both the same
But one was born
The other achieved fame.

The man is talented
And has many a friend
They opened a restaurant
His name he did lend.

They are two different things
Making burgers and song
The business went sour
It didn't take long.

He repaid his friends
Why did he act
Was it business or friendship
Which is fact?

Business the court held
It's deductible they feel
We disagree with the answer
But let's not appeal.

Recommendation:
Nonacquiescence.

Reviewers:

DAVID C. FEGAN
Attorney

JOEL GERBER
Acting Chief Counsel

By: CLIFFORD M. HARBOURT
Senior Technician Reviewer
Branch No. 2
Tax Litigation Division

SECTION E. UNRELEASED DOCUMENTS

1. Advance Pricing Agreements (APA)

Advance pricing agreements are made between taxpayers and the IRS regarding income allocation between commonly-controlled entities. Companies that segment their operations between countries with different tax rates and structures can enter into APAs with both the United States and the other country if the two countries have a tax treaty.

In 2000, the IRS began issuing an annual report concerning APAs.[171] Code section 6110(b)(1)(B) exempts APAs from release to the public.

2. Closing Agreements

Closing agreements memorialize the parties' agreement regarding specific taxpayer-IRS disputes. As a condition of the agreement, the IRS has occasionally forced publication of certain closing agreements with exempt organizations but otherwise resisted releasing these documents. Code section 6110(b)(1)(B) exempts closing agreements from release to the public.

3. Technical Assistance

As this text went to press, Tax Analysts was seeking disclosure of technical assistance memoranda issued to national office program managers, to component offices within the chief counsel office, to specific taxpayers, and to state government agencies.[172]

SECTION F. LOCATING IRS DOCUMENTS

1. Officially Published Documents in Internal Revenue Bulletin

a. Finding Lists

You can find citations to these documents using print or electronic sources. Print sources include Code-based looseleaf services, such as Stan-

---

[171] See, e.g., Ann. 2002-40, 2002-15 I.R.B. 747, for the report covering 2001. You can also find these reports on the IRS website.

[172] Disclosable technical assistance memoranda are covered in Subsection D.18. Briefs in Tax Analysts v. Internal Revenue Service can be located on LexisNexis at 2002 TNT 13-41 (Tax Analysts), 2002 TNT 48-42 (government), and 2002 TNT 86-75 (government). See 2002 TNT 116-8 for the Circuit Court's June 2002 opinion.

dard Federal Tax Reporter and United States Tax Reporter. You can also use topic-based looseleaf services such as Federal Tax Coordinator 2d and Rabkin & Johnson, Federal Income, Gift and Estate Taxation. Both types of looseleaf service are discussed in detail in Chapter 12. Another print source is the Service's own Bulletin Index-Digest System (Chapter 16), although it is useful only for 1954-1993/94 material.

Because revenue rulings and procedures, notices, and announcements carry numbers that don't correspond to Code or regulations sections, CD-ROM (Chapter 18) and online (Chapter 19) services are excellent tools for locating them. You can search many electronic databases by topic, Code or regulations section, or prior ruling. Use case citators to find acquiescences.

b. Digests

Unlike finding lists, digests provide descriptions that help you decide if a particular item is likely to be useful. Keep in mind that a digest's usefulness is a function of its compiler's expertise and its frequency of supplementation.

You can locate digests in a looseleaf service such as United States Tax Reporter (Chapter 12), in newsletters such as Tax Notes (Chapter 15), and in the Service's Bulletin Index-Digest System (Chapter 16; 1954-1993/94 material only).

c. Texts

Numerous services contain texts of Internal Revenue Bulletin items. Most of those listed below are available in both print and electronic formats.

Looseleaf services such as Standard Federal Tax Reporter and United States Tax Reporter include the text of current year rulings in their print services; electronic services may include older rulings or provide links to them on other databases. The Rulings volumes of Mertens, Law of Federal Income Taxation include full text of revenue rulings and procedures since 1954 but do not carry other Internal Revenue Bulletin documents. Looseleaf services are discussed further in Chapter 12.

Print versions of daily newsletters such as Highlights and Documents or Daily Tax Report carry Internal Revenue Bulletin items as they are released; electronic versions include prior releases. They are discussed in detail in Chapter 15.

The print versions of the Internal Revenue Bulletin and Cumulative Bulletin (Chapter 16) include text of all items issued for a particular week (or six-month period); various online services include these documents but do not have full retrospective coverage. If you have a citation to a pre-1954 Code item, a print or microform Cumulative Bulletin may be the only place you can locate it.

d. A Note on Searching in Electronic and Print Sources

In using electronic sources, you must differentiate between those that allow searching by topic and those that include the relevant information but do not provide a means to find it using word or Code section searches. This distinction is particularly important for online services. If you can't find the item without knowing its citation, the source is less valuable than one that allows access based on Code sections or other search terms.

Illustrations 9-3 through 9-8 involve a quest for a revenue ruling discussing whether expenses associated with quitting smoking qualify as medical expenses. We begin with the IRS website and move to one other online, one print, and one CD-ROM service.

The IRS website includes a page that gives access to the Internal Revenue Bulletins. That page does not provide a mechanism to search for individual items if you don't know which Bulletin you want. Alternatively, you might try using the Advanced Search function, on another page of the IRS site, and search for the terms medical and smoking. That search also produces no Internal Revenue Bulletin items. Illustrations 9-3 and 9-4 illustrate our unsuccessful search. We must try other services.

Illustration 9-3. Internal Revenue Bulletin List on IRS Website

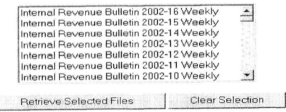

Internal Revenue Bulletins

The Internal Revenue Bulletin (IRB) is the authoritative instrument of the IRS for announcing all substantive ruling necessary to promote a uniform application of tax law.

IRBs are offered here in Adobe PDF format. The Adobe Acrobat reader is available for free and is required to view and print PDF files.

Please Select the file(s) you wish to download.

    Internal Revenue Bulletin 2002-16 Weekly
    Internal Revenue Bulletin 2002-15 Weekly
    Internal Revenue Bulletin 2002-14 Weekly
    Internal Revenue Bulletin 2002-13 Weekly
    Internal Revenue Bulletin 2002-12 Weekly
    Internal Revenue Bulletin 2002-11 Weekly
    Internal Revenue Bulletin 2002-10 Weekly

    Retrieve Selected Files   Clear Selection

➔There is no tool for finding an individual ruling without a citation.

Illustration 9-4. Advanced Search Option on IRS Website

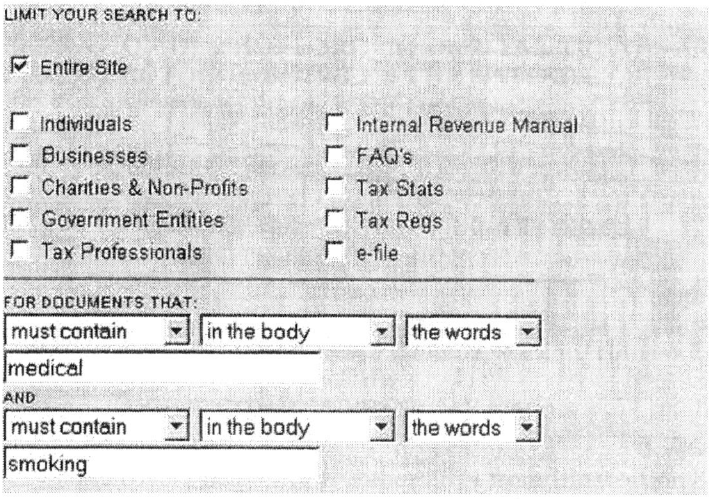

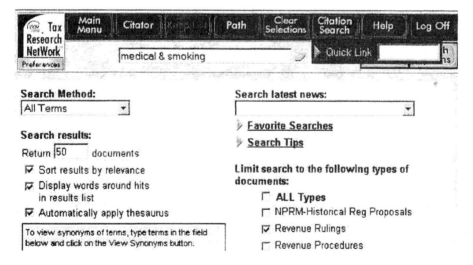

→This search yielded no Internal Revenue Bulletin items.

→The Advanced Search option also allows you to specify dates.

Illustration 9-5. Search on Tax Research NetWork

→Tax Research NetWork allows you to search the entire Bulletin or specific items, in this case revenue rulings. It can search for synonyms.

Illustration 9-6. Search Results on Tax Research NetWork

Terms searched for: cigaret, cigarette, cigarette smoking, medical, smoking, tobacco .

Documents are displayed in ranked order, best matches first. 4 documents matched your query.

1. ● REV-RUL. 99FED ¶46,455. **Medical expenses: Deductibility: Stop-smoking programs.--** Revenue Ruling 99-28, I.R.B. 1999-25, 6, (June 10, 1999)
   99-28, I.R.B. 1999-25, 6, June 10, 1999.
   [Code Sec. 213]
   Medical expenses: Deductibility: **Stop-smoking** programs.--The IRS has announced that the costs of

2. ● REV-RUL. **Rev. Rul. 65-71. 1965-1 CB 601**
   SECTION 5704--EXEMPTION FROM TAX
   26 CFR 270.232: Experimental purposes.
   Where **tobacco** products are to be removed for testing by a selected panel, primarily

3. ● REV-RUL. **Rev. Rul. 66-124. 1966-1 CB 338**
   26 CFR 270.232: Experimental purposes.
   Where cigars and **cigarettes** are to be removed for testing by a selected panel, primarily by

4. ● REV-RUL. **Medical expenses: program to stop smoking., Rev. Rul. 79-162,** 1979-1 CB 116. (Jan. 01, 1979)
   Rev. Rul. 79-162, 1979-1 CB 116
   Section 213.--**Medical,** Dental, Etc., Expenses
   26 CFR 1.213-1: **Medical,** dental, etc., expenses.
   (Also Section 262; 1.262-1.)

➡️Each item found included both terms. Items 1 and 4 are relevant. Note the synonyms in the search terms.

You can locate Internal Revenue Bulletin material using tables in print sources, but you will be limited to one search term. [See Illustration 9-7.] You are more likely to find the desired information using a looseleaf service with extensive annotations and footnotes. [See Illustration 9-8.]

Illustration 9-7. Excerpt from Mertens Code-Rulings Table

1954-2000 CODE-RULINGS TABLE			
Code Sec.	**Rev. Rul.**	**Code Sec.**	**Rev. Rul.**
213(d)(1) . . . 87-106, 97-9, 99-28, 2000-24		216(a) . . 58-421, 59-257, 62-178, 70-92, 73-15, 87-130, 90-36, 92-60	

➡️Mertens lists three rulings not listed in Tax Research NetWork. They aren't relevant because they don't involve smoking. The Mertens search was based on Code section 213(d)(1), which defines medical care.

➡️Mertens failed to list Rev. Rul. 79-162, which Tax Research NetWork located, because it was revoked by Rev. Rul. 99-28.

Illustration 9-8. Excerpt from Federal Tax Coordinator 2d

¶ K-2117   Programs to stop smoking.

The costs of a smoking-cessation program are deductible as amounts paid for medical care. This is the case even though the taxpayer hasn't been diagnosed as having any specific disease, and participation in the program isn't suggested by a physician. 37 For the deductibility of drugs or medications designed to alleviate nicotine withdrawal, see ¶ K-2137.

> 37   Rev Rul 99-28, 1999-1 CB 1269.

✍ **RIA client letter:** A sample client letter on deducting the cost of a smoking-cessation program as a medical expense appears in Client Letters at ¶ 1377.

Before June 10, '99, 37.1 IRS had ruled that the cost of a program to quit smoking wasn't deductible, 37.2 but IRS revoked that ruling. 37.3 Since the revocation applies retroactively (see ¶ T-9975), taxpayers who (i) paid for smoking-cessation programs in recent years, (ii) didn't include such costs in computing their medical expenses, and (iii) otherwise had sufficient medical expenses to claim a deduction, should consider filing amended returns to include the smoking-cessation program costs in their deductible expenses. Other taxpayers should check their earlier returns to determine whether adding these expenses would give them enough medical expenses to claim a medical expense deduction. 38

> 37.1 IR 1999-55, 6/10/1999.
> 37.2 Rev Rul 79-162, 1979-1 CB 116 before revoked by Rev Rul 99-28, 1999-1 CB 1269.
> 37.3 Rev Rul 99-28, 1999-1 CB 1269.
> 38   IR 1999-55, 6/10/1999.

➔Federal Tax Coordinator, a topic-based looseleaf, discusses the issue you are researching. The footnote references cover the relevant revenue rulings.

➔This excerpt comes from the OnPoint CD-ROM. Federal Tax Coordinator 2d is also available in print and online. The CD-ROM and online versions include hyperlinks to discussion and primary source materials. Illustration 18-5 shows a portion of the service's table of contents.

2. Other Officially Published Documents

You can easily find IRS forms, instructions, and explanatory publications using the IRS website. Unlike Internal Revenue Bulletin items, these items can be found by using word searches. The site includes these documents in full text. Other CD-ROM (Chapter 18) and online (Chapter 19) services also make these documents available.

RIA publishes IRS forms in RIA's Complete Federal Tax Forms service. CCH includes forms in CCH Federal Tax Forms; it includes approximately 150 explanatory publications in CCH IRS Tax Publications. Tax Management Portfolios (Chapter 12) often reproduce forms.

3. Publicly Released Documents

Because the IRS issues so many of these documents, your library is more likely to provide access to them electronically than through a print service. Some libraries may carry CCH IRS Letter Rulings Reporter, a full-text service that allows you to search for letter rulings, technical advice memoranda, and other publicly released documents by Code section and topics. This service is also available electronically.

CCH and other publishers also offer print versions of the Internal Revenue Manual. Because of the Manual's detailed structure, it is easier to find materials using electronic versions.

Texts of publicly released documents are included in numerous CD-ROM and online research sources. These include OneDisc, LexisNexis, Westlaw, Tax Research NetWork, and TaxBase. You can search these services by Code section or by phrases describing the issue you are researching.

With one exception, electronic services operate the same way for publicly released documents as they do for documents published in the Internal Revenue Bulletin. That exception relates to the numbering system. As noted in Section D, services may assign their own names to documents issued by the chief counsel's office. If you are not sure which name a particular service uses for chief counsel items, search across all possible databases rather than limiting yourself. Fortunately, all publishers use the same names for the most common items: letter rulings, technical advice memoranda, actions on decisions, field service advice, and service center advice.

Although the IRS website provides free access to publicly released documents, its current site arrangement does not make finding them as easy as it could. To find publicly available documents, you may have to start with Freedom of Information Act, Chief Counsel Documents Online, or Internal Revenue Manual pages. Because there is no single page on the site that specifically lists all available documents, try using the Advanced Search function or the Site Map to search for these documents by type.

The IRS website divides documents into the following categories for searching by document number: actions on decisions; service center advice; chief counsel notices; chief counsel bulletins; and written determinations. The written determinations category includes private letter rulings, technical advice memoranda, field service advice, and other information that must be disclosed.

Illustration 9-9. IRS Website AOD Finding List

Actions on Decisions (AOD)

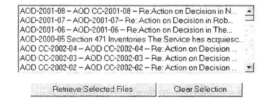

➜The files can be retrieved as PDF documents.

SECTION G. UNIFORM ISSUE LIST (UIL)

The **Uniform Issue List** is a Code-section-based index of issues. The IRS assigns UIL numbers to documents released to the public pursuant to Code section 6110, which is discussed in Section D. This list is prepared by chief counsel office personnel.[173] AOD 1984-022 [Illustration 9-2] includes two UIL numbers, both involving Code section 162. The IRS publishes the list in Publication 1102; this publication is not revised annually. Shepard's Federal Tax Citator includes a section that provides citations to the UIL.

The IRS varies in the terminology used for UIL numbers. The terms UIL, UILC, or Index may precede the actual UIL number in a document.

The IRS website lets you sort documents classified as written determinations based on document number or UIL number. As of June 2002, numbers are initially sorted by their digits rather than by their actual Code section number. As a result, documents based on Code section 1041 and 1042 follow those based on section 104; documents based on section 105 begin after those based on section 1042.

SECTION H. CITATORS FOR IRS DOCUMENTS

The IRS reviews its pronouncements for continued relevance. In addition, some revenue rulings have been subjected to judicial scrutiny. The status of these items can be determined from CD-ROM (Chapter 18) and online (Chapter 19) services and from the following citator and citator-like services.

- Shepard's Federal Tax Citator (Chapter 11)

- RIA Citator (Chapter 11)

- CCH Standard Federal Tax Reporter—Citator (Chapter 11)

- Mertens, Law of Federal Income Taxation—Rulings (Chapter 12) (since 1954)

- IRS Bulletin Index-Digest System (Chapter 16) (1954-1993/94 only)

The Mertens and IRS services have several limitations. First, they include only IRS action. Second, they cover only revenue rulings and procedures. Third, they are likely to remove an item from their database if the Service

---

[173] See IRM 30.7.3.1 (Jan. 14, 1994).

revokes it. Because the IRS service is no longer published, it should be considered an updating service of last resort.[174]

The print citators are more useful. They include judicial action and may even cover documents such as private letter rulings.

You are likely to get better results using an electronic service, which allows you to use the cited item as your search term. Within categories of electronic resources, online services are more likely than are CD-ROMs to have the most recent updates. Subscription-based sites are far more likely to provide updating information than are other sites.

Illustrations 9-10 through 9-13 use electronic versions of citators from CCH, RIA, Shepard's, and Westlaw to illustrate differences in citator results for the same revenue ruling. If your library has print versions of the CCH, RIA, or Shepard's tax citators, try doing this search using those versions. West's KeyCite, shown in Illustration 9-13, does not have a print version.

Illustration 9-10. CCH Citator Results for Rev. Rul. 79-98

CCH-CITATOR, 2002FED, Main Finding Lists, Rev. Rul. 79-98

Rev. Rul. 79-98 , 1979-1 CB 103

ANNOTATED AT ... 2002FED ¶11,029.50

1979 CCH ¶6488

Cited in:

Sealy Power, Ltd., CA-5, 95-1 USTC ¶50,103, 46 F3d 382

SMC Corp., DC, 80-2 USTC ¶9642

Clarified by:

Rev. Rul. 84-85

→The CCH Citator indicates that the ruling was cited in two cases and clarified by a later ruling.

→ The Tax Research NetWork version provides hyperlinks to citing material.

---

[174] The Internal Revenue Bulletins contain Current Actions on Previously Published Items information but do not cumulate that information over multiple years.

Illustration 9-11. RIA Citator Results for Rev. Rul. 79-98

SUBSEQUENT APPELLATE HISTORY (1 citing reference) • Hide Subsequent Appellate History

Clarified by:
Rev Rul 84-85, 1984-1 C.B. 10, Rev. Rul. No. 84-85 (I.R.S. 1984)

CITING DECISIONS (3 citing decisions)

5TH CIRCUIT - COURT OF APPEALS

Cited by:
Sealy Power v. Commissioner, 46 F.3d 382, 1995 U.S. App. LEXIS 2901, 75 A.F.T.R.2d (RIA) 1213, 95 TNT 44-73, 95-1 U.S. Tax Cas. (CCH) P50103 (5th Cir. 1995)

Cited by:
75 A.F.T.R.2d (RIA) 1213 p.1226

U.S. TAX COURT

Cited by:
Oglethorpe Power Corp. v. Commissioner, T.C. Memo 1990-505, 1990 Tax Ct. Memo LEXIS 558, 60 T.C.M. (CCH) 850, T.C.M. (RIA) P90505 (T.C. 1990)

➔The RIA citator indicates that the ruling was cited favorably in three cases, that its reasoning was followed in one case, and that it was clarified by a later ruling.

➔The Westlaw version did not provide hyperlinks to the citing material.

Illustration 9-12. Shepard's Results for Rev. Rul. 79-98

Rev Rul 79-98
1979-1 CB 103

Clarified
Rev Rul 84-85, 1984-2 CB 10

Cited favorably
Sealy Power, Ltd. v. Com.., 75 AFTR 2d 95-1213, 95-1226--95-1227, 46 F3d 382, 395, 396 (CA5)

Cited favorably
Oglethorpe Power Corp., 1990 PH TC Memo 90,505, 90-2471, 90-2473

Cited favorably (1)
SMC Corp. v U.S., 46 AFTR 2d 80-5827, 80-5829 (DC TN)

Reasoning followed (1)
Mitchell, James E., In re, 64 AFTR 2d 89-5535, 89-5538 (Bktcy Ct WA)

➔Shepard's on LexisNexis located two citing cases and the clarifying later ruling.

➔Shepard's provides hyperlinks to these items.

Illustration 9-13. KeyCite Results for Rev. Rul. 79-98

Citing References
(Showing 32 documents)

Positive Cases
★ ★ ★ Discussed

▷ 1 Sealy Power, Ltd. v. C.I.R., 46 F.3d 382, 395+, 75 A.F.T.R.2d 95-1213, 95-1213+, 95-1 USTC P 50,103, 50103+ (5th Cir. Feb 15, 1995) (NO. 93-4260)

★ ★ Cited

▶ 2 Oglethorpe Power Corp. v. C.I.R., 1990 WL 136701, *136701+, T.C. Memo. 1990-505, 1990-505+, 60 T.C.M. (CCH) 850, 850+, T.C.M. (P-H) P 90,505, 90505+ (U.S.Tax Ct. Sep 24, 1990) (NO. 37767-86, 2873-88, 3690-88)

Administrative Materials

3 Field Service Advisory, 1996 WL 33107156, *6 (IRS FSA Jul 16, 1996) ★ ★

C 4 TAM 9414004, 1993 WL 622701, (IRS TAM Apr 08, 1994) (NO. 9414004) ★ ★ ★

➔KC Citing Ref found 32 documents. Although it listed only two citing cases, it found numerous other documents, including field service advice and technical advice memoranda as well as secondary sources.

➔KC History listed only the clarifying revenue ruling. That ruling was not listed in KC Citing Ref. Chapter 19 discusses KC History and KC Citing Ref.

➔KeyCite provided hyperlinks to the citing material.

SECTION I. JUDICIAL DEFERENCE

The items discussed in this chapter receive less government and public review than do Treasury regulations. As indicated by the excerpts below, judges vary in the amount of deference paid these pronouncements. Although items released as a result of FOIA litigation are not precedential, many courts take note of their holdings.

Decisions giving deference to rulings and other IRS documents must be judged in light of the Supreme Court's *Mead* decision, which involved a Customs Service ruling letter. The Court held: "We agree that a tariff classification has no claim to judicial deference under *Chevron,* there being no indication that Congress intended such a ruling to carry the force of law, but we hold that under *Skidmore v. Swift & Co.,* 323 U.S. 134 (1944), the ruling is eligible to claim respect according to its persuasiveness."[175]

1. Officially Published Documents

• Revenue rulings are not binding precedent, but are entitled to some weight, as reflecting an interpretation of the law by the agency entrusted with its interpretation. Such rulings, however, do not require this court to apply a mistaken view of the law to a particular taxpayer. In particular,

---

[175] United States v. Mead Corp., 533 U.S. 218, 221 (2001). See Chapter 8 for a brief discussion of *Chevron.*

Supreme Court precedent makes clear that if a revenue ruling is found to be unreasonable or contrary to law, it is binding neither on the Commissioner nor this court, based on the rationale that the Congress, and only the Congress, has the power to make law. Vons Companies, Inc. v. United States, 51 Fed. Cl. 1, 12 (2001).[176]

• We note that, in any event, revenue rulings are not entitled to any special deference. Bhatia v. Commissioner, 72 T.C.M. (CCH) 696, 699 n.5 (1996).

• Revenue rulings represent the official IRS position on application of tax law to specific facts. ... They relate to matters as to which the IRS is the "primary authority." ... Revenue rulings are accordingly entitled to precedential "weight." Salomon Inc. v. United States, 976 F.2d 837, 841 (2d Cir. 1992).

2. Other IRS Documents

• Nor are we persuaded by the preamble or technical advice memorandum upon which petitioners rely. In addition to the obvious fact that these documents also are not items of legislative history, these documents are afforded little weight in this Court. Allen v. Commissioner, 118 T.C. No. 1, n.12 (2002), 2002 WL 14007.

• The interpretation of Rev. Proc. 71-21 contained in the General Counsel Memorandum and the IRS decision under the Revenue Procedure is not reflected in a regulation adopted after notice and comment and probably would not be entitled to *Chevron* deference. *See Mead*, ... Here, however, as noted above, we are not dealing with an agency's interpretation of a statute and issues of *Chevron* deference, but with the IRS's interpretation of an ambiguous term in its own Revenue Procedure. In such circumstances, substantial deference is paid to an agency's interpretations reflected in informal rulings.... In the context of tax cases, the IRS's reasonable interpretations of its own regulations and procedures are entitled to particular deference. American Express Co. v. United States, 262 F.3d 1376, 1382-83 (Fed. Cir. 2001).

---

[176] The court later revised the first two sentences to read as follows: "Taxpayers generally may rely on a revenue ruling to support their interpretation of a provision of the Code, provided the ruling is unaffected by subsequent legislation, regulations, cases or other revenue rulings. Such rulings do not require this court to apply a mistaken view of the law to a particular taxpayer." (89 A.F.T.R.2d 2002-301 (2001)). The court also stated its view regarding letter rulings, technical advice memoranda, and general counsel memoranda.

• Such private letter rulings "may not be used or cited as precedent," § 6110(j)(3), and we do not do so. It does not follow that they are not relevant here. Transco Exploration Co. v. Commissioner, 949 F.2d 837, 840 (5th Cir. 1992).

• Although this ruling cannot be cited as precedent under 26 U.S.C. § 6110(J)(3) [sic], it highlights the confusion this section has engendered at the IRS. More importantly, the fact that the IRS has done an about face since 1986 makes us even more reluctant to adopt their interpretation of this statute without an understandable articulation of a tax policy supporting it. Estate of Spencer v. Commissioner, 43 F.3d 226, 234 (6th Cir. 1995).

• In *Herrmann*, the court would not rely on the GCM to interpret the plan involved because the GCM was fact specific to the plan for which it was written. The court, however, did rely on its interpretation of the Code section involved because it assumed the IRS would insist upon a uniform interpretation of the section. Here, where there is no case law in point, it is arguably permissible to use GCMs to *instruct* the court on how the IRS itself interprets § 501(c)(5), since they constitute the only real guidance as to what the IRS considers a labor organization for the purposes of a § 501(c)(5) exemption. Morganbesser v. United States, 984 F.2d 560, 563 (2d Cir. 1993).

• While recognizing that the IRM does not represent law and is in no way binding upon this court, the court believes that the manual reflects the more reasonable interpretation of the Revenue Code's mandate in this instance. Thus, the manual's agreement with the court's own independent reading of the statute bolsters the court's conclusion. Anderson v. United States, 71 A.F.T.R.2d 93-1589, 93-1591, 93-1 U.S.T.C. ¶ 50,249, at 87,958 (N.D. Cal. 1993), rev'd, 44 F.3d 795, 799 (9th Cir. 1995) ("But the IRS correctly concedes that its internal agents' manual does not have the force of law, *see Schweiker v. Hansen,* ..., and makes no *Chevron* argument for deference to this language from its manual, not promulgated as a regulation.")

3. IRS Litigating Positions

• We now hold that the IRS' position in the *amicus* brief was an informal agency policy pronouncement not entitled to *Chevron* deference. Matz v. Household International Tax Reduction Investment Plan, 265 F.3d 572, 574 (7th Cir. 2001).

SECTION J. PROBLEMS

1. Who drafted

   a. Rev. Rul. 88-12   d. Rev. Proc. 99-30   g. Ann. 95-8

   b. Rev. Rul. 90-32   e. Notice 88-3   h. Ann. 2002-8

   c. Rev. Proc. 90-40   f. Notice 96-12

2. Which 1939 Code sections are discussed in

   a. I.T. 3441   c. Mim. 5968

   b. M.T. 35   d. Rev. Rul. 49

3. What is the most recent revenue ruling involving Code section

   a. 104   c. 543   e. 1244

   b. 264   d. 1035   f. 2056

4. What is the most recent revenue ruling referring to Treasury regulation section

   a. 1.102-1   c. 1.471-3   e. 1.704-1

   b. 1.368-1   d. 1.513-1   f. 20.2053-1

5. What is the most recent revenue ruling or procedure mentioning T.D.

   a. 8954   c. 7397   e. 6153

   b. 7717   d. 7160   f. 6091

6. What is the status of the item listed? What later pronouncement effectuated the status change?

   a. Rev. Rul. 55-290   d. Rev. Proc. 92-98   g. Notice 2001-10

   b. Rev. Rul. 60-345   e. Rev. Proc. 83-78   h. Notice 97-26

   c. Rev. Rul. 75-17   f. Rev. Proc. 77-37   i. Notice 88-129

7. What is the most recent judicial decision that discusses deference and revenue rulings? What did the court hold?

8. List all current year revenue procedures indicating matters on which the IRS will not grant a ruling.

9. Find a current year notice announcing a regulations project.

10. What did the most recently issued IRS announcement involve?

11. What is the most recent revenue procedure providing the procedures for

    a. applying Article 10(2)(a) of the U.S.-United Kingdom income tax treaty

    b. requesting a Statement of Value to substantiate the value of art for tax purposes

    c. filing Form 1042-S electronically

    d. establishing a Treasury Direct Account with the IRS

12. Which IRS publication is titled

    a. Community Property   c. Older Americans' Tax Guide

    b. Selling Your Home   d. Tax Benefits for Adoption

13. Who drafted or approved

    a. PLR 200140017   d. TAM 199932049   g. AOD 1999-009

    b. PLR 199901029   e. FSA 199949031   h. AOD 2002-001

    c. TAM 200004001   f. FSA 200212027   i. SCA 199950009

14. Which Code sections are discussed in

    a. PLR 200217059   c. FSA 200125019

    b. TAM 200121006   d. GCM 39888

15. What is the most recent PLR or TAM involving Code section

    a. 83   b. 164   c. 856

16. What is the most recent PLR or TAM citing Treasury regulation section

    a. 1.213-1   b. 1.611-1   c. 26.2601-1

17. What is the status of the item listed? What later pronouncement effectuated the status change?

    a. PLR 8529027   c. TAM 8737002   e. AOD 1996-003

    b. PLR 9610034   d. GCM 39732   f. FSA 200033002

18. What is the most recent judicial decision that discusses deference and technical advice memoranda? What did the court hold?

19. Locate the document asked for below and indicate the Code section(s) involved:

    a. a 1999 PLR citing to Rev. Rul. 54-395

    b. a 2001 TAM citing to Rev. Rul. 75-462

    c. a 1999 TAM citing to Rev. Rul. 54-97

    d. a 1999 FSA citing to Rev. Proc. 91-51

    e. a 2002 FSA citing to Rev. Rul. 89-96

    f. a 1999 SCA citing to Rev. Rul. 74-611

20. Which GCM was issued to explain the ruling listed?

    a. PLR 8640071   c. Rev. Rul. 89-96

    b. PLR 9236042   d. Rev. Rul. 90-38

21. Which subsequent GCM changed the status of the GCM listed below, and what issue was involved?

    a. 38166   c. 35481   e. 34000

    b. 36413   d. 34073   f. 33851

22. Which IRM part deals with the Taxpayer Advocate Service?

23. Locate a PLR involving the following facts and indicate its holding.

   a. whether physical touching that left no observable bodily harm was a personal physical injury

   b. a state university that plans to offer a tuition reduction plan that covers its employees' spouses and domestic partners

   c. a VEBA that provides health coverage to employees' domestic partners

   d. whether racing fuel with an octane rating of 110 is subject to the gasoline excise tax

24. Locate a TAM involving the following facts and indicate its holding:

   a. whether a passenger van used to transport special education students qualified as an "automobile bus"

   b. whether a radio station license was of "like kind" to a television station license

   c. the appropriate generation assignment for the children of the transferor's step-brother

   d. the appropriate interest rate on an employment tax refund paid to a state-chartered educational institution that filed a Form 990-T

25. Locate an AOD involving the following decision and indicate its holding:

   a. McLeod v. United States (1967 District Court)

   b. Hahn v. Commissioner (1998 Tax Court)

   c. May Department Stores Co. v. United States (1996 Court of Federal Claims)

   d. Sealy Power Ltd. v. Commissioner (1995 Fifth Circuit)

   e. Goree v. Commissioner (1994 T.C. Memo.)

26. Locate an FSA involving the following facts and indicate its holding:

   a. a donation of the corporate records of a company that can trace its history to before the Civil War

b. marketing and advertising costs a firm incurred before its product received regulatory approval from the U.S. government

c. contributions made by a professional sports team in settlement of a league-wide antitrust suit

d. the appropriate classification of the Everglades Agricultural Privilege Tax

27. Locate an SCA involving the following facts and indicate its holding:

a. whether the Code prevents a State from requiring an employer identification number when abandoned property is claimed

b. a refund of a decedent's tax overpayment to his girlfriend

c. obtaining a Utah driver's license using a TIN instead of a social security number

d. when the statute of limitations begins running on a Form 1040 initially filed without a Schedule A and refiled four years later with a Schedule A

28. Provide a citation indicating IRS acquiesce or nonacquiesce in

a. Jordan Marsh Co. v. Commissioner, 3 B.T.A. 553 (1926)

b. Finley Peter Dunne v. Commissioner, 29 B.T.A. 1109 (1934)

c. Al Jolson v. Commissioner, 3 T.C. 1184 (1944)

d. Pelham G. Wodehouse v. Commissioner, 19 T.C. 487 (1952)

e. Fred MacMurray v. Commissioner, 21 T.C. 15 (1953)

29. Locate a judicial decision that

a. discusses bootstrapping and revenue ruling 76-125

b. indicates that revenue ruling 91-21 may be self-serving

30. Print the first page of the closing agreement entered into between the IRS and the Bishop Estate

31. What did the *Vons* case in Subsection I.1 say about general counsel memoranda?

32. For the case listed below, find as many of the following items as you can: (1) a publicly released IRS document, issued before the decision, with facts that resemble those of the case; (2) any subsequent IRS notice of acquiescence or nonacquiescence; (3) any AOD issued with respect to the decision; and (4) any appellate court decisions.

a. Lassiter v. Commissioner, 83 T.C.M. (CCH) 1139 (2002)

b. Sutherland Lumber-Southwest, Inc. v. Commissioner, 255 F.3d 495 (8th Cir. 2001)

c. North Dakota State University v. United States, 255 F.3d 599 (8th Cir. 2001)

33. Your law firm's managing partner wants to prepare a handbook covering potential tax issues. Print out the first page of the guidance described below.

a. a 2002 chief counsel advice discussing whether "of counsel" attorneys are employees for employment tax purposes

b. a 2001 field service advice discussing the tax consequences to an employee posted overseas of employer-paid tax return preparation assistance

c. a 1997 technical advice memorandum discussing the employment tax consequences of referral fees paid to attorneys who had retired from the firm

d. a 1996 technical advice memorandum discussing whether a law clerk, who was also a law student, was an employee or independent contractor

e. a 1994 technical advice memorandum discussing whether a law firm could take a current deduction for outlays that would later be billed to clients

f. a 1993 letter ruling discussing whether an attorney could deduct payments in settlement of a malpractice claim brought by former clients

34. You have been assigned several clients for whom you expect to do tax controversy work. Locate and print out the first page of the following documents.

a. MSSP Audit Guide for grain farmers

b. MSSP Audit Guide for child care providers

c. MSSP Audit Guide for barber shops

d. a chief counsel document discussing whether the receipt of 50 money orders, for $500 each, triggered the Code section 6050I reporting requirement

e. a field service advice indicating whether acceptance of a taxpayer's Offer in Compromise results in discharge of indebtedness income

35. Print out the most recent quarterly list of expatriates from the Federal Register (see Code section 6039G).

36. Print the first page of a

a. technical advice memorandum indicating whether a cheese-curing facility is a manufacturing facility for purposes of Code section 144

b. revenue ruling indicating whether an S corporation can accrue contributions under Code section 170(a)(2)

c. notice discussing the Code section 4261 excise tax and future regulations

d. 1999 litigation guideline memorandum discussing using writs of ne exeat republica

e. technical assistance memorandum discussing the appropriate depreciation classification for a hotel's magnetic stripe keycard system

37. Find the following documents, for which you have only a number. Indicate the type of document and the issue involved. These are not I.R.B. items.

a. 200220026	d. 200145040	g. 199949003
b. 2002-021	e. 200028035	h. 199938031
c. 200142007	f. 199951006	i. 9815008

38. What information appears in T. 114, 1944 C.B. 710?

39. In 2002, the IRS announced it would begin issuing TEAMs. What does the first TEAM issued this year involve?

PART FOUR

PRIMARY SOURCES: JUDICIAL

Chapter 10. Judicial Reports

CHAPTER 10. JUDICIAL REPORTS

SECTION A. INTRODUCTION

This chapter discusses the courts that decide tax cases, both initially and on appeal, and the reporter services in which you can locate judicial opinions. It also discusses sources that publish briefs filed in tax cases, lists name changes for several courts, and indicates when each court began hearing tax cases.

Your goals for this chapter include locating pertinent decisions, judging their relevance in a particular jurisdiction, and updating your research to include cases that are working their way through the litigation and appeals processes. Because Congress can usually "overrule" a judicial decision it disagrees with by amending the statute, remember to check recently passed and pending legislation before deciding that you can rely on a particular case as precedent. In addition, you must also check IRS litigating positions; the IRS may choose not to follow an adverse lower court decision.

SECTION B. COURT ORGANIZATION

1. Trial Courts

Four courts serve as trial courts for tax disputes: District Courts; the Court of Federal Claims; the Tax Court; and Bankruptcy Courts.[177]

a. United States District Courts

Because District Courts are courts of general jurisdiction, their judges rarely develop as high a level of expertise on tax law questions as do judges of the Tax Court or even of the Court of Federal Claims. Taxpayers must pay the amount in dispute and sue for a refund as a condition to litigating in District Court, the only tribunal where a jury trial is available.

---

[177] In addition, the United States Court of International Trade hears cases involving tariffs and related tax matters. See, e.g., Princess Cruises, Inc. v. United States, 22 Ct. Int'l Trade 498 (1998). Many, but not all, CIT cases also appear in Federal Supplement. Appeals go to the Court of Appeals for the Federal Circuit.

A significant number of District Court decisions are not published in Federal Supplement but may be located in other reporter services.[178]

b. United States Court of Federal Claims

Although the Court of Federal Claims does not hear tax cases exclusively, the percentage of such cases it hears is likely to be greater than that heard in the average District Court. As in the District Court, a taxpayer must first pay the disputed amount before bringing suit.

Prior to October 1, 1982, this court was called the United States Court of Claims and the Court of Claims of the United States. Trials were conducted by a trial judge (formerly called a commissioner), whose decisions were reviewed by Court of Claims judges; only the Supreme Court had jurisdiction over appeals from its decisions. Between October 1, 1982, and October 28, 1992, this court was called the United States Claims Court.

c. United States Tax Court

Because Tax Court judges hear only tax cases, their expertise is substantially greater than that of judges in the other trial courts. Tax Court cases are tried by one judge, who submits an opinion to the chief judge for consideration. The chief judge can allow the decision to stand or refer it to the full court for review.[179] The published decision will indicate if it has been reviewed; dissenting opinions, if any, will be included. In some instances, special trial judges will hear disputes and issue opinions.[180]

There are three types of Tax Court decisions, two of which can result in appeals. The government printing office publishes **Regular Opinions**; these present important legal issues. Other publishers print **Memorandum**

---

[178] These include American Federal Tax Reports (A.F.T.R.) and U. S. Tax Cases (U.S.T.C.), discussed in Section C.5., CD-ROM materials (Chapter 18), and online services (Chapter 19). Freedom of Information Act litigation forced the Justice Department to make all District Court tax opinions available to the public. United States Department of Justice v. Tax Analysts, 492 U.S. 136 (1989).

[179] "Court review is directed if the report proposes to invalidate a regulation, overrule a published Tax Court case, or reconsider, in a circuit that has not addressed it, an issue on which we have been reversed by a court of appeals." Mary Ann Cohen, *How to Read Tax Court Opinions*, 1 Hous. Bus. & Tax L.J. 1, 5-6 (2001).

[180] The Supreme Court upheld this practice in Freytag v. Commissioner, 501 U.S. 868 (1991). The special trial judges were called commissioners until 1984. Taxpayers have sought access to special trial judges' reports. See, e.g., Justice Department brief to Eleventh Circuit in In re Ballard, available on LexisNexis at 2001 TNT 23-26.

Opinions, which involve well-established legal issues and are primarily fact-based.[181] The Tax Court also has a **Small Cases** division that taxpayers can elect to use for disputes of $50,000 or less. The **Summary Opinions** issued in those cases cannot be appealed or used as precedent. Until 2001, they were not published in any reporter service or on the Tax Court website.[182]

A taxpayer can sue in the Tax Court without paying the amount in dispute prior to litigating. Taxpayers also had this privilege in the Tax Court's predecessor, the Board of Tax Appeals.

Table 10-1. Names Used by Tax Court and Court of Federal Claims

United States Tax Court (since 1970)	United States Court of Federal Claims (since Oct. 29, 1992)
Tax Court of the United States (October 22, 1942-1969)	United States Claims Court (Oct. 1, 1982-Oct. 28, 1992)
Board of Tax Appeals (1924-October 21, 1942)	United States Court of Claims (1948-Sept. 30, 1982)
	Court of Claims of the United States (1863-1948)

d. United States Bankruptcy Courts[183]

In addition to deciding priority of liens and related matters, United States Bankruptcy Courts may issue substantive tax rulings. District Court judges or Bankruptcy Appellate Panels review Bankruptcy Court decisions.[184]

---

[181] Memorandum decisions have been appealed as far as the Supreme Court. See, e.g., Commissioner v. Duberstein, 363 U.S. 278 (1960).

[182] I.R.C. § 7463(b). The increase to $50,000 in 1998 is likely to increase the percentage of taxpayers using this litigation route. The previous limit was $10,000.

[183] These courts came into existence in 1979; bankruptcy trustees appointed by District Court judges previously administered these cases. See Pub. L. No. 95-598, § 201(a), 92 Stat. 2549, 2657 (1978). Bankruptcy judges are currently appointed by Court of Appeals judges. See Bankruptcy Amendments and Federal Judgeship Act of 1984, Pub. L. No. 98-353, § 104(a), 98 Stat. 333, 336.

[184] See, e.g., In re Michaud, 199 B.R. 248 (Bankr. D.N.H. 1996), aff'd, Michaud v. United States, 206 B.R. 1 (D.N.H. 1997); In re Mosbrucker, 220 B.R. 656 (Bankr. D.N.D. 1998), aff'd, 227 B.R. 434 (B.A.P. 8th Cir. 1998), aff'd, 99-2 U.S.T.C. ¶ 50,883, 84 A.F.T.R.2d 99-6457 (8th Cir. 1999)(unpublished opinion). Each circuit decides if

Bankruptcy cases often have two captions. One caption begins with "In re." The other follows the format used for most cases "Plaintiff v. Defendant." Table 10-2 shows how a 1999 Bankruptcy Court case involving Guardian Trust Company (Henderson, Trustee) is captioned in three reporter services.

Table 10-2. Case Captions for Bankruptcy Court Decisions

Bankruptcy Reporter: In re Guardian Trust Co., 242 B.R. 608 (Bankr. S.D. Miss. 1999)

U.S. Tax Cases: In re Guardian Trust Company, 99-2 U.S.T.C. ¶ 50,819 (Bankr. S.D. Miss. 1999)

American Federal Tax Reporter: Henderson v. United States, 84 A.F.T.R.2d 99-5940 (Bankr. S.D. Miss. 1999)

➔If you are looking for a particular bankruptcy case, note both the debtor and the trustee's names so that you can find the case no matter which case reporter or citator service you are using.

2. Courts of Appeals

When your research uncovers trial court decisions, you should trace those decisions to the appellate court level. This is particularly important if decisions conflict with each other and none comes from your jurisdiction.

Decisions of District Courts and the Tax Court are appealed to the Court of Appeals for the taxpayer's geographical residence[185] and from there to the Supreme Court. Even if the Tax Court disagrees with a particular Circuit Court precedent, it will follow it if that court would hear the appeal.[186] After appellate reversal in several circuits, the Tax Court is likely to change its

---

it will use a Bankruptcy Appellate Panel (BAP) and whether the BAP will hear all cases. For example, the Sixth Circuit currently follows a mixed procedure. Bankruptcy decisions from Ohio and the Western District of Tennessee go through the BAP; decisions from Kentucky, Michigan, and the rest of Tennessee go through the District Courts.

[185] From 1924 to 1926, decisions of the Board of Tax Appeals (the Tax Court's predecessor) were appealed to District Court. Revenue Act of 1924, ch. 234, § 900(g), 43 Stat. 253, 336; Revenue Act of 1926, ch. 27, § 1001(a), 44 Stat. 9, 109.

[186] Golsen v. Commissioner, 54 T.C. 742 (1970).

position for future litigation.[187]

Two Courts of Appeals are of relatively recent vintage. The Eleventh Circuit was carved out of the Fifth Circuit in 1981. If you represent a taxpayer who lives in the Eleventh Circuit, you should also consider Fifth Circuit decisions issued before October 1, 1981.[188]

The second recently established court is the Court of Appeals for the Federal Circuit, which was formed in 1982 to review decisions of what is now the Court of Federal Claims. Because the Supreme Court reviews so few Court of Appeals decisions, the Court of Federal Claims-Federal Circuit route offers a forum-shopping opportunity. Taxpayers living in circuits where appellate court decisions involving similar issues are adverse can avoid the law of their home circuits by suing in the Court of Federal Claims.[189]

In December 1989, the Federal Courts Study Committee recommended abolishing the present system for resolving tax controversies. The Committee recommended substituting a single trial court—the Tax Court—with appeals going to a specialized appellate court.[190] That suggestion, or variants using other courts, occasionally resurfaces.[191]

---

[187] See, e.g., Fazi v. Commissioner, 102 T.C. 695 (1994).

[188] See, e.g., Estate of Kosow v. Commissioner, 45 F.3d 1524, 1529 (11th Cir. 1995), citing a 1972 Fifth Circuit decision. Because the Tenth Circuit was split from the Eighth Circuit in 1929, you are unlikely to find Eighth Circuit precedent relevant to research involving the Tenth Circuit. Splitting the Ninth Circuit has been discussed several times.

[189] See Ginsburg v. United States, 184 Ct. Cl. 444, 396 F.2d 983 (1968), for a discussion of this phenomenon in the court's predecessor, the Court of Claims.

[190] FEDERAL COURTS STUDY COMM., TENTATIVE RECOMMENDATIONS FOR PUBLIC COMMENT (1989). Earlier in 1989, an ABA committee had proposed assigning trial court jurisdiction to the Tax Court. ABA STANDING COMMITTEE ON FEDERAL JUDICIAL IMPROVEMENTS, THE UNITED STATES COURT OF APPEALS: REEXAMINING STRUCTURE AND PROCESS AFTER A CENTURY OF GROWTH (1989).

[191] "If Congress decides to centralize tax appeals, the Federal Circuit provides a readily available forum for that purpose, one that already adjudicates appeals in tax cases coming to it from the Court of Federal Claims, and whose docket would be capable of absorbing appeals from the Tax Court or the district courts or both." COMMISSION ON STRUCTURAL ALTERNATIVES FOR THE FEDERAL COURTS OF APPEALS, TENTATIVE DRAFT REPORT (OCT. 1998), excerpted in Tax Notes today file on LexisNexis at 98 TNT 234-78.

3. Supreme Court

As noted above, decisions from the Circuit Courts can be appealed to the United States Supreme Court. The Supreme Court hears cases involving both constitutional challenges and those involving statutory interpretation. The Court is unlikely to grant certiorari in a case involving only statutory interpretation unless there is a conflict between two or more circuits.

SECTION C. LOCATING DECISIONS

1. Finding Lists

If you need to find judicial decisions involving a particular statute, treaty, regulation, or ruling, you can compile a preliminary reading list using the annotated looseleaf services and treatises discussed in Chapter 12. You can also use the following services for that purpose:

- Shepard's Citations; Shepard's Federal Tax Citator (Chapter 11)

- RIA Citator (Chapter 11)

- CCH Standard Federal Tax Reporter—Citator (Chapter 11)

- West's KeyCite (Chapter 11)

- Bulletin Index-Digest System (Chapter 16) (1954-1993/1994)

2. Locating Citations

If you know the name of a case, but not its citation, how do you locate its text? Several sources will be useful in this type of search. CD-ROM (Chapter 18) and online (Chapter 19) services are particularly helpful because you can include facts and issues in your search request.[192] These services may include screens in which you can enter party names and as much information as you know and retrieve a case. [See Illustration 10-1.]

If you know the taxpayer's first name and last names, you can use the RIA and CCH citators (Chapter 11); both list taxpayers alphabetically. United States Tax Reporter (Chapter 12) also includes a Table of Cases. If you lack the taxpayer's first name, but do know the jurisdiction, you might instead consult the alphabetical list of parties in West's Federal Practice Digest 4th.

---

[192] CD-ROM services don't always include a citation to a case reporter service.

That service does not include the Tax Court.[193]

If you know who the other party is, you can narrow your search among various tax reporter services. If, for example, the case is captioned "Taxpayer v. Commissioner," it arose in the Tax Court. Cases captioned "Taxpayer v. United States" arose in a District Court or the Court of Federal Claims.[194] Cases whose captions include "In re" often began in Bankruptcy Court, but reporter services differ in their captioning of bankruptcy cases. [See Table 10-2.]

Illustration 10-1. Using Get a Document in LexisNexis

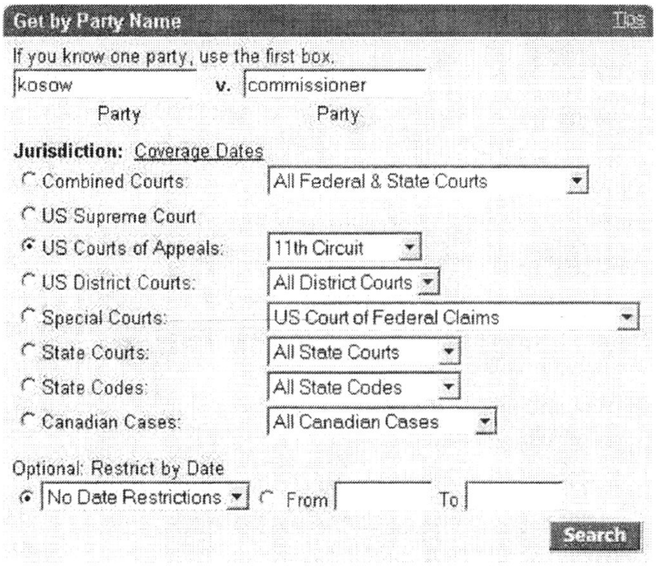

➔I knew both the taxpayer's name and the court but not the year.

---

[193] These materials are particularly useful if CCH and RIA omit the case from their citators. Such omission is possible if nontax aspects of a case are more important than tax aspects. See, e.g., United States v. Rosengarten, 857 F.2d 76 (2d Cir. 1988), omitted from CCH, RIA, and Shepard's tax citators.

[194] Knowing where to start is particularly useful if you use print reporter services and lack access to the CCH and RIA citators and electronic services. If the case arose in the Tax Court, you can use the CCH Tax Court Reporter's Table of Decisions, including the Current and Latest Additions supplements to ascertain the CCH Decision Number. You can obtain a citation by cross-referencing those numbers to the official reports or the CCH Tax Court Memoranda service using cross-reference tables in Volume 2 of this service. You can locate cases originating in other trial courts, as well as all appeals court decisions, through A.F.T.R.'s Table of Cases, which is cumulated throughout each five-year period in the A.F.T.R. volumes.

3. Digests of Decisions

Digests are useful for locating decisions omitted from the annotations discussed in Chapter 12. You can also use them in deciding which of many digested cases to read first.

Warren, Gorham & Lamont publishes several specialized digests. These include Corporate Tax Digest, Pass-Through Entity Tax Digest, Estate and Gift Tax Digest, Real Estate Tax Digest, and Tax Procedure Digest.

The IRS Bulletin Index-Digest System (Chapter 16) digests cases between 1954 and 1993/1994. Services such as Standard Federal Tax Reporter and United States Tax Reporter, both discussed in Chapter 12, digest cases in their compilation and updating volumes or in their newsletters. Newsletters such as Tax Notes and Daily Tax Report, both described in Chapter 15, digest cases in every issue.

4. Texts of Decisions[195]

With the exception of Tax Court decisions, you can locate federal court decisions involving taxation in the sets listed in Table 10-3. You can also locate these and Tax Court decisions online (Chapter 19), in microform (Chapter 17), and in CD-ROM format (Chapter 18). Online and CD-ROM services may have limited retrospective coverage; remember to check when each service began including a court's decisions. Retrospective coverage on individual court websites may be even more limited than it is on subscription-based electronic services. Various newsletters (Chapter 15) also print texts or digests; several of these are available online as well as in print.

Coverage of Tax Court decisions varies.[196] The government published Regular decisions by the Tax Court's predecessor, the Board of Tax Appeals in the Board of Tax Appeals Reports (B.T.A.). The government did not publish B.T.A. Memorandum decisions. Prentice-Hall printed both Regular and Memorandum decisions.

The government also publishes Tax Court Regular decisions in Tax Court

---

[195] Early Cumulative Bulletins included lower federal court decisions either as Court Decisions (Ct. D.) or as Miscellaneous Rulings. Because the disparate labels make these items virtually impossible to locate, they are omitted from these lists. See Fundamentals of Legal Research ch. 4 for an extensive discussion of case reports.

[196] Table 10-1 lists relevant dates and court names for the Tax Court and Board of Tax Appeals. Although the Board began in 1924, it did not issue Memorandum decisions until 1928.

of the United States Reports and United States Tax Court Reports; both are cited as T.C. It does not officially publish Tax Court Memorandum decisions.

Both Commerce Clearing House and Research Institute of America (which acquired the Prentice-Hall service) publish Tax Court decisions in a variety of formats. Their reporter services are discussed in Subsection C.5.

Table 10-3. Print Reporter Services Other Than Tax Court

	Supreme Court	Court of Appeals	District Court	Bankr. Court.	Federal Claims
U.S.	1796-				
S. Ct.	1882-				
L. Ed.	1796-				
A.F.T.R.	1796-	1880-	1882-	1979-	1876-
U.S.T.C.	1913-	1915-	1915-	1979-	1924-
F.		1880-	1882-1932		1929-1932 1960-1982
F. Supp.			1932-		1932-1960
Ct. Cl.					1863-1982
Cl. Ct.					1982-1992
Fed. Cl.					1992-
B.R.				1979-	

→Several reporter services are in second or third series (e.g., F., F.2d, F.3d).

→Only A.F.T.R. and U.S.T.C. print cases from all these courts.

→Coverage for the Court of Federal Claims reflects its name changes. [See Table 10-1.]

→The Cumulative Bulletin (Chapter 16) has included Supreme Court decisions since 1920; it calls them Ct. D.

→A.F.T.R. volumes 1-4 reprint cases by reporter service (e.g., Federal Reporter, United States Reports) and not in strict chronological order.

→Until 1912 so-called Circuit Courts decided cases; reports are found in Federal Cases and Federal Reporter.

5. Tax-Oriented Case Reporter Services

Most of the sets listed above are published by the Government Printing Office or by West and are used the same way for tax research as for nontax research. The sets published by Research Institute of America and Commerce Clearing House differ enough from the others to warrant further discussion.

a. American Federal Tax Reports and U.S. Tax Cases

The use of these sets can be coordinated with the use of each publisher's looseleaf reporting service, A.F.T.R. with RIA United States Tax Reporter and U.S.T.C.[197] with CCH Standard Federal Tax Reporter. Each service publishes decisions from all courts except the Tax Court, and each includes "unpublished" decisions omitted from Federal Supplement and Federal Reporter.[198]

Each service first includes decisions in an Advance Sheets volume of the related looseleaf reporting service. This initial publication in conjunction with the looseleaf services results in recent decisions being available in print on a weekly basis. While both services are supplemented weekly, each occasionally prints decisions before the other does.

These cases also appear in the listings of new material in the services' update volumes (Recent Developments for United States Tax Reporter; New Matters for Standard Federal Tax Reporter). The listings appear in Code section order and are cross-referenced to discussions in the services' compilation volumes. As a result, you can locate a recent case when you know the Code section involved but not the taxpayer's name, and you can immediately find a discussion of the topic in the compilation volumes. The daily newsletters (Chapter 15), which are probably the only more current print source of these cases, often print only partial texts or digests and don't provide full-year cumulative indexes.

The reference method is important if you use these services. CCH cites decisions in the U.S.T.C. advance sheets and bound volumes by paragraph number (e.g., 88-1 U.S.T.C. ¶ 9390). RIA cites to decisions in A.F.T.R. by

---

[197] The earliest volumes of this service print all Supreme Court decisions and those lower court decisions of "genuine precedent value ...." *Foreword* to 1 U.S.T.C. (1938). When CCH began issuing two volumes per year, it expanded coverage.

[198] See, e.g., Alexander v. United States, 88-1 U.S.T.C. ¶ 9390, 62 A.F.T.R.2d 88-5228 (N.D. Ga. 1988); Estate of McLendon v. Commissioner, 96-1 U.S.T.C. ¶ 60,220, 77 A.F.T.R.2d 96-666 (5th Cir. 1995) (unpublished opinion).

page number (e.g., 62 A.F.T.R.2d 88-5228).

The bound volumes include all types of tax cases—income, estate and gift, and excise; the individual Advance Sheets volumes do not. The different types of cases appear in Advance Sheets sections accompanying each publisher's looseleaf service for the particular area of tax law.

b. Tax Court Reports

Both CCH and RIA publish Tax Court reporters. RIA publishes bound volumes of the Tax Court Memorandum Decisions. A CD-ROM covers both Tax Court and Board of Tax Appeals Regular and Memorandum decisions.

The CCH Tax Court Reporter has three looseleaf volumes. Volume 1 contains Memorandum decisions and Volume 2 contains Regular decisions. Volume 3, which is discussed in Section D, contains information about pending litigation. Volume 1 has an alphabetical Table of Decisions, while Volume 2 provides cross-references to CCH case numbers.

c. Citation Format for CCH and RIA Reporter Services

Citation formats for the services published by CCH and RIA vary depending upon whether you follow the guidelines established by The Bluebook, by TaxCite, or by the ABA Tax Section Committee on Government Submissions.[199] Depending on the format adopted, you are likely to encounter any of the Table 10-4 citation formats.

Table 10-4. Citation Formats for CCH and RIA Reporters

American Federal Tax Reports: AFTR; A.F.T.R.; A.F.T.R. (P-H); A.F.T.R. (RIA); AFTR2d; A.F.T.R.2d; A.F.T.R.2d (RIA)
U.S. Tax Cases: USTC para.; U.S.T.C. ¶; U.S. Tax Cas. (CCH)
Tax Court Reports: T.C.R. (CCH) Dec.; T.C.R. Dec. (P-H) ¶; T.C.R. Dec. (RIA) ¶; Tax Ct. Rep. (CCH); Tax Ct. Rep. Dec. (P-H); Tax Ct. Rep. Dec. (RIA)
Tax Court Memorandum Decisions: T.C. Memo; TCM; para. #, P-H memo T.C.; T.C.M. (CCH); T.C.M. (P-H) ¶; T.C.M. (RIA) ¶; T.C.M. (P-H); T.C.M. (RIA)
Board of Tax Appeals Memorandum Decisions: B.T.A. Mem. Dec. (P-H) ¶; B.T.A.M. (P-H)

[199] The ABA Section of Taxation is one of TaxCite's participants. Although TaxCite bears a 1995 copyright, the Tax Section's 2001-2002 Directory lists other citation forms for these services.

6. Parallel Citations

Online and CD-ROM services make cases accessible without regard to reporter service. If you use bound volumes for your research, you may find that the volume for which you have a citation is not on the library shelf. Because so many case reporters cover each court level, you may be able to find that case in another set. All you need is the correct citation for the other reporter service.

Because general reporter services print nontax as well as tax decisions, numerous volumes cover each year's cases. Looking up the case name in several volumes is a tedious method of finding another printing. You can accomplish this task more quickly by locating the case citation in one of the tools listed below and obtaining a parallel citation to the same decision in another reporter.

- Shepard's Federal Tax Citator (Chapter 11)

- RIA Citator (Chapter 11)

- CCH Standard Federal Tax Reporter—Citator (Chapter 11)

- Federal Tax Coordinator 2d (Chapter 12)

- United States Tax Reporter Table of Cases (Chapter 12)

Shepard's is the most likely to print citations for all the reporter services. The other sources are limited in their cross-referencing and change the cross-references included from time to time.

SECTION D. PENDING LITIGATION, BRIEFS, AND PETITIONS

You can use the United States Tax Reporter Current and Supplementary Tables of Cases or the Standard Federal Tax Reporter current year's Case Table to determine if appeals have been filed in recent tax cases. These services are described in Chapter 12.

Cases pending decision by the Tax Court appear in volume 3 of the CCH Tax Court Reporter, which contains digests (abstracts) of petitions the editors deem noteworthy. The digests identify cases whose outcome might affect the results of a current research effort. Unfortunately, they are not indexed, and the Code section does not appear as a heading. CCH arranges cases by docket numbers; these numbers appear in the alphabetical Petitioners Table.

The CCH Tax Court Reporter also contains Motion and Trial Calendars and a section for New Tax Disputes. The Disputes section contains explanations of newsworthy petitions—e.g., those presenting novel theories or involving previously unexplored areas of the Code. Updating is weekly.

Because the IRS often indicates its recommendation about appealing adverse decisions in actions on decisions and notices of acquiescence (Chapter 9), you should also research these documents before deciding if appeals are likely in cases of interest.

Briefs are relevant in determining which arguments the taxpayers and government have raised for court consideration. Tax Analysts covers pending litigation in the Court Filings section of Tax Notes (Chapter 15); its online version prints the full text of taxpayer petitions and government briefs. [See Illustration 10-2.] Supreme Court briefs are also available in Law Reprints—Tax Law Series and in microform services (Chapter 17).

Illustration 10-2. Digest of Tax Court Petition from Tax Notes

---

Section 61 - Gross Income Defined

OAKLAND RAIDERS DENY $10 MILLION IN ORDINARY INCOME. The Oakland Raiders, a limited partnership, has contested the Service's determination that it failed to report $10 million in ordinary income in 1992 based on funds received from Spectacor Management Limited Partnership in 1990.

The Oakland Raiders contends that the characterization of the Spectacor transaction is pending before the Tax Court in Docket Nos. 16256-95 and 24614-95. It further contends that no event occurred in 1992 that required it to recognize additional ordinary income from the transaction.

The partnership also claims that the proposed adjustments are time-barred and that it is entitled to $1.3 million of additional deductions for contributions to a retirement plan. *The Oakland Raiders Limited Partnership v. Commissioner,* T.C. Dkt. No. 20581-96 (Filed: Sept. 23, 1996).
Full Text Citation: *Doc 97-4476 (10 pages)*

→The Document number can be used to locate the full text. Doc stands for Document, not Docket. The Docket number is 20581-96. Recent documents also include TNT citations for finding the document online.

SECTION E. CITATORS FOR DECISIONS AND HEADNOTES

There are four commonly used print citators for judging the relative authority of any tax decision, and many libraries own all of them. Although there is substantial overlap in their coverage, each citator contains some information the others lack. All four are discussed in Chapter 11.

• Shepard's Federal Citations; Shepard's United States Citations; Shepard's Bankruptcy Citations

• Shepard's Federal Tax Citator

• RIA Citator

• CCH Standard Federal Tax Reporter—Citator

CD-ROMs (Chapter 18) and online services (Chapter 19) also include access to citators or provide citator-like functions. One citator, West's KeyCite, is available only in electronic format.

IRS action with regard to cases it has lost can be located in the Bulletin Index-Digest System (1954-1993/94) (Chapter 16) or in a service covering IRS documents (Chapter 9).

As discussed in Chapter 11, different volumes of Shepard's Federal Tax Citator provide citations for cases irrespective of where they appear (e.g., appellate court cases published in Federal Reporter, A.F.T.R. and U.S.T.C.). Each reporter service makes its own decision regarding the headnotes or syllabus numbers it assigns a case. If you read a case in one service and are interested in a particular syllabus issue, make sure the citator you use is keyed to that service.

SECTION F. EVALUATING DECISIONS

1. In General

Courts must determine how much weight to give opinions in cases cited by the taxpayer or government. An individual court, whether Tax Court, District Court, or Court of Federal Claims, will give its own decisions far more deference than it will give decisions of the other trial courts.

If a Court of Appeals has ruled, that opinion will be binding precedent for District Court, Bankruptcy Court, and Tax Court cases that will be appealed in that circuit. Otherwise, the opinion will be persuasive precedent. Supreme Court decisions are binding precedent for all courts.

If a court ruled against the government position, and the IRS issues a notice of acquiescence, an action on decision, or other document explaining why it won't appeal, the precedential value of the decision is further enhanced. Instead of acquiescing, the IRS announcement may indicate it will continue litigating. [See, e.g., Illustration 3-9.] These IRS documents are discussed in Chapter 9.

2. Unpublished Opinions

There is a difference between an **unpublished opinion** and an opinion to which you cannot get access. Many services include decisions issued under no-publication rules. You may want to find these decisions, as they shed light on the court's thinking. However, you cannot cite them as precedent if you are writing a brief or other submission to the court.

There is also a difference, as noted earlier in this chapter, between an officially published opinion and one available through other reporter services. Unless designated by court or statute as not precedential, both sets of opinions can be cited as precedential or persuasive authority. Although unofficial reporters may include official pagination, they do not have to do so. If you need to cite official pagination, you must use reporters that provide that information. If courts abandon the requirement of citing to print page numbers, and more decisions are posted online, the distinction between official and other publication sources will continue to diminish.

3. Statements Regarding Deference

If no appeals have been taken, you may be tempted to accord greater weight to a Tax Court decision than to a decision of another trial court. Although the Tax Court judges have specialized knowledge, the degree of deference their decisions receive is not necessarily greater than that given decisions from other trial courts.

The items below illustrate statements regarding deference to decisions.

• We review the Tax Court's construction of the tax code de novo.... Although we presume that the Tax Court correctly applied the law, we give no special deference to the Tax Court's decisions. Best Life Assur. Co. of Calif. v. Commissioner, 281 F.3d 828, 830 (9th Cir. 2002).

• The Commissioner also argues that a sufficient explanation had been provided, relying upon an older body of case law that purports to grant great deference to the Tax Court.... In these cases, however, the Tax Court provided some justification for its conclusions in a manner that allowed us to understand and reconstruct the Tax Court's rationale. In the case at hand, the Tax Court merely announced the discount it applied to the Estate's stock without any explanation. Estate of Mitchell v. Commissioner, 250 F.3d 696,

703 n.6 (9th Cir. 2001).

• A finding is clearly erroneous when, although there is evidence to support it, a review of the entire record leaves the reviewing court with the definite and firm conviction that a mistake has been made.... This standard of review requires that we accord great deference to the values established by the tax court, but it does not render us a mere rubber stamp. Gross v. Commissioner, 272 F.3d 333, 343 (6th Cir. 2001).

• For the following reasons, pursuant to 28 U.S.C. § 1334(c)(1), we voluntarily ABSTAIN: (1) This adversary proceeding involves a classic two-party dispute, the outcome of which will have little or no effect on the estate;[3] (2) there is litigation currently pending before the United States Tax Court, Docket # 4516-88; (3) the litigation requires the resolution of complex issues of tax law, some of which are unsettled or are questions of first impression; (4) there is a specialized forum for hearing this kind of dispute (i.e., the United States Tax Court); and (5) resolution of the issues would require this Court to interpret decisions of the United States Tax Court.[4] .... In the circumstances, and in deference to its expertise in the subject matter of the litigation, this adversary proceeding is transferred to the United States Tax Court for hearing and adjudication. In re Williams, 209 B.R. 584, 585 (Bankr. D.R.I. 1997) (footnotes omitted).

SECTION G. PROBLEMS

1. Give the preferred citation, including taxpayer name, court involved, and year, for the case found at

    a. 10-2 C.B. 276 (1931)   c. 2001-2 U.S.T.C. ¶ 50,766

    b. 1947-1 C.B. 97   d. 28 A.F.T.R.2d 71-5839

2. Give the preferred citation, including court involved and year, for all decisions involving the following taxpayers.

    a. Sally Conforte   c. Hershey Chocolate Co.

    b. General Lead Batteries Co.   d. William W. Saunders

3. Was the lower court affirmed or reversed on appeal?

    a. 16 B.T.A. 136   c. 24 Cl. Ct. 64

    b. 520 F. Supp. 1207   d. 196 B.R. 542

4. An friend of yours, who majored in literature, claims that literary concepts are totally absent from tax decisions. Prove your friend wrong by locating a decision including the quotation indicated.

a. "The lady doth protest too much, me thinks."

b. "It is like going to see Shakespeare's Hamlet and finding no Hamlet on the stage, nothing rotten in the state of Denmark, and no ghost frightening the palace guards."

c. "Calculation of taxes is not a reprise of Jarndyce v. Jarndyce, the legendary suit in Charles Dickens' Bleak House, in which resolution came about only because legal fees ate up the whole of an estate."

d. "Concededly, this does not mean simply a 'clue' which would be sufficient to intrigue a Sherlock Holmes. But neither does it mean a detailed revelation of each and every underlying fact."

e. "This divergence is so out of the ordinary that, upon an initial reading of section 1256, a person might feel like Dorothy did upon finding herself transported to the Land of Oz, and, speaking to her dog, said: 'Toto, I've a feeling we're not in Kansas anymore.'"

f. "The attempt of the majority herein to alleviate by fiat the alleged 'harshness' and 'inequity' of the statute ... may be as wide of the mark as the attempt portrayed in Gilbert and Sullivan's 'Mikado' to 'let the punishment fit the crime.'"

g. "We can borrow an illustration from O. Henry's 'Gift of the Magi', transforming it in milieu and feeling-tone."

5. In which case does the following language appear?

a. "He could not draw a conjurer's circle around the whole matter by his own declaration that to write any word upon the government blank would bring him into danger of the law."

b. "The tax collector's presumption of correctness has a herculean muscularity of Goliathlike reach, but we strike an Achilles' heel when we find no muscles, no tendons, no ligaments of fact."

c. "Leave it to the IRS to turn a family reunion into a taxable event."

d. "Baxley's assertion that the defendant is not the same individual as named in the complaint because he does not spell his name in all capital letters does, in fact, fail the 'laughable' test. Thus, despite knowing what was coming, when Baxley stated his contention at the hearing, I spontaneously laughed. This, it seems to me, establishes the frivolousness of the contention."

e. "ORDER DETERMINING THAT THE INTERNAL REVENUE SERVICE IS STILL NAUGHTY AND NOT NICE"

f. "The petition and amended petition contains little more than unintelligible gobbledygook."

g. "Do we now give license to challenge that orthodoxy? Restaurants do not sell tobacco products anymore, and liquor may give them pause, but can fancy French restaurants (or large food service operations) now argue that they need not inventory their comestibles since they are inherently a service business, with peas, carrots, truffles, and boeuf being integral to that service?"

6. You are interested in locating judicial decisions involving the following:

a. The value, for estate tax purposes, of shares of stock in the company producing Korbel champagne

b. a theft loss claimed by the producer/promoter of the New Kids on the Block musical group

c. a bad debt deduction claimed by the now-deceased owner of the Kansas City Royals

d. the appropriate year for taxing payments a government employee received from the KGB

e. whether royalties received by the ex-wife of a member of the Eagles were taxable to her or to her husband

f. whether a musician who toured with Rod Stewart was an employee or an independent contractor

g. whether the Code section 1056 limits applied to the sale of an interest in the partnership that owned the Denver Broncos

h. the number of shares in the corporation owning the Cincinnati Bengals to be included in an owner's estate

i. whether the IRS's tax lien was superior to another creditor's rights to royalties earned by the composer of "Rockin' Pneumonia and Boogey Woogey Flu"

j. the deductibility of certain post-acquisition costs incurred by the company that purchased the Ladies' Home Journal magazine

7. Locate judicial decisions involving the following issues; indicate the outcome, including any later judicial action.

a. a 2000 District Court decision appealable to the Eleventh Circuit that cites Fifth Circuit precedent regarding a spouse's interest in homestead property titled solely in the other spouse's name

b. a 2000 District Court decision determining the appropriate year to treat the cost of a home, built for a taxpayer with multiple chemical sensitivity, as a medical expense

c. a 1987 Tax Court decision involving a casualty loss claimed by a man who, in the course of burning his wife's clothing, set his house on fire

d. a 1991 Tax Court decision involving a casualty loss deduction for a car that was towed and crushed after the city pound could not determine who owned it

e. a 1999 Tax Court decision involving a surgeon in which the IRS claimed that nerve damage didn't constitute permanent loss of a bodily function

f. a 1995 Tax Court decision determining whether a tax-exempt organization was liable for unrelated business income tax on "instant bingo" games

g. a 1999 District Court decision determining whether a man convicted of racketeering could deduct the fees he paid his defense attorneys as business expenses

h. a 1998 Tax Court decision determining when a professor, who guaranteed success on a money-back basis, had to report fees he received for teaching a bar review course

i. a 1999 Tax Court decision determining whether an attorney could deduct, in the year he retired, the full cost of a malpractice policy in effect for an indefinite period and covering past acts

j. a 1999 District Court case determining whether payments made to induce faculty members to relinquish their tenure rights and retire early produced capital gains or ordinary income for the payees

k. a 2001 Tax Court decision discussing whether a junk yard could deduct the cost of cat food

l. a 1999 Court of Federal Claims decision discussing whether a taxpayer could use Code section 1341 to compute his tax after he repaid funds fraudulently obtained by his wholly-owned corporation

8. In each case below, the Tax Court overruled its prior holding on an issue. Provide the citation for the case you find and the earlier case.

a. a 2001 decision in which the court held it has jurisdiction under Code section 6330(d)(1)(A) whether or not the taxpayer received a proper hearing opportunity

b. a 2002 decision regarding whether Treas. Reg. § 1.861-8(e)(2) permits netting of interest income and expense

c. a 1996 decision regarding whether a surviving spouse had a qualifying income interest if passage of that interest to the spouse depended on the executor's making a QTIP election

d. a 1964 decision regarding whether salvage value is different from the amount received upon the sale of an asset unless the asset is sold at or near the end of its useful life

9. Print out the first page of the Tax Court petition filed by

a. a deceased taxpayer who owned a minority interest in the corporation that produced Little Debbie snack foods

b. a taxpayer claiming an amortization deduction allocable to a favorable position in the National Basketball Association draft

c. a taxpayer, albeit in a totally unrelated matter, whose family name is the same as that of the department store known for Frango Mints

d. the taxpayer who starred in the movie versions of both Grease and Saturday Night Fever

e. the deceased husband of Anna Nicole Smith

f. a deceased taxpayer and his widow who claimed they did not materially participate in the operations of the corporation owning the Tampa Bay

Buccaneers

g. a Swedish tennis professional who claimed certain endorsement income was not U.S.-source income

h. a former New York Yankee who owned stock in All-Pro Sports

10. Print out the first page of the brief described below.

a. the Department of Justice brief to the appellate court in a case involving the corporation staging the Kentucky Derby

b. the taxpayer's brief to the appellate court in a case involving an ad in USA Today claiming that Bill Clinton's political positions were contrary to Bible teachings

c. the Department of Justice brief to the appellate court in a case involving foreign tax credits and the Ontario Mining Tax

d. the taxpayer's brief to the appellate court in a case involving whether advances and rent credits provided the Oakland/Los Angeles/Oakland Raiders football team were valid loan amounts

11. Provide a citation to the decision described and indicate its holding

a. a 2002 summary judgment resolution finding that GCM 34190 was not helpful

b. a 2000 appellate court decision rejecting IRS reliance, in TAM 9715002, on a regulation

c. a 2001 summary judgment resolution indicating that the judge's result was consistent with PLR 9616012

d. a 2001 appellate court decision citing Notice 98-5 as evidence the IRS had "consciously chosen to try to stack the deck this way"

12. Locate these Bankruptcy Court decisions and indicate the substantive tax issue (i.e., not priority of liens) each involved.

a. a 1999 decision regarding the vice president of Tri-D Inc.

b. a 2000 decision regarding the sole shareholder of a corporation that owned a Christmas tree farm

c. a 1999 decision regarding taxpayers who lived in a mobile home while traveling to craft shows

d. a 2001 decision regarding interest on a corporation's trade debt and institutional debt

13. Find the listed case in the reporter listed and in A.F.T.R., and U.S.T.C. and indicate how many syllabus numbers it has in each reporter service.

a. Wertz v. United States, 51 Fed. Cl. 443 (2002)

b. Boca Investerings Partnership v. United States, 167 F. Supp. 2d 298 (D.D.C. 2001)

c. U.S. Freightways Corp. v. Commissioner, 270 F.3d 1137 (7th Cir. 2001)

d. Eberl's Claim Service, Inc. v. Commissioner, 249 F.3d 994 (10th Cir. 2001)

14. You have been asked to give a speech about the difference between a business and a hobby for tax purposes. Print the first page of the documents requested for the following activities, which you plan to use as examples.

a. brief filed—taxpayers owned a Lamborghini Countach

b. brief filed—taxpayers raised water buffalo and South African goats

c. trial court decision—taxpayer wrote about brothels

d. trial court decision—taxpayer began gold mining in 1995

e. trial court decision—taxpayer ran health, wealth and healing ministry

15. Give a citation to the most recent decision you can find citing

a. the New York Times Style Manual

b. Merriam-Webster's Collegiate Dictionary

c. any other dictionary your instructor assigns

PART FIVE

SECONDARY SOURCES

Chapter 11. Citators

Chapter 12. Looseleaf Services, Encyclopedias, and Treatises

Chapter 13. Legal Periodicals

Chapter 14. Form Books and Model Language

Chapter 15. Newsletters

Chapter 11. Citators

Section A. Introduction

You can use the citator services discussed in this chapter to judge whether a particular statute, treaty, regulation, ruling, or judicial decision has been criticized, approved, or otherwise commented upon in a more recent proceeding. Although they cover relatively few tax-oriented periodicals, you can also use citators to determine if a judicial opinion has cited a particular periodical article or if an article has cited a particular decision.

Goals for this chapter include determining coverage and format differences for each citator and citator-like service. You should also feel comfortable using word searches in electronic services in lieu of using print or electronic citators.

Section B. Terminology

This chapter discusses services that are called **citators** and services that perform citator-like functions. I refer to the latter as **updating services** or as **citator-like services**. In their print versions, citators and updating services group statutes, judicial decisions, or other documents in a particular format (for example, by year of decision, alphabetically, or by type of tax). Each item is followed by a list of later items that cite to it.

A later item may merely cite the earlier item as authority or it may discuss the earlier item and indicate agreement or disagreement with its holding. The discussion may center on the earlier item as a whole or on a particular issue involved in that item.

In this chapter, the earlier material is referred to as the **cited** item; any later material that refers to it is a **citing** item. Subdivisions such as **headnote** or **syllabus** numbers, which refer to issues, are referred to by either term throughout this text.

Section C. Citator Format and Coverage

This section provides a brief overview of differences in citator format and coverage. Detailed descriptions of each citator appear in Sections D through G.[200] Section I provides information about citator-like services.

Several citators described in this chapter are available in both print and electronic formats. Although the descriptions focus on print materials, both print and electronic searching are discussed. Because of updating frequency and the ability to search the equivalent of multiple print citator volumes, you are likely to prefer using electronic citators if you can find the same material in both formats.

Illustrations of citator results for a revenue ruling appear in Chapter 9. Illustrations in Section H of this chapter cover a judicial decision.

1. Arrangement

Citators follow a variety of format conventions, the most important of which relate to judicial decisions. The major distinction is between citators that arrange cases by reporter service citation and those that arrange them alphabetically. A second distinction relates to the overall arrangement of multivolume services.

Citators published by Shepard's arrange cited cases by numerical reporter citations. Citators published by Commerce Clearing House (CCH) and Research Institute of America (RIA) arrange them by taxpayer name. When using the CCH and RIA services, you should note the taxpayer's first name to make your search easier, particularly if the taxpayer has a common surname. Likewise, note that alphabetization rules may vary between print citators, particularly for names that begin with numbers (e.g., 21 West Lancaster precedes Twenty Mile Joint Venture in RIA but not in CCH). Alphabetization rules are irrelevant if you use an electronic citator service.

Each service follows a different format for classifying items into citator volumes. CCH divides its citator service to correspond to its separate income, estate and gift, and excise tax services. RIA does not make this distinction.[201] Shepard's uses separate volumes for different courts and reporter services.

When listing citing items for judicial decisions, RIA subdivides citing cases by syllabus number. Within each number, it arranges items by rank of court; within each rank, it lists the earliest items first. Shepard's print service

---

[200] Because each citator has a different scope and format, the separate discussions in Sections D through G treat each cited primary authority in the same order.

[201] Shepard's and West's KeyCite are not associated with looseleaf services.

arranges citing items by circuit and then by rank of court; it lists the earliest items first. The electronic Shepard's follows this arrangement but lists the most recent items first. West's KeyCite arranges citing judicial decisions by category (e.g., positive, cited, mentioned); within each category, it lists them by court. For each court, it lists the most recent items first.

2. Syllabus Number and Judicial Commentary

The print and online Shepard's and RIA citators (and the online KeyCite) use syllabus numbers to indicate issues and words or letter symbols to indicate judicial commentary (e.g., distinguished, explained); CCH does neither. Although many users prefer using citators that provide this information, illustrations in Section H display the potential for misleading results.

3. Miscellaneous Differences

CCH uses fewer citing cases than do the others; it limits its coverage to citing cases that affect the cited case's "effectiveness as precedent." The online Shepard's and KeyCite include numerous secondary sources as citing items. All services are more likely than the general Shepard's print service to include Tax Court (particularly Memorandum decisions) and IRS material as citing items.

SECTION D. SHEPARD'S CITATIONS; FEDERAL TAX CITATOR

Shepard's publishes a general version that is useful for traditional legal research, including tax research, and a special Shepard's Federal Tax Citator version. The general Shepard's is discussed first; differences in the specialized version are noted in each category. Except as noted in the discussion, Shepard's on LexisNexis follows the general Shepard's coverage.

Because its overall coverage is general, Shepard's is the best-known citator. It is divided both chronologically and by cited authority into hardbound volumes and softbound supplements. As a result, searches using the print Shepard's take longer than those using another system. You can avoid this problem using the online version.[202]

Shepard's includes several valuable features, such as citations to A.L.R. and to Lawyers' Edition annotations. The Shepard's Federal Tax Citator

---

[202] Federal Citations and United States Citations are available in CD-ROM versions only until December 31, 2002.

includes citations to articles in specialized tax periodicals.[203] The online Shepard's service includes more secondary source material than is found in the print volumes.

1. Constitution, Statutes, and Treaties

a. General

If a constitutional provision, statute or treaty has ever been interpreted, or a statute's validity passed upon, by any federal court (other than the Tax Court in a Memorandum decision), a citation to the decision will appear in Shepard's Federal Statute Citations.[204] That service also indicates any subsequent congressional amendments or repeal of statutory material. Federal Statute Citations does not use revenue rulings and procedures as citing material.

Symbols indicate how the court ruled in each case involving validity. Shepard's groups citing decisions by jurisdiction in chronological order. It does not indicate the state for District Courts.[205]

Shepard's arranges cited statutes in Code section order; TITLE 26 contains the bulk of tax statutes. The citator uses subdivisions as small as paragraphs and clauses.

Shepard's eliminated its coverage of treaties in 1995. Earlier volumes included treaties and listed them in order of their volume and page number in United States Treaties and Other International Agreements (U.S.T.); no indication of country name appears.

b. Federal Tax

Federal Tax Citator never included the Constitution or treaties as cited material. In addition to the traditional case reporters covered in the general service, it provides U.S.T.C. and A.F.T.R. citations for cases that cite to statutes.

---

[203] Shepard's initially cited to Tax Law Review; the most recent volumes include citations to Journal of Taxation and to TAXES—The Tax Magazine.

[204] Court rules of practice and material in Statutes at Large (but omitted from U.S.C.) are included as cited material in this volume. Use the Statutes at Large section of this citator for statutory provisions that were not codified. See Chapter 5 for a discussion of codified and uncodified statutes.

[205] Shepard's Federal Circuit Table provides that information.

2. Regulations and IRS Documents

a. General

Shepard's Code of Federal Regulations Citations is arranged in C.F.R. section order; tax regulations are listed as TITLE 26. Symbols indicate how each court ruled on challenges to the regulation's validity.

This citator indicates action by federal courts other than the Tax Court; it does not use revenue rulings and procedures as citing material. It provides citations to law review articles discussing the regulations.

The general Shepard's service does not provide citations to material interpreting IRS documents. The online Shepard's lets you Shepardize IRS documents but does not necessarily provide relevant case citations. Illustration 11-1 shows the results from Shepardizing Revenue Ruling 87-22, discussed and illustrated in Chapter 3.

Illustration 11-1. Online Shepardizing of Revenue Ruling 87-22

PRIOR HISTORY (0 citing references) ◆ Hide Prior History

▸ (CITATION YOU ENTERED):
    Rev Rul 87-22, 1987-1 C.B. 146, 1987-14 I.R.B. 41, Rev. Rul. No. 87-22 (I.R.S. 1987)❶

CITING DECISIONS (1 citing decision)

ADMINISTRATIVE AGENCY DECISIONS

    Cited by:
    Rev Proc 87-15, 1987-1 C.B. 624, 1987-14 I.R.B. 47, Rev. Proc. No. 87-15 (I.R.S. 1987)❶

➔Compare these results to those in Illustration 3-7.

b. Federal Tax

Several sections of Federal Tax Citator cover regulations. Its C.F.R. section divides regulations into three categories–final, temporary, and proposed–and separately provides citations for items in each category. These items are arranged by regulations section number. Federal Tax Citator has a separate section citing to Treasury Decisions; these items are arranged by T.D. number. Finally, within the section that covers IRS material, it provides citations to Notices of Proposed Regulations; this section is arranged by the project numbers discussed in Chapter 8.

When citing to regulations, Federal Tax Citator cites to A.F.T.R. and U.S.T.C. as well as to the reporter services normally covered by the general service. Although Federal Tax Citator also fails to provide cross-references between C.F.R. sections and T.D. numbers, it does provide Tax Court citations to both T.D.s and regulations sections. The general Shepard's service does not do so.

Federal Tax Citator provides citations to revenue rulings, revenue procedures, private letter rulings, technical advice memoranda, and a variety of other IRS documents. Citing material includes judicial decisions and IRS documents (including documents that are not published in the Internal Revenue Bulletin). Federal Tax Citator also includes citations to UIL numbers (discussed in Chapter 9). Coverage of IRS material expanded significantly in the 1998-2002 Supplement volumes.

3. Judicial Decisions

a. General

Shepard's arranges case citations by level of court being cited. Different sets cover different courts. Two different sets of Federal Citations[206] cover Court of Appeals, District Court, and Court of Federal Claims decisions. United States Citations volumes trace Supreme Court decisions. Shepard's also publishes Bankruptcy Citations. There are no volumes covering Tax Court decisions as cited cases.

Each set provides citations for all citing cases; Tax Court Memorandum decisions are rarely listed as citing cases. Both cited and citing cases are listed by volume and page number, rather than by taxpayer name. These sets do not use revenue rulings and procedures as citing material.

Print version citations indicate the relevant page of the citing decision. The electronic version [Illustration 11-7] indicates both the first page of the citing decision and the page where the citation to the earlier item appears.

Standard symbols indicate whether or not later decisions follow the cited decision. Syllabus numbers being discussed are indicated for jurisdictions other than the Tax Court. Citing cases are listed by circuit.[207]

You can locate citations to articles discussing decisions (other than Tax

---

[206] Volumes 1-15 (1995 edition) covers the Federal Reporter; volumes 16-21 cover the Federal Supplement, Court of Claims, Claims Court, and Federal Claims Reporters. Hardbound and softbound supplements cover these reporter services.

[207] In all volumes, cases are arranged by level of court, starting with the Supreme Court. Within each grouping, the earliest cases are listed first. Although Shepard's indicates syllabus numbers, citing cases are not arranged with regard to these numbers.

Court) in Shepard's Federal Law Citations in Selected Law Reviews.

b. Federal Tax

The Federal Tax Citator volumes expand on the items covered by the general Shepard's service. Federal Tax Citator includes Tax Court Regular and Memorandum decisions as cited and citing cases. It indicates IRS acquiescences and nonacquiescences in adverse decisions; the online Shepard's also provides this information. Federal Tax Citations also includes other IRS documents and law review articles as citing material.

The Federal Tax Citator volumes use multiple versions of a case as cited material. You can, for example, check a Supreme Court decision through separate sections for United States Reports; United States Supreme Court Reports, Lawyers' Edition; Supreme Court Reporter; A.F.T.R.; and U.S.T.C. The Lawyers' Edition and Supreme Court Reporter sections omit Tax Court citations to Supreme Court decisions. Each reporter's section contains parallel citations to other case reporters.

Federal Tax Citator arranges citing cases by circuit. Although it indicates the syllabus number for cited cases, it does not list syllabus numbers in the sections covering A.F.T.R., U.S.T.C., or Tax Court Reports. [See Illustrations 11-5 and 11-6.]

Table 11-1. General Shepard's Volumes Covering Taxation

Cited Item	Shepard's Volumes
Constitution	Federal Statute Citations
Statutes	Federal Statute Citations
Treaties	Federal Statute Citations (only until 1995)
Regulations	Code of Federal Regulations Citations
Revenue Rulings	not covered
District Court	Federal Citations
Federal Claims	Federal Citations
Bankruptcy Court	Bankruptcy Citations
Court of Appeals	Federal Citations
Supreme Court	United States Citations

SECTION E. RIA CITATOR

The RIA Citator covers all federal taxes in each volume. Because of the alphabetical format, it does not subdivide volumes by level of court. This service consists of several hardbound and softbound volumes, which are supplemented monthly.[208]

RIA's format requires more time than would a comparable effort using the CCH service described below, but the time will be well spent. For most items it cites, the RIA Citator is the most useful of the various print citators.[209] Using the online version avoids the extra time commitment.

1. Constitution, Statutes, and Treaties

The RIA Citator does not give citations for materials construing the Constitution, statutes, or treaties.

2. Regulations and IRS Documents

Each volume has a Treasury Decisions and Rulings section covering IRS material, including private letter rulings. RIA lists cited regulations in T.D. (rather than regulations section) number order; it lists revenue rulings, revenue procedures, and other documents in numerical order.

RIA uses letters to indicate whether the subsequent material approved, rejected, or otherwise affected the cited item. Subsequent material includes judicial decisions, revenue rulings, letter rulings, and revenue procedures.

Case citations for citing decisions include citations to RIA case reporter services (A.F.T.R., RIA Tax Court Reports, and RIA Tax Court Memorandum Decisions) and citations to the official and West publications. With the exception of District Court subdivisions (e.g., DC NY instead of S.D.N.Y.), RIA indicates the geographical jurisdiction of each court hearing a case.

Citations for cited revenue rulings and procedures are given to the appropriate volume of the Cumulative Bulletin or to United States Tax Reporter. Letter rulings are listed by document number followed by a reference to United States Tax Reporter.

3. Judicial Decisions

The Court Decisions section of each volume lists cited and citing cases by taxpayer name. RIA lists cited cases alphabetically; it arranges citing cases

---

[208] The first series covers federal tax cases from 1796 to 1954. The second series begins with 1954.

[209] Shepard's Code of Federal Regulations Citations is, however, better for Treasury regulations because it cites by C.F.R. section. RIA and CCH cite to T.D.s, which can contain multiple regulations sections, and are less likely to be cited items.

according to the pertinent RIA syllabus number of the cited case. Within syllabus groupings, RIA lists cases by rank of the citing court, starting with the Supreme Court. Within each group of courts, the earliest cases generally appear first. Geographical jurisdiction is indicated for cited and citing decisions, but District Court subdivisions are not indicated.

RIA uses letters to indicate whether or not subsequent decisions follow the cited decision. Citations to subsequent decisions indicate the page where reference to the cited case is made, not the first page of the citing material. The online version gives both the first page and the citing page. Case citations are given to the RIA case reporters as well as to the official and West services.

This citator also includes citations to revenue rulings, letter rulings, and revenue procedures discussing the cited decision. It indicates IRS acquiescence or nonacquiescence in adverse judicial decisions. Citations for revenue rulings and procedures are given to the appropriate volume of the Cumulative Bulletin or to United States Tax Reporter; letter rulings and T.D.s are cited by number, followed by a reference to United States Tax Reporter.

SECTION F. CCH STANDARD FEDERAL TAX REPORTER—CITATOR[210]

You can use the two volumes in this service to locate both citing material and CCH topical discussions. Although these volumes list non-Tax Court cases involving estate and gift taxes and excise taxes, actual citations to those cases appear only in the Citator sections of Federal Estate and Gift Tax Reporter and Federal Excise Tax Reporter. Materials are supplemented quarterly. If you access the CCH Citator online through LexisNexis or the CCH Tax Research NetWork, you avoid using separate citator volumes.

While its compactness makes it the easiest system to use, this citator has the fewest useful features and omits, through editorial selection, many citing cases. It does provide paragraph cross-references to discussion in the SFTR compilation volumes.

1. Constitution, Statutes, and Treaties

No citations are given for materials construing the Constitution, statutes, or treaties.

---

[210] The remainder of this looseleaf service is described in Chapter 12.

2. Regulations and IRS Documents

The second citator volume contains Finding Lists for these items. Cited regulations are listed in T.D. (rather than regulations section) number order; rulings and procedures are listed in numerical order. Selected letter rulings are covered as cited material. Supplementation is included in the Current Finding Lists.[211]

Case citations for decisions discussing these items include citations to the CCH case reporter services (U.S.T.C., CCH Tax Court Reporter, and CCH Tax Court Memorandum Decisions); many citations include the official and West publications. CCH Decision numbers are given for Tax Court materials. The editors provide no indication as to how non-IRS citing material dealt with the cited material.

Cited rulings and procedures have their location in the Cumulative Bulletin or Internal Revenue Bulletin indicated. CCH lists citing items issued by the IRS only by number.

3. Judicial Decisions

This citator contains a main case table and quarterly supplements. Although citing cases from all jurisdictions are listed, CCH maintains its compact form by limiting itself to cases commented on or cited in SFTR.

CCH lists both cited and citing cases by taxpayer name. It lists cited cases alphabetically. It indicates geographical jurisdiction for decisions rendered by District Courts (but not subdivisions within a state) or Courts of Appeals.

CCH does not indicate which syllabus number is involved in the citing case; likewise, it does not indicate whether the citing material follows or distinguishes the cited decision. Its case citations refer to the CCH case reporters and to the official and West services. Citations to subsequent decisions in services other than U.S.T.C. indicate the first page of the citing case, not the page where reference is made to the cited material.[212]

CCH also includes numerical citations to revenue rulings, letter rulings, and revenue procedures discussing the cited decision. CCH also indicates IRS acquiescence or nonacquiescence in adverse judicial decisions.

---

[211] New rulings (without citing matter) are included weekly in the SFTR New Matters volume.

[212] Citations to U.S.T.C. are to the paragraph number assigned the case, not to the U.S.T.C. page number.

SECTION G. WEST'S KEYCITE

When LexisNexis acquired full ownership of Shepard's, Westlaw substituted its KeyCite system for Shepard's citators. Unlike the systems discussed in Sections D through F, KeyCite is available only online. After you locate a primary source on Westlaw, you click the KeyCite icon to obtain citations to later materials included in the Westlaw database. Alternatively, if you already have a citation, you can go directly to KeyCite and enter that citation.

When you use KeyCite, Westlaw takes you to a KC History screen. This screen provides citations and hyperlinks to the decision's prior and subsequent history and to so-called negative holdings.[213] To obtain a more complete list, including positive and neutral citations and secondary source materials, select the KC Citing Ref option.

Citing material is arranged by category (e.g., Discussed, Cited, Mentioned). Within categories, judicial decisions are arranged by level of court. Within each level, the most recent material is listed first. KeyCite indicates both the first page and the citing page for later material. If the number of citing sources is large enough, categories may be subdivided into topics.

Differences between KC History and KC Citing Ref are covered in more detail below in the discussion of various primary sources. Because KeyCite generally provides hyperlinks to the citing material, the discussion below does not indicate to which reporter service citations are made.

1. Constitution, Statutes and Treaties

KC Citing Ref provides citations to cases that have interpreted constitutional provisions. It also lists articles and other secondary source materials. KC Citing Ref provides citations to cases that have interpreted or discussed the constitutionality of statutes; cases are arranged by issue.[214] KeyCite also indicates IRS interpretations.

KC History alerts you to pending legislation and provides information about prior amendments to the statute.

---

[213] Flags indicate varying degrees of negative history. Stars indicate the depth of treatment. [See Illustration 11-14.]

[214] The service includes pre-1954 Code cases, but with some erroneous results. For example, KeyCiting 26 USC 213 (medical expenses) yielded Klein v. Commissioner, 84 F.2d 310 (7th Cir. 1936). That case had nothing to do with medical expenses but did involve section 213 of the Revenue Act of 1924.

2. Regulations and IRS Documents

KC Citing Ref provides citations to judicial decisions, officially published and publicly available IRS documents, and secondary sources interpreting regulations and IRS documents. It uses flags to indicate negative history items. KC History provides T.D. numbers and dates for regulations. It provides dates for IRS documents; if the document appears in the Cumulative Bulletin, KC History also provides that information.

3. Judicial Decisions

KC History provides negative history and IRS action (e.g., acquiescences). KC Citing Ref includes positive and neutral history and citations by administrative agencies, including IRS documents such as revenue rulings and field service advice.

SECTION H. ILLUSTRATIONS

The illustrations below indicate the results obtained using *Fox v. Commissioner* as the cited case in four print and four online citator services. Illustration order follows the order of Sections D through G; online services are illustrated after print versions.

The citing case of *Oelze v. Commissioner* will be used to indicate different results reached by different citators. *Oelze* begins this section as Illustration 11-2. Other relevant citator differences are covered in the notes accompanying the illustrations.

- Shepard's Federal Citations (print) [Illustration 11-3]

- Shepard's Federal Tax Citator (print) [Illustrations 11-4 through 11-6]

- Shepard's Citations (online) [Illustration 11-7]

- RIA Citator 2nd (print) [Illustration 11-8]

- RIA Citator 2nd (online) [Illustration 11-9]

- CCH Standard Federal Tax Reporter—Citator (print) [Illustration 11-10]

- CCH Tax Research NetWork—Citator (online) [Illustration 11-11]

- Westlaw KeyCite (online) [Illustrations 11-12 through 11-15]

Illustration 11-2. Text of Oelze v. Commissioner

53 A.F.T.R. 2d 84-912 (726 F.2d 165)

PER CURIAM:

The petition for rehearing is denied.

In this petition for rehearing, the taxpayer, Richard E. Oelze, urges this court to follow the holding of the United States Court of Appeals for the Seventh Circuit in Fox v. Commissioner, 718 F.2d 251 [52 AFTR 2d 83-6083] (7th Cir.1983) and hold that the Tax Court may not dismiss a taxpayer's petition for redetermination of tax liability for failure to comply with discovery orders unless the court first finds that the taxpayer's failure to comply is willful and in bad faith, and that the taxpayer totally failed to respond to the discovery orders.

[1] In Eisele v. Commissioner, 580 F.2d 805 [42 AFTR 2d 78-5886] (5th Cir.1978), this court, in a half-page per curiam opinion, affirmed dismissal by the Tax Court pursuant to Rule 104, noting simply that the dismissal is "explicitly authorized" by the rules. In the case before us here, it is unnecessary to decide whether this circuit should follow the Seventh Circuit in imposing stricter standards for dismissals for failure to comply with discovery orders, pursuant to Eisele. This is true because even under the analysis of Fox, the Tax Court's dismissal is justified in this case. The taxpayer's continued failure to cooperate with the Commissioner, the necessity for four orders to comply with the Commissioner's discovery requests, the taxpayer's continuous reliance on a baseless fifth amendment claim, and the taxpayer's last-minute attempt to comply with the discovery order all demonstrate that Oelze acted wilfully. Additionally, the Tax Court issued four separate discovery orders, some explicitly warning the taxpayer that failure to comply would result in dismissal of the case. Though the taxpayer finally did partially comply with one of the orders, he did so only after repeated and total failure to supply the Commissioner with the information he requested. Such partial compliance under these circumstances cannot serve to exonerate the taxpayer from willful failure to comply with the orders of the court.

Oelze's petition for rehearing is Denied.

→The *Oelze* decision appears in three case reporter services. The version above comes from A.F.T.R. You can also find this case in F.2d and U.S.T.C.

→Note the language in the opinion: "In the case before us here, it is unnecessary to decide whether this circuit should follow the Seventh Circuit in imposing stricter standards for dismissals .... This is true because even under the analysis of Fox, the Tax Court's dismissal is justified in this case." Does this indicate agreement with the holding in *Fox*?

→Note also the [1]. A.F.T.R. assigned one syllabus number to *Oelze.*

Illustration 11-3. Excerpt from Shepard's Federal Citations

—251—	—251—	—251—
Fox v Internal	Fox v Internal	Fox v
Revenue	Revenue	Commissioner
1983	1983	1983
	Cir. 7	Cir. 7
s 60TCt 1058	147F3d635	239F3d^{5}936
s60TCt 1123		
125FRD321		
125FRD339		
Cir. 4		
916F2d^{4}174		
Cir. 5		
f 726F2d^{5}165←		
Cir. 7		
852F2d^{2}283		
995F2d^{2}1381		
830FS^{2}1230		
e 110FRD^{2}267		
Cir. DC		
777F2d44		
c 82TCt 601		
88TCt 1499		
88TCt1500		
99TCt541		
1983TCM#786		
1984TCM#567		
1984TCM#638		
1984TCM#639		
1990TCM#637		
Wyo		
882 P2d820		

→The print Shepard's volumes applicable to the *Fox* decision are in the Shepard's Federal Citations set that covers the Federal Reporter. As of mid-May 2002, that set has five components—1995, Supplement 1995-1999, Supplement 1999-2000, Supplement 2000-2001, and Cumulative Supplement May 1, 2002.

→Only three of the components had citations to *Fox*. Column 1 reproduces the citations from 1995 volume 12; column 2, from 1995-1999 volume 2; column 3, from 2000-2001 volume 1.

→Note the change in the 2000-2001 volume to "Commissioner" instead of "Internal Revenue."

→*Oelze* is marked with a ← in all illustrations for Shepard's.

Illustration 11-4. Excerpt from Federal Tax Citator: Fed. Rep.

—251—
Fox v Internal
Revenue
1983
(52AF2d6083)
(83UTC¶ 9622)
s 60TCt 1058
s 60TCt 1123
f 53AF2d912←
   56AF2d6465
   66AF2d5721
f 84UTC¶ 9274←
   85UTC¶ 9815
   90UTC¶ 50538
c 82TCt601
   88TCt1499
   88TCt1500
   99TCt541
c 82TCt#46
   88TCt#81
   88TCt#84
   99TCt#28
   1983TCM#786
   1984TCM#567
   1984TCM#638
   1984TCM#639
   1990TCM#637
   125FRD321
   125FRD339
      Cir. DC
   777F2d44
      Cir. 4
   916F2d^{4}174
      Cir. 5
f 726F2d^{5}165←
      Cir. 7
   852F2d^{2}283
   995F2d^{2}1381
   830FS^{2}1230
e 110FRD^{2}267
      Wyo
   882 P2d820

—251—
Cir. 6
75AF2d1500
95UTC¶50227

—251—
Cir. 7
81AF2d2468
98-2UTC¶50511
147F3d635
239F3d^{5}936

→The Shepard's Tax volumes covering Federal Reporter and applicable to the *Fox* decision are 1995 (column 1), Supplement 1996-1998 (column 2), and Supplement 1998-2002 (column 3).

→Tax Court (TCt) decisions are cited twice, by page and decision number.

Illustration 11-5. Excerpt from Federal Tax Citator: A.F.T.R.

—6083—	—6083—	—6083—
Fox v Internal	Cir. 6	Cir. 7
Revenue	75AF2d1500	81AF2d2468
1983		147F3d635
(83UTC¶ 9622)		239F3d936
(718F2d251)		

```
      (83UTC¶ 9622)
      (718F2d251)
  s  60TCt 1058
  s  60TCt 1123
  f  53AF2d912←
     56AF2d6465
     66AF2d5721
  c  82TCt601
     88TCt1499
     88TCt1500
     99TCt541
  c  82TCt#46
     88TCt#81
     88TCt#84
     99TCt#28
     1983TCM#786
     1984TCM#567
     1984TCM#638
     1984TCM#639
     1985TCM#84
     1990TCM#637
     125FRD321
     125FRD339
        Cir. DC
     777F2d44
        Cir. 4
     916F2d174
        Cir. 5
  f  726F2d165←
        Cir. 7
     852F2d283
     995F2d1381
  e  110FRD267
        Wyo
     882 P2d820
```

→The print Shepard's Tax volumes covering A.F.T.R. and applicable to the *Fox* decision are 1995 (column 1), Supplement 1996-1998 (column 2), and Supplement 1998-2002 (column 3).

→Tax Court (TCt) decisions are cited both by page and decision number.

→The materials covering A.F.T.R. delete the superscript indicating issue even for Federal Reporter cases. Compare Illustration 11-4.

Illustration 11-6. Excerpt from Federal Tax Citator: U.S.T.C.

—¶ 9622—	—¶ 9622—	—¶ 9622—
Fox v Internal	Cir. 6	Cir. 7
Revenue	95UTC¶ 50227	98-2UTC¶ 50511
1983		147F3d635
(52AF2d6083)		239F3d936
(718F2d251)		

```
s  60TCt 1058
s  60TCt 1123
f  84UTC¶ 9274←
   85UTC¶ 9815
   90UTC¶ 50538
c  82TCt601
   88TCt1499
   88TCt1500
   99TCt541
c  82TCt#46
   88TCt#81
   88TCt#84
   99TCt#28
   1983TCM#786
   1984TCM#567
   1984TCM#638
   1984TCM#639
   1990TCM#637
   125FRD321
   125FRD339
      Cir. DC
   777F2d44
      Cir. 4
   916F2d174
      Cir. 5
f  726F2d165←
      Cir. 7
   852F2d283
   995F2d1381
e  110FRD267
      Wyo
   882 P2d820
```

→The print Shepard's Tax volumes covering U.S.T.C. and applicable to the *Fox* decision are 1995 (column 1), Supplement 1996-1998 (column 2), and Supplement 1998-2002 (column 3).

→Tax Court (TCt) decisions are cited both by page and decision number.

→The materials covering U.S.T.C. delete the superscript indicating issue even for Federal Reporter cases. Compare Illustration 11-4.

Illustration 11-7. Excerpt from Shepard's on LexisNexis

Fox v. Commissioner, 718 F.2d 251, 1983 U.S. App. LEXIS 16239, 52 A.F.T.R.2d (RIA) 6083, 37 Fed. R. Serv. 2d (Callaghan) 1233, 83-2 U.S. Tax Cas. (CCH) P9622 (7th Cir. 1983)

CITING DECISIONS (26 citing decisions)

4TH CIRCUIT - COURT OF APPEALS

Cited by:
Hillig v. Commissioner, 916 F.2d 171, 1990 U.S. App. LEXIS 18188, 66 A.F.T.R.2d (RIA) 5721, 17 Fed. R. Serv. 3d (Callaghan) 1164, 90-2 U.S. Tax Cas. (CCH) P50538 (4th Cir. 1990)*{Caution}*
> Cited by:
> 916 F.2d 171 p.174

5TH CIRCUIT - COURT OF APPEALS

Followed by:
Oelze v. Commissioner, 726 F.2d 165, 1983 U.S. App. LEXIS 14118, 53 A.F.T.R.2d (RIA) 912, 84-1 U.S. Tax Cas. (CCH) P9274 (5th Cir. 1983)*{Analysis}*
> Followed by:
> 726 F.2d 165 p.165

6TH CIRCUIT - COURT OF APPEALS

Cited by:
McFerren v. Commissioner, 1995 U.S. App. LEXIS 4732, 75 A.F.T.R.2d (RIA) 1498, 95 TNT 58-11, 95-1 U.S. Tax Cas. (CCH) P50227 (6th Cir. 1995)*{Analysis}*
> Cited by:
> 75 A.F.T.R.2d (RIA) 1498 p.1500
> 95-1 U.S. Tax Cas. (CCH) P50227

7TH CIRCUIT - COURT OF APPEALS

Cited by:
Golant v. Levy (In re Golant), 239 F.3d 931, 2001 U.S. App. LEXIS 2057, 37 Bankr. Ct. Dec. (LRP) 106, 48 Fed. R. Serv. 3d (Callaghan) 1116 (7th Cir. Ill. 2001)*{Analysis}*
> Cited by:
> 239 F.3d 931 p.936

Cited by:
Shepherd v. Commissioner, 147 F.3d 633, 1998 U.S. App. LEXIS 13610, 81 A.F.T.R.2d (RIA) 2466, 98-2 U.S. Tax Cas. (CCH) P50511 (7th Cir. 1998)*{Positive}*
> Cited by:
> 147 F.3d 633 p.635

Cited by:
Crown Life Ins. Co. v. Craig, 995 F.2d 1376, 1993 U.S. App. LEXIS 12943, 26 Fed. R. Serv. 3d (Callaghan) 113 (7th Cir. Ill. 1993)*{Caution}*
> Cited by:
> 995 F.2d 1376 p.1381

Cited by:
Patterson v. Coca-Cola Bottling Co., 852 F.2d 280, 1988 U.S. App. LEXIS 9965, 11 Fed. R. Serv. 3d (Callaghan) 952 (7th Cir. Ill. 1988)*{Analysis}*
> Cited by:
> 852 F.2d 280 p.283

7TH CIRCUIT - U.S. DISTRICT COURTS

Not followed by:
Select Creations v. Paliafito Am., 830 F. Supp. 1223, 1993 U.S. Dist. LEXIS 11858 (E.D. Wis. 1993)*{Caution}*

➔In its Full option, Shepard's on LexisNexis cited 26 cases and articles in Virginia Tax Review and University of California-Davis Law Review. In its Quick option, it cited five cases.

➔The LexisNexis version includes hyperlinks to the citing materials.

Illustration 11-8. Excerpt from RIA Citator 2nd

FOX, GEORGE J. v COMM., 52 AFTR2d 83-6083, 718
    F2d 251 (USCA 7, 10-6-83)
k—Vermouth, Jon W., 88 TC 1499, 88 PH TC 763 [See
    52 AFTR2d 83-6086, 718 F2d 254]
e—Figura, Donald W., 1984 P-H TC Memo 84-2304 [See
    52 AFTR2d 83-6086]
q-l—Oelze, Richard E. v Comm., 53 AFTR2d 84-913,
    726 F2d 165 (USCA 5)
e-1—Aruba Bonaire Curacao Trust Co., Ltd., Trustee v
    Comm., 56 AFTR2d 85-6469, 777 F2d 44 (CADC)
q-1—Dusha, Edward P., 82 TC 601, 605, 82 PH TC 303,
    315
e-1—Douglas, Floyd E., 1983 PH TC Memo 83-3288
f-1—Kuhn, Cynthia J., 1984 PH TC Memo 840-2600
f-1—Baranski, Richard R. & Geraldine A., 1984 PH TC
    Memo 84-2603
e-1—Williamson, Lucas F., Jr., 1985 PH TC Memo
    85-390

FOX, GEORGE J. v COMM., 52 AFTR2d 83-6083, 718
    F2d 251, 83-2 USTC ¶9622, (CA 7, 10-6-83)
e—Hillig, Bernard J. v Comm., 66 AFTR 2d 90-5723, 916
    F2d 174, (CA4), [See 52 AFTR2d 83-6085, 718 F2d 255]
e-1—McFerren, Charles S. v. Com., 75 AFTR 2d 95-1500,
    (CA6)
e-1—Harper, Wally, 99 TC 541, 99 TCR 274
f-1—Geodesco, Inc., 1990 PH TC Memo 90-3107, 90-3108

FOX, GEORGE J. v COMM., 52 AFTR2d 83-6083, 718
    F2d 251, 83-2 USTC ¶9622, (CA 7, 10/6/83)

e—Shepherd, Charles E. v. Com., 81 AFTR 2d 98-2468,
    147 F3d 635, (CA7), [See 52 AFTR 2d 83-6085, 718 F2d
    255]

➔Because *Fox* was decided after 1977, I ignored all volumes of the original Prentice-Hall Citator and the first volume of RIA Citator 2nd.

➔To obtain all citations to *Fox*, I checked bound volumes for 1978-1989 (volume 2), 1990-1996 (volume 3), 1997-2001 (volume 4). Those results appear in order above. The April 2002 Cumulative Supplement had no additional cases.

➔Note the reference to q-1. RIA uses this notation to indicate that *Oelze* questioned the result in the first syllabus number in *Fox*. In its print version of *Fox*, P-H assigned the case only one syllabus number. In F.2d, West assigned it seven numbers.

Illustration 11-9. Excerpt from RIA Citator 2nd on Westlaw

FOX, GEORGE J. v COMM.
52 AFTR 2d 83-6083, **718 F2d 251**, 83-2 USTC ¶ 9622
CA7
10/6/1983

Cited favorably
Hillig, Bernard J. v Comm., 66 AFTR 2d 90-5721, 90-5723, 916 F2d 171, 174 (CA4) [See 52 AF

Cited favorably
Shepherd, Charles E. v. Com., 81 AFTR 2d 98-2466, 98-2468, 147 F3d 633, 635 (CA7) [See 52 .

Cases reconciled
Vermouth, Jon W., 88 TC 1488, 1499, 88 PH TC 763 [See 52 AFTR 2d 83- 6086, 718 F2d 254]

Cited favorably
Figura, Donald W., 1984 PH TC Memo 84,567, 84-2304 [See 52 AFTR 2d 83- 6086]

Decision questioned (1)
Oelze, Richard E. v Comm., 53 AFTR 2d 84-912, 84-913, 726 F2d 165, 165 (CA5)

➔The online citator lists 14 citing cases, categorized as "cited favorably," "cases reconciled," "decision questioned," and "reasoning followed."

➔RIA lists cases with no syllabus number first and then those it assigned syllabus number 1. Within groups, cases are listed by court level; within each level, the earliest cases are listed first.

Illustration 11-10. Excerpt from CCH SFTR Citator

Fox, George
• CA-7—(aff'g unreported TC), 83-2 USTC ¶ 9622; 718 F2d 251
McFerren, CA-6, 95-1USTC ¶ 50,227
Harper, TC, Dec. 48,610, 99 TC 533
Shepherd, CA-7, 98-2 USTC ¶ 50,511, 147 F3d 633
Oelze, CA-5, 84-1 USTC ¶ 9274, 726 F2d 165
Geodesco, Inc., TC, Dec. 47,039(M), 60 TCM 1452, TC Memo. 1990-637
Dusha, Dec. 41,123, 82 TC 592
Douglas, TC, Dec. 40,715(M), 47 TCM 791, TC Memo. 1983-786

➔CCH provides both U.S.T.C. and F.2d citations.

➔CCH does not indicate how *Oelze* treated *Fox*; it indicates only that it cited *Fox*. In addition, it does not include syllabus numbers.

➔CCH lists seven other decisions, all in the main Citator section.

Illustration 11-11. Excerpt from CCH Tax Research NetWork

CCH-CITATOR, 2002FED, Main Citator Table, Fox, George

Fox, George

- **CA-7**--(aff'g unreported TC), 83-2 USTC ¶9622; 718 F2d 251

  McFerren, CA-6, 95-1 USTC ¶50,227

  Harper, TC, Dec. 48,610, 99 TC 533

  Shepherd, CA-7, 98-2 USTC ¶50,511, 147 F3d 633

  Oelze, CA-5, 84-1 USTC ¶9274, 726 F2d 165

  Geodesco, Inc., TC, Dec. 47,039(M), 60 TCM 1452, TC Memo. 1990-637

  Dusha, TC, Dec. 41,123, 82 TC 592

  Douglas, TC, Dec. 40,715(M), 47 TCM 791, TC Memo. 1983-786

➔The online CCH Citator provided the same seven items as the print version.

➔Neither version of the CCH Citator lists later decisions by court, by year, or alphabetically.

➔The online CCH service provides hyperlinks to the citing material.

Illustration 11-12. Excerpt from Westlaw KeyCite Access

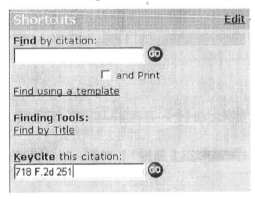

➔With an online citator, you can find citations after you've read the original case. If don't need to read the case, you can go directly to a citator screen and enter the cited case. This illustration shows that method on KeyCite.

Illustration 11-13. Excerpt from Westlaw KC History

FOR EDUCATIONAL USE ONLY
History
(Showing 3 documents)

Direct History

➡ 1 Fox v. C.I.R., 718 F.2d 251, 52 A.F.T.R.2d
       83-6083, 37 Fed.R.Serv.2d 1233, 83-2
       USTC P 9622 (7th Cir. Oct 06, 1983) (NO.
       81-2869, 81-2870)

Negative Indirect History
Disagreed With by
  2 Dusha v. Commissioner of Internal
      Revenue, 82 T.C. No. 47, 82 T.C. 592, Tax

➡KC History yielded the case itself and two negative citations. It did not list *Oelze*.

Illustration 11-14. Excerpt from Westlaw KC Citing Ref

FOR EDUCATIONAL USE ONLY
Citing References
(Showing 41 documents)

Negative Cases
Disagreed With by
  1 Dusha v. Commissioner of Internal
      Revenue, 82 T.C. 592, 601+, 82 T.C. No. 47,
      47+, Tax Ct. Rep. (CCH) 41,123, 41123+
      (U.S.Tax Ct. Apr 09, 1984) (NO. 23713-82)
      ✯✯✯✯✯ HN: 2,5,7

➡KC Citing Ref yielded 41 documents, including 22 cases classified as negative or positive (discussed, cited, mentioned), two administrative proceedings, and 17 secondary sources.

➡KC Citing Ref found *Oelze* and classified it as "cited," one of the positive categories. [Illustration 11-15.]

Illustration 11-15. Excerpt from Westlaw KC Citing Ref

★ ★ ★ Discussed

C 3 Geodesco, Inc. v. C. I. R., 1990 WL 205212, *205212+, T.C. Memo. 1990-637, 1990-637+, 60 T.C.M. (CCH) 1452, 1452+, T.C.M. (P-H) P 90,637, 90637+ (U.S.Tax Ct. Dec 18, 1990) (NO. 43972-86, 36394-87) ❞ HN: 2,5

★ ★ Cited

H 4 Roger J. Spott, D.D.S., P.A. v. C.I.R., 875 F.2d 316, 316+ (4th Cir. May 22, 1989) (Table, text in WESTLAW, NO. 88-2926, 88-2927) HN: 2,5

H 5 Oelze v. C.I.R., 726 F.2d 165, 165+, 53 A.F.T.R.2d 84-912, 84-912+, 84-1 USTC P 9274, 9274+ (5th Cir. Dec 28, 1983) (NO. 83-4084) HN: 6

C 6 McFerren v. C.I.R., 48 F.3d 1219, 1219+, 75 A.F.T.R.2d 95-1498, 95-1498+, 95-1 USTC P 50,227, 50227+ (6th Cir. Mar 08, 1995) (Table, text in WESTLAW, NO. 94-1035) HN: 2,5

▷ 7 In re Golant, 239 F.3d 931, 936, 48 Fed.R.Serv.3d 1116, 37 Bankr.Ct.Dec. 106, 106 (7th Cir.(Ill.) Feb 12, 2001) (NO. 00-1205) HN: 2,5

→Note the flag for *In re Golant*.

SECTION I. UPDATING SERVICES IN LIEU OF CITATORS

The citator services discussed above cover most types of primary authority. You can also determine continued validity for revenue rulings and procedures using two services discussed in greater detail in Chapters 12 and 16. However, these services have an inherent limitation. They use only IRS material as citing material and ignore judicial decisions citing to rulings.

If you are interested in finding only IRS material or if you need a citator that uses a Code section format, these are available:

• Mertens, Law of Federal Income Taxation—Rulings (Chapter 12)

• IRS Bulletin Index-Digest System (Chapter 16) (1954-1993/94)

There are several differences between these services. The IRS service has separate volumes for each tax—income, estate and gift, and excise. It subdivides cited material by Code section and, when relevant, by regulations section. Mertens subdivides cited material by Code section, often using smaller subdivisions such as subsections and paragraphs.

The IRS service provides digests of citing items elsewhere in the service. Mertens subscribers have access to the full text of the revenue rulings and procedures used as cited and citing items.

SECTION J. PROBLEMS

1. Your instructor will assign you a primary source item to check in as many citators as are available to you. Make a list of differences in citing documents and a list of any differences in treatment. If you find differences in treatment, go to the actual citing ma\erial to determine which citators were correct.

2. Using Shepard's Federal Tax Citator, make a list of documents involving UIL

   a. 354.00-00

   b. 3121.05-00

   c. 6201.07-03

   d. 7872.00-00

3. Several of the problems in other chapters are easily completed with a citator. If you initially completed a problem using a citator, redo it using a different publisher's service and compare your results.

CHAPTER 12. LOOSELEAF SERVICES, ENCYCLOPEDIAS, AND TREATISES

You may wish to consult explanatory materials early in the research effort, perhaps even before you read the relevant statutes.[215] The texts described in this chapter may provide insight into the problem being researched, and you can draw upon their liberal use of citations for a preliminary reading list of cases and administrative pronouncements. Each is updated at frequent intervals, and most have at least one related newsletter.

While general research texts would list some of these materials as looseleaf services and others as legal encyclopedias or treatises,[216] those classifications are less significant in this context than are classifications based upon their formats. Most of them take a subject matter approach, but two of the best-known services are arranged in Code section order.

SECTION A. CODE SECTION ARRANGEMENT

The Commerce Clearing House[217] and Research Institute of America[218] looseleaf services take essentially the same approach. Each service's **compilation volumes** print the full texts of Code sections and Treasury regulations along with editorial explanations. An annotation section listing cases and rulings follows each section. Users wanting ready access to the text of the law while they are reading explanations of it will appreciate this format.

---

[215] In appropriate cases you can use these textual materials to ascertain which statutes are involved. In addition, you should consult these materials whenever you desire additional textual information.

[216] See Fundamentals of Legal Research chs. 14, 16 and 18, for further discussion of these research tools. The annotated law reports discussed in that text's Chapter 7 also provide textual material.

[217] Standard Federal Tax Reporter (income tax); Federal Estate and Gift Tax Reporter; Federal Excise Tax Reporter. CCH also publishes subject matter format services (e.g., Federal Tax Service, an online service).

[218] United States Tax Reporter—Income Taxes; United States Tax Reporter—Estate & Gift Taxes; United States Tax Reporter—Excise Taxes. RIA also publishes subject matter format services (e.g., Federal Tax Coordinator 2d).

Because of the arrangement described above, problems involving multiple Code sections do not receive comprehensive discussion. Although the publishers supplement their looseleaf materials with newsletters, special pamphlets, and planning aids, Code-based services are not as suited as are subject-based services for learning about issues involving several Code sections.

Although each service is arranged in Code section order, all materials are assigned paragraph numbers. A "paragraph" can be several pages long or the size of a traditional paragraph. Unless noted otherwise, each service cross-references between paragraph numbers, not between page numbers.

These services have subject matter indexes; their format makes Code section indexes unnecessary. New material is sent to subscribers weekly for insertion in the compilation volumes or in a separate updating volume. These new developments are indexed according to the paragraph in the main compilation to which they relate, i.e., in Code section order.

Libraries often carry both services,[219] and users eventually develop a preference for one or the other. As each service's annotations are editorially selected, use of both can reduce the risk of missing a valuable annotation although it may substantially increase research time. The extra material obtained rarely justifies the additional time involved.

The two services are discussed individually below.

1. Standard Federal Tax Reporter

The discussion of this CCH looseleaf service follows the format in which it is arranged. Several volumes, such as the Citator, are discussed in greater detail elsewhere in this text; appropriate cross-references to those discussions appear here. A Taxes on Parade newsletter provides cross-references to SFTR and to CCH's Federal Tax Service.

a. Code Volumes. These volumes print, in Code section order, all provisions involving income, gift and estate, employment, and excise taxes as well as procedural provisions. A brief explanation of amendments (including the Public Law number and section and effective dates) follows each Code provision. These explanations include information about prior statutory language. These volumes are updated at intervals following Code amendments.

Volume I contains tables providing cross-references between the 1939 and

---

[219] The library may carry the looseleaf, CD-ROM, or online version.

1954 Codes (Tables I and II). Table III indicates sections of the 1986 Code that refer to other sections [Illustration 5-8].[220] As the Code itself is not fully cross-referenced, this table is valuable for researching an unfamiliar area. But, because related Code sections may not refer to each other at all, you should also use the annotated materials discussed in this chapter to familiarize yourself with interrelated Code sections.

Volume I includes lists of Acts Supplementing the 1954 and the 1986 Codes. These lists provide the Public Law number, bill number, date, and Statutes at Large citation for each act; they include popular names for several acts. These lists are in Public Law number order. Each act is arranged in act section order; the list indicates every Code section affected by an act section. Coverage begins in 1971.[221]

Volume I also includes a Public Laws Amending the Internal Revenue Code section. It lists Public Law number and Congress, popular name, and enactment date. These materials begin in mid-1954 and are in Public Law number order.

Volume I includes both a Topical Index [Illustration 3-2] and a Table of Contents listing all Code sections in order.

Volume II prints the text of non-Code statutory provisions affecting federal taxes in the Related Statutes section. That section has a subject matter table of contents. Volume II also includes subject matter and Code section lists of 1954-1966 amendments to the 1939 Code. The Code section list includes Public Law number and Congress, act section, and SFTR paragraph number.

b. Index Volume and Compilation Volume 1. Both volumes provide useful tables and other reference material. Because it covers the annotations in addition to the Code, the topical index in the Index volume is far more detailed than the index in Code volume I. The Index volume also includes:

- Tax calendars
- IRS Service Center addresses
- Exemption and Standard Deduction Amounts
- Tax rates since 1909
- Withholding tables
- Depreciation tables—Bulletin F; class life ADR; MACRS

---

[220] As of mid-May 2002, this table was current through January 1, 1999.

[221] Some libraries may have retained a special 1971 SFTR publication covering earlier acts.

- Annuity tables, including valuation for life estates and remainders
- Savings bond redemption tables
- Interest rate tables
  applicable federal rates since 1984
  interest on overpayments/underpayments
- Low income housing credit rates and recapture information
- Per diem rates
- Checklists
  for completing tax returns
  income and deductions
  medical expenses—summary of rulings and cases
  real property tax dates by state
  tax elections
  information return filing
  disaster areas declared in preceding year
- Tax terms—explanatory definitions of commonly used jargon

Compilation volume 1 includes the following reference material:

- Tax planning by topic—e.g., choice of entity; filing status
- Inflation adjustments for several years—by topic and Code section
- Return preparer information
- Who Is the Taxpayer?—discussion and annotations
- Constitutional and tax protest materials, including annotations

c. Compilation Volumes. Volumes 1-18 contain, in Code section order, the full text of the Code, proposed, temporary, and final regulations,[222] and digest-annotations to revenue rulings and revenue procedures, publicly available IRS documents such as letter rulings, and judicial decisions. [Illustration 12-1.] An alphabetical index is provided whenever the annotations section is lengthy. There is an editorial explanation, including citations to the annotations, for each Code provision.

Immediately after each Code section, the editors indicate which Public Laws have amended it and print text of, or citations to, committee reports; a brief T.D. history also follows regulations sections. The pre-amendment text is omitted for both Code and regulations sections. If a regulation does

---

[222] Because regulations are printed in Code section order, regulations from different parts of 26 C.F.R. (or even from other titles of C.F.R.) appear together. Because regulations from other C.F.R. titles follow their own prefix system, it is critical that your citation indicate Treas. Reg. (or 26 C.F.R.) for Treasury regulations and the other C.F.R. title for other regulations. See, e.g., 40 C.F.R. § 20.1, which appears in SFTR with Code section 169. If this were a Treasury regulation, the prefix 20 would indicate an estate tax regulation and the 1 following it would indicate Code section 1 (which covers income tax rates).

not reflect Code amendments, SFTR indicates that fact at the top of each page.

The compilation volume covering taxation of foreign income also includes summaries of United States tax treaties.

Repealed tax provisions may be re-enacted in whole or part. Volume 18 includes annotations arising under expired laws, such as excess profits taxes. These will be useful for historical research as well as in the event of re-enactment.

Volume 18 also lists IRS and Tax Court forms (numerically and alphabetically), IRS publications (numerically), Treasury and IRS personnel, and IRS procedural rules.

d. New Matters Volume. The compilation volumes' annotations receive little updating during the year involved. Instead, recent material is indexed in the New Matters volume (volume 19). Because the Cumulative Index (including a Latest Additions supplement) is based on the paragraph numbers used in the compilation volumes, it is easy to use the New Matters volume to find recent developments. [Illustrations 12-2 and 12-4.]

SFTR reproduces the updating material as follows:

• New Matters volume—texts of revenue rulings and procedures; digests of Tax Court Regular and Memorandum Opinions

• U.S.T.C. Advance Sheets volume—texts of decisions rendered by all other courts

• Compilation volumes—Code and regulations.

The New Matters volume digests a limited number of publicly available IRS documents. [Illustrations 12-3 and 12-5.]

The New Matters volume has several other helpful features. In addition to a Topical Index of current year developments, there are sections devoted to highlights of important new developments (CCH Comments and CCH Tax Focus and Features). These items, which are covered in the Topical Index, also contain cross-references to the compilation volumes.

This volume prints preambles for current year Treasury Decisions. It also indicates where all final and temporary regulations appear in the SFTR service.

A Case Table (including a supplement for Latest Additions) lists each year's decisions alphabetically. It indicates (1) which trial court is involved and where the decision appears in the U.S.T.C. Advance Sheets or SFTR New Matters volumes;[223] (2) appeals by either side and IRS acquiescence or nonacquiescence in unfavorable decisions; and (3) outcome at the appellate level.

A Supreme Court Docket, which also lists cases alphabetically, includes a brief digest of the issues involved and their disposition. This table includes cases in which the Court denies certiorari.

A Finding List of Rulings cross-references current year IRS documents to the appropriate paragraphs in volume 19. Consult this list in addition to the Finding Lists in the SFTR Citator when checking the status of IRS items.

e. U.S. Tax Cases (U.S.T.C.) Advance Sheets Volume. This volume contains the preambles to proposed income tax regulations. Lists of proposed income tax regulations appear in both topical and Code section formats; the topical format is arranged chronologically rather than alphabetically.

This volume also contains the texts of income tax decisions rendered by courts other than the Tax Court.[224] You can locate these items using the Cumulative Index to Current Year Developments in the New Matters volume. Decisions appear in the order in which they are received rather than in Code section order. These decisions will later be issued in hardbound volumes as part of the U.S.T.C. reporter service discussed in Chapter 10.

f. Citator. You can use these volumes, which list decisions alphabetically, to determine if subsequent decisions have affected earlier items. The Citator also covers revenue rulings, revenue procedures, other IRS items, and Treasury Decisions.

The Citator provides cross-references to discussions of cases and rulings in the compilation volumes. The second volume includes citations to committee reports for sections amending the 1954 and 1986 Codes. These materials are in Code section order. The SFTR Citator is discussed in Chapter 11.

---

[223] It does not indicate the state for District Court and does not print every unreported District Court decision. Bankruptcy Court cases are listed as BC-DC (Bankruptcy Court-District Court).

[224] Preambles and recent court decisions involving estate and gift taxes or excise taxes appear in the CCH services covering those topics. Court decisions involving all taxes appear in the U.S.T.C. hardbound volumes.

Illustration 12-1. Excerpt from SFTR Compilation Volume

CCH-ANNO, 2002FED ¶7438.80, Certain Fringe Benefits: Working condition fringe benefits.--

Related Documents:		
⅋⅋ [IRC]	⅋⅋ [Current Developments]	⅋⅋ [CCH Explanations]

Certain Fringe Benefits: Working condition fringe benefits.--

An airline failed produce sufficient evidence showing that its employees maintained adequate records of their actual meal expenses to meet the substantiation requirements under Code Sec. 274(d) ; thus, it was not entitled to deduct meal allowances paid to the employees as "working condition fringe" benefits. The taxpayer was adequately apprised that a withholding obligation existed. Its reliance on revenue rulings to meet the substantiation requirements ignored the inclusion of lodging within the deemed substantiation limit and consideration of employee circumstances on an individual basis. Thus, the allowances were properly included in the employees' wages and were subject to employment tax withholding.

American Airlines, Inc., CA-FC, 2000-1 USTC ¶50,236 , 204 F3d 1103.

The IRS properly determined that one of the taxpayers was required to include in her gross income the lease value of a corporate automobile she used during the years in issue to the extent she used the automobile for personal reasons. The taxpayer failed to show that the automobile constituted a working condition fringe benefit under Code Sec. 132 . She did not produce any evidence corroborating her self-serving testimony that she reimbursed the corporation for any personal usage of the car.

➔The annotation section for SFTR's print volumes contains the same information as this online version; the print version uses a two-column format.

➔The online version includes hyperlinks to Current Developments. The print version uses the Developments Tables in the New Matters volume. Illustrations 12-2 through 12-5 illustrate different updating results.

Illustration 12-2. Excerpt from SFTR Current Developments Online

REL_FED2002CDSET_CFD(CD)2002FED7438.80
2 documents.

1. ● REV-PROC, 2002FED ¶46,103. Income and exclusions: Certain fringe benefits: Working condition fringe benefits: Substantiation requirements: Adequate records.-- Revenue Procedure 2001-56, I.R.B. 2001-51, (Nov. 29, 2001)
2. ● MISC-DOC, 2002FED ¶47,332, FSA 200137039, June 19, 2001.

➔The online version located two documents, a revenue procedure and a field service advice. It pulled only from ¶ 7438.80 above. Compare the print version in Illustration 12-4.

Illustration 12-3. Excerpt from SFTR New Development Online

FSA 200137039, June 19, 2001., June 19, 2001

[Code Secs. 132 , 911 and 3401]

Expatriate employees: Gross income: Wages: Working condition fringe benefits: Foreign earned income exclusion.--The value of income tax return preparation services provided to expatriate employees was includible in gross income because the benefits were not excludable as a working condition fringe. Moreover, the value of the income tax preparation services constituted wages subject to FICA and FUTA tax. However, for withholding purposes, Chief Counsel determined that the value of the benefit may have been excludable if the employer reasonably believed that the benefit was excludable from the recipient-employee's gross income under Code Sec. 911 and the regulations thereunder. BACK REFERENCES: ¶7438.80 , ¶28,049.025 and ¶33,506.1869 .

➔The online version provides hyperlinks to the Code sections and to the original SFTR paragraphs.

Illustration 12-4. Excerpt from SFTR Print Current Developments

From Compilation Paragraph No.	To New Development Paragraph No.
Code Sec. 132—Certain fringe benefits	

7438 .12 Whitehead, TCM—Taxpayers required to include lease value of employer-provided vehicles in gross income	47,814
.77 2002 Inflation adjustments—Rev. Proc.	46,115
.80 Employer paid tax preparation services not excludable as working condition fringe—Letter Ruling	47,332
.80 Reimbursements of salary-reduction amounts paid for health insurance premiums not excludable; Rev. Rul. 61-146 distinguished—Rev. Rul.	46,226

→The document in ¶ 47,332 really is field service advice, not a letter ruling.

→The print version pulls from all of ¶ 7438 and included more items than the online version, which pulled only from ¶ 7438.80. The online version was linked to the actual subparagraph we used in the compilation volume.

Illustration 12-5. Illustration from SFTR Print New Development

[¶ 47,332]   FSA 2001371039, June 19, 2001

[Code Secs. 132, 911 and 3401]

Expatriate employees: Gross income: Wages: Working condition fringe benefits: Foreign earned income exclusion.—The value of income tax return preparation services provided to expatriate employees was includible in gross income because the benefits were not excludable as a working condition fringe. Morever, the value of the income tax preparation services constituted wages subject to FICA and FUTA tax. However, for withholding purposes, Chief Counsel determined that the value of the benefit may have been excludable if the employer reasonably believed that the benefit was excludable from the recipient-employee's gross income under Code Sec. 911 and the regulations thereunder. **Back references:** ¶ 7438.80, ¶ 28,049.025 and ¶ 33,506.1869.

2. United States Tax Reporter—Income Taxes

Prentice-Hall revamped its Federal Taxes service in 1990, improving the layout to make the materials easier to locate and read. Research Institute of America continued the new format when it acquired and renamed this service.

The discussion of USTR follows the format in which it is arranged. Several of its volumes, and the RIA Citator, are discussed in greater detail elsewhere in this text; this section includes appropriate cross-references to those discussions.

a. Code Volumes. The two Code volumes print, in Code section order, all provisions involving income, gift and estate, employment, and excise taxes as well as procedural provisions.[225] Historical information follows Code provisions that have been amended. Historical material includes the Public Law number, the Public Law section number, and the effective date of any amendments. Prior statutory language is provided for several sections; this material can also be obtained from Cumulative Changes, discussed in Chapter 16.

Volume I contains a Topic Index to the Code [Illustration 3-1] and a listing of all Code sections. Volume I also contains an Amending Acts section. This section includes Public Law number, date, act title or subject, and Cumulative Bulletin or Statutes at Large citation for acts since 1954. This section is not separately indexed.

b. Index Volume. Volume 1 contains an extensive index, using paragraph numbers, to all of the material in the compilation volumes discussed below. This index uses different typefaces to denote Code section numbers and locations, location of topical discussions, and location of regulations text. Volume 1 also includes a Glossary, which provides succinct definitions of terms (both words and phrases) used by tax practitioners.

c. Tables Volume. Volume 2 contains main, supplementary, and current Tables of Cases and main and supplementary Tables of Rulings. These tables cross-reference cases and rulings to the appropriate discussions in the compilation volumes or in the Weekly Alert newsletter.[226] RIA provides case citations to several different reporter services in addition to A.F.T.R. Special notations indicate paragraph numbers for decisions printed in RIA's Tax Court Memorandum Decisions service. A Supreme Court docket listing indicates petitions filed and granted.

The case tables are not citator supplements. The main table merely lists cases discussed in SFTR. The supplementary and current tables indicate appeals action and IRS acquiescences for cases previously reported in the main table. The rulings tables, which cover both Internal Revenue Bulletin and other documents, do indicate prior or subsequent IRS action; they do not indicate judicial action.

d. Compilation Volumes. Volumes 3-15A contain, in Code section order, the full text of the Code; final, temporary and proposed regulations; and digest-annotations to revenue rulings, letter rulings and other IRS releases, and judicial decisions. Texts of committee reports (or Cumulative

---

[225] Repealed Code sections are included in the Code and compilation volumes.

[226] The Weekly Alert provides cross-references to both Federal Tax Coordinator and United States Tax Reporter.

Bulletin citations) are also included. Paragraph numbers assigned to these materials correspond to the Code section involved.

USTR indexes each compilation section and its annotations; it occasionally provides Overviews for related groups of sections. Italicized material indicates changes in both Code and regulations sections. There is an extensive editorial explanation, including citations to the annotations, for each Code provision.

e. Recent Developments Volume. The Recent Developments Volume (volume 16) contains a Cross Reference Table that cross-references from USTR paragraphs to updating material. Use this table to determine if a recent ruling or decision has been issued in any area of interest. [See Illustration 12-6.]

USTR reproduces the updating material in the Recent Developments volume (texts or digests of IRS rulings and procedures), in the A.F.T.R.2d Decisions Advance Sheets volume (texts of decisions rendered by courts other than the Tax Court), or in the Weekly Alert newsletter (digests of Tax Court decisions).

The Recent Developments volume provides Public Law number, title or subject, and relevant dates for acts since 1987.

f. A.F.T.R.2d Decisions Advance Sheets Volume. Volumes 17 and 17A contain the texts of recent income tax decisions from all courts except the Tax Court.[227] You can locate these items by Code section using the Cross Reference Tables in the Recent Developments volume. Decisions appear in the order they were received rather than in Code section order. Decisions printed in this volume will later be issued in hardbound volumes as part of the A.F.T.R. reporter service discussed in Chapter 10.

g. Federal Tax Regulations Volume. Volume 18 prints the preambles to proposed regulations. Coverage is chronological. A Finding List is in Code section order; it lists regulations without an underlying Code section first. This list indicates Federal Register publication date.

h. Citator. The RIA Citator is not part of USTR and does not cross-reference to it. You can use this citator with any looseleaf service to determine the status of both judicial decisions and IRS items. A full discussion of the RIA Citator appears in Chapter 11.

---

[227] Recent court decisions involving estate and gift taxes or excise taxes appear in the RIA services covering these topics. Court decisions for all taxes appear in the A.F.T.R. hardbound volumes.

Illustration 12-6. Excerpt from USTR Cross Reference Table

From ¶	To ¶/Page	Listed in Code Section Order
	IRC §263A	Capitalization Rules for Inventory Costs
263A4.	86,128	Internet site correction. Announc 2002-30
263A4.	86,141	Correction to prop. regs. for § 263 clarification. Announc 2002-35
263A5.01(17)	3.11	*Plastic Engineering & Technical Services Inc:* Solely owned plastics corp.'s royalty payments as exclusive licensee of owner's patented hot manifold assembly system. TCMem
	IRC §267	Related Parties—Disallowance of Losses or Accrued Expenses and Interest
2675.19(10)	*2002-536*	*Henricksen aff:* Refund claim based on net operating loss sustained upon sale of business inventory to brother. CA
	IRC §274	Disallowance of Certain Entertainment, Gift and Travel Expenses
2745.02(5)	86,179	Recreation center's deduction of business expenses. LtrRul 200214007

→Note the three types of To ¶/Page listings. Three items (86,128, 86,141, and 86,179) appear in full text or as digests in the Current Developments volume. One item (3.11) appears in the Weekly Alert newsletter. Those four items are paragraph references. The fifth item (2002-536) is a page reference to the A.F.T.R. Advance Sheets volume.

SECTION B. SUBJECT ARRANGEMENT: MULTIPLE TOPICS

The second group of materials is quite varied; many libraries lack at least one of them or carry others not discussed here. Each covers a wide range of topics using a subject matter arrangement.

If you use several services, you will get quicker access to relevant items in the second (or later) service by using tables for cases and other primary sources. Once you have obtained these items from one service, you can use them to locate relevant discussion in the other service. If the second service lacks these tables,[228] you can enter it from its topical or Code section index.

---

[228] For example, Tax Management Portfolios lack case and rulings tables. They have excellent Code and topical indexes.

1. Federal Tax Coordinator 2d

This weekly service contains excellent discussions of all areas of taxation, with minimal coverage of employment taxes. Federal Tax Coordinator identifies most items by paragraph number; text of Code, regulations, and treaties is identified by page number. The Weekly Alert newsletter provides cross-references to both Federal Tax Coordinator and United States Tax Reporter.

Material in each volume is discussed in the following paragraphs.

a.   Topic–Index Volume and Volume 1. The Topic–Index Volume contains an extensive Topic Index, which you can use to locate appropriate discussion in the text volumes. The index has main and current sections.

Volume 1 includes several Finding Tables that indicate where items are discussed in the text volumes. These tables cover the Internal Revenue Code, Public Laws since 1991, other United States Code titles, temporary and final regulations, Treasury Decisions for the past six months, Labor regulations, and proposed regulations.

Volume 1 includes tables indicating where you can find discussion of recent Public Law and proposed regulations provisions and a table for T.D.s issued in the previous six months. The Public Law table is in act section order. Volume 1 also includes a table covering non-Internal Revenue Code statutes discussed in this service. There is also a table of Code sections that is not tied to discussion in the service.

b. Volume 2. This volume contains a Rulings and Releases Table giving cross-references to discussions in the text volumes. The table arranges each type of IRS document chronologically. Letter rulings are included.

Volume 2 also includes an alphabetical list of cases with cross-references to discussions in the text volumes. This list includes citations to various case reporter services, often including both A.F.T.R. and U.S.T.C. in addition to reporters such as Federal Reporter.

A Supreme Court Docket and a Court of Appeals Docket indicate where discussion of pending cases appears in the text volumes. The Supreme Court materials classify cases as recently decided, petition granted, petition denied, and petition filed.

c.   Volume 3. Volume 3 includes sample letters to clients on a wide variety of topics. It also includes planning checklists, tax tables, a tax calendar, interest and annuity tables, and tables showing where tax return forms are discussed in the text. Other reference items, such as federal rates and per diem amounts, appear in the text volumes. A Current Legislation Table lists acts since 1994 by Public Law number, subject, and relevant dates.

d. Text Volumes. The text volumes (4-26, including some additional volumes such as 10A and 14A) are arranged by chapters using a subject matter approach. Discussions in each chapter include liberal use of citations and analysis of as yet unresolved matters.

Each chapter has the following arrangement: a Detailed Reference Table for topics included; cross-references to topics of potential relevance discussed in other chapters; discussion of each topic, including footnote annotations; and text of Code and regulations sections applicable to the chapters being discussed. Chapters are subdivided into topics, and then into paragraphs. [See Illustration 12-7.]

Volume 20 contains the texts of United States income, estate, and gift tax treaties and textual material dealing with the treaties. United States and OECD model treaties are also included. Although this service prints only treaties currently in effect, it does include a list of treaties awaiting ratification or exchange of instruments of ratification.

Illustration 12-7. Excerpt from Federal Tax Coordinator Text

Ordinary Income Property Contributions

K-3160. Appreciated ordinary income property contributions.

Except as provided in ¶ K-3178 *et seq.*, in the case of a contribution of "ordinary income property"[21] (as defined in ¶ K-3161), the contribution amount must be reduced by the amount (referred to as "ordinary income") which would have been recognized as gain other than long-term capital gain if the property had been sold by the donor at its fair market value at the time of its contribution to the charitable organization.[22] (For a discussion of capital gains in general, see ¶ I-5000 *et seq.*; for discussion of when capital gain is long-term, see ¶ I-8901 *et seq.*)

✓ *illustration:* A donor bought stock for $4,000 and contributed it to charity four months later. At that time, the stock was worth $6,000, and the long-term holding period was more than one year. Because the $2,000 of appreciation is short-term gain, the donor's charitable deduction is only $4,000.

→Federal Tax Coordinator uses paragraphs for most cross-references.

e. Proposed Regulations. Volumes 27 and 27A contain proposed regulations reproduced in the order in which they were issued, along with preambles and Federal Register citations. A cross-reference table lists the proposed regulations in Code section order. Proposed regulations issued as temporary regulations are instead reproduced in the textual volumes.

f. Internal Revenue Bulletin. Volume 28 contains reprints of the weekly Internal Revenue Bulletin. Because the material in volume 28 is not indexed by Code section or by subject matter anywhere in this service, it will be difficult to locate a particular item without an Internal Revenue Bulletin citation.

2. Tax Management Portfolios

BNA issues three series of Tax Management Portfolios: U.S. Income; Foreign Income;[229] and Estates, Gifts, and Trusts. Each series is subdivided into several softbound volumes that cover narrow areas of tax law in great depth.[230] Each Portfolio refers to other Portfolios containing information relevant to a particular problem.

In addition to a Table of Contents, each Portfolio includes a Detailed Analysis section (Section A) with extensive footnoting (including references to IRS letter rulings). A Working Papers/Worksheets section (Section B) includes checklists, forms that can be used as models in drafting documents, and texts of relevant IRS materials. A Bibliography & References section (Section C) includes citations to regulations, legislative history, court decisions, and rulings. Books and articles are listed by year of publication.

BNA supplements the Portfolios with Changes & Analysis sheets, or completely revises them, whenever warranted by new developments.

BNA provides several methods for locating relevant Portfolios. The looseleaf Portfolio Index includes the Classification Guides; these are lists of Portfolios in each series arranged by major category (such as Life Insurance). Each series also has a detailed Master Subject Index. [See Illustration 12-8.] A Master Code Section Index covers all series; it indicates the main Portfolio on point with an asterisk (*).

Numerical IRS Forms and IRS Publications Finding Tables are cross-referenced to appropriate Portfolios.

The Tax Management Memorandum, a biweekly analysis of current developments, unsettled problems, and other significant items, includes cross-references to discussions in the Portfolios. Tax Management Weekly Report (Chapter 15) includes updating material before it is added to the Portfolios. The Weekly Report also includes Code section indexes.

---

[229] See also Chapter 7.

[230] Subdivisions are so narrow that several portfolios may cover one Code section.

Illustration 12-8. Excerpt from U.S. Income Master Subject Index

ATHLETES
Bonuses, reasonableness of compensation, 390:A-20
Employees vs. independent contractor, 391:A-56
Injury protection payments received outside workers' compensation, 522:A-5
Meals and lodging expenses, 519:A-39
Multiemployer plans, 359:C&A:A-2
Player contracts amalgamation rule, 563:A-99
State income allocation, 366:A-33
Travel expenses, 519:A-39

ATHLETIC FACILITIES
Employees and contingent workers, 399:A-52
Fringe benefit, 373:A-76; 394:A-33, A-42; 399:A-52; 501:A-56

➔Note the reference to the Changes & Additions (C&A) page in Portfolio 359. These materials will be integrated into Section A when the Portfolio is revised.

3. Mertens, Law of Federal Income Taxation

The original Mertens service contained five sets of volumes: treatise; Code; Code commentary; regulations; and rulings. Although the revised service includes only treatise, Code commentary, and rulings, the Code and regulations materials are still useful for historical research.

a. Treatise. The treatise volumes closely resemble general encyclopedias such as Am. Jur. 2d and C.J.S. in format.[231] Material is presented by subject matter with extensive footnoting. Each chapter contains cross-references to relevant materials found elsewhere in the service. A section digesting revenue rulings, revenue procedures, and IRS acquiescences appears at the end of many chapters; this material is divided by topic. Treatise materials are supplemented monthly; supplements are cumulated semiannually.

Discussions include extensive historical background information. Because its discussions are so thorough, Mertens is frequently cited in judicial decisions.[232] However, that very thoroughness can be a drawback; using the treatise materials for background knowledge can be very time-consuming.

A **Tables Volume** (with main and supplementary sections) contains tables indicating where primary source materials are discussed. These

---

[231] Fundamentals of Legal Research discusses these encyclopedias in Chapter 16. Although each covers a wide variety of topics, discussions of taxation appear in separate volumes within each service and are thus quite accessible.

[232] See, e.g., Nelson v. Commissioner, 110 T.C. 114, 127 (1998).

include the Internal Revenue Code, other United States Code titles, Treasury regulations, other Code of Federal Regulations titles, and IRS materials. IRS materials covered include items printed in the Cumulative Bulletin, letter rulings, technical advice memoranda, and field service advice. Two other tables provide Cumulative Bulletin citations for revenue rulings and revenue procedures.

Because citations for Supreme Court decisions listed in the **Table of Cases Volume** include United States Reports, United States Supreme Court Reports, Lawyers' Edition, and Supreme Court Reporter, you can use that table to some extent to obtain parallel citations. The tables rarely provide parallel citations for lower court decisions.

The **Index Volume** contains a detailed subject matter index. The monthly Developments & Highlights newsletter in the **Current Materials Volume** includes lists of recent tax articles.

b. Code. Each Code volume contains all income tax provisions enacted or amended during a particular time period (one or more years). Textual notations (diamond shapes and brackets) indicate additions and deletions. A historical note indicates Act, section, and effective date and can be used to reconstruct the prior language. The subject matter index in the looseleaf current volume cross-references each topic to applicable Code sections. This material does not cover the 1986 Code.[233]

c. Code Commentary. Looseleaf volumes of Code Commentary provide useful short explanations of statutory provisions as well as cross-references to the discussions in the treatise materials.

d. Regulations. Regulations materials have undergone change since the mid-1990s. In a separate service, but using the Mertens name, the publisher currently issues a softbound set of regulations in force (volumes 1 through 5) and proposed regulations (volume 6). Regulations appear in Code section order; there is also a subject matter table of contents. New matter issued during the year is filed in a looseleaf Current Developments binder. The service also includes looseleaf volumes containing the preambles issued since 1985 to proposed, temporary, and final regulations.

Many libraries also hold the discontinued regulations service. That service's volumes include the texts of all income tax regulations issued or amended during a particular time period (two or more years). Publication is in Code section order.

---

[233] Mertens currently publishes annual softbound Code volumes, but they are not tied to the Law of Federal Income Taxation service.

The discontinued volumes have several useful features. Textual notations (diamond shapes and brackets) indicate deletions, additions, and other changes in amended regulations. A historical note, from which you can determine the regulation's prior wording, follows. This facilitates research into early administrative interpretations. Each volume also contains a section reproducing the preamble to the Treasury Decision or Notice of Proposed Rulemaking announcing each proposed and final regulation.

e. Rulings. The Rulings volumes contain the texts of revenue rulings and procedures. Notices, announcements, and other IRS items are excluded. Each volume covers a particular time period and includes rulings in numerical order, followed by procedures in numerical order. Mertens adds current items monthly.

The looseleaf current volume has Code–Rulings and Code–Procedures Tables, which provide chronological listings of every revenue ruling or procedure involving income tax Code sections or subsections. [See Illustration 3-5.] In addition, a Rulings Status Table lists the most recent revenue ruling or procedure affecting the validity of a previously published item. Mertens indicates the effect on the earlier item (e.g., modified, revoked). A separate section includes Cumulative Bulletin citations for this material.

4. Rabkin & Johnson, Federal Income, Gift and Estate Taxation

This service originally had three segments: treatise; Code and Congressional Reports; and Regulations. Only the treatise materials are currently being updated.

Supplementation is monthly, with New Matter pages appearing near the beginning of each volume. Subscribers also receive Taxes Today, a monthly report letter.

a. Treatise. The treatise materials consist of explanatory materials and two volumes of reference material designed to facilitate research in the remainder of the set. It is arranged in chapters; each chapter is divided into sections that use chapter numbers in their prefixes. Cross-referencing is done by section number.

The first two volumes (1 and 1A) contain tables and other user aids. Volume 1 includes the following indexes and tables, which cross-reference to discussions in the treatise volumes: topical Index; Table of Statutory References (Internal Revenue Code and other parts of United States Code); Table of Cases; and Table of Regulations, Rulings and Releases (publicly available IRS materials in addition to revenue rulings). The Table of Cases indicates if a case is discussed more than once in a text section. Use this feature to avoid missing all discussion of that case in longer text sections.

Volume 1A includes a detailed User's Guide to using Rabkin & Johnson. This volume also contains tax calendars and checklists of deductions (arranged by the tax form involved). Tax forms are listed numerically; IRS publications are listed alphabetically. In addition to rates, the Tax Rates section includes imputed interest rates, annuity valuation tables, depreciation tables, and similar helpful tables. Tax Court and IRS Practice Rules also appear in this volume.

Volumes 2 through 5 contain textual discussion of the law. Because this treatise is not arranged in Code section order, it integrates discussions of various aspects of a problem in each section.

While discussions are thorough, they do not purport to cover all types of authority. Letter rulings are rarely discussed or cited as authority "[b]ecause they lack precedential value."[234]

b. Code and Congressional Reports. Volumes 6 through 7B contain the text of the Code in Code section order.[235] You can use the Legislative History notes following each Code subsection to determine how amendments changed prior statutory language. These notes indicate the act, section, and date for amendments, but they do not provide a citation to Statutes at Large.

The legislative history notes refer to congressional committee reports explaining each provision. Relevant excerpts from these reports, including full citations, appear at the end of each Code section. These materials cover only the 1954 Code.

Volume 6 contains a topical index to the Code materials. Volume 7B (Appendix) includes tables cross-referencing 1939 and 1954 Code sections. Because these tables were printed in 1963, they miss section number changes that occurred after 1963. There are no cross-reference tables for the 1986 Code.

c. Regulations. Volumes 8 through 12 include the text of 1954 Code regulations. Regulations are printed in numerical order and are preceded by

---

[234] 1A RABKIN & JOHNSON, FEDERAL INCOME, GIFT AND ESTATE TAXATION § G 1.03[6], at 1A-G (also available in LexisNexis FIGETX file).

[235] This service omits miscellaneous excise taxes other than those involving registration required obligations, public charities, private foundations, qualified pension plans, real estate investment trusts, and the crude oil windfall profit tax.

T.D. numbers and dates for the original version and amendments.[236] There is no list of regulations in T.D. number order. Regulations sections are cross-referenced to subject matter discussions in the treatise volumes.

Volume 12A printed selected proposed regulations in numerical order. That volume's Table of Contents contains a numerical list of included provisions. Both the Table of Contents and the heading for each proposed regulation indicate the Federal Register date and a cross-reference to treatise discussion. The volumes do not include preambles.

Table 12-1. Cross-Referencing in Looseleaf Services

Service	Method	Updates Found In
SFTR	¶	New Matters; USTC Adv. Sheets
USTR	¶/Page	Compilations; Recent Dev.; AFTR Adv. Sheets; Weekly Alert
Fed. Tax Coordinator	¶	Inserted in chapter
Tax Mgt Portfolios	Page	Beginning of Portfolio; Weekly Report
Mertens	§	Beginning of volume
Rabkin & Johnson	§	Beginning of volume

SECTION C. SUBJECT ARRANGEMENT: LIMITED SCOPE

Various publishers issue textual materials discussing a limited number of Code sections, such as those covering S corporations.[237] These texts are extremely useful for research involving very complex areas of tax law. In recent years the number of texts covering a particular topic, and the number of topics covered, have both grown explosively. You can locate at least one text on almost any topic, from tax problems of the elderly to estate planning for farmers. While these materials are periodically supplemented, their updating is rarely as frequent as that for the services in sections A and B.

The following materials are a representative sample.

• Bittker & Eustice, Federal Income Taxation of Corporations and Shareholders

• Casey, Federal Tax Practice

• Casner & Pennell, Estate Planning

---

[236] Federal Register dates are instead given for IRS procedural rules. These materials do not include the text of a regulation's prior versions.

[237] Form books (Chapter 16) may also include extensive textual material.

• McKee, Nelson & Whitmire, Federal Taxation of Partnerships and Partners

• O'Connell, Divorce Taxation

• Schneider, Federal Taxation of Inventories

Other potential sources include law school casebooks or textbooks, which may include copious notes. CLE providers such as Practicing Law Institute regularly publish softbound volumes of course materials. Finally, the multivolume Bittker & Lokken, Federal Taxation of Income, Estates and Gifts, provides thorough treatment of difficult issues.

SECTION D. PROBLEMS

1. Using SFTR, locate the paragraph reference in the compilation volumes assigned by your instructor. Then use the updating material in the New Matters volume to find all updating references to the original item. Provide a citation to each new item that includes its location in SFTR and its "official" location (e.g., I.R.B. for a revenue ruling).

2. Repeat problem 1 using USTR and the Recent Developments volume.

3. Indicate the Tax Management Portfolios concerned with Code section

a. 32   c. 271   e. 7702

b. 144   d. 883

4. Indicate who authored

a. Tax Management Portfolio: Employee Benefits for the Contingent Workforce

b. Tax Management Portfolio: Testamentary Capacity and Validity of Wills

c. Mertens chapter: Deduction of Net Operating Losses

d. Mertens chapter: Community Property

5. Is there a Tax Management Portfolio covering the Slovak Republic?

Chapter 13. Legal Periodicals

Section A. Introduction

This chapter provides information about periodical literature. It covers various methods for locating citations to articles and the articles themselves. It also discusses methods for determining if a judicial opinion has cited an article.

Although periodical literature is a secondary source, and articles cannot be used as authority for avoiding the substantial understatement penalty, they are still important research tools. Because articles generally appear more quickly than do treatise supplements, they are valuable tools for learning about new or amended Code sections, regulations, and judicial decisions. In addition, articles may provide citations to primary source materials that you can use as authority.

Section B. Categorizing Periodicals

Commentary on particular tax problems appears in various legal periodicals. These include general focus, student-edited law reviews, publications that focus on a broad variety of tax-related topics, and publications that specialize in a particular area of taxation.

Although general focus, student-edited law reviews occasionally include tax articles, other sources generally carry a larger number of relevant items.[238] These other sources include law school-based law reviews (student- or faculty-edited[239]) that focus on taxation, tax-oriented periodicals published by professional groups or commercial entities, and tax-oriented newsletters. Although not technically periodicals, tax institute proceedings contain useful information and can be accessed using several periodical indexes.

---

[238] See William J. Turnier, *Tax (and Lots of Other) Scholars Need Not Apply: The Changing Venue for Scholarship*, 50 J. Legal Educ. 189 (2000).

[239] These publications may have student editors, who edit work that has been selected through a faculty review process.

Table 13-1 lists representative titles in several categories.

Table 13-1. Representative Periodical Titles

Type	Title
Student-edited	Akron Tax Journal
Student-edited	Virginia Tax Review
Faculty-reviewed	Florida Tax Review
Faculty-reviewed	Tax Law Review
Faculty-reviewed	The Tax Lawyer
General tax focus	Journal of Taxation
General tax focus	TAXES–The Tax Magazine
Specialized focus	Real Estate Taxation
Newsletter	Tax Notes
Institute	Institute on Estate Planning
Institute	Institute on Federal Taxation

SECTION C. CITATIONS TO PERIODICALS

Your search for relevant publications may begin in a variety of sources. For example, looseleaf services such as Tax Management Portfolios and newsletters such as Tax Notes include lists of articles. Citators may also provide citations to articles. Several publications digest articles. Digests may limit themselves to a particular topic or cover a general range of topics; they generally cover fewer articles than do the other tools.

Although the materials mentioned in the preceding paragraph are useful, periodical indexes are the most comprehensive sources for compiling lists of articles. This section divides indexes into three categories—general legal indexes, specialized indexes, and other indexes.

General legal periodical indexes such as Index to Legal Periodicals and Current Law Index cover all areas of law. Two specialized indexes, Federal Tax Articles and Index to Federal Tax Articles cover only tax-related materials. The third category of indexes covers areas related to law, such as political science, economics, and history and nontax specialized legal topics (such as indexes to articles published in other countries).

The tax-oriented and general indexes differ in their indexing methods, publication frequency, and lists of publications covered. All are available in print versions; the general indexes are also available in electronic formats. Law-related indexes are available in a variety of formats.

You can use the publications below to generate lists of articles. Publications are categorized by type—indexes, looseleaf services, newsletters, citators, miscellaneous, and digests.

1. General Legal Periodicals Indexes

a. Current Law Index; Legal Resource Index; LegalTrac

Current Law Index (CLI) indexes articles by subject, author/title, case name, and statute. Its Table of Statutes includes a heading for Internal Revenue Code. Because that section lists articles in Code section order, CLI is the most convenient print-based general index for researching articles by section.

CLI covers more publications than does Index to Legal Periodicals. It includes several tax-oriented publications, including Tax Notes. It began publication in 1980, limiting its usefulness to more recent materials.

An online version, Legal Resource Index (LRI), is available through Westlaw and LexisNexis. The publisher also offers an electronic version, LegalTrac, as a CD-ROM product and online through InfoTrac Web. These electronic materials cover material indexed since 1980.

CLI is published monthly in print and cumulated quarterly and annually. The LegalTrac CD-ROM is cumulated monthly; the online version is updated daily. LRI is updated at least weekly on Westlaw and LexisNexis.

Illustration 13-1. Excerpt from Legal Resource Index on Westlaw

Query: AU(jerome ...	Edit Query ☰
Database(s): LRI	26 Doc(s)
Go to: [ ] GO	◁ 1-20 ▷
Print ▾	WestClip

☐ 1. TITLE: Divorce: a window for estate planning opportunities. AUTHOR: Adams, Frank T.; Hesch, Jerome M. YEAR: Publication Date: May 8, 2000. Page: 163-184. 2000 WL 717625 (LRI), 41 Tax Mgmt. Memorandum 163 <<Full Text Available>>

☐ 2. TITLE: Beyond the basic freeze: further uses of deferred payment sales. AUTHOR: Hesch, Jerome M. YEAR: Publication Date: Annual 2000. Page: CH16(53). 2000 WL 1598909 (LRI), 34 Inst. on Est. Plan. CH16

➔This search asked for Jerome Hesch as author. The search produced a list of 26 documents; the same search in Index to Legal Periodicals yielded four. [See Illustration 13-2.]

b. Index to Legal Periodicals & Books; WilsonWeb; WilsonDisc

Index to Legal Periodicals[240] includes tax articles in its subject matter listings. It indexes articles by subject/author, case name, and act name. Because it indexes by statute, it is not searchable by Code section.

ILP indexes fewer tax-related publications than do the other indexes, and it imposes page minimums for indexed material. Because ILP began publication in 1908, it is useful for historical research.

Both Westlaw and LexisNexis carry ILP. The publisher also offers its own online service, WilsonWeb. WilsonDisc is a CD-ROM product. Because Wilson's electronic offerings cover material indexed since mid-1981, they allow rapid searching for current material but not for earlier items.

ILP is published monthly and cumulated quarterly and annually. The CD-ROM version is cumulated monthly. WilsonWeb is updated weekly. The Westlaw and LexisNexis versions of ILP are updated at least weekly.

Illustration 13-2. Excerpt from Index to Legal Periodicals on Westlaw

Query: au(jerome ...   Edit Query   ▤
Database(s): ILP   4 Doc(s)
Go to: ◉

Print   ▾   WestClip

☐   1. TITLE: Beyond the basic freeze: further uses of
deferred payment sales. AUTHOR: Hesch, Jerome M.;
Manning, Elliott. YEAR:2000. Page: 16.1-.53. 2000 WL
1126055 (ILP), 34 Inst. on Est. Plan. 16.1

☐   2. TITLE: Family deferred payment sales, installment
sales, SCINs, private annuity sales, OID and other
enigmas. AUTHOR: Hesch, Jerome M.; Manning, Elliott.
YEAR: 1992. Page: 3.1-.169. 1992 WL 483425 (ILP), 26
Inst. on Est. Plan. 3.1

→Compare the results in Illustrations 13-1 and 13-2.

---

[240] ILP began covering books in 1994.

2. Tax-Oriented Periodicals Indexes

a. Federal Tax Articles

This looseleaf reporter contains summaries of articles on federal taxes appearing in legal, accounting, business, and related periodicals. It also covers proceedings and papers delivered at major tax institutes.

Contents appear in Code section order; each item receives a paragraph cross-reference number. The service is published monthly; contents are cumulated at six-month intervals.

There are topic and author indexes. Each has main and current subdivisions. There is a List of Publications division; several publications covered in the looseleaf volume weren't included in that list.

Federal Tax Articles is cumulated into bound volumes at regular intervals. Bound volumes currently cover 1954-67, 1968-72, 1973-78, 1979-84, 1985-89, and 1990-96. The looseleaf volume contains the most recent material.

Federal Tax Articles has advantages and disadvantages. It is relatively timely. It covers a wide array of publications. Its use of Code sections facilitates searching. However, its use is limited to 1954 and later materials. Searching through its multivolume format is more time-consuming than searching electronically, but it is not available in an electronic format.

Illustration 13-3. Excerpt from Federal Tax Articles

2374	**1996 Article Summaries-Reports 401-406**	407 7-96

¶ 2981 Alternative minimum tax imposed (Code Sec. 55)

.074 Repeal of AMT Depreciation. Bruce H. Barnett. 47 Tax Executive, November/December 1995, p. 471.

Presents the proposed legislation that would require use of the same depreciation method for regular tax purposes and for alternative minimum tax (AMT) pur-

poses. Observes that compliance with the proposal would be difficult, and notes that the depreciation rules have been amended many times. Believes that the AMT should be repealed in its entirety. Suggests ways for taxpayers to comply with the provision if it is enacted.

→The author index cross-references articles by paragraph number to the Code section listing. The author index does not separately list articles.

b. Index to Federal Tax Articles

This multivolume work covers tax literature contained in legal, specialized tax, accounting, and economics journals, and nonperiodical publications. It includes comprehensive coverage of nontax journals.

Contents appear in topical order. There are separate topical and author indexes but no Code section index. The most recent entry appears first in each listing of articles.

Coverage begins with 1913. Volumes I-III cover through mid-1974. There are cumulation volumes for 1974-81, 1982-83, 1984-87, 1988-92, and 1993-96. Subsequent material appears in the quarterly cumulative supplement volume. This index is updated less frequently than the other indexes and is available only in a print version.

Because Index to Federal Tax Articles begins coverage with 1913, it is an excellent source for locating discussions of early developments in taxation. It covers a wide array of publications. Although you cannot search by Code section, searching by topic may yield more generalized information. Depending on your familiarity with an area, that can be an advantage or disadvantage. As was true for Federal Tax Articles, searches are more time-consuming than those done with electronic services.

Illustration 13-4. Excerpt from Index to Federal Tax Articles

WINTER 2002 CUMULATIVE SUPPLEMENT

Children—*Cont'd*

The Population Crisis: The Stork, The Plow, and The IRS, Mona L. Hymel, 77 North Carolina Law Review No. 1, 13 (1998)

Deductibility of Private School Costs for

Choice of Business Entity—*Cont'd*

More Than Meets the Eye: Selected Tax Issues in the Use of "Disregarded" Single Member Entities, Carolyn Joy Lee and Steven G. Frost, 58 New York University Institute on Federal Taxation 13 (2000)

3. Other Periodicals Indexes

General legal research texts discuss law-related periodicals indexes.[241] Representative titles include Business Periodicals Index, Index to Periodical Articles Related to Law, and Social Sciences Index. If your problem involves another country, indexes such as Index to Foreign Legal Periodicals and European Legal Journals Index may be useful.

---

[241] See, e.g., Fundamentals of Legal Research ch. 17.

4. Looseleaf Services

Looseleaf services include a variety of finding aids. Those that list articles are discussed briefly below. Each service is discussed in greater detail in Chapter 12.

a. Tax Management Portfolios

The Bibliography & References section of each Portfolio lists articles by year of publication. Updating material appears in the Portfolio's Changes & Analysis section; this section cross-references to the Bibliography & References materials. Tax Management Portfolios are also available online.

b. Mertens, Law of Federal Income Taxation

Mertens lists current articles by topic in the Recent Tax Articles section of its monthly Developments & Highlights newsletter. Although Mertens is an income tax service, the lists include articles on estate planning. The monthly lists are not cumulated.

5. Newsletters

Calling Tax Notes a newsletter understates its importance. Tax Notes includes original articles in each weekly issue.[242] It also includes lists of articles published elsewhere in its Tax Bibliography section. This section is indexed by Code section. Articles that do not fit neatly into Code section categorization are listed by topic. Tax Notes is available as an archived CD-ROM. It is available online (Tax Notes Today) through LexisNexis. Tax Analysts also has its own electronic subscription service, TaxBase.

Consult your librarian to determine if the library subscribes to other newsletters that survey relevant periodical literature.

6. Citators

You can locate articles discussing primary source materials such as statutes and cases using a print citator. Unfortunately, only Shepard's citators provide this information, and their coverage is extremely limited. Shepard's Federal Law Citations in Selected Law Reviews indicates if a constitutional provision, statute, regulation, or case has been cited in a law review article. However, it covers relatively few law reviews, none of them tax-oriented, and it does not cover Tax Court decisions. Even Shepard's

---

[242] Tax Notes is described more fully in Chapter 15.

Federal Tax Citator covers very few tax-oriented publications.

Online citators give better results. KeyCite Citing Ref and Shepard's Full options (Chapter 11) both provide periodical citations for Tax Court cases.

7. Miscellaneous Sources

a. Institutes. The New York University Institute on Federal Taxation has published Consolidated Indexes of its proceedings at irregular intervals. These indexes are arranged by subject, author, title, case name, statute, regulation, and ruling. The second volume of each annual Institute includes current indexes and tables. Other institutes also provide current indexes of their proceedings.

b. Bibliographies. Bibliographies compiled by a librarian or by another researcher may be available. Likely sources include the library's reference section and law review symposium issues covering a particular area of law.

Tax Policy in the United States: A Selective Bibliography with Annotations (1960-84) was published by the Vanderbilt University Law Library in cooperation with the ABA Section of Taxation. This looseleaf covers articles, books, and government documents dealing with tax policy. Each item is explained briefly. There are author and subject indexes.

c. Websites. If you are searching for articles by a particular author, don't neglect to check the web. The author may list publications in a resume or publications section. Law and accounting firms and educational institutions are likely to provide this information about their employees.

8. Digests

a. Monthly Digest of Tax Articles

This periodical presents significant current articles in abridged form. Descriptions are more detailed than are the summaries printed in Federal Tax Articles, but fewer articles receive coverage. Newkirk Products, Inc., also offers an Internet Articles Library covering tax, estate and financial planning, and employee benefits.

b. WG & L Journal Digest

Previously published as the Journal of Taxation Digest, this service covers articles published in the Journal of Taxation and several other Warren, Gorham & Lamont publications. Coverage begins with 1977, and the publications covered have varied over time. Digests are arranged by topic; the most recent items appear first. Cross-references are given to relevant articles digested under other topical headings. Each annual volume has Code section and subject indexes.

Illustration 13-5. Partial List of Publications by Evelyn Brody

Charities in Tax Reform: Threats to Subsidies Overt and Covert, 66 TENN. L. REV. (1999).

The Limits of Charity Fiduciary Law, 56 MD. L. REV. 1400 (1999).

Introduction to Nonprofit Symposium Issue, 23 J. CORP. L. 581 (1998).

Of Sovereignty and Subsidy: Conceptualizing the Charity Tax Exemption, 23 J.L. & CORP. L. 585 (1998).

Institutional Dissonance in the Nonprofit Sector, 41 VILL. L. REV. 433 (1997).

Charitable Endowments and the Democratization of Dynasty, 39 ARIZ. L. REV. 873 (1997).

➔This list is from www.kentlaw.edu/faculty/scholarship/brody_pubs.html.

SECTION D. TEXTS OF PERIODICALS

1. Print

If your library subscribes to publications printing articles you wish to read, you can easily locate them. Many libraries shelve all periodicals together in alphabetical order; a library with an alcove devoted to a particular subject area may shelve specialized periodicals in the alcove. No matter which shelving method it uses, the library is likely to keep a periodical's most current issues on reserve until they are cumulated and bound.

2. Online

If your library does not subscribe to a particular publication, or it is in use by another researcher, try locating it online in Westlaw or LexisNexis. Both online services carry numerous publications in full text. In addition, individual periodicals may include full-text articles on their own websites. If you use a service such as Westlaw or LexisNexis, you can also find articles on particular topics (e.g., Code sections or cases) by using those topics as search terms.

Hein-On-Line[243] represents an attempt to provide full-text access to articles, particularly those published before 1980. The collection can be searched by author, title, or words in text; searchers can use Boolean search terms. It allows direct access by citation, and includes an electronic table of contents for each volume. Each page is reproduced as originally published. As of mid-May 2002, it includes Florida Tax Review; new publications are added regularly.

Illustration 13-6. Excerpt from Hein-On-Line

700 *VIRGINIA LAW REVIEW* [Vol. 35

THE TAX COURT'S INFLUENCE ON THE TAX LAW*

THE efficiency of the Tax Court of the United States was recognized by the Supreme Court of the United States when, in 1943, Justice Jackson wrote an opinion which contained the following words:

"The court is independent, and its neutrality is not clouded by prosecuting duties. Its procedures assure fair hearings. Its deliberations are evidenced by careful opinions. All guides to

→This article appears at 35 VA. L. REV. 700 (1949).

3. CD-ROM

Matthew Bender's Authority CD-ROM includes texts for articles from the New York University, University of Miami, and University of Southern California tax institutes. CD-ROM archive versions of Tax Notes include articles printed in that publication. Some law reviews, such as Harvard Law Review, are available in CD-ROM format.

4. Microform

William S. Hein & Co., Inc., provides numerous periodicals in microform. Libraries established after a particular periodical issue went out of print may acquire it in microform. Libraries may also purchase microform versions of periodicals if space is at a premium.

---

[243] Hein-On-Line is a collaborative venture of William S. Hein & Co., Inc., Cornell Information Technologies, and Cornell University Law Library. It is available by subscription.

SECTION E. CITATORS FOR ARTICLES

Section C covered using citators to find citations to articles discussing various primary source materials. This section discusses determining if a court has cited a particular article in one of its opinions.

Shepard's Law Review Citations indicates if an opinion has cited an article. Only two of the publications currently covered—Tax Law Review and TAXES—focus on taxation. Shepard's Law Review Citations does not cover the Tax Court.

Instead of using a print citator for this purpose, you will obtain more accurate results using a CD-ROM or online search on Westlaw, LexisNexis, or other electronic service covering judicial decisions. Use part of the article's title as your search term and search in the relevant judicial database.

SECTION F. PROBLEMS

Your instructor may assign one or more of the sources listed in this chapter for answering the questions below. If you have carte blanche to decide among sources, try using multiple sources so that you can compare their relative value. Unless you receive contrary instructions, your search can include articles in professional journals, newsletters, and institutes in addition to articles in law reviews.

1. Provide citations to as many articles as you can for each author for the publication periods listed below.

   a. Steven Bank (2000 and later)

   b. David Brennen (2000 and later)

   c. Joseph Bankman (2000 and later)

   d. Leandra Lederman (2000 and later)

   e. Wendy Gerzog (2000 and later)

   f. Steve Johnson (1990-1999)

   g. Deborah Geier (1990-1999)

   h. Beverly Moran (1990-1999)

i. Carolyn Jones (1980-1989)

j. Marjorie Kornhauser (1980-1989)

k. Martin Ginsburg (1970-1979)

l. Lester Snyder (1970-1979)

m. Bernard Wolfman (1960-1969)

n. Boris Bittker (1950-1959)

o. Erwin Griswold (1940-1949)

p. Charles Lowndes (1930-1939)

q. Roswell Magill (1920-1929)

2. Complete the citation for the following articles.

a. A Populist Political Perspective of the Business Tax Entities Universe: "Hey the Stars Might Lie But the Numbers Never Do"

b. Heteronormativity and Federal Tax Policy

c. Locke, Property, and Progressive Taxes

d. The Pink Panther Meets the Grim Reaper: Estate Taxation of the Fruits of Crime

e. An Obituary of the Federal Estate Tax

f. For Haven's Sake: Reflections on Inversion Transactions

g. Strange Loops and Tangled Hierarchies

h. The (Not So) Little House on the Prairie: The Hidden Costs of the Home Mortgage Interest Deduction

i. Keeping Kosher, The Epistemology of Tax Expenditures

j. Death and Tobacco Taxes

k. Taxation and the Human Body: An Analysis of Transactions Involving Kidneys

   l. Order in Multiplicity: Aristotle on Text, Context, and the Rule of Law

   m. Harry Potter and the Tax Accounting Myths

3. Complete the citation for the following 1940-1979 articles.

   a. Section 1348: The Death of Mickey Mouse?

   b. Mergers, Taxes, and Realism

   c. "Primarily for Sale": A Semantic Snare

   d. Learned Hand's Contribution to the Law of Tax Avoidance

   e. Sexism in the Code: A Comparative Study of Income Taxation of Working Wives and Mothers

   f. Federal Taxes and the Radiating Potencies of State Court Decisions

   g. Becoming More Inevitable? Death and Taxes—and Taxes

4. Complete the citation for the following pre-1940 articles

   a. Joseph A. Hill, The Civil War Income Tax

   b. Edwin B. Whitney, The Income Tax and the Constitution

   c. Edwin R.A. Seligman, Are Stock Dividends Income?

   d. Hugh Satterlee, The Income Tax Definition of Reorganization

   e. Thomas Reed Powell, Stock Dividends, Direct Taxes, and the Sixteenth Amendment

5. Update the articles search from Illustrations 13-1 and 13-2 using all indexes available for your use.

6. Find the most recent article you can discussing the case listed. If possible, find discussion in text rather than in footnotes.

   a. Gitlitz v. Commissioner

   b. Schmidt Baking Company, Inc. v. Commissioner

   c. United States v. Cleveland Indians Baseball Co.

d. Cotnam v. Commissioner

e. United States v. Fior D'Italia, Inc.

f. Lunsford v. Commissioner (use the 2001 decision)

g. Arkansas Best Corp. v. Commissioner

7. Find the most recent article you can discussing the Code section listed. If possible, find discussion in text rather than in footnotes.

a. 41   c. 303   e. 1311

b. 108   d. 482   f. 7872

8. Find the most recent article you can discussing the act listed. If possible, find discussion in text rather than in footnotes.

a. Community Renewal Tax Relief Act of 2000

b. Economic Growth and Tax Relief Reconciliation Act of 2001

c. FSC Repeal and Extraterritorial Income Act of 2000

d. Retirement Equity Act of 1984

e. Small Business Job Protection Act of 1996

9. Locate an article discussing tax legislation enacted last year.

10. Find the most recent article you can discussing the United States income tax treaty with the country listed. If possible, find discussion in text rather than in footnotes.

a. Luxembourg   c. Mexico

b. Canada   d. Japan

11. Find the most recent article you can discussing the document listed. If possible, find discussion in text rather than in footnotes.

a. Rev. Proc. 2002-28   c. Circular 230   e. Ann. 2002-2

b. Treas. Reg. 1.861-18   d. Rev. Rul. 99-28

12. Find the most recent article you can discussing the topic listed. If possible, find discussion in text rather than in footnotes.

a. corporate inversions

d. qualified state tuition programs

b. step transaction doctrine

e. treaty override

c. private annuities

f. marriage penalty

13. Do a web search to find articles on a topic your instructor assigns.

14. Provide the title and citation for two articles: (A) one written about the case below; and (B) the other written by the taxpayer involved in that case.

a. 493 F.2d 608   b. 1988 WL 524934   c. 877 F.2d 1364

Chapter 14. Form Books and Model Language

Section A. Using Forms, Checklists, and Model Language

The drafter's choice of language may determine the tax consequences of a contract, law suit settlement, or other legal matter. To avoid adverse consequences, you might consider adapting a form book's model language. The author's comments explain why particular language avoids tax problems. [See Illustration 14-1.] You can also use checklists to guide you in drafting your own form. The IRS occasionally provides model language in revenue procedures and other documents and even in tax return forms.

Illustration 14-1. Excerpt from Tax Practice Series

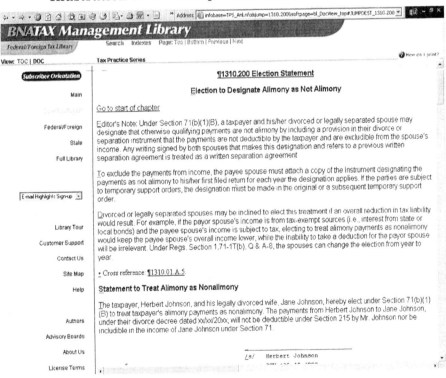

→ The language above is one part of a marital dissolution form. Note the explanatory statements preceding the sample language.

SECTION B. FORM BOOKS AVAILABLE

The following list illustrates the range of available materials. Forms are most useful if the author includes citations to authority.

- Bittker, Emory & Streng, Federal Income Taxation of Corporations & Shareholders: Forms

- Lowell, Tilton, Sheldrick & Donohue, U.S. International Taxation: Agreements, Checklists & Commentary

- Mancoff & Steinberg, Qualified Deferred Compensation Plans–Forms

- McGaffey, Legal Forms with Tax Analysis

- Murphy's Will Clauses: Annotations and Forms with Tax Effects

- Rabkin & Johnson, Current Legal Forms with Tax Analysis

- Robinson, Real Estate Forms: Tax Analysis & Checklists

In addition to using form books, you can find model language in looseleaf services, articles,[244] and tax institute proceedings. For example, several Tax Management Portfolios[245] include model language in their Working Papers section. Section D discusses online sources of forms.

SECTION C. FINDING FORMS AND OTHER DOCUMENTS

You can find drafting language relatively easily using a form book, because relevant forms or checklists will be listed by topic or Code section or will appear along with the topical discussion. You can use the publication's table of contents or relevant tables of authority to locate forms. The method of publication, print or electronic, should not matter. [See Illustration 14-2.]

You can locate relevant IRS language using an electronic search (online or CD-ROM) using such search terms as "model language," "prototype language," or "sample language."

---

[244] See, e.g., James F. Gulecas, Old Trusts—New Tricks (With Forms), Prac. Tax Law., Winter 2002, at 27.

[245] The Portfolios are described in detail in Chapter 12.

Illustration 14-2. Excerpt from Murphy's Will Clauses

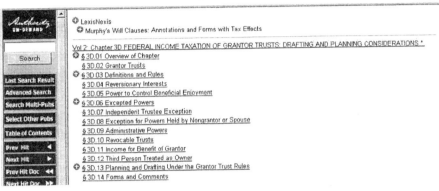

→Note that forms are listed at the end of the chapter's table of contents. Murphy's Wills Clauses is available in print and electronically. This screen print is from Matthew Bender Authority On-Demand, a LexisNexis product.

SECTION D. PUBLICATION FORMAT FOR FORMS

Although form books are available in print, materials published in electronic formats have an added advantage. Users can download forms and customize them for their clients' needs. In some instances, a CD-ROM may accompany a print form book.

Westlaw and LexisNexis include form books in their databases (e.g., West's Legal Forms on Westlaw; LEXIS Clause Library – Estates, Gifts and Trusts on LexisNexis). Publishers such as BNA provide form book materials to Westlaw and LexisNexis and also include them in their own subscription databases (e.g., BNATAX Management Library [Illustration 14-1]).

Internal Revenue Service forms are available online through commercial services and also through the IRS website, www.irs.gov. If you use the IRS website, you can find IRS model language if you know the citation for the form, revenue procedure, or notice you are seeking.[246] As Illustrations 9-3 and 9-4 illustrate, the IRS website currently includes no means of searching the Internal Revenue Bulletin database. You must retrieve each I.R.B. individually to browse its contents. If you instead seek a publication or form, you may be able to find it with a topic search.

---

[246] If you have the citation, you can obtain the model language from your library's print version Internal Revenue Bulletin or Cumulative Bulletin. You would use electronic materials if you wanted to download the language.

SECTION E. PROBLEMS

1. Locate a form or checklist covering tax consequences of a

    a. shareholder cross-purchase agreement

    b. support agreement for spouses who are separated but not divorced

    c. QTIP trust

    d. stock bonus plan

    e. private annuity

2. Locate a revenue procedure that provides model language for

    a. informing employees of how they will be taxed on their use of demonstrator vehicles

    b. complying with the requirements of the Uniformed Services Employment and Reemployment Rights Act of 1994 and Code section 414(u)

    c. a "rabbi" trust

    d. transferring prizes in a manner that satisfies Code section 74(b)

3. Locate an IRS notice that provides model language for

    a. required changes to plan qualification requirements under Code section 401(a) made because of the Economic Growth and Tax Relief Reconciliation Act of 2001

    b. a QDRO

    c. sample language to assist plan administrators in preparing spousal consent forms that meet the requirements of Code section 417

4. Locate an IRS announcement providing a notice employers can give employees explaining the I.R.C. § 25B retirement contribution credit.

5. What is the purpose of IRS Form 5305-R?

6. Locate an IRS announcement in Spanish giving a safe harbor explanation that can be given employees who receive rollover distributions.

Chapter 15. Newsletters

Section A. Introduction

Researchers in any area must update their findings or risk citing obsolete sources. When the research involves taxation, the odds of change are extremely high and the number of sources to consult may appear endless. Although keeping current requires a significant time commitment, it pays off in the long run. Regular self-education ultimately reduces your research time.

Newsletters are convenient tools for keeping up with changes in the law. While they are no substitute for updating with a citator or the new matter section of a looseleaf service, they offer the opportunity for a leisurely review of changes occurring during a predetermined time period.

Several newsletters print texts or digests of primary source material. These materials are then maintained on electronic databases. If your library has sufficient shelf space to maintain print copies, or you have electronic access, you can also use newsletters to locate and read primary source materials.

Section B. Categorizing Newsletters

Methods for categorizing newsletters include frequency of publication, subject matter, relation to looseleaf services, and publication format.

1. Frequency of Publication

Newsletters may appear daily, weekly, or even monthly. Daily and weekly newsletters either offer longer excerpts from cases and rulings than do their monthly counterparts or cover a wider range of topics. To avoid extraordinary length, monthly newsletters must limit their breadth or depth of coverage. The IRS's practice of issuing advance revenue rulings and revenue procedures, notices, and announcements makes daily and weekly newsletters particularly attractive. They may carry this information several weeks before it appears in the Internal Revenue Bulletin.

Online publication represents the ultimate in frequency. Because electronic databases can update their newsletter files daily, subscribers enjoy instant access while avoiding the library shelving problems associated with daily newsletters. A significant number of newsletters are available online in addition to being published in print versions.

2. Subject Matter

Newsletters may be general in scope, covering all (or at least most) areas of tax. Unless a general purpose newsletter is relatively long, or published very frequently, it gives limited attention to various areas or to particular types of authority. Other newsletters may limit coverage to a particular specialty, such as the estate tax or oil and gas taxation. Still others may cover a particular type of authority, such as pending legislation.

3. Relation to Looseleaf Services

Publishers of looseleaf services provide subscribers with pamphlet-type newsletters summarizing major events of the week or other relevant time period. Their summaries may be quite terse, but these newsletters offer the advantage of cross-references to discussion in the relevant looseleaf. CCH Taxes on Parade and RIA Weekly Alert are examples of this group.

In other instances, a looseleaf service subscription may not include a newsletter. Tax Management Weekly Report falls into this category; it is not included in the subscription to either Tax Management Portfolios or Tax Practice. Even though not included in a subscription, a newsletter may include cross-references to a publisher's looseleaf service. Tax Management Weekly Report includes updating material keyed to the Tax Management Portfolios.

Finally, some newsletters have no relation to any looseleaf service. Some of these, including Tax Notes, provide cross-references to sources printing full texts of items digested in the newsletter. Others provide no cross-reference service, leaving the choice of full-text reference source to the reader.

4. Publication Format

Most newsletters are available in a variety of formats, but print and online are the predominant formats. CD-ROM or microform publication is useful if shelf space is limited and you want permanent access to the publication. The descriptions in Section C indicate the publication format.

SECTION C. DESCRIPTIONS OF NEWSLETTERS

It is impossible to provide detailed descriptions of all available newsletters in this short a text. Although I limited this section to a handful of newsletters (and four publishers), you should not overlook other resources available in print or online. This is particularly important for relatively specialized areas.

1. Daily Tax Report; Tax Management Weekly Report

Both of these newsletters are currently available in print and on Westlaw and LexisNexis.

a. Daily Tax Report

This newsletter is an invaluable aid in following current developments in the law. [See Illustration 15-1.] Each separately paginated issue includes a section describing congressional activity, including bills passed and introduced, committee hearings, and committee reports.

Daily Tax Report prints full or partial texts of judicial decisions; full texts of most revenue rulings and procedures; summaries of other IRS materials (e.g., private letter rulings); and texts of proposed, temporary, and final regulations.

The indexes follow a subject matter format. Newsletter subscribers can access full text documents online using Tax Management's TaxCore.

Illustration 15-1. Excerpt from Daily Tax Report

G-2 (No. 13)	TAX, BUDGET & ACCOUNTING
get cheated out of their retirement savings by unfair pension rules." 　During the early 1980s, Congress enacted legislation to respond to certain business transactions where corporate insiders received large payments, called "golden parachutes," the release said. They were called golden	than 2 million, or 1.8 percent, over the previous year. Adjusted gross income (AGI) grew $439.5 billion, or 8.1 percent—a drop of almost 1 percent from the 9 percent growth between 1997 and 1998, IRS said. 　The bulletin noted, however, that several

→Daily Tax Report includes news reports in addition to full texts or digests of primary source material.

b. Tax Management Weekly Report

The Weekly Report primarily serves as a digest rather than full text service for primary source material. It focuses on news and analysis of current issues. Short articles appear in its Focus section.

The Weekly Report prints digests of court decisions, revenue rulings and procedures, and regulations. It also covers private letter rulings and other IRS material. It is particularly useful for subscribers to Tax Management Portfolios, as it includes cross-references and updating information for Portfolio material.

The Weekly Report is pre-punched for filing in a looseleaf binder.

Illustration 15-2. Excerpt from Weekly Report on Westlaw

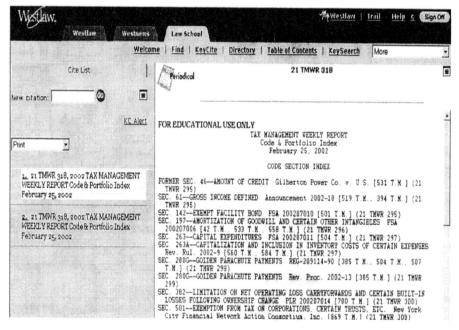

→ Weekly Report is also available on LexisNexis. Note the references to updating material for the Portfolios.

2. Daily Tax Highlights & Documents; Tax Notes

a. Daily Tax Highlights & Documents

Highlights & Documents is printed daily in subparts. The first contains brief reports of important events ("News Highlights"); the second provides full texts or lengthy summaries of the most significant items ("Documents"). Items covered include court decisions; revenue rulings and procedures; letter rulings and other IRS documents; legislative action; and proposed and final regulations. There is lengthy coverage, often including full text, of comments on Treasury regulations.

Each daily issue concludes with an Abstracts & Citations section. This section provides document reference numbers for items included in full text in Tax Notes Today (available on LexisNexis) and in Tax Analysts' online TaxBase service.

All documents are pre-punched for insertion into notebooks. Highlights & Documents has a monthly index (cumulated quarterly).

Illustration 15-3. Excerpt from Highlights & Documents

ABSTRACTS & CITATIONS

Section 38 • Investment Credit

Proposed Legislation

S. 1886 Would Provide Credit for Supported Elderly Housing S. 1886, introduced by Sen. Christopher J. Dodd, D-Conn., would provide a credit for the purpose of constructing assisted living housing for low- and moderate-income Americans. Assisted Living Tax Credit Act **Full Text Citations:** AccServ & Microfiche: Doc 2002-690 (36 original pages); Electronic 2002 TNT 12-51

Section 83 • Property Transferred for Services

Practice Articles

The Split-Dollar Life Insurance Regimes Burgess J.W. Raby, Esq., and William L. Raby, CPA, discuss the tax consequences of split-dollar life insurance arrangements and the IRS's recent moves to stop the aggressive use of these arrangements. **Full Text Citations:** AccServ & Microfiche: Doc 2002-1281 (5 original pages); Electronic 2002 TNT 12-71

→Materials in the Abstracts & Citations section are arranged in Code section order.

b. Tax Notes

This weekly newsletter contains a comprehensive collection of recent tax-oriented material. In addition, it is readily accessible through quarterly indexes. These are divided in highly usable fashion into categories covering the various types of information printed in Tax Notes.

Tax Notes includes digests of revenue rulings and procedures, other IRS documents, court opinions, and briefs and petitions. It also includes summaries of committee reports, testimony at hearings, bills, and statements in Congressional Record. It also includes information about public hearings on regulations and summaries of comments received on proposed regulations. Tax Notes publishes one or more articles in each issue. Its Bibliography section lists recent tax articles published elsewhere. Lists are in Code section or subject order.

Tax Notes is virtually complete in itself for most readers' purposes. It is also an excellent tool for locating prior year items. Full text information, such as statements at hearings on legislation and regulations, texts of tax articles, and IRS documents are available online in Tax Notes Today.

You can access this service through LexisNexis or the publisher's web-based service (TaxBase); document numbers appear in each weekly newsletter. Some libraries may also have these documents in a Tax Analysts' Microfiche Database.

Illustration 15-4. Excerpt from Tax Notes

SUMMARIES/IRS REGULATIONS

In response, some writers have criticized the proposed guidance, while others have offered suggestions for improvement.

Their specific comments are as follows:

- Austin J. Belton of the U.S. Small Business Administration, Washington, has enclosed records back to 1998 outlining efforts to bring about the credit. He says the SBA would like clarification of its role in the oversight and administration of new markets tax credit companies. *Doc 2002-7161 (32 original pages); 2002 TNT 59-17*

as part of an estate to make the election available if the power is held jointly. (For a summary of REG-106542-98, see Tax Notes, Dec. 25, 2000, p. 1695; for the full text see *Doc 2000-33612 (10 original pages), 2000 TNT 248-9,* or *H&D*, Dec. 18, 2000, p. 2651.) That change, says Gans, is consistent with the statutory language and legislative history.

Full Text Citations: *Doc 2002-6944 (2 original pages); 2002 TNT 58-16*

➔This excerpt is from the Public Comments on Regulations section of Tax Notes. If full text appears in Highlights & Documents, that citation appears in addition to a citation to Tax Notes Today.

3. Federal Tax Day News and Documents; Federal Tax Weekly

These newsletters are available online through LexisNexis and through the Tax Research NetWork. CCH includes links to primary source material discussed in these newsletters. There are also links to discussion in online versions of CCH looseleaf services.

Federal Tax Weekly is received by subscribers to the CCH Federal Tax Service. Online users can access it as a PDF file.

Illustration 15-5. Excerpt from Federal Tax Day

← Back to Search Results List	⊡ Previous Document In List	🖨 Print Text Only	Read Previous
Add Document to Keep List	⊡ Next Document In List	Export to File	Read Next

Federal Taxes · Current Features and Journals · Federal Tax Day · INTERNAL REVENUE SERVICE ·   #13 of 1348

NEWS-FEDERAL, 2002TAXDAY, 04/05/2002, Item #.1, Nonconventional Source Fuel Credit Inflation Adjustment Factor Given for 2001 (Notice)
Nonconventional Source Fuel Credit Inflation Adjustment Factor Given for 2001 (Notice)

The reference price that is to be used in determining the availability of the Code Sec. 29 tax credit for the production of fuel from nonconventional sources for calendar year 2001 is $21.86. Since this amount does not exceed $23.50, multiplied by the inflation adjustment factor, the Code Sec. 29(b)(1) phaseout of the credit will not occur for any qualified fuel based on the above reference price. The inflation adjustment factor for calendar year 2001 is 2.0917, and the nonconventional source fuel credit for 2001 is $6.28 per barrel-of-oil equivalent of qualified fuels.

Nonconventional Source Fuel Credit Notice,

Nonconventional Source Fuel Credit Notice, 2002FED ¶46,408

Other References:

Code Sec. 29

    CCH Reference · 2002FED ¶4051.04

➔Note the hyperlinks to primary source materials and to discussion in other CCH publications, including Standard Federal Tax Reporter.

4. Daily Tax Bulletin; Federal Tax Bulletin

The biweekly Federal Tax Bulletin supplements the TaxExpert CD-ROM. It includes reports on major legislative, administrative, and judicial action and brief digests of other items. Each issue has a Code section index; indexes are not cumulated. Subscribers can receive the print newsletter by e-mail. They also can access full-text documents using TaxExpert Online, Kleinrock's online service. The Daily Tax Bulletin is archived online.

Illustration 15-6. Excerpt from Federal Tax Bulletin

Employment Taxes

Rudman v. Commissioner, 118 T.C. No. 21 (4/29/02): The Tax Court held that the use of a floor broker did not substantially alter the normal course of a taxpayer's commodities trading activity and, thus, the earnings the taxpayer realized are subject to self-employment tax. Code Section 1402.

Select Rehab, Inc. v. United States, No. 3:CV-01-1278 (M.D. Pa. 4/8/02): A district court held that the taxpayer had acted reasonably and in good faith in treating its employee physicians as independent contractors. Therefore, the taxpayer was entitled to the safe harbor relief from liability for employment taxes provided in Section 530 of the Revenue Act of 1978. Code Section 3121.

➔Subscribers who receive Federal Tax Bulletin by e-mail can use the hyperlinks to access full text documents on TaxExpert Online. The e-mail version lacks a Code section index but allows electronic searching.

Illustration 15-7. Excerpt from Daily Tax Bulletin

March 12, 2002

Economic Stimulus Bill Contains Several Tax Provisions Affecting 2001 Tax Returns

Document: None
Code Section: None
Kleinrock's Analysis Section: None

On Saturday, March 9, President Bush signed The Job Creation and Worker Assistance Act of 2002 (Pub. L. 107-147) into law. The Act contains several tax provisions which may affect 2001 tax returns already filed – a bonus depreciation deduction, an extension of the net operating loss carryback period, and special tax benefits for the area of New York affected by the terrorist attacks. In addition, the Act closes a loophole used by shareholders of bankrupt S corporations and extends certain tax provisions which had expired at the end of 2001. It also creates a special deduction from gross income for certain expenses incurred by elementary and secondary school teachers.

To see a PDF of the Act, click here

➔Note the full-text PDF option.

PART SIX

COLLECTIONS OF PRIMARY SOURCE MATERIALS

Chapter 16. Print Materials

Chapter 17. Microforms

Chapter 18. CD-ROM

Chapter 19. Online Legal Research

CHAPTER 16. PRINT MATERIALS

The materials described below, and referred to in other chapters, print several types of material used in tax research.[247] Except as indicated below, they contain no textual discussion of the materials presented.

SECTION A. TREASURY AND IRS MATERIALS

1. Internal Revenue Bulletin; Cumulative Bulletin; Bulletin Index-Digest System

The three IRS-generated series contain the text of almost every nonjudicial primary authority. As the discussion below indicates, the Bulletin Index-Digest System (Index-Digest) was an excellent aid to using the other two series. Unfortunately, it ceased publication after the 1993/94 edition. As a result, citators and looseleaf services are probably the best print sources for locating citations to these items.[248]

The primary source materials printed in these volumes are available in microform (Chapter 17), CD-ROM (Chapter 18), and online (Chapter 19) services offered by a variety of vendors. Government-sponsored websites also include many of these materials.

a. Internal Revenue Bulletin

The weekly[249] Internal Revenue Bulletin (I.R.B.) is divided into four parts. Part I prints the text of all revenue rulings, final regulations, and Supreme

---

[247] Categories—Treasury and IRS Materials and Legislative and Administrative History Materials—reflect the primary use I make of each service.

[248] You can also search citators and looseleaf services online or simply perform an electronic search through an IRS database looking for a particular topic. For example, you might search for revenue rulings after 2000 dealing with divorce by performing the following Westlaw search: DIVORCE & DA(AFT 12/31/2000) in the FTX-RR database.

[249] Budget constraints occasionally result in a less-frequent publications schedule. See Ann. 93-82, 1993-22 I.R.B. 31, regarding semimonthly publication in June through September 1993. The IRS briefly considered eliminating the Cumulative Bulletin in 1998. See Ann. 99-36, 1999-1 C.B. 925.

Court tax decisions issued during the week; publication is in Code section order. Part II covers treaties, including Treasury Department Technical Explanations (Subpart A), and tax legislation, including committee reports (Subpart B). Part III contains notices and revenue procedures, while Part IV, "Items of General Interest," is varied in content. Its coverage includes disbarment notices, announcements, and notices of proposed rulemaking. Federal Register dates and comment deadlines are provided in addition to the preambles and text of proposed regulations. The I.R.B. also prints notices of IRS acquiescence or nonacquiescence for judicial decisions against the government.

Each I.R.B. was separately paginated until mid-1999. I.R.B. issues are now paginated successively over a six-month period.

Although the Bulletin has indexes and finding lists, they are unwieldy. A subject matter index appears in the first I.R.B. issued each month. It covers material published since the last six-month cumulation and is subdivided by type of tax.

Each issue contains a Numerical Finding List for each type of item; these lists lack any tie-in to Code sections and cover no more than six months. A Finding List of Current Action on Previously Published Items indicates IRS, but not judicial, action.

Because of its index format, the Bulletin is best used to locate material for which you already have a citation[250] or as a tool for staying abreast of recent developments. I.R.B. items are shown in Illustrations 3-6 and 9-1.

b. Cumulative Bulletin

Every six months the material in the I.R.B. is republished in a hardbound Cumulative Bulletin (C.B.). The C.B. began publication in 1919. Volumes initially were given Arabic numerals (1919-1921). Although volume spines may show Arabic numerals, the IRS used Roman numerals for 1922 through 1936 volumes. Since 1937, volumes have been numbered by year (e.g., 1937-1). With the exception of 1943-1945, there have been two volumes annually (with occasional extra volumes for extensive legislative history material) since 1920; the -1, -2 numbering system for each year began in 1922.

The C.B. format has varied over time. Before 1998, it largely followed that of the weekly service with three exceptions. First, major tax legislation and

---

[250] You can locate citations in citators, looseleaf services, periodical articles, and newsletters.

committee reports generally appeared in a third volume rather than in the two semiannual volumes.[251] Second, only disbarment notices and proposed regulations appeared from Part IV.[252] Finally, rulings appeared in the C.B. in semiannual Code section order; this bore no relation to their numerical order.

In 1998, the IRS ceased recompiling items in the C.B. Instead, C.B.s are simply bound versions of the individual I.R.B.s. If an item appears in the I.R.B., it will also appear in the C.B. Successive pagination for the I.R.B.s began in mid-1999.

At the time it changed format, the C.B. added a Code Sections Affected by Current Actions listing. Although this provides additional assistance in using six-month's worth of material, it does not make searching over longer periods of time any easier. The other C.B. indexes and finding lists are as difficult to use as are their counterparts in the I.R.B.

Table 16-1. Cumulative Bulletin Format Changes

Year	Numbering	Other Major Changes
1919	1, 2, 3	
1922	I-1, I-2, II-1	Rulings divided by type of tax
1937	1937-1, 1937-2	
1939		Committee reports added
1953		End of separate table of contents by type of tax
1974		End of separate section for 1939 Code
1981		Proposed Regulations added
1993		Acquiescences no longer limited to Tax Court regular decisions
1998		Six-month rearrangement of I.R.B. items ceased

c. Bulletin Index-Digest System

The IRS issued the Index-Digest in four services: Income Tax; Estate and Gift Tax; Employment Tax; and Excise Tax. The Income Tax service, which is the focal point for this discussion, was supplemented quarterly; the other services received semiannual supplementation. New softbound cumulations generally were issued every two years. The last cumulation covered 1954

---

[251] Committee reports for 1913 through 1938 appear in 1939-1 (pt. 2) C.B. Committee reports for the 1954 Code's enactment never appeared in the C.B.

[252] These are printed in Part III or immediately following it through 1997. Proposed regulations, which appear as a separate category, were added in the 1981-1 volume. The C.B.'s format differed from the above description until the 1974-2 volume.

through 1993 for income tax and 1994 for the other taxes.

You can use the Index-Digest to obtain I.R.B. or C.B. citations for revenue rulings and procedures, Supreme Court and adverse Tax Court decisions, Public Laws, Treasury Decisions, and treaties. In addition, it digests the rulings, procedures, and court decisions.

The following paragraphs explain using the final (1954-1993/94) Index-Digest to locate citations and digests.

(1) Statutes and Regulations

You can locate specific Code and regulations sections that were added or amended in the Finding Lists for Public Laws and Treasury Decisions. A C.B. citation is given for the first page of each Public Law involved.

Still another Finding List, "Public Laws Published in the Bulletin," is useful for locating committee report citations and popular names for the various revenue acts. It is in Public Law number order.

(2) Rulings and Procedures

The Finding Lists for Revenue Rulings, Revenue Procedures, and other Items can be used in various ways to locate relevant rulings and procedures. These items appear in Code and regulations section order in the "Internal Revenue Code of 1986" section, and in ruling and procedure number order in the "Revenue Rulings" and "Revenue Procedures" sections of these lists. The Index-Digest lists revenue rulings and procedures involving treaties by country in the "Revenue Rulings and Revenue Procedures under Tax Conventions" section. The service covers both 1954 and 1986 Code items.

None of these Finding Lists provides C.B. citations. Instead, citations are given to a digest of each item in the Index-Digest itself; the C.B. citation follows the digest. Although you must take an extra step to obtain the citation, the format frequently saves time; a glance through the digest may indicate the item is not worth reading in full text.[253] [See Illustration 16-1.]

Because the digests are arranged by subject matter, you can locate pertinent rulings even if you do not know the underlying Code or regulations section. The subject matter divisions are so numerous that the same item may be digested under several different headings.

---

[253] Unfortunately, the digest may not include a pertinent holding, in which case exclusive use of the digest would yield inadequate results.

If you want to know if a particular ruling or procedure has been modified or otherwise affected by subsequent IRS action, you can obtain this information from the "Actions on Previously Published Revenue Rulings and Revenue Procedures" section of the Finding Lists. Judicial decisions affecting a ruling are not indicated. Whenever a subsequent ruling affects an earlier item, a C.B. citation is given for the updating material.

(3) Judicial Decisions

The Finding Lists for Revenue Rulings, Revenue Procedures, and Other Items can be used to locate all Supreme Court decisions and adverse Tax Court decisions in which the IRS has acquiesced or nonacquiesced.

Supreme Court decisions appear alphabetically in the "Decisions of the Supreme Court" section of the Finding Lists. The Index-Digest lists them by the IRS-assigned Court Decision (Ct.D.) number in the "Internal Revenue Code of 1986" materials, arranged according to the applicable Code and regulations sections.

Tax Court decisions are listed alphabetically in the "Decisions of the Tax Court" section of the Finding Lists; they are listed by T.C. citation in the "Internal Revenue Code of 1986" materials.

As with rulings and procedures, references to Supreme Court decisions in the Finding Lists give only the digest number.[254] The official and Cumulative Bulletin citations follow the digest of the case. Again, because the digests have a subject matter format, you can locate decisions directly from the digests without first consulting the Finding Lists.

Illustration 16-1. Excerpt from Bulletin Index-Digest System

| **Allowances** they are not ordained, commissioned, or licensed as ministers of the gospel. §1.107-1. (Sec. 22(b), '39 Code; Sec. 107, '86 Code.) Rev. Rul. 59-270, 1959-2 C.B. 44 .... | **22.47 Rental; minister; traveling evangelist.** An ordained minister, who performs evangelistic services at churches located away from the community in which he maintains his permanent home may exclude .... | nished by the National Guard to officers and enlisted personnel while on active duty is not includible in the gross income of the recipients. §1.61-2 (Sec. 61, '86 Code.) Rev. Rul. 60-65, 1960-1 C.B. 21. |

→The Index-Digest lists digest numbers (e.g., 22.47) after Code and regulations sections. The actual digests appear in a separate Index-Digest section.

---

[254] Tax Court citations appear in both the Finding Lists and the digests. The Finding Lists indicate acquiescences; the digests provide citations for them.

2. U.S. Code Congressional & Administrative News—Federal Tax Regulations

The annual Federal Tax Regulations volumes contain the text of all income, estate and gift, and employment tax regulations in force on the first day of the year. These materials include references to the T.D. number, date, and Federal Register publication for both original promulgation and all amendments. However, this service omits T.D. numbers for original promulgation of pre-existing regulations republished in 1960 in T.D. 6498, 6500, or 6516. The final volume for each year includes a subject matter index.

3. Cumulative Changes

See Subsection B.3.

SECTION B. LEGISLATIVE AND ADMINISTRATIVE HISTORY MATERIALS

1. Internal Revenue Acts—Text and Legislative History; U.S. Code Congressional & Administrative News—Internal Revenue Code

You can use these services in researching the texts and histories of 1954 and 1986 Code sections.

Internal Revenue Acts, issued each year in pamphlet form, prints the full text of newly enacted statutes in chronological order. Hardbound volumes cumulate the material in one or more years' pamphlets.

Texts of selected committee reports and Congressional Record statements appear in the second section of each pamphlet. Each pamphlet includes a subject matter index; tables indicate Code sections affected and cross-reference Public Law section numbers to pages in Statutes at Large. The cross-reference table lists acts by name through 1996. Later pamphlets instead include a separate Popular Name table for acts. This series is excerpted from the general U.S. Code Congressional & Administrative News service and cross-references to material printed there but omitted here.

The annual Internal Revenue Code volumes contain the text of all Code sections in effect when the most recent congressional session ended. Dates, Public Law numbers, and Statutes at Large citations appear in the brief history of enactment and amendment following each section. Editorial notes indicate effective dates and provide some information about prior language.[255] The final volume for each year contains a subject matter index.

2. Primary Sources

Primary Sources is an excellent tool for locating significant proposed legislation and deriving the legislative history of existing Code sections. It also covers the Employee Retirement Income Security Act (ERISA). Although it no longer follows pending legislation through Congress, it does provide legislative history updates for changes in the Code.

Extensive legislative histories appear for selected Code sections. The sections chosen for inclusion are traced back to their original 1954 Code versions;[256] all changes are presented. [See Illustration 16-2.] Materials presented for each Code section include presidential messages, committee reports, Treasury Department testimony at hearings, and discussion printed in Congressional Record.

The legislative histories are published in several series, each of which covers several years.[257] Within each series, material appears in Code section order. Each series contains a Master Table of Contents in Code section order; these tables cover the current series and all prior series. Primary Sources limits its coverage to Code sections affected by the Tax Reform Act of 1969 or by subsequent legislation.

3. Cumulative Changes

This multivolume looseleaf service tracks changes in the Code and Treasury regulations. There are series for the 1939, 1954, and 1986 Codes and regulations; many libraries lack the 1939 Code series. Cumulative Changes covers employment taxes and provides limited coverage of excise taxes.

The Code and regulations materials appear separately, arranged in Code section order. The 1954 service includes parallel citation tables for the 1939 and 1954 Codes.

---

[255] Primary Sources provides such information for 1969 and subsequent amendments.

[256] Series I also includes the 1939 Code version for many Code sections.

[257] Series I begins with sections affected by the Tax Reform Act of 1969; Series II begins with the 1976 Tax Reform Act; Series III begins with the Revenue Act of 1978; Series IV begins with the Economic Recovery Tax Act of 1981; Series V begins with the Tax Reform Act of 1986.

a. Internal Revenue Code

A chart for each Code section indicates its original effective date. The chart includes the Public Law number, section, and enactment and effective dates of each amendment and the act section prescribing the effective date. The chart covers Code section subdivisions (subsections, paragraphs, and even smaller subdivisions). It does not include Statutes at Large citations.

The format of Cumulative Changes changed slightly in the mid-1990s. It now prints citations for effective dates rather than the dates themselves. Illustration 16-3 includes both formats for Code section 51.

Illustration 16-2. Excerpt from Primary Sources

<table>
<tr><td>IV-26</td><td></td><td>§168 [1981] pg.(i)</td></tr>
</table>

SEC. 168 – ACCELERATED COST RECOVERY SYSTEM

Table of Contents

Page

STATUTE — [As Added by the Economic Recovery Tax Act of 1981 (P.L. 97-34)] . . . . §168 [1981] pg.1

LEGISLATIVE HISTORY

    Background
        97th Congress, 1st Sess. (H.R. 3849)
           Treasury Dept. Tech. Explanation of H.R. 3849 . . . §168 [1981] pg. 28

    House of Representatives
        Ways and Means Committee
           Committee Hearings
               Statement of Donald Regan, Sec'y of Treasury §168 [1981] pg. 34
           Committee Report . . . . §168 [1981] pg. 35

    Senate
        Finance Committee
           Committee Hearings
               Statement of Donald Regan, Sec'y of Treasury §168 [1981] pg. 43
           Committee Press Releases
               No. 81-19 (June 24, 1981) . . . . §168 [1981] pg. 44
               No. 81-21 (June 26, 1981) . . . . §168 [1981] pg. 45
           Committee Report . . . . §168 [1981] pg. 46
        Senate Discussion
           Vol. 127 Cong. Rec. (July 20, 1981) . . . . §168 [1981] pg. 55
           Vol. 127 Cong. Rec. (July 23, 1981) . . . . §168 [1981] pg. 58

→Primary Sources excerpts a wide range of legislative history documents.

The pages following each chart reproduce each version (except the current one) since the provision's original introduction in the relevant Code. The current version can be found in any service that includes the current Code.

b. Treasury Regulations

Tables of amendments cover all regulations sections for each tax; individual sections do not have their own charts. Each table indicates the original and all amending T.D. numbers and filing dates and provides a Cumulative Bulletin or Internal Revenue Bulletin citation. Cross-references to United States Tax Reporter are also given. A final table, in T.D. number order, indicates the purpose, date and C.B. or I.R.B. citation for each regulation issued.[258]

The tables follow the regulations part designations illustrated in Chapter 8; as a result, they do not follow a strict Code section numerical sequence. The 1954 series includes tables for regulations that have been redesignated or replaced.

Immediately following the tables, the editors print prior versions of each regulation. Older materials note changes in italics and use footnotes to indicate stricken language; recent materials do not use this format. Cumulative Changes includes the T.D. number and the dates of approval and of filing for each version of a regulation.

4. Barton's Federal Tax Laws Correlated

Five hardbound volumes trace income, estate, and gift tax provisions from the Revenue Act of 1913[259] through the Tax Reform Act of 1969.

a. 1909 through 1952

The five hardbound volumes reproduce in Code or act section order the text of the various tax acts. Because the acts are lined up in several columns on each page, it is possible to read across a page and see every version of a

---

[258] Although T.D. 6500, a 1960 republication of existing income tax regulations is not formally included, Cumulative Changes does list the original pre-1960 T.D. A cautionary note warns the user to remember that pre-1960 regulations were republished in T.D. 6500. T.D. 6498 (procedure and administration) and T.D. 6516 (withholding tax) receive similar treatment. None of these T.D.s appears in the Cumulative Bulletin.

[259] The original second edition (vol. 1) also contained the text of the income tax laws from 1861 through 1909. The reproduced second edition omits this material.

particular section for the period that volume covers.[260] Whenever possible, Barton's uses different typefaces to highlight changes.

The first two volumes provide a citation to Statutes at Large for each act. Volume 1 includes case annotations, and each volume has a subject matter index. The volumes covering the 1939 Code include tables indicating amending acts and effective dates for 1939 Code sections. Volume 5 has a retrospective table cross-referencing sections to pages in the four previous volumes.

b. 1953-1969

The looseleaf sixth volume does not print the text of Code sections. Its Tables instead provide citations to primary sources that print the desired material. Tables A-D are in Code section order; Table E is in Public Law number order.

Table A provides the history of the 1954 Act. It indicates Statutes at Large page; House, Senate, and Conference report page (official and U.S. Code Congressional & Administrative News); 1939 Code counterpart; Revenue Act where the provision originated; and relevant pages in volumes 1-5.

Table B covers amendments to the 1954 Code. For each section it provides Public Law number, section, and enactment date; Statutes at Large citation; House, Senate, and Conference report numbers and location in the Cumulative Bulletin; comment (e.g., revision, amendment); and effective date information.

Table C is similar to Table A, but it covers the 1939 Code. It gives the 1954 Code section; the origin of the 1939 Code provision; and cross-references to volumes 1-5.

Table D is the same as Table B, but it covers post-1953 changes to the 1939 Code.

Table E provides citations to legislative history for all acts from 1953 through 1969. It also provides the following information for each act: Public Law number; date of enactment; congressional session; Statutes at Large, Cumulative Bulletin, and USCCAN citations for the act; congressional sessions, dates, and Cumulative Bulletin and USCCAN citations for House, Senate, and Conference report numbers; and Congressional Record citations for floor debate. Acts are not cited by popular name.

---

[260] Volume 1 covers 1913-1924; volume 2 covers 1926-38; volume 3 covers 1939-43; volume 4 covers 1944-49; volume 5 covers 1950-52.

Illustration 16-3. Excerpt from Cumulative Changes

3-2000	Section 51. Amount of Credit	§ 51—p. 3

[See definitions preceding chart on page 1 of this section.]

SEC. 751 '86 I.R.C.	SUBSECTIONS					
	(f)—(h)	(i)(1)	(i)(2)	(i)(3)	(j)	(k)
Pub. Law 99-514, 10-22-86				Added by 1701(c) 1701(e)* Note 1		Redesig. 1878(f)(1) 1881* Note 1
AMENDING ACTS						
Pub. Law 103-66 8-10-93		13302(d) 13303* 8-10-93				

Public Law	Law Sec.	IRC Sec.	Eff. Date
P.L. 104-188	1201(a)	51(a)	1201(g)*
	1201(e)(1)	51(a)	1201(g)*
	1201(f)	51(c)(1)	1201(g)*
	1201(d)	51(c)(4)	1201(g)*
	1201(b)	51(d)	1201(g)*
	1201(e)(1)	51(g)	1201(g)*
	1201(c)	51(i)(3)	1201(g)*
	1201(e)(5)	51(j) Heading	1201(g)*
P.L. 105-34	603(b)(2)	51(d)(2)(A)	
	603(c)(2)	51(d)(9)-(11) Redes (10)-(12)	
	603(d)(2)	51(i)(3)	
P.L. 105-277	1002(a)	51(c)(4)(B)	1002(b)
	4006(c)(1)	51(d)(6)(B)(i)	

5. Seidman's Legislative History of Federal Income and Excess Profits Tax Laws[261]

Although Seidman's stops in 1953, it remains useful for determining the legislative history of provisions that originated in the 1939 Code or even earlier.[262] This series follows each act, beginning with the most recent, presenting the text of Code sections, followed by relevant committee reports and citations to hearings[263] and the Congressional Record.[264] Because Seidman's uses different type styles, you can easily ascertain where in Congress a provision originated or was deleted. [See Illustration 16-4.[265]]

Seidman's prints proposed sections that were not enacted along with relevant history explaining their omission. This information can aid you in interpreting provisions Congress did enact.

Although its coverage has great breadth, Seidman's does not print every Code section. It omits provisions with no legislative history, items lacking substantial interpretive significance, and provisions the editor considered long outmoded. Seidman's does not cover gift, estate, or excise taxes.

Seidman's has three indexes. The Code section index lists each section by act and assigns it a key number. The same key number is assigned to corresponding sections in subsequent acts. The key number index indicates every act, by section number and page in the text, where the item involved appears. A subject index lists key numbers by topic.

Volume II of the 1953-1939 set contains a table cross-referencing 1953 and 1954 Code sections covered in Seidman's. [See Illustration 6-4.]

---

[261] The two volumes covering 1939 through 1953 include both taxes. Separate volumes for the income tax and the excess profits tax were used for the earlier materials, covering 1861 through 1938 and 1917 through 1946, respectively.

[262] I.R.C. § 263, for example, contains language taken almost verbatim from § 117 of the 1864 Act. See Act of June 30, 1864, ch. 173, 13 Stat. 223, 281-82.

[263] Seidman's cites relevant page numbers in the hearings and indicates appearances by Treasury representatives.

[264] Seidman's cites to relevant pages and reproduces the text itself in some instances.

[265] Illustration 16-6 covers the report excerpted in Illustration 16-4.

Illustration 16-4. Excerpt from Seidman's

for key to statute type]   1934 ACT   381

SEC. 164 DIFFERENT TAXABLE YEARS.   Sec. 164

If the taxable year of a beneficiary is different from that of the estate or trust, the amount which he is required, under section 162(b), to include in computing his net income, shall be based upon the income of the estate or trust for any taxable year of the estate or trust (whether beginning on, before, or after January 1, 1934) ending within his taxable year.

Committee Reports

Report–Ways and Means Committee (73d Cong., 2d Sess., H. Rept. 704).–Section 164. Different taxable years: The present law requires a beneficiary of an estate or trust to include in his income amounts allowed as a deduction to the estate or trust under 162(b). In order to continue this policy, it is necessary in view of the policy adopted in section 1 to add additional language to provide for cases where the estate or trust has a taxable year beginning in 1933 and ending in 1934 (p.32)

Report–Senate Finance Committee (73d Cong., 2d Sess., S. Rept. 558).–Same as Ways and Means Committee Report. (p.40)

SEC. 166 REVOCABLE TRUSTS.   Sec. 166

Where at any time **(96)** <del>\<during the taxable year\></del> the power to revest in the grantor title to any part of the corpus of the trust is vested–

→The 1934 Act predated the first Internal Revenue Code. Section numbers do not correspond to the system used for the 1954 and 1986 Codes.

→Note how Seidman's indicates language stricken on the Senate floor.

6. The Internal Revenue Acts of the United States: 1909-1950; 1950-1972; 1973-

a. Original Series

This set, edited by Bernard D. Reams, Jr., provides the most comprehensive legislative histories of all the services discussed in this chapter. In addition to each congressional version of revenue bills, the 144 original volumes (1909-1950) contain the full texts of hearings, committee reports, Treasury studies, and regulations. Official pagination is retained for relevant documents. In addition to income and excise taxes, this set includes estate and gift, social security, railroad retirement, and unemployment taxes. This set is available in print and microfiche.

An Index volume contains several indexes for locating relevant materials. A chronological index lists each act and every item comprising its legislative history. That index indicates the volume, but not the page, where each item is located.[266] Other indexes cover miscellaneous subjects, such as hearings on items that did not result in legislation; Treasury studies; Joint Committee reports; regulations; congressional reports; congressional documents; bill numbers; and hearings. Unfortunately, there is neither a Code section nor a subject matter index.

Full text materials appear by type of document rather than by the act involved. All hearings are printed together, as are all bills, laws, studies, and regulations. You will need to use several volumes to assemble all materials for a particular law or provision. This is by no means a substantial drawback to using this set; assembling the same materials from elsewhere in the collection (assuming they are all available) would be far more difficult.

b. Subsequent Series[267]

Professor Reams subsequently compiled materials to extend this set's coverage to later years. The later volumes are similar in coverage and format to the 1909-50 materials, although hearings receive less attention.

The 1954 volumes include committee reports, hearings, debates, and the final act. Revenue bills and Treasury studies do not appear. Because the IRS Cumulative Bulletins do not cover the 1954 Act, these materials are particularly valuable. A two-volume update published in 1993 includes fifty House and Senate bills missing from the original volumes.

Additional sets cover 1950-51, 1953-72, 1969, 1971, 1975, 1976, 1978, 1980, 1984, 1985 (Balanced Budget), 1986, 1987 (Balanced Budget), 1988, 1990, and 1993. Another set, covering the Taxpayer Relief Act of 1997, was edited by William Manz. Several sets are available only in microform.

7. Legislative History of the Internal Revenue Code of 1954

Prepared for the Joint Committee on Internal Revenue Taxation in 1967, this volume covers all changes made in the 1954 Code from its enactment through October 23, 1965. Arranged in Code section order, it contains full text of the 1954 language and of all changes made. It also includes the text

---

[266] Individual volumes aren't consecutively paginated.

[267] I have used libraries that shelve other legislative history materials between sets of the Reams materials. Check the library catalog to determine which sets your library has.

of ancillary provisions (which are in other parts of U.S.C. or not in U.S.C. at all) and citations to Statutes at Large.

There are four sets of tables: 1939 Code sources of each 1954 Code provision; corresponding sections of the two Codes; post-1954 Code amendments to the 1939 Code; and amendatory statutes. The last table includes the Public Law number; date approved; bill number; House, Senate, and Conference Committee report numbers; Act name; and Statutes at Large citation.

Illustration 16-5. Excerpt from The Internal Revenue Acts of the United States Index Volume

REVENUE ACT OF 1934	
	Volume
BILL IN ITS VARIOUS FORMS	
Compiler's note	74
Introduced: 73d Cong., 2d session. H.R. 7835. In the House of Representatives February 9, 1934. Mr. Doughton of North Carolina introduced the following bill, which was referred to the Committee on Ways and Means and ordered to be printed	74
House committee print No. 1. (Confidential committee print No. 1). 73d Cong., 2d session H.R. (7835). In the House of Representatives February (2), 1934. Mr. introduced the following bill, which was referred to the Committee on Ways and Means and ordered to be printed	74
Reported to the House: 73d Cong., 2d session. H.R. 7835 (Report No. 704). .... of the Union and ordered to be printed	74

→The report excerpted in Illustration 16-4 (Seidman's) appears in full text in volume 100 of The Internal Revenue Acts of the United States. [See Illustration 16-6.]

→The text missing from the third entry ("Mr. introduced") is also omitted in the original Index volume.

**Illustration 16-6. Excerpt from The Internal Revenue Acts
of the United States Volume 100**

> Section 148(b). Profits of taxable year declared: This subsection is entirely rewritten, not with any view to a change in policy, but with the intent to set forth in more definite language the present policy.
>
> Section 164. Different taxable years: The present law requires a beneficiary of an estate or trust to include in his income amounts allowed as a deduction to the estate or trust under section 162(b). In order to continue this policy, it is necessary in view of the policy adopted in section 1 to add additional language to provide for cases where the estate or trust has a taxable year beginning in 1933 and ending in 1934.
>
> Section 168 (Revenue Act of 1932). Capital net gains and losses: This section is omitted from the bill in view of the change of policy in taxing capital gains.
>
> Section 182. Tax on partners: this section represents a change in section 182 of existing law in two respects: First, because of the change in the policy of treating fiscal-year returns, a new section (sec. 188) is carried in

→The Internal Revenue Acts reprints reports in the format used by Congress; all sections for each act appear in order. Compare the treatment in Seidman's [Illustration 16-4], which groups reports by act or Code section.

→Because there was no Internal Revenue Code in 1934, some act sections merely repeat sections enacted in previous years. Other act sections change earlier language or add entirely new provisions.

8. Eldridge, The United States Internal Revenue System

This reprint of early legislative materials is a useful complement to The Internal Revenue Acts of the United States, discussed in Subsection B.6. It includes texts of revenue acts passed through 1894. There is extensive textual material as well as annotations for the various acts. It also contains a descriptive history of the various acts.

9. Cumulative Bulletin

See Subsection A.1.

CHAPTER 17. MICROFORMS

SECTION A. ADVANTAGES AND DISADVANTAGES

Microforms have three important advantages. The first relates to space. As primary and secondary source materials proliferate, libraries can use microforms to reduce their space needs. A second advantage relates to availability. Certain historical materials are currently available only in microform. A third advantage relates to cost. Once the library has purchased materials in microform, it has no obligation to make further outlays to ensure its access to those materials.

There are several reasons why other formats may be preferable to microforms. These relate to availability, ease of searching, mobility, space, and security.

Availability may be the most critical factor. Many publishers are eliminating microform products and switching to CD-ROMs and online services.[268] Even if a publisher no longer updates a microform service, these materials remain valuable for historical research.

Navigation and mobility are also important. Electronic sources are easier to navigate and permit word and phrase searching. Microforms are effectively used only if the compiler has indexed them well. In addition, electronic materials do not tie the researcher to a fixed place. Unlike microforms, which require a reader or reader-printer, a researcher with the appropriate computer configuration can use electronic materials anywhere.

Space and security are relevant factors for many libraries. Web-based systems require no library storage space; CD-ROMs require relatively little space. Although microforms require less space than their print counterparts, they do require more than the electronic versions. Finally, microforms share a problem with looseleaf services; the individual forms can be misfiled or pilfered from the library.

---

[268] CCH switched from ultrafiche to CD-ROM and online versions for case reporter services. Tax Analysts also uses CD-ROM and online sites for material from its Microfiche Database. These materials include Tax Notes in addition to primary source materials.

Section B. Format

Microforms are available in a variety of formats, including microfilm, microfiche, and ultrafiche. You can use a reader-printer to produce a copy of materials you locate.

Section C. Available Materials

Government publications available in microform include Congressional Record, Statutes at Large, Federal Register, Code of Federal Regulations, and the Cumulative Bulletin. Other materials include Tax Court and Supreme Court case reporter services. Many libraries include briefs filed with the United States Supreme Court in their microform collections.

You are also likely to find legislative history materials available in microform. Publishers using this format include Congressional Information Service (part of LexisNexis) and William S. Hein & Co., Inc.

The CIS/Microfiche Library includes committee hearings, reports, and prints and public laws since 1970. Libraries can customize their purchases to include only certain types of documents. The CIS/Index, available in print or online, provides abstracts of publications and a separate index.[269]

Several series of Hein's Internal Revenue Acts of the United States (Chapter 16) are available in microform. These include the sets for 1909-1950, 1950-51, 1954, 1953-72, 1978, and 1984.

Some libraries may own ultrafiche copies of Tax Management Primary Sources–Series I (Chapter 16).

Law reviews and other periodicals may also be available in microform. Representative publications available from Hein include Akron Tax Journal, American Journal of Tax Policy, Tax Law Review, Tax Lawyer, and several tax institutes.[270]

Because the number of materials and the microform format used varies, always consult a librarian about microform access before concluding that your library lacks a particular resource.

---

[269] See http://www.lexis-nexis.com/academic/3cis/cisMnu.htm for a listing of CIS publications.

[270] Hein-On-Line, a web-based source for periodicals, is discussed in Chapter 13.

Chapter 18. CD-ROM

Section A. Advantages and Disadvantages

CD-ROMs store significant amounts of information yet require little storage space. In many areas of research, CD-ROM and online services have supplanted microform as an alternative to print materials.

Although CD-ROM materials may be updated less frequently than looseleaf services or other research tools are,[271] they have offsetting advantages. The CD-ROM format lets you perform more efficient searches than can be accomplished using print services. Some CD-ROM publishers even provide a direct link to their online services. This option reduces your online time, an important factor if you are billed based on that time.

Most looseleaf services print recent developments in separate subdivisions, sometimes even in separate volumes. Update CDs integrate new material directly into the original text. Because all material is on the same CD,[272] researchers don't have to worry about filing errors or damaged pages.

CD-ROMs are not a perfect substitute for print versions of primary source materials. The CD may not use the citation form you need for a brief or article; even if it does, it may not show page numbers for individual sections of text. In some instances, the citation provided is erroneous. In addition, you must remember that a CD-ROM is only as current as the underlying material it includes. A publisher that updates a particular print treatise quarterly will not necessarily update it more frequently in CD-ROM.

A potential disadvantage of CD-based services relates to access. Unless the service is networked, only one researcher can use it at a time. In contrast, several researchers can simultaneously use different volumes of a print reporter service; they can search the same volumes simultaneously when using an online service.

---

[271] Several CD-ROM services offer updating options. Check the option in use (for example, monthly or quarterly) so that you don't erroneously assume your CD-ROM reflects the most recent changes in the law.

[272] Some services require multiple CD-ROMs. In that case, you will be prompted to insert the appropriate CD if your computer is not attached to a CD changer.

Section B. Search Strategies

1. Similarity to Searching Print Materials

You can use CD-ROM materials much as you would print items. In the case of treatises, for example, you can locate a topic in the table of contents and then review that text segment or download it for later reading.

As is true for other types of research, you must consider synonyms if your concept can be expressed in different ways.[273] In addition, just as print publishers use different cross-referencing methods, CD-ROM publishers may use different search commands. Table 18-1 lists common search commands.

2. Search Strategies Unique to Electronic Materials

A major difference between print and electronic services relates to the latter's use of hypertext links. When you click on a link, you are transported to other text sections or to primary source materials such as the Code or Treasury regulations. To return to the original text, you merely click on the appropriate command. Illustrations 9-8 and 18-5 depict using hypertext links in the RIA OnPoint service. Although it appears similar to conducting a search using multiple print volumes, using links is not the same. Be careful to backtrack rather than exit the service if you want to retrace your steps.

Another difference relates to your initial search strategy. Rather than using indexes or tables to find material, you can use electronic services to find primary source material directly. As shown in Illustration 18-9, these services offer several search fields and also let you specify words that must appear in the document.

Electronic services also allow more sophisticated searching. You can specify Boolean connectors (e.g., and, or, and not). You can also take advantage of wild card symbols (e.g., deduct* for deduct, deducting, deduction, deducted, deductions, and deductible) to expand your search results.

Because search commands vary, you should read the user's guide for each service. You might find it useful to compile a short command list for each service included in your library's collection. Remember also to check the contents; electronic services often expand or contract their coverage based

---

[273] Check to see if the CD-ROM includes a thesaurus feature. If you insert a $ sign at the end of a word on OneDisc, OnPoint, or Tax Practice Plus, each retrieves synonyms. [See Illustration 18-6.] TaxExpert does not offer this feature.

on market demand.

3. Differences Between CD-ROM and Online Services

Online services are likely to include more primary and secondary sources than a single CD-ROM, thus avoiding the need to change CDs.[274] Online services are more likely to let you narrow searches by year. Online services also use their own search command structure. If you use a particular service's CD version, don't be surprised if you must use different commands online. You are most likely to encounter different search commands if you use a general online service rather than one offered by the CD's publisher.[275]

SECTION C. REPRESENTATIVE MATERIALS

The sources discussed below are a sampling of the materials available. Some are CD-ROM versions of the publisher's print materials. In other cases, the publisher makes the item available only in an electronic format.

1. Tax Analysts

a. OneDisc

Subscribers to Tax Analysts' OneDisc can select monthly, quarterly, or annual update options. Sources covered include:

• Legislative Materials

  Internal Revenue Code
  New Legislation
  Joint Committee on Taxation Blue Book for prior Congress

• Regulations

  Temporary and Final Treasury Regulations
  Preambles for Treasury Decisions
  Proposed Regulations (including Preambles)
  BATF Regulations

---

[274] Government-sponsored and other nonsubscription online services may use hyperlinks both within their websites and to other sites.

[275] For example, if you search Federal Tax Coordinator 2d using OnPoint, you can add letters at the end of a word using an asterisk (*). If you use Westlaw, the comparable command is an exclamation point (!).

- Treasury and IRS

  IRS Regulatory Agenda
  IRS Business Plan (with Tax Analysts annotations)

- IRS Materials (check Chief Counsel Advice CD-ROM for prior year items that are publicly available rather than officially published by the IRS)

  Revenue Rulings and Revenue Procedures
  Announcements and Notices
  Letter Rulings and Technical Advice Memoranda
  Actions on Decisions
  General Counsel Memoranda
  Field Service Advice
  Legal Guideline Memoranda
  Service Center Advice
  Chief Counsel Notices
  Legal Memoranda
  Information Letters
  Compliance Officer Memoranda
  Technical Assistance
  Market Segment Specialization Program Papers and Market
     Segment Understandings
  Industry Specialization Papers and Settlement Guidelines
  IRS Publications
  IRS Penalties Handbook
  Circular 230

- Judicial

  Court Opinions (summaries of older material and text of newer items; check separate CDs for retrospective coverage)

- Other

  Tax Law Baedeker (a guide to federal tax law)
  Tax Directory of Federal and State Officials

The OneDisc includes tables of IRS information such as rates, inflation adjustments, interest on under- and overpayments, the kiddie tax, and applicable federal rates. Several of the looseleaf services described in Chapter 12 also provide the type of information included in these tables.

b. Tax Legislative History and Tax Treaties[276]

Tax Analysts publishes both Tax Legislative History, U.S. Tax Treaties, and Worldwide Tax Treaties CDs. The legislative history materials cover the period since 1986 and include committee reports, Congressional Record material, and other documents. The United States treaty materials cover all tax treaties between the United States and another country and include a variety of primary source documents. The worldwide service includes treaties to which the United States is not a party. These services are available in quarterly or annual updating.

c. IRS Material and Judicial Opinions

OneDisc includes the most recent court opinions and Chief Counsel items. Older materials appear on separate CDs. If an item is included on a separate CD, the OneDisc signals you to insert it.

The Chief Counsel Advice CD includes materials from 1980 through the preceding year. This service is also available online and in print. Tax Analysts also publishes an Internal Revenue Manual CD, which is available with quarterly or annual updating, and a Forms Disc covering federal and state tax return forms and instructions. Judicial decisions are included in the Federal Courts Collection service.

Illustration 18-1. Tax Analysts OneDisc and Court Decisions 1 Disc

→The next three illustrations use the OneDisc and a Court Decisions CD to find a judicial opinion involving validity of year-end divorces.

→The exercise below was completed using words (divorce December AND valid*) as the search terms. I could instead have used criteria such as Code section, case name, citation, or jurisdiction (assuming I knew them).

---

[276] These materials are discussed further in Chapter 6 (Legislative Histories) and Chapter 7 (Treaties).

Illustration 18-2. Search Using OneDisc

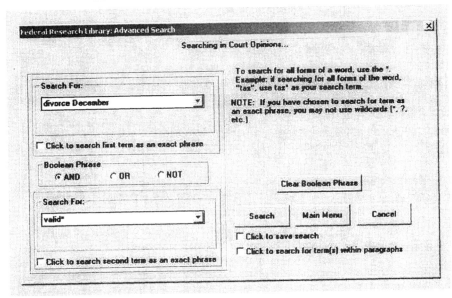

→I selected the Court Opinions section of OneDisc. I could have conducted the same search directly in the Court Decisions CD. Beginning with OneDisc ensures including current year items.

→The Advanced Search function allows limited Boolean searching (AND, OR, NOT), using an asterisk (*) to find multiple forms of a word, specifying that words must appear as an exact phrase, and searching for terms within a paragraph. Use the Help function to find other search commands.

Illustration 18-3. Excerpt from Items Found Using OneDisc

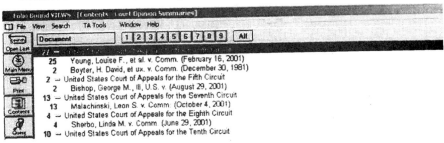

→The search located approximately 30 opinions. Assume you remembered hearing about the *Boyter* case and selected it to read.

→Note that decisions are grouped by court level.

Illustration 18-4. Excerpt from Court Decisions Disc

WINTER, Chief Judge:

Taxpayers (H. David Boyter and his sometime wife, Angela M. Boyter), both of whom are domiciled in Maryland, ask us to reverse the Tax Court and to rule that for the tax years 1975 and 1976 they successfully avoided the "marriage penalty" of the Internal Revenue Code. The "marriage penalty" results from the fact that a man and woman who are husband and wife on the last day of the taxable year, each having separate income, are taxed, in the aggregate, in a greater amount if they file either joint or separate income tax returns than would be the case if they were unmarried. /1/ The Tax Court ruled that the Boyters were legally married at the end of tax years 1975 and 1976, and therefore were subject to the higher tax rate, since their purported Haitian and Dominican Republic divorces (granted on December 8, 1975 and November 22, 1976, respectively) were invalid under the law of Maryland, the state of the Boyters' domicile. The Tax Court therefore sustained the Commissioner's deficiency assessments for unpaid taxes. In view of this conclusion the Tax Court apparently thought it unnecessary to decide the Commissioner's alternative argument that even if the divorces would be recognized in Maryland, the taxpayers should be treated as husband and wife for federal income tax purposes under the "sham" transaction doctrine.

➔The Court Decisions disc gives a citation to Tax Notes Today but does not give an official citation.

➔The Boyters divorced in December 1975 and November 1976. If both divorces had occurred in November, my search would not have located this decision. Perhaps I should have eliminated "December" as a search term and included "sham" instead of "valid*." Deleting "December" increases the number of records the system retrieves.

➔If I use "sham$" instead of "sham," my search yields opinions that include "fraud" and "fraudulent."

d. Other Tax Analysts Products

Your library may also have CD-ROM versions of Tax Notes (Chapter 15), a Tax Directory, or the Exempt Organization Tax Review.

2. Research Institute of America

a. OnPoint

RIA offers two products that include a variety of research tools, OnPoint and Public Domain Library. Both are updated monthly.

The OnPoint service offers several combinations of sources on CD-ROM. Materials available include primary source, citator, looseleaf service, and treatise materials. In addition to the sources normally included in each service, subscribers can add selected other RIA services. Two examples of OnPoint services appear below.

System 1 includes Federal Tax Coordinator 2d, Federal Tax Handbook, various practice aids, the Internal Revenue Code, Treasury regulations, revenue rulings and revenue procedures, IRS publications, and legislation.

System 3 includes United States Tax Reporter, Federal Tax Handbook, the Internal Revenue Code, Treasury regulations, revenue rulings and revenue procedures, IRS publications, tax treaties, legislation (including selected committee reports), and current year decisions from American Federal Tax Reports.

The Public Domain Library includes the following items (coverage dates vary):

- Legislative Materials

    Internal Revenue Code and Code history

- Regulations

    Final and Temporary Regulations
    Preambles to Final Regulations
    Proposed Regulations (including Preambles)

- IRS Materials

    Revenue Rulings and Revenue Procedures
    Announcements and Notices
    Letter Rulings and Technical Advice Memoranda
    Actions on Decisions
    General Counsel Memoranda
    Field Service Advice
    Service Center Advice
    Disclosure Litigation Bulletins and other IRS Documents
    Delegation Orders

- Judicial

    Court Opinions from RIA case reporter services

- Other

    RIA Citator 2nd
    Federal Taxes Handbook; Handbook Topic Index
    Federal Taxes Weekly Alert
    Tax Planning and Practice Guides

Illustration 18-5. Excerpt from Federal Tax Coordinator Contents

```
✧ Chapter J-4690 Income: Taxable and Exempt, Non-Wage Withholding
⟶ Chapter K Deductions: Taxes, Interest, Charitable, Medical, Others
  ✧ ¶K-1000 Deductions Allowed by Law.
  ✧ ¶K-1100 Personal Expenses.
  ✧ ¶K-2000 Medical Expenses—General Rules.
  ⟶ ¶K-2100 Expenditures Which Qualify as Medical Expenses—Other Than Travel and Transportation Expenses.
      ¶K-2102 Medical expenses as deductible personal expenses.
      ¶K-2103 Medical expenses versus general health expenses.
      ¶K-2104 Medical professional services as medical expenses.
      ¶K-2105 Expenditures prescribed or recommended by a medical professional.
      ¶K-2105.1 Diagnostic tests and DNA collection as medical expenses.
      ¶K-2106 Illegal treatments.
      ¶K-2107 Medical treatments by unlicensed persons, where license is legally required.
      ¶K-2108 Psychoanalysis and psychological counseling costs as medical expenses.
      ¶K-2109 Cosmetic surgery and similar procedures as medical expenses.
      ¶K-2110 Discretionary medical costs.
      ¶K-2111 Nursing and attendant services.
      ¶K-2112 Allocating costs between nursing and non-nursing services.
      ¶K-2113 What are nursing services.
      ¶K-2114 "Nontraditional" medical care, therapy, services, etc., not performed by medical professionals.
      ¶K-2115 Health club, spa, etc. expenses as medical expenses.
      ¶K-2116 Weight-loss programs.
      ¶K-2117 Programs to stop smoking.
      ¶K-2118 Alcoholism treatment
```

➔The contents list reflects subject matter rather than Code section arrangement. This service is arranged by paragraph rather than by page or section.

➔A **+** sign indicates additional subheadings in the table of contents; click to reach them. A **-** sign indicates there are no additional subheadings.

➔ If you double click on a paragraph, you jump to descriptive text. From there, you can jump to additional explanatory material or to primary source material. Navigation buttons let you move back and forth. This screen includes ¶K-2117. Clicking it takes us to the discussion in Illustration 9-8.

Illustration 18-6. Excerpt from Federal Tax Coordinator 2d

Retrieve by Paragraph Number and/or Keywords

```
mediator
mediators
mediator's
medica
medicaid
medical
medically
medicare
medicated
medication
medications
medicinal
medicine
medicines
```

Paragraph Number or Numbers:

For example, A-1001

Fill in one or more of the fields.

Keywords

medical$

Records with hits - 1515

```
medical - 1283
healing - 7
pharmaceutical - 41
therapeutic - 31
medicinal - 3
curative - 16
```

OK   Cancel   Help

➔Using medical$ in Keywords yields several synonyms.

b. Legislative History

RIA offers a Pending and Enacted Legislation CD-ROM. It covers laws, bills, and committee reports and begins with 1995. Updating is monthly.

c. IRS Material and Judicial Opinions

RIA offers an IRS Letter Rulings & Memoranda CD-ROM, marketed with the OnPoint logo. This service covers private letter rulings, technical advice memoranda, actions on decisions, and general counsel memoranda. It also includes the Internal Revenue Code and Code history, regulations and preambles, and the Weekly Alert newsletter.

An IRS Practice CD-ROM covers the Internal Revenue Manual, the Market Specialization Program, Market Segment Understandings, Industry Specialization Program Papers, Circular 230, and the AICPA Statements of Responsibilities in Tax Practice. This service is updated quarterly.

RIA offers three CD-ROM services covering judicial opinions: American Federal Tax Reports (monthly updating); Tax Court Cases (monthly updating); and Tax Cases 1860-1953.

The RIA Citator 2nd, covering cases and rulings since 1954, is also available as a monthly subscription.

d. Other RIA Products

RIA offers two CD-ROMS, Elections & Compliance Statements and Tax Advisors Planning System, that provide language for completing IRS election forms or assist in drafting documents. Each is updated monthly.

3. Bureau of National Affairs

Bureau of National Affairs publishes two of its services in CD-ROM versions. The Portfolios Plus Library covers the Tax Management Portfolios; the Tax Practice Plus Series covers the Tax Practice service. The Portfolios are discussed in more detail in Chapter 12, covering looseleaf services.

Both services include topical discussion authored by tax professionals and primary source material. Updating is monthly.

Each service includes the following primary source material:

- Legislative Materials

Internal Revenue Code
Selected legislation and committee reports

• Regulations

Final, Temporary, and Proposed Regulations

• IRS Materials

Revenue Rulings and Revenue Procedures
Announcements and Notices
Letter Rulings, Technical Advice Memoranda, and other IRS documents
IRS Publications
Industry Specialization Papers
Circular 230

In addition, the Portfolios Plus Library includes tax treaties and judicial opinions (dates vary by level of court).

Illustration 18-7. Excerpt from Tax Practice Series CD-ROM

→Tax Practice offers several search options, including Analysis & Client Letters, a variety of primary sources, and practice aids.

→The Portfolios Plus CD-ROM [Illustration 18-11] has a similar screen.

Illustration 18-8. Tax Practice Plus Global Search Screen

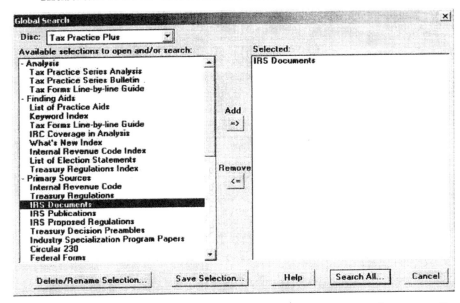

→Tax Practice Plus lets us select multiple databases to search at once. In this case I selected only the IRS Documents database.

Illustration 18-9. Tax Practice Plus Search Template

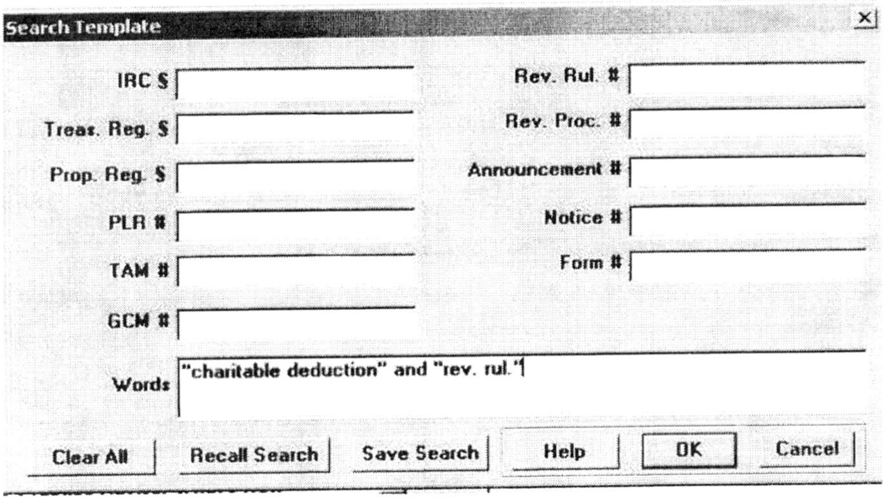

→Let's search for a revenue ruling covering charitable deductions.

→This search template is excellent if we know the document number. Because I didn't, I added "rev. rul." in an attempt to narrow my search.

Illustration 18-10. Tax Practice Plus Specialized Search Option

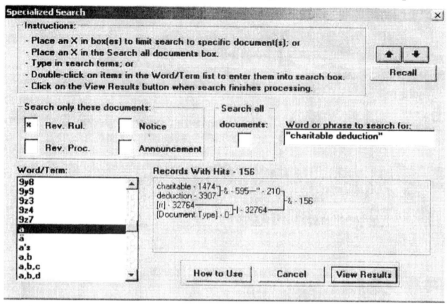

→I got better results using the Specialized Search shown above. Results are listed by year.

Illustration 18-11. Excerpt from Portfolios Plus List of Portfolios

→The print Portfolios (Chapter 12) have Classification Guides for topics.

4. Commerce Clearing House

CCH offers several of its services in CD-ROM format. These include Standard Federal Tax Reporter (including full text of primary sources); Federal Tax Service; Tax Court Reports; Tax Treaties; and the Internal Revenue Manual. Most series are updated monthly.

5. Kleinrock

The TaxExpert CD-ROM includes analysis and primary sources. Illustrations 18-12 through 18-15 use TaxExpert to search for IRS notices or announcements for the tax treaty with Denmark illustrated in Chapter 7.

Illustration 18-12. Multiple Database Search Choices on TaxExpert

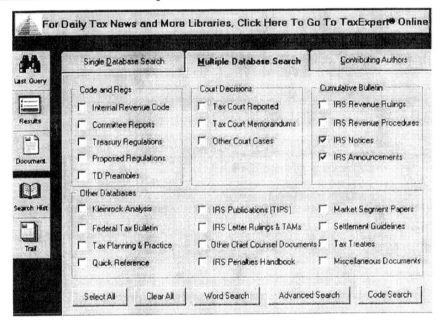

➔I selected the IRS Notices and IRS Announcements databases.

➔Note the direct link to TaxExpert Online. See Illustrations 15-7, 19-18, and 19-19.

Illustration 18-13. Word Search on TaxExpert

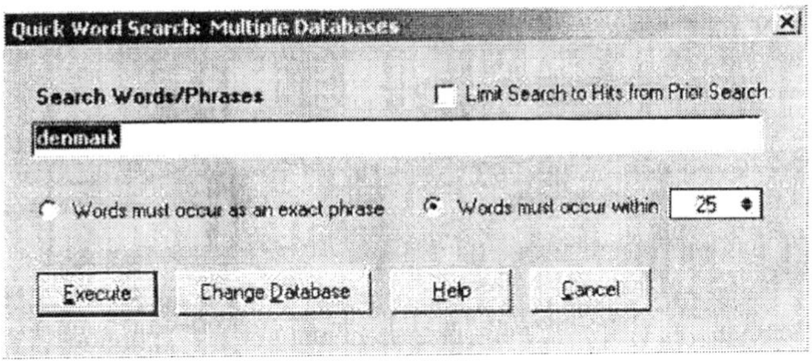

➔Note the ability to search within hits.

Illustration 18-14. Results Obtained with TaxExpert

Word Search: "denmark".

1. Notices 87-56
2. Notices 87-52
3. Notices 84-15
4. Announcement 2000-59
5. Announcement 99-88

➔TaxExpert located five items. I started with Announcement 2000-59, which is closest in time to the treaty's effective date.

**Illustration 18-15. Excerpt from Announcement 2000-59
on TaxExpert**

ANNOUNCEMENT 2000-59

    Changes apply to Tables 1 and 2 in Publication 515, Withholding of Tax
on Nonresident Aliens and Foreign Corporations (For Withholding in 2000),
and in Publication 901, U.S. Tax Treaties. These changes are needed to
reflect the new income tax treaty with Denmark. The provisions for taxes
withheld at source are effective for amounts paid or credited on or after
May 1, 2000. For other taxes, the provisions are effective for tax years
beginning on or after January 1, 2001.

6. LexisNexis

LexisNexis offers several Matthew Bender titles in CD-ROM format. These include Rhoades and Langer on U.S. International Taxation and Tax Treaties; Rabkin & Johnson, Current Legal Forms with Tax Analysis; and various tax institutes (New York University, University of Miami, University of Southern California).

LexisNexis offers other publications (e.g., Murphy's Will Clauses) on a Tax and Estate Planning CD-ROM or on a Business Law Library CD-ROM. These CDs are part of the Matthew Bender Authority series.

7. Warren, Gorham & Lamont

Warren, Gorham & Lamont offers several treatises on CD-ROM. Representative titles include Bittker & Lokken, Federal Taxation of Income, Estates & Gifts; Saltzman, IRS Practice & Procedure; and Bishop & Kleinberger, Limited Liability Companies: Tax & Business Law.

8. Clark Boardman Callahan

Mertens TaxLink is a CD-ROM version of the Mertens, Law of Federal Income Taxation looseleaf service discussed in Chapter 12. The CD-ROM also includes the Internal Revenue Code.

9. Other Publishers

Several publishers provide tax treaties (see Chapter 7), periodicals indexes (Chapter 13), and forms (Chapter 14) in CD-ROM format. The IRS offers tax forms in CD-ROM. Potomac Publishing offers a Statutes at Large CD-ROM and another CD-ROM that lists the titles of all public laws since 1789 (both with online options).

The items above are illustrative. Consult your library CD-ROM collection to determine which materials are available.

Table 18-1. Common CD-ROM Search Connectors and Wildcards

And	Both terms must appear
Or	Either term must appear (both terms may appear)
Not	Only the first term may appear
Xor	Only the first or only the second term may appear
/N	Second term must follow first by no more than N words
@N	First and second terms must be within N words of each other
?	Replaces a single character (used anywhere in word)
*	Replaces one or more characters
%	Finds all verb forms of word (used at end of word)
$	Finds synonyms for word (used at end of word)

→Check the CD-ROM service you are using to ascertain the search connectors and wildcard symbols.

SECTION D. PROBLEMS

You can solve many of the problems in earlier chapters using CD-ROM services. If you used a particular CD-ROM service in an earlier chapter and you have access to other services, try solving that problem using a different service.

CHAPTER 19. ONLINE LEGAL RESEARCH

SECTION A. INTRODUCTION

This chapter continues the discussion of electronic research begun in Chapter 3 and continued in Chapters 9, 11, and 18. In addition to discussing advantages and disadvantages of online research, it describes three types of service: general focus subscription services; tax-oriented subscription services; and other online services. This chapter also includes a brief discussion of search engines, directories, and portals.

SECTION B. ADVANTAGES AND DISADVANTAGES

Online legal research systems have many useful features. First, they bring research materials together in one readily accessible location. Libraries with tax alcoves require several shelf ranges to house the relevant information; libraries without alcoves may shelve these items on several floors. An online system requires only a computer, a modem or other online access tool, and a printer.

The Internet provides a quick means for transmitting and accessing both text and graphics. More important than the time saved in gathering the material is the ability to do searches that are virtually impossible to accomplish using print materials. Because the service responds to queries based on words appearing or not appearing in its database, you could easily use an online system to locate all opinions by a particular judge[277] or all decisions rendered in 2001, at every court level, involving the medical expense deduction. Although CD-ROM searches can yield similar results, online services often include more material and are updated more frequently.

Given these advantages, why isn't research conducted solely online? That question was raised in Chapter 3, Section C, in comparing print and electronic services. As noted there, online services may be less suited than print materials for certain research tasks, such as using looseleaf services to familiarize yourself with a topic. Older material may not be available in an online database, and tax-oriented articles indexes are not available in any

---

[277] See the example for Judge Marvel in Chapter 3.

online service. Publisher consolidation, discussed in Chapter 1, is also a factor. If you have access only to Westlaw, for example, you currently lack access to Shepard's and CCH publications. Even if an online service carries a particular source, your subscription option may not cover it.

Cost constraints may limit the time you can spend online. If your final product requires accurate page numbers, a final check of print sources may be necessary to assure yourself that you have made no citation errors. As the discussion in Chapter 3 indicates, there is no "best source" for tax research.

Keep two important rules in mind. First, you must check the time period covered for materials made available online. Don't assume a source included in an online service begins its coverage with the first print volume of that service. Coverage for many sources begins at a later date online than it does in print. This is true for both subscription and free services.

Second, remember that different systems use different search commands, rules for wildcard searches, or methods for indicating you want to use a Boolean search. You will not achieve the desired results unless you tailor your search to the rules imposed by the service you are using.[278]

SECTION C. AVAILABLE MATERIALS

Some subscription-based services include tax materials in a general database. Others focus exclusively on taxation. Nonsubscription services vary in their coverage; they may include data from a variety of sources or may focus on a single type of information. They may provide links to relevant materials rather than including text in their databases.

Materials available online may also be available in print or on CD-ROM, often from the same publisher. Several publishers offer their own online services and also include their materials on services such as Westlaw or LexisNexis.

D. ONLINE SUBSCRIPTION SERVICES—GENERAL FOCUS

Although they do not focus on tax, two commercial services, LexisNexis and Westlaw, have extensive tax databases. Two others, Loislaw and

---

[278] I noted a print service analogy in Chapter 12, dealing with looseleaf services. Those services vary in using page, paragraph, and section numbers for categorizing and cross-referencing information.

VersusLaw, currently include fewer tax materials. Services frequently expand the number of sources and time periods covered.[279] They also delete sources, generally substituting others. Changes on LexisNexis and Westlaw often reflect the parent companies' acquisitions of other publishers.

Each of these services differs slightly in its coverage and search commands. All allow you to specify particular words that must appear or be absent in a document; if the words must be in a desired proximity, you can include that limitation. You can use these systems to locate decisions involving damages within five words of the term personal injury, or for decisions involving damages but not personal injury. You can limit your search to particular types of authority (e.g., only Tax Court) or to particular dates.

Before formulating a search query, you should become familiar with the search term symbols used on the system being accessed. In addition to each service's explanatory texts, other guides are available.

The discussion in this section relates to each service's web-based service. Since Westlaw began offering a web-based option, I use it more frequently than I used its dial-up service. Because LexisNexis includes Tax Notes, my newsletter of choice, I often use it instead of Westlaw. Until Loislaw and VersusLaw significantly expand the materials they include, they will be of limited use for many tax research projects.

Subsections 1 through 4 compare general subscription-based services. The discussion includes database contents, proximity connectors, wildcard characters, synonyms, and citators. I searched for the same items in all four services—Tax Court decisions in 2001 that mention *Chevron* (Chapter 8).[280]

1. LexisNexis

a. Database Contents

The LexisNexis tax library, FEDTAX, is divided into files.[281] There are also files for state taxes and for various publishers. FEDTAX materials are accessed through individual files (e.g., CASREL for judicial decisions and

---

[279] For some tools (e.g., articles indexes), you may need to extend LexisNexis and Westlaw searches to their nontax libraries.

[280] I chose a single court because VersusLaw did not allow simultaneous searching in all of the courts discussed in Chapter 10.

[281] Although I mention them, you do not need to know library or file names to use the web-based LexisNexis system.

IRS material; TXLAWS for statutes and regulations); an OMNI file combines most primary source material.

Within each database, you can click on an icon to see dates of coverage. LexisNexis's coverage of the Supreme Court begins in 1790; its Tax Court coverage begins in 1924 with the Board of Tax Appeals.

Secondary source files cover tax-oriented law reviews, Shepard's Citations, and services published by Bureau of National Affairs/Tax Management, Commerce Clearing House, Matthew Bender, Kleinrock, Research Institute of America, Tax Analysts, and Warren, Gorham & Lamont.

b. Proximity Connectors, Wildcard Characters, and Synonyms

LexisNexis uses several connectors in searches:

AND	both terms must appear
OR	at least one of the terms must appear
AND NOT	only the first term may appear
W/n	terms must appear within n words of each other; either can appear first (n can be any number up to 255)
W/s	terms must appear within the same sentence
W/p	terms must appear within the same paragraph
W/seg	terms must appear in the same segment (e.g., case caption, text)
PRE/n	First term must precede second by no more than n words

If you use multiple words without a connector, LexisNexis treats them as a phrase.

LexisNexis also lets you state proximity connectors in the negative (e.g., NOT W/s). You can exclude documents unless the term appears AT LEAST a stated number of times, and you can specify that the term must appear in all capital letters or only as a plural.

LexisNexis allows you to use an exclamation point (!) as a wild card symbol to expand words by any number of letters following the !. You can use an asterisk (*) to add missing letters anywhere except at the beginning of the word. Each * represents a single missing letter.

LexisNexis does not automatically add synonyms to your search. If you use the Select Words and Concepts option, it suggests possible search terms based on those you have already selected. LexisNexis also allows you to use natural language searching instead of using Boolean connectors.

c. Citator

LexisNexis includes the Shepard's Citator. Symbols to the left of cases indicate that you will find updating material using the citator; click on these symbols to go directly to the citator results. [See Illustration 19-4.]

Illustration 19-1. LexisNexis Directory of Sources

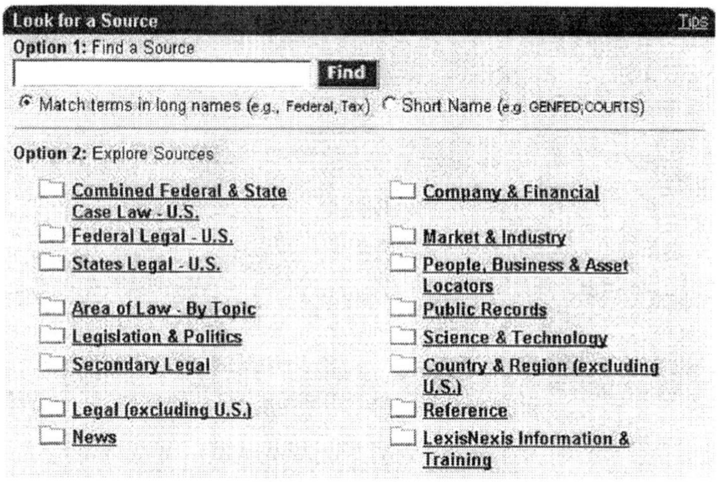

→Click on the link next to the folder icon to obtain a contents list. For this search, I used the Area of Law - By Topic option and selected Taxation.

Illustration 19-2. LexisNexis Court List

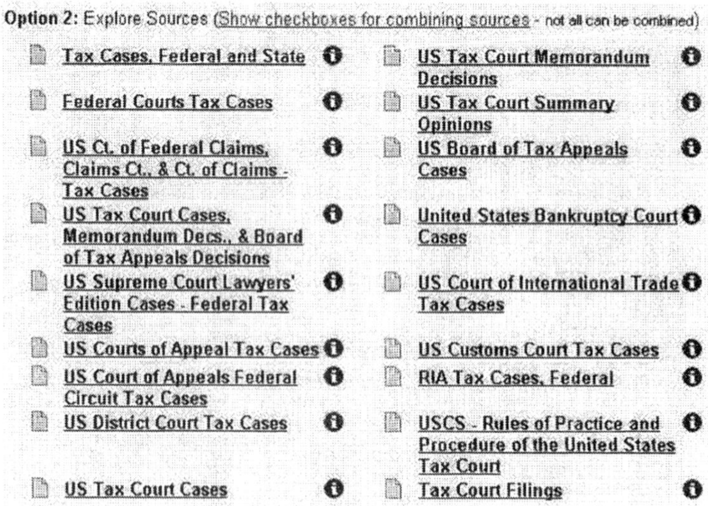

→Click the ❶ for information about each option.

Illustration 19-3. LexisNexis Search

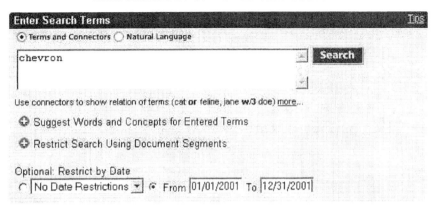

→I selected the US Tax Court Cases, Memorandum Decs., & Board of Tax Appeals Decs. file because it includes Regular, Memorandum, and Summary decisions.

→The Date Restriction option is part of the search screen. Use the Restrict Search option to limit the search by court, judge, attorney, and several other items. Compare this Date Restriction format to the format used for Westlaw in Illustration 19-7.

Illustration 19-4. Partial List of LexisNexis Results

⌐Select for FOCUS™ or Delivery

⌐ ▲ 1. Lunsford v. Comm'r, No. 18071-99L, UNITED STATES TAX COURT, 117 T.C. 159; 2001 U.S. Tax Ct. LEXIS 48; 117 T.C. No. 16, November 30, 2001, Filed

> **OVERVIEW:** In an appeal challenging a proposed tax levy, the court held that, when determining whether it had subject matter jurisdiction, the court would not look behind the notice of determination to evaluate the adequacy of the administrative hearing.

> **CORE TERMS:** levy, notice of determination, collection, notice, judicial review, collection action, correspondence, invalid, purported, notice of deficiency...

⌐ ◆ 2. N.Y. Football Giants, Inc. v. Comm'r, No. 8563-00, UNITED STATES TAX COURT, 117 T.C. 152; 2001 U.S. Tax Ct. LEXIS 46; 117 T.C. No. 15, October 30, 2001, Filed

> **OVERVIEW:** Tax court lacked jurisdiction to determine whether built-in gains tax applied to S corporation as the proposed built-in gains adjustments to its tax returns were subchapter S items to be determined in unified audit and litigation proceeding.

→LexisNexis located four cases. I can use the hyperlinks to go directly to those cases. LexisNexis cites to the official and LexisNexis citation and to the CCH Tax Court Memorandum decisions. It uses symbols to indicate I can find additional information by Shepardizing.

→When I search within the cases found, LexisNexis lets me navigate directly to the place where the term is used.

→A Show Hits option (not illustrated above) lets me display the term sought in context.

2. Westlaw

a. Database Contents

The Westlaw tax database, FTX-ALL, gives access to virtually every type of primary source material.[282] These materials can also be accessed separately through individual databases (e.g., FTX-CSRELS for judicial decisions and IRS material; FTX-CODREG for statutes and regulations).

Within each database, you can click on an icon to see dates of coverage. Westlaw's coverage of the Supreme Court begins in 1790; its Tax Court coverage begins in 1924 with the Board of Tax Appeals.

Secondary source files cover tax-oriented law reviews, RIA Citator 2nd and West's KeyCite, and services published by Bureau of National Affairs/Tax Management, Research Institute of America, Warren, Gorham & Lamont, and other West Group entities (e.g., the Mertens service discussed in Chapter 12).

b. Proximity Connectors, Wildcard Characters, and Synonyms

Westlaw uses several search connectors:

&	both terms must appear
space	at least one of the terms must appear
%	only the first term may appear
/n	terms must appear within n words of each other
/s	terms must appear within the same sentence
/p	terms must appear within the same paragraph
+n	first term must precede the second by no more than n words
+s	first term must precede the second in same sentence
+p	first term must precede the second in same paragraph
" "	terms must appear in order (a phrase)

Westlaw allows you to use a single exclamation point (!) as a wild card symbol (root expander) to expand words by any number of letters following the !. You can use an asterisk (*) to add missing letters anywhere but at the beginning of the word. Each * represents a single missing letter. Westlaw also allows searches based on West topics and key numbers.

Westlaw does not automatically add synonyms. If you use the Thesaurus option, it suggests search terms based on those you selected. Westlaw offers

---

[282] Although I mention the database names, you do not need to know them to use the web-based Westlaw service.

both Natural Language and Boolean search options.

c. Citator

Westlaw offers two citators, RIA 2nd Citator and KeyCite. KeyCite is the default option in the court database. You can instead enter the RIA Citator 2nd directly and type the case you want to check (by party or by citation).

Illustration 19-5. Westlaw Directory

- U.S. Federal Materials
- U.S. State Materials
- International/Worldwide Materials
- Topical Materials by Area of Practice
- Westnews (News and Business Databases)
- WestDockets
- Public Information, Records and Filings
- Law Reviews, Bar Journals & Legal Periodicals
- Forms, Treatises, CLEs and Other Practice Material
- Legal News, Highlights and Notable Trials
- Directories and Reference Materials
- Databases Listed by Provider
- KeyCite, ALR and American Jurisprudence
- WestlawPRO and Westlaw Libraries
- What's New and Customer Information

→The Westlaw directory can be expanded wherever a plus $\boxed{+}$ appears to provide a more-detailed contents list. For this search, I used the Topical Materials by Area of Practice option. Within that option, I selected Taxation.

Illustration 19-6. Westlaw Court List

Federal Tax Cases - Other Databases
- Cases - All Courts (FTX-CS) ❶
- - Supreme Court (FTX-SCT) ❶
- - Courts of Appeals (FTX-CTA) ❶
- - District Courts (FTX-DCT) ❶
- - Court of Federal Claims (FTX-FEDCL) ❶
- - Tax Court (FTX-TCT) ❶
- Federal Tax Cases & IRS Releases Combined (FTX-CSRELS) ❶
- Federal Taxation - Headnotes (FTX-HN) ❶

→I selected the Tax Court database. Click ❶ for database information.

Illustration 19-7. Westlaw Search

Database: Federal Taxation - Tax Court Cases (FTX-TCT) ❶

Terms and Connectors query:

```
chevron & DA(AFT 01/01/2001 & BEF 12/31/2001)
```

Search

Recent Queries ▼

▶ Connectors/Expanders Reference List

▶ Field Restrictions

▶ Thesaurus

▶ Preferred Terms

➔I used the Field Restrictions option to limit the date. That option also allows me to limit my search by court, judge, attorney, and other items.

➔This search put me at risk of missing some cases. The LexisNexis date search option [Illustration 19-3] is From/To. The Westlaw date search is After/Before. To be sure of finding all cases decided in 2001, I should have selected 12/31/2000 for AFT and 01/01/2002 for BEF.

Illustration 19-8. Westlaw Results

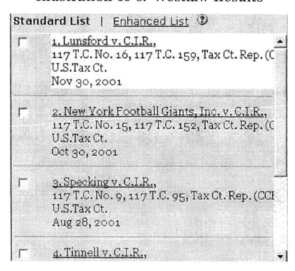

Standard List | Enhanced List ❓

☐ 1. Lunsford v. C.I.R.,
117 T.C. No. 16, 117 T.C. 159, Tax Ct. Rep. (C
U.S.Tax Ct.
Nov 30, 2001

☐ 2. New York Football Giants, Inc. v. C.I.R.,
117 T.C. No. 15, 117 T.C. 152, Tax Ct. Rep. (C
U.S.Tax Ct.
Oct 30, 2001

☐ 3. Specking v. C.I.R.,
117 T.C. No. 9, 117 T.C. 95, Tax Ct. Rep. (CCI
U.S.Tax Ct.
Aug 28, 2001

☐ 4. Tinnell v. C.I.R.,

➔Westlaw located four cases. Hyperlinks take me directly to them.

➔When I search these cases, Westlaw lets me navigate directly to the place where the term appears.

➔An Enhanced List option (not illustrated above) displays the term sought in context.

3. Loislaw

a. Database Contents

Loislaw does not have a separate tax database. Its coverage of federal taxation is currently limited to primary source materials (although it offers access to several nontax treatises[283] published by Aspen). Judicial decisions covered include those from the Tax Court, District Courts, Bankruptcy Court, Courts of Appeals, and the Supreme Court. Loislaw also offers access to the United States Code, slip laws, the Constitution, Code of Federal Regulations, and the Federal Register.

Within each database, you can click a button for information about how up-to-date the materials are. Retrospective coverage varies by database. As of April 2002, Supreme Court coverage begins in 1899; Tax Court coverage begins in 1942, thus omitting cases from the Board of Tax Appeals.

Although Loislaw is a lower-cost alternative to LexisNexis and Westlaw, its utility is limited by its lack of IRS documents, legislative history materials, and secondary source materials.

The Choose a Type of Law option covers all courts; the Choose a Jurisdiction option lets you search only one court at a time. If you select the Choose a Type of Law option, you can select more than one, but less than all, courts.

b. Proximity Connectors, Wildcard Characters, and Synonyms

Loislaw uses five connectors in searches. You can express them as words or symbols:

And	&	both terms must appear
Or	|	at least one of the terms must appear
Not	%	only the first term may appear
Near	/	terms must appear within 20 words of each other
Nearx	/x	terms must appear within x words of each other

Loislaw allows you to use an asterisk (*) as a wild card symbol to find variations of search terms.

Loislaw does not add synonyms for you, and it does not have a thesaurus you can use to find similar terms.

---

[283] Several of these treatises are in areas related to tax, such as elder law, family law, and business entities.

c. Citator

The Loislaw citator is GlobalCite. You activate it within the item you are viewing and it provides a link to the later items. GlobalCite does not currently use symbols to indicate if the later item agrees with the earlier one. It does place the cited item in context on the GlobalCite screen.

Illustration 19-9. Loislaw Court List

Choose the jurisdiction you would like to search:

Federal Libraries	Federal Circuits	
U.S. Supreme Court Reports	1st	8th
U.S. Tax Court	2nd	9th
Recent U.S. Supreme Court Developments	3rd	10th
U.S. Supreme Court Rules	4th	11th
U.S. Code	5th	Federal
Public Laws of the United States	6th	DC
U.S. Constitution	7th	
Code of Federal Regulations		
Federal Register		
Federal Rules		Recent Federal Circuit
U.S. Sentencing Comm. Guidelines Manual		Court Opinions

➔You enter Loislaw through one of three options, Choose a Jurisdiction, Choose a Type of Law (case, statute, administrative), or Choose a Book (treatises).

➔Choose a Jurisdiction also includes District Court and Bankruptcy Court opinions. Choose a Type of Law shows all court levels and allows you to select which of them (one or more) you wish to search.

Illustration 19-10. Loislaw Search

U.S. Tax Court

CURRENCY   SELECTCITE

Search Entire Document

| chevron |

Official Citation

| |

Appellant and Appellee Names

| |

Docket Number

| |

Appellate Court

| |

Decided Date

| 2001 |

➔This search used the Tax Court database. The "Appellant and Appellee Names" option is misleading, as the Tax Court is a trial court. This is a standard screen for federal court cases.

➔The currency button provides the database's beginning and ending date.

Illustration 19-11. Loislaw Results

U.S. Tax Court

LUNSFORD v. COMMISSIONER OF INTERNAL REVENUE, 117 T.C. 159

(2001)

Docket No. 18071-99L.

Filed November 30, 2001.

This case arises from a petition for judicial review filed under section 6330(d) (1)(A).[fn1] The issue for decision is whether this Court has jurisdiction to review respondent's determination to proceed with collection by way of levy. At the time petitioners filed their petition, they resided in Asheville, North Carolina. When this case was called for trial, the parties submitted the case fully stipulated. For convenience, we combine the facts, which are not in dispute, with our opinion.

U.S. Tax Court

NEW YORK FOOTBALL GIANTS v. COMM., INTERNAL REV., 117 T.C. 152

(2001)

Docket No. 8563-00.

Filed October 30, 2001.

➔Loislaw found three cases. It missed *Tinnell*, a Memorandum decision.

➔You can jump to each case using hyperlinks but not to the search term.

4. VersusLaw

a. Database Contents

VersusLaw does not offer a separate tax database. Its coverage of federal taxation is limited to primary source materials. Judicial decisions covered include those from the Tax Court, Court of Federal Claims, a limited number of District Courts, Courts of Appeals, and the Supreme Court. VersusLaw also offers online Code of Federal Regulations and United States Code services.

Within each database you click a link to determine the dates of coverage. As of April 2002, Supreme Court coverage begins in 1900; Tax Court coverage begins in 1999. Retrospective coverage for several other courts is quite limited.

Although VersusLaw does not let you search every court level simultaneously, you can search the Tax Court, Supreme Court, and Court of Federal Claims simultaneously. You can also search all of the District Courts it covers together with the Supreme Court or search the Courts of Appeals together with the Supreme Court.

b. Proximity Connectors, Wildcard Characters, and Synonyms

VersusLaw uses six connectors in searches:

adj	the terms must be adjacent to each other (this is VersusLaw's default option)
and	both terms must appear
or	at least one of the terms must appear
not	only the first term may appear
near/n	terms must appear within n words of each other
w/n	second term must appear within n words following the first

Versuslaw includes a useful table comparing its connectors to those used in LexisNexis and Westlaw.

VersusLaw lets you use an asterisk (*) as a wild card symbol to substitute for any string of characters and a question mark (?) as a wild card symbol to substitute for a single character. You can use a plus (+) to find any variant of a word, including one in which additional letters precede rather than follow the word indicated (e.g., mediate+ should yield mediated and immediate, among other words). Parentheses are used to group alternate search terms.

VersusLaw does not add synonyms for you, and it does not have a thesaurus option.

c. Citator

VersusLaw does not have a citator. You can simulate citator results by using a case or other item as a search term. Because this method won't yield editorial comments, you must read the later items to determine if they agree with the earlier one. And, because you must search some court databases separately, this process is almost as inefficient as using a multivolume print citator.

Illustration 19-12. VersusLaw Directory

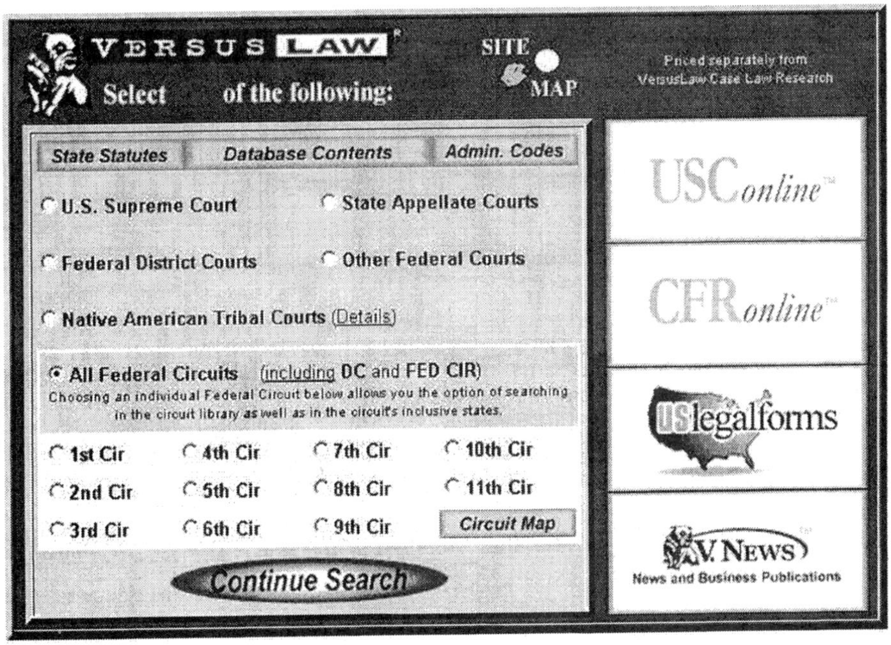

→You enter VersusLaw through this screen.

→Select Other Federal Courts to find the Tax Court.

Illustration 19-13. VersusLaw Search

Search Query

VERSUS LAW

[Search other jurisdictions.]

Please complete the following 5 steps.

➡ 1. **SELECT JURISDICTION(S).** Select the jurisdiction(s) you want to search.

☐ U.S. Supreme Court   ☐ Court of International Trade

☐ Board of Immigration Appeals   ☑ U.S. Tax Court

☐ Board of Patent Appeals (Coming Soon) ☐ U.S. Court of Appeals for the Armed Forces

☐ Court of Federal Claims

☐ **All the above jurisdictions** (make sure no other boxes are selected or it won't work)

➡ 2. **ENTER YOUR SEARCH** in the box below. Need help? – see below

| chevron |
| |

➡ 3. **DATE RANGE (optional)** (format mm/dd/yyyy) FROM: 01/01/2001   TO: 12/31/2001

➡ 4. **NUMBER OF RESULTS TO VIEW:** 50 ▾   ➡ 5. **SUBMIT SEARCH.**   SUBMIT

➡This screen also has a Court Coverage Dates link (not illustrated above).

Illustration 19-14. VersusLaw Results

4 documents found (4 returned) for Search Query: *(chevron)AND*
***20010101<=dates<=20011231*.**

To view case in full-text format, click on case name. Use the Back function of your browser to return to this page to view the next case. [U] in the case name means the case is unpublished.

USTC   Lunsford v. Commissioner of Internal Revenue, No. 18071-99L (U.S.T.C. 11/30/2001)

USTC   New York Football Giants, Inc. v. Commissioner of Internal Revenue, No. 8563-00 (U.S.T.C. 10/30/2001)

USTC   Specking v. Commissioner of Internal Revenue, No. 12010-99 (U.S.T.C. 08/28/2001)

USTC   United States Tax Court v. Commissioner of Internal Revenue, No. 20318-97 (U.S.T.C. 05/04/2001)

➡VersusLaw found all four cases. However, the fourth case is incorrectly captioned; it is actually *Tinnell v. Commissioner*.

➡Note that VersusLaw uses both USTC and U.S.T.C. as abbreviations for Tax Court. Remember that U.S.T.C. is also a CCH case reporter service that does not include Tax Court cases. See Chapter 10.

SECTION E. ONLINE SUBSCRIPTION SERVICES—TAX FOCUS

The services discussed in this section provide access to a variety of primary and secondary source materials. I used two of them—Tax Research NetWork and TaxExpert Online—to replicate the search from Section D (finding Tax Court decisions in 2001 that mentioned the *Chevron* case).

1. Tax Research NetWork

Commerce Clearing House materials are included on LexisNexis. CCH also offers its own web-based service, Tax Research NetWork. The materials below discuss using this service.

a. Database Contents

Tax Research NetWork includes the Internal Revenue Code, committee reports, regulations, treaties, IRS materials (including items such as revenue rulings, letter rulings, field service advice, and the Internal Revenue Manual), and judicial decisions. The service includes Standard Federal Tax Reporter and CCH Federal Taxes, CCH newsletters and journals, a citator, and various practice aids. It does not include Federal Tax Articles.

Supreme Court coverage begins in 1913; Tax Court coverage begins in 1924 with the Board of Tax Appeals.

b. Proximity Connectors, Wildcard Characters, and Synonyms

Tax Research NetWork uses prescribed search methods. You select the method in the Search Options Screen. Unless you select Boolean, the method itself determines the option. If you select Boolean, you must use the connectors to get the results you want.

ALL TERMS	all of the terms must appear
ANY TERM	at least one of the terms must appear
NEAR	terms must be within 20 words of each other
EXACT PHRASE	terms must appear in order exactly as typed

Boolean:

AND	both terms must appear
OR	either term must appear
NOT	only the first term may appear
W/n	the first term must appear within n words of the second (n can be no more than 127)
W/sen	the first term must appear within 20 words of the second
W/par	first term must appear within 80 words of the second

Tax Research NetWork lets you use a single exclamation point (!) as a wild card symbol to expand words by any number of letters at the end of a word. You can use an asterisk (*) to add missing letters anywhere except the beginning of the word. Each * represents a single missing letter.

Tax Research NetWork has a Thesaurus function. It will search on synonyms if you enable that option.

c. Citator

Tax Research NetWork includes the CCH Citator. The looseleaf version of this citator (Chapter 11) is divided into three services, one for each of CCH's Code-based looseleaf services. The online version is not divided in this manner. If, for example, you seek both income and gift tax cases that cite to a particular tax case, you can find them online with a single search.

Illustration 19-15. Excerpt from Tax Research NetWork Directory

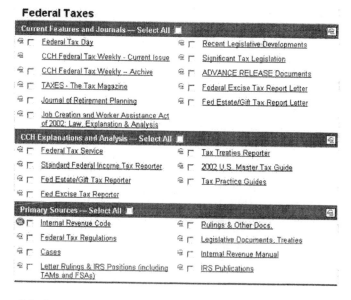

Federal Taxes

Current Features and Journals — Select All

Federal Tax Day	Recent Legislative Developments
CCH Federal Tax Weekly - Current Issue	Significant Tax Legislation
CCH Federal Tax Weekly -- Archive	ADVANCE RELEASE Documents
TAXES - The Tax Magazine	Federal Excise Tax Report Letter
Journal of Retirement Planning	Fed Estate/Gift Tax Report Letter
Job Creation and Worker Assistance Act of 2002: Law, Explanation & Analysis	

CCH Explanations and Analysis — Select All

Federal Tax Service	Tax Treaties Reporter
Standard Federal Income Tax Reporter	2002 U.S. Master Tax Guide
Fed Estate/Gift Tax Reporter	Tax Practice Guides
Fed Excise Tax Reporter	

Primary Sources — Select All

Internal Revenue Code	Rulings & Other Docs.
Federal Tax Regulations	Legislative Documents, Treaties
Cases	Internal Revenue Manual
Letter Rulings & IRS Positions (including TAMs and FSAs)	IRS Publications

→Because this is a tax-oriented service, all items in the directory are potentially relevant. For this search, I selected Cases.

→Note that the Tax Research NetWork directory refers to Standard Federal Tax Reporter (Chapter 12) as Standard Federal Income Tax Reporter.

Illustration 19-16. Tax Research NetWork Search

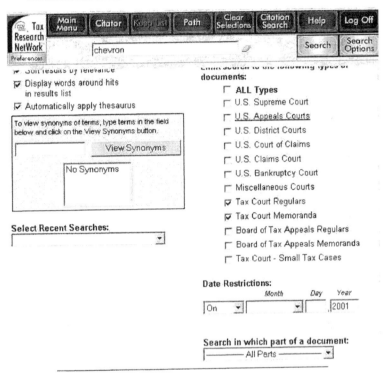

→I used "On" and "2001" as restrictions.

→Because I wanted a particular case name, I ignored the thesaurus.

Illustration 19-17. Tax Research NetWork Search Results

Terms searched for: chevron .

Documents are displayed in ranked order, best matches first. 4 documents matched your query.

1.● TC. [CCH Dec. 54,552] . Joseph D. and Wanda S. Lunsford v. . [Liens and levies: Determination to proceed with levy: Tax Court jurisdiction to review: Collection Due Process hearings: Opportunity for hearing: Summary record of assessment, Form 4340 Sufficiency of notice.], (Nov. 30, 2001)
Benefit Guar. Corporation v. LTV Corp., supra, and a third case, **Chevron**, U.S.A., Inc. v. Natural Res. Def. Council, Inc., 467 U.S. 837 (1984).

2.● TC. [CCH Dec. 54,533] . New York Football Giants, Inc. v. Commissioner. [S corporations: Tax on built-in gains: Subchapter S items defined.], (Oct. 30, 2001)
if it is arbitrary, capricious, or manifestly contrary to the statute, **Chevron** U.S.A. Inc. v. Natural Res. Def. Council, Inc., 467 U.S. 837, 844

3.● TC. [CCH Dec. 54,470] . Joseph D. Specking, et al.[1] v. Commissioner, [Gross income: Exclusions: Wages: Specified U.S. possession, qualification as: Johnston Island: Foreign country, qualification as: Bona fide residency test: U.S. possessions: Foreign earned income. Tax home.], (Aug. 28, 2001)
"whether Congress has directly spoken to the precise question at issue." **Chevron** U.S.A. Inc. v. Natural Res. Def. Council, Inc., 467 U.S. 837, 842

4.● TCM. [CCH Dec. 54,327(M)] . James Tinnell v. Commissioner. Deductions: Losses: Nonprofit activities: Mining: Profit motive.--, (May 04, 2001)
major oil companies in the United States; i.e., Phelps Dodge, Texaco, **Chevron**, Exxon; and major mining companies in the United States; i.e., Kenicott, Mobil,

→This search retrieved all four cases.

→Another method for searching would be to use the citator and enter *Chevron* as the cited case. Because the desired *Chevron* case is not a tax case, that option is not available.

2. TaxExpert Online

LexisNexis includes Kleinrock's newsletters and analytical materials in its database. Kleinrock also offers its own web-based service, TaxExpert Online. The materials below discuss this service.

a. Database Contents

TaxExpert Online includes the Internal Revenue Code, committee reports, regulations, preambles (since 1995), treaties, IRS materials (including items such as letter rulings, field service advice, and the penalties handbook from the Internal Revenue Manual),[284] and judicial decisions. The service includes back issues of Daily Tax Bulletin and various practice aids.

Supreme Court coverage begins in 1984; the service covers "key cases" from 1917. TaxExpert Online begins Tax Court coverage in 1954 and does not include the Board of Tax Appeals.

b. Proximity Connectors, Wildcard Characters, and Synonyms

Tax Expert Online has three search method options: treat words as a phrase; find words within 25 words of each other; or enter your own syntax. If you choose to enter your own syntax, you can select from four connector commands and can use words or symbols for three of them:

AND	&	both terms must appear
OR	|	at least one of the terms must appear
NOT	~	only the first term may appear

To search for terms within N words of each other, you must structure your command as follows: NEAR((term1, term2, ...), N). Make sure that all terms subject to this command are in a single parenthetical phrase *and* that the proximity number (N) follows a comma and shares a second parentheses with the desired terms.

TaxExpert Online lets you use a percentage sign (%) to add all possible endings to a word. You use one or more underlines (_) to add as many additional characters as you specify anywhere in the word.

TaxExpert Online does not have a thesaurus feature.

---

[284] Coverage dates for IRS materials vary widely. For example revenue rulings begin in 1954; revenue procedures, in 1955; notices, in 1980; and announcements, in 1993. Coverage for publicly released items begins as early as 1990 for letter rulings and as late as 1999 for documents such as field service advice.

c. Citator

TaxExpert does not have a citator. You can simulate citator results by using a case or other item as a search term. You must read the later items to determine if they agree with the earlier one.

Illustration 19-18. TaxExpert Online Directory and Search

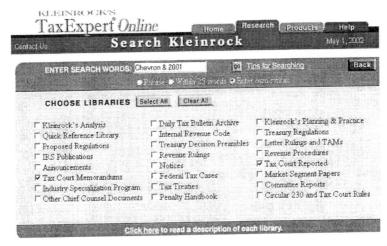

→I selected both Tax Court files and the enter your own syntax option.

Illustration 19-19. TaxExpert Results

Search found 13 documents from 29914 searched. Search Query is *Chevron & 2001*

1. Square D Company v. Commissioner, 118 T.C. No. 15
2. Lunsford v. Commissioner, 117 T.C. No. 16
3. New York Football Giants, Inc. v. Commissioner, 117 T.C. No. 15
4. Specking v. Commissioner, 117 T.C. 9
5. Estate of Richard R. Simplot v. Commissioner, 112 T.C. 130
6. Alumax Inc. v. Commissioner, 109 T.C. 133
7. Estate of Willis Edward Clack v. Commissioner, 106 T.C. 131
8. Redlark v. Commissioner, 106 T.C. 31
9. Estate of Lucille P. Shelfer v. Commissioner, 103 T.C. 10
10. Brandon v. Commissioner, 91 T.C. 829
11. Tinnell v. Commissioner, T.C. Memo 2001-106
12. Owens v. Commissioner, T.C. Memo 1997-538
13. Exxon Corporation v. Commissioner, T.C. Memo 1992-92

→My search yielded all four cases and nine others. The unwanted cases all used the term "Chevron" but were not decided in 2001. For example, Simplot mentioned a purchase from Chevron and Code section 2001.

3. Checkpoint

LexisNexis and Westlaw both include materials from Research Institute of America. RIA also offers its own service, Checkpoint. Users can customize Checkpoint to include various primary and secondary source materials. Available options include the Code, committee reports, regulations and their preambles, treaties, IRS materials, judicial decisions, Federal Tax Coordinator 2d, United States Tax Reporter, and the RIA Citator. Checkpoint search options include using connectors and a thesaurus feature.

4. TaxBase

LexisNexis includes materials from Tax Analysts. Tax Analysts also offers a separate subscription-based option, TaxBase, which users can customize to include various primary and secondary source materials. Available sources include the Code, committee reports, regulations and their preambles, IRS materials, treaties, judicial decisions, Tax Notes Today, and Worldwide Tax Daily. Unlike CCH and RIA, Tax Analysts does not have its own citator service. Its extensive database permits you to conduct citator-like searches using case names or other words as search terms. [See Illustrations 18-2 and 18-3, illustrating its OneDisc CD-ROM.]

5. TaxCore

Westlaw and LexisNexis include materials from Tax Management. Tax Management also offers TaxCore, which is included with subscriptions to Daily Tax Report and available separately to other users. Available sources include the Code, committee reports, testimony at hearings, regulations and their preambles, IRS materials, and judicial decisions.

Illustration 19-20. Documents Covered on TaxCore

BNA, Inc.

TaxCore®

▼ Sec. 42 Low-income housing credit
   ▼ 03/26/2001
      PLR 200112051 - IRC Section 42 - Low-income housing credit
   ▼ 03/05/2001
      PLR 200109011 - IRC Section 42 - Low-income housing credit
      PLR 200109012 - IRC Section 42 - Low-income housing credit
      PLR 200109013 - IRC Section 42 - Low-income housing credit
      PLR 200109014 - IRC Section 42 - Low-income housing credit
▼ Sec. 59 Other definitions and special rules
   ▼ 03/12/2001
      FSA 200110019 - IRC Section 59 - Other definitions and special rules

SECTION F. OTHER ONLINE SERVICES

There are a variety of useful websites available. Some provide primary source material directly; some provide hypertext links to other websites; some perform both functions. Unfortunately, websites often change address or cease to exist altogether. You are likely to find that many of your searches lead you to at least a few nonexistent sites.

The following list, which includes a sampling of nonsubsctription sites, includes the current URL for each site.

1. Government Sites[285]

a. Government Printing Office (http://www.access.gpo.gov)

This site provides text of, or links to, documents generated by all branches of the federal government. It offers PDF format for many documents, thus allowing you to cite original pagination.

This site allows limited searching by terms; you do not need an exact citation to find many of the covered documents.

Illustration 19-21. Excerpt from Resource Listing on GPO Access

Legislative

Congressional Publications | U.S. House of Representatives | U.S. Senate
Other Legislative Branch Publications and Resources on GPO Access
Legislative Branch Web Sites Hosted by GPO Access

Congressional Publications

- Congressional Bills, 103rd Congress forward
- Congressional Committee Prints, 105th Congress forward
- Congressional Directory, 104th Congress forward
- Congressional Hearings, 105th Congress forward
- Congressional Pictorial Directory, 105th Congress forward
- Congressional Record, 1994 forward

➔GPO Access has directories for legislative, executive, other administrative, and judicial documents. It also links to other government sites.

---

[285] Many government sites link to each other. Online access to government documents is attributable to the Government Printing Office Electronic Information Access Enhancement Act of 1993, Pub. L. No. 103-40, 107 Stat. 112.

b. Library of Congress THOMAS (http://thomas.loc.gov)

Users can find texts of bills, note the progress of bills in Congress, and gain access to the Congressional Record, committee reports, and hearings.[286] Coverage dates vary.

Illustrations 19-22 through 19-24 illustrate several features available on the THOMAS website.

Illustration 19-22. Search Options on THOMAS

The Library of Congress

THOMAS
Legislative Information on the Internet

In the Spirit of Thomas Jefferson, a service of The Library of Congress

Congress Now: House Floor This Week | House Floor Now | Senate Schedule

Search Bill Text 107th Congress (2001-2002):

Bill Number [   ]   Word/Phrase [   ]   [Search] [Clear]

Quick Links: House of Representatives | House Directory | Senate | Senate Directory | GPO

LINKS	LEGISLATION	CONGRESSIONAL RECORD	COMMITTEE INFORMATION
About THOMAS	**Bill Summary & Status** 93rd - 107th	**Most Recent Issue**	**Committee Reports** 104th - 107th
THOMAS FAQ		**Text Search** 101st - 107th	
Congress & Legislative Agencies	**Bill Text** 101st - 107th		House Committees: Home Pages, Schedules, and Hearings
How Congress Makes Laws: House | Senate	**Public Laws By Law Number** 93rd - 107th	**Index** 104th - 107th	
		Roll Call Votes: House Senate	**Senate Committees:** Home Pages, Schedules, and Hearings
Résumés of Congressional Activity			

→You can use THOMAS to find various versions of a bill, trace its history, and read it as a public law.

---

[286] Chapter 6 provides additional information about websites providing legislative history material.

Illustration 19-23. Search Using THOMAS

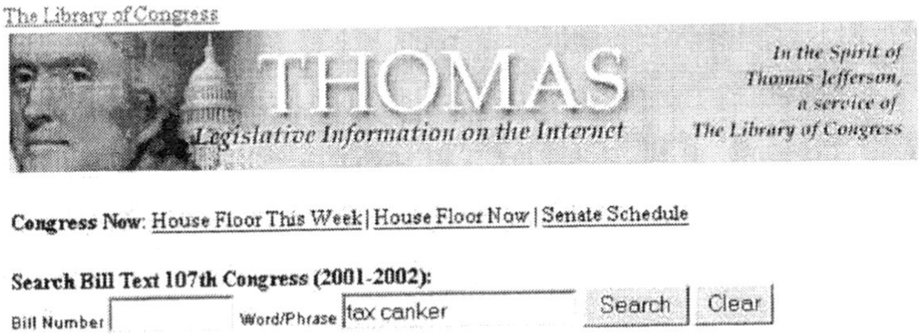

Congress Now: House Floor This Week | House Floor Now | Senate Schedule

Search Bill Text 107th Congress (2001-2002):

Bill Number [   ]   Word/Phrase [tax canker   ]   [Search] [Clear]

➔You can search for legislation by bill number or by terms.

➔If THOMAS locates bills using "tax" or "canker" or both terms, it will link me to their text and to status information.

➔You can search for bills from earlier Congresses by using the Bill Summary & Status and Bill Text options shown in Illustration 19-22.

Illustration 19-24. Partial Results from THOMAS Search

THIS SEARCH	THIS DOCUMENT	GO TO
Next Hit	Forward	New Bills Search
Prev Hit	Back	HomePage
Hit List	Best Sections	Help
	Doc Contents	

50 Bills from the 107th Congress ranked by relevance on *"tax canker "*.

    0 bills containing your phrase **exactly as entered**.
    0 bills containing all your search words **near each other in any order.**
    2 bills containing all your search words **but not near each other.**
    48 bills containing **one or more of your search words.**

Listing of 2 bills containing all your search words **but not near each other.**

  1 . Growers' Tax Fairness Act of 2001 (Introduced in House)[H.R. 2822. IH]
  2 . Economic Security and Recovery Act of 2001 (Reported in Senate)[H.R. 3090. RS]

➔THOMAS located two bills (H.R. 2822, and H.R. 3090) including both terms and 48 other bills including at least one of them. Several bills in the latter group were on point.

➔THOMAS provides links to each of the bills it found.

c. Treasury Department (http://www.treas.gov)

The most useful parts of this site are pages for the Office of Tax Policy page (www.treas.gov/taxpolicy), which provides text for recent tax treaties and Treasury testimony at congressional hearings, and for the Office of Tax Analysis (www.treas.gov/ota), which includes analytical reports on tax policy issues. See Chapters 6 (Legislative Histories) and 8 (Treasury Regulations) for additional information about Treasury materials.

d. Internal Revenue Service (http://www.irs.gov)

The IRS site includes text of tax forms and publications, Internal Revenue Bulletins, the Internal Revenue Manual, IRS releases that are not included in the I.R.B., and income tax treaties. The site also includes links to the United States Code, Code of Federal Regulations, and Federal Register.

This site is not as easy to navigate as it could be. The Search function and Site Tree ease the process, but some items are still difficult to locate.[287] IRS materials are discussed in Chapter 9. That chapter includes additional illustrations from the IRS website.

e. White House Home Page (http://www.whitehouse.gov)

This site provides text of presidential speeches, including bill-signing messages. It also provides links to such support functions as the Office of Management and Budget.

f. Federal Judiciary Home Page (http://www.uscourts.gov)

This site provides links to individual courts. The Opinions page of the Supreme Court site (www.supremecourtus.gov) includes a Case Citation Finder. This service provides the preferred citation, as determined by the Reporter of Decisions, for all Supreme Court decisions scheduled for publication in a bound volume since 1790.

g. United States Tax Court Home Page (www.ustaxcourt.gov)

This site provides text of Regular, Memorandum, and Summary Opinions. You can search the site by judge, date, taxpayer name, and opinion type. It currently includes Regular and Memorandum decisions since 1999 and Summary decisions since 2001. You cannot search by topic or Code section.

---

[287] In May 2002, the links to the United States Code, Code of Federal Regulations, and Federal Register all appeared on a page whose heading is Tax Regulations.

Illustration 19-25. Excerpt from Tax Court Case Search Page

Historical Opinions

Historical Opinions Search Options (TC and Memorandum Opinions starting 01/01/99; Summary Opinions starting 01/01/01 *)

Search Options Help

Release Date:	(Format: MM/DD/YY)
Case Name Keyword:	(e.g., petitioner's last name)
Judge:	All Judges ▼
Opinion Type:	All Types ▼
Sort By:	Case Name ▼
	Search Reset

2. Other Sites

The sites below are a sample of those available. Each provides access to a variety of primary and secondary source materials. Because they focus on law, these sites might be considered special purpose search engines or directories (Section G). In addition to primary source material, these sites provide links to other relevant sites.

• Cornell Law School Legal Information Institute [See Illustration 8-5.] (http://www.law.cornell.edu)

• FindLaw (http://www.findlaw.com)

• Hieros Gamos (http://www.hg.org/; www.hg.org/tax.html for tax)

• Villanova   University   School   of   Law   Tax   Master (http://vls.law.vill.edu/prof/maule/taxmaster/taxhome.htm)

• Washburn University School of Law (http://www.washlaw.edu)

SECTION G. USING SEARCH ENGINES

Online sites have Uniform Resource Locator (URL) addresses, most of which begin with http://www. This text provides URL locations for several government, commercial, nonprofit, and academic sites. Those sites represent only a small portion of what is available online.

Navigating online can be a daunting task if you lack a site's URL or if you don't know if a site exists. Fortunately, you can use search engines and related services to locate information based on key words.

Search engines are unlikely to lead you to as much primary source material as you can locate using the subscription services discussed in Sections D and E. They are likely to find articles and other analysis that don't appear on those sites. If information is posted to a site in PDF format, your search engine may not locate it.[288]

No matter how you locate your material, remember to determine the last time it was updated. Materials posted to websites may be current, but there is no requirement that they be.

1. Search Engines, Directories, and Portals

A **search engine** is a program built on a database of individual websites. The engine searches these sites to find search terms the user specifies. If the search engine doesn't include a particular site in its database, your search results will not include information contained on the site.

Search engines differ not only in the sites they include. They also utilize different command structures for entering searches.[289] Before using a search engine, make sure you know its rules for Boolean searches, whether it automatically searches for synonyms, whether you can restrict a search to a particular web page segment or date, and how it treats phrases.

Rather than using a single search engine, you might try a metasearcher, which performs the search using several search engines at once.[290] A metasearcher doesn't separately compile individual websites.

---

[288] See Thomas R. Keefe, *The Invisible Web: What You Can't See Might Hurt You,* RES. ADVISOR, May 2002, at 1.

[289] For a discussion of Boolean searching, see Diana Botluk, *Search Engines Comparison 2001,* at http://www.llrx.com/features/engine2001.htm (Aug. 1, 2001) (last visited May 1, 2002). This article also discusses features of several search engines.

[290] For example, MetaCrawler (http://www.metacrawler.com) allows you to search using any or all of About, AltaVista, Ask Jeeves, FindWhat, Kanoodle, LookSmart, MetaCatalog, OpenDirectory, Overture, and Sprinks. Metor (http://www.metor.com) uses AltaVista, Entireweb, FAST Search, Google, HotBot, Lycos, and Overture. Metasearchers may change the engines they use over time.

Directories provide links to websites based on subjects. A major difference between directories and search engine relates to their compilation. Editors select websites for inclusion in a directory using criteria established for the particular directory. Search engines use programs ("spiders" and "robots") to search the web for material to add and index.

Web **portals** are entry ports into the web that offer a variety of services, including search engines or directories. They also offer services such as e-mail and shopping.

As is the case for subscription-based services, these services can be general in focus or can cover a single topic.

2. Sample Search

On May 1, 2002, I submitted the search words **casualty loss deduction** to six services: AltaVista; Excite; Findlaw; Google; HotBot; and Lycos. I entered the terms exactly the same way in each service.

I did not specify any chronological or geographical limitations. I did not narrow the search after receiving a source's initial response. I did not enclose the words in quotation marks.

My results (first two items reproduced) from each service appear below. These results illustrate the importance of using search commands, particularly if you are looking for a particular type of material.

AltaVista: 3,255 results

How to Use The Index-Digest System
To find the topical category you need, scroll down through the blue text listings which ... the Service has ruled on the allowance of a **casualty loss deduction** for damages caused by the bursting of a ...
taxboard.com/Tax-Bulls/IndexDigest/indexdigesthelp.html •• Translate
More pages from taxboard.com

Disaster Response Information
... Contracts Business Finances (Series of Publications) **Casualty Loss Deduction** for Tax Purposes After the Storm: ... a Tree Worth? (pdf format) **Casualty Loss Deduction** for Tax Purposes (pdf format) When ...
www.ces.ncsu.edu/disaster/ •• Related pages •• Translate
More pages from www.ces.ncsu.edu

Excite: did not indicate number of results

1. IRS Provides An Option For Determining Casualty Loss Deduction

IRS Provides An Option For Determining Casualty Loss Deduction One of hardest provisions for timber owners to live with is the IRS s position on how timber casualty losses are to be treated. The Internal Revenue Code itself and accompany IRS

www.fnr.purdue.edu

2. Casualty-loss deductions limited by IRS regulations

Arizona Central News contains information and links about the Phoenix metro area, also known as the Valley of the Sun.

www.azcentral.com

Findlaw: 109 results

Guide to Home Ownership: **Casualty** Losses

... year's return to claim the **deduction**. Any insurance reimbursements or federal disaster relief grants are subtracted from the **casualty loss**, along with a $100 ...

http://consumer.pub.findlaw.com/newcontent/homeownership/chp9_a_7.html

http://consumer.pub.findlaw.com/money/taxes/le10_iglossary.html

... **Casualty loss**. A **loss** caused by the complete or partial destruction ... allowed by Congress for various purposes. **Deduction**. A subtraction from taxable income. ...

http://consumer.pub.findlaw.com/money/taxes/le10_iglossary.html

Google: 29,400 results

Chicago Tribune | Qualifying for tax break on **casualty loss**

... be uninsured. Or the insurance company must have refused to pay the entire **loss**, so the uninsured portion then may qualify as a **casualty loss deduction**. However ...

chicagotribune.com/classified/realestate/chi-0201250323jan25.story - 25k - Cached - Similar pages

The Basics -- Let the IRS share your disaster and theft losses - ...

... areas To claim a **casualty loss deduction**, you will need Form 4684 to calculate and report your **loss** and Schedule A to itemize your **loss deduction**. Attach both ...

money.msn.com/articles/tax/reduce/1389.asp - 19k - Cached - Similar pages

HotBot: 6,100 results

1. **IRS Provides An Option For Determining Casualty Loss Deduction**

1/3/2001 http://www.fnr.purdue.edu/ttax/new_developments/99-56explanation.htm

See results from this site only.

2. **Casualty-loss deductions limited by IRS regulations**

Arizona Central News contains information and links about the Phoenix metro area, also known as the Valley of the Sun.

4/18/2002 http://www.azcentral.com/home/home2/0224casualtyloss24.html

See results from this site only.

Lycos: 12,542 results

1. <u>File Manager For Forms - IRS</u> - Select a file format. For additional information about a format click on the format name below. (PDF format allows you to view your form electronically on most computers. The freely available Adobe Ac
http://www.irs.gov/forms_pubs/forms.html Fast Forward »»

2. <u>The Home Office **Deduction**</u> - The Taxpayer Relief Act of 1997 included a modification of the IRS's definition of " principal place of business" that will permit a larger number of taxpayers to qualify for the home-office **deduction**
http://www.acctsite.com/articles/homeofficededuction.htm Fast Forward »»

SECTION H. PROBLEMS

You can solve many of the problems in earlier chapters using online services. For some them, online or CD-ROM searches are your only viable option. Those problems lack sufficient identifying information to allow searches using print materials. To practice your online research skills, try the following additional tasks.

1. Find recently introduced legislation on a topic your instructor selects and follow its history.

2. Track the progress of a regulations project your instructor selects.

3. Find all IRS documents released this year that mention a Code section your instructor selects.

4. Download a presidential tax return.

5. Find articles posted on the web on a topic your instructor selects. Concentrate on websites for law and accounting firms.

6. Refine the "casualty loss deduction" search using the options available on the search engines used in Section G. What refinements did you need to produce more relevant results?

PART SEVEN

APPENDIXES

Appendix A. Commonly Used Abbreviations

Appendix B. Alternate Citation Forms

Appendix C. Potential Research Errors

Appendix D. Bibliography

Appendix E. Publishers of Publications Described in Text

Appendix F. Commonly Owned Publishers

APPENDIX A. COMMONLY USED ABBREVIATIONS

> NOTE: Abbreviations may appear with or without periods, depending on the service you use. The list below presents some items in both formats.

A	Acquiescence
Acq.	Acquiescence
AF; AF2d	American Federal Tax Reports
A.F.T.R.; A.F.T.R.2d	American Federal Tax Reports
ALI	American Law Institute
Am. Jur.	American Jurisprudence
Ann.	Announcement
ANPRM	Advance Notice of Proposed Rulemaking
AOD	Action on Decision
APA	Advance Pricing Agreement; Administrative Procedure Act
App.	Appeals
A.R.M.	Committee on Appeals and Review Memorandum
A.R.R.	Committee on Appeals and Review Recommendation
Art.	Article
A.T.	Alcohol Tax Unit; Alcohol and Tobacco Tax Division
Bankr.	Bankruptcy
BAP	Bankruptcy Appellate Panel
BATF	Bureau of Alcohol, Tobacco, and Firearms
BNA	Bureau of National Affairs
B.R.	Bankruptcy Reporter
BTA	Board of Tax Appeals
Bull.	Bulletin
CA	Court of Appeals
CB; C.B.	Cumulative Bulletin
CBO	Congressional Budget Office
CBS	Collection, Bankruptcy and Summons Bulletin
CC	Chief Counsel
CCA	Chief Counsel Advice or Advisory
CCDM	Chief Counsel Directives Manual
CCH	Commerce Clearing House
CCM	Chief Counsel Memorandum
CCN	Chief Counsel Notice
CEA	Counsel of Economic Advisors

C.F.R.	Code of Federal Regulations
Ch.	Chapter
CIR	Commissioner of Internal Revenue
Cir.	Circuit; Circular
CIS	Congressional Information Service
C.J.S.	Corpus Juris Secundum
Cl.	Clause
Cl. Ct.	Claims Court Reporter
CLI	Current Law Index
C.L.T.	Child-Labor Tax Division
CO	IRS Corporate Division
Comm.	Commissioner; Commission; Committee
Comm'r	Commissioner
Comp.	Compilation; Compliance
Con.	Concurrent
Conf.	Conference
Cong.	Congress
Const.	Constitution
CPE	Continuing Professional Education
CRS	Congressional Research Service
C.S.T.	Capital-Stock Tax Division
C.T.	Carriers Taxing Act of 1937; Taxes on Employment by Carriers
Ct.	Court
CTB	Criminal Tax Bulletin
Ct. Cl.	Court of Claims
Cum. Bull.	Cumulative Bulletin
D.	Decision; District
D.C.	Treasury Department Circular
Dec.	Decision
Del. Order	Delegation Order
Deleg. Order	Delegation Order
Dept. Cir.	Treasury Department Circular
Dist.	District
Dkt.	Docket
DLB	Disclosure Litigation Bulletin
D.O.	Delegation Order
Doc.	Document
E.A.S.	Executive Agreement Series
EE	IRS Employee Plans and Exempt Organization Division
Em. T.	Employment Taxes
E.O.	Executive Orders

EO	Exempt Organizations
E.P.C.	Excess Profits Tax Council Ruling or Memorandum
E.T.	Estate and Gift Tax Division or Ruling
Ex.	Executive
Exec. Order	Executive Order
F.; F.2d; F.3d	Federal Reporter
Fed.	Federal; Federal Reporter
Fed. Cl.	Court of Federal Claims
Fed. Reg.	Federal Register
Fed. Supp.;	
Fed. Supp. 2d	Federal Supplement
FI	IRS Financial Institutions and Products Division
FOIA	Freedom of Information Act
FR	Federal Register
FSA	Field Service Advice
F. Supp.;	
F. Supp.2d	Federal Supplement
FTC; FTC2d	Federal Tax Coordinator
GAO	General Accounting Office
GATT	General Agreement on Tariffs and Trade
GCM	General Counsel Memorandum
G.C.M.	Chief Counsel's Memorandum; General Counsel's Memorandum; Assistant General Counsel's Memorandum
Gen. Couns. Mem.	General Counsel Memorandum
GL	IRS General Litigation Division
GPO	Government Printing Office
GSA	General Services Administration
H	House of Representatives
H.R.	House of Representatives
HRG	Hearing
IA	IRS Income Tax and Accounting Division
ICM	IRS Compliance Officer Memorandum
IIL	IRS Information Letter
IL	IRS International Division
ILM	IRS Legal Memoranda
ILP	Index to Legal Periodicals
INTL	IRS International Division
Int'l	International
IR	Information Release
IRB	Internal Revenue Bulletin

IRC	Internal Revenue Code
IRM	Internal Revenue Manual
IR-Mim.	Published Internal Revenue Mimeograph
IRS	Internal Revenue Service
ISP	Industry Specialization Program
I.T.	Income Tax Unit or Division
ITA	IRS Technical Assistance
ITC	International Tax Counsel
JEC	Joint Economic Committee
JCT	Joint Committee on Taxation
Jt.	Joint
KC	KeyCite
L.	Law; Legal; Letter
L. Ed.	United States Supreme Court Reports, Lawyers' Edition
LGM	Litigation Guideline Memorandum
L.M.	Legal Memorandum
LMSB	IRS Large & Mid-Size Business Operating Division
L.O.	Solicitor's Law Opinion
LR; L & R	IRS Legislation and Regulations Division
LRI	Legal Resource Index
LTR	Private Letter Ruling
Ltr. Rul.	Private Letter Ruling
M.A.	Miscellaneous Announcements
Mem.	Memorandum
Memo.	Memorandum
Mim.	Mimeographed Letter; Mimeograph
MS.	Miscellaneous Unit or Division or Branch
MSSP	Market Segment Specialization Paper
M.S.U.	Market Segment Understanding
M.T.	Miscellaneous Division or Branch
NA	Nonacquiescence
NARA	National Archives and Records Administration
Nonacq.	Nonacquiescence
NPRM	Notice of Proposed Rulemaking
NSAR	Non Docketed Service Advice Review
O.	Solicitor's Law Opinion
O.D.	Office Decision
OECD	Organisation for Economic Co-operation and Develop-

	ment
Off. Mem.	Office Memorandum
OMB	Office of Management and Budget
Op. A.G.	Opinion of Attorney General
OTA	Treasury Department Office of Tax Analysis
OTP	Treasury Department Office of Tax Policy
Para.	Paragraph
PDF	Portable Document Format
PH; P-H	Prentice-Hall
PLR	Private Letter Ruling
Priv. Ltr. Rul.	Private Letter Ruling
Prop.	Proposed
PS	IRS Passthroughs and Special Industries Division
P.T.	Processing Tax Decision or Division
Pt.	Part
P.T.E.	Prohibited Transaction Exemption
Pub.	Public; Published
Rec.	Record
Reg.	Register; Registration; Regular; Regulation
Rep.	Report; Reports; Representatives; Reporter
Res.	Resolution
Rev. Proc.	Revenue Procedure
Rev. Rul.	Revenue Ruling
RIA	Research Institute of America
RIN	Regulation Identification Number
RISC	Regulatory Information Service Center
RP	Revenue Procedure
RR	Revenue Ruling
S.	Senate; Solicitor's Memorandum
SAM	Strategic Advice Memorandum
SB/SE	IRS Small Business/Self-Employed Operating Division
SCA	Service Center Advice
S. Ct.	Supreme Court
Sec.	Section
Sess.	Session
SFTR	Standard Federal Tax Reporter
Sil.	Silver Tax Division
S.M.	Solicitor's Memorandum
Sol. Op.	Solicitor's Opinion
S.P.R.	Statement of Procedural Rules
S.R.	Solicitor's Recommendation
S.S.T.	Social Security Tax and Carriers' Tax; Social Security

	Tax; Taxes on Employment by Other than Carriers
S.T.	Sales Tax Unit or Division or Branch
Stat.	United States Statutes at Large
T.	Temporary; Tobacco Division; Treaty
TAM	Technical Advice Memorandum
T.B.M.	Advisory Tax Board Memorandum
T.B.R.	Advisory Tax Board Recommendation
T.C.	Tax Court Reports
TCM	Tax Court Memorandum Opinion
TC Memo	Tax Court Memorandum Opinion
T. Ct.	Tax Court
T.D.	Treasury Decision
TEAM	Technical Expedited Advice Memorandum
TECH	Assistant Commissioner, Technical
Tech. Adv. Mem.	Technical Advice Memorandum
Tech. Info. Rel.	Technical Information Release
Tech. Mem.	Technical Memorandum
TE/GE	IRS Tax Exempt/Government Entities Operating Division
Temp.	Temporary
T.I.A.S.	Treaties and International Acts Series
T.I.R.	Technical Information Release
TLB	Tax Litigation Bulletin
TLC	Tax Legislative Counsel
TM	Technical Memorandum
Tob.	Tobacco Branch
TRAC	Tip Reporting Alternative Commitment
Treas.	Treasury Department
Treas. Dep't Order	Treasury Department Order
Treas. Reg.	Treasury Regulation
T.S.	Treaty Series
UIL	Uniform Issue List
UNTS	United Nations Treaty Series
U.S.	United States Reports
U.S.C.	United States Code
U.S.C.A.	United States Code Annotated
USCCAN	United States Code Congressional & Administrative News
U.S.C.S.	United States Code Service
U.S.T.	United States Treaties and Other International Agreements
U.S. Tax Cas.	U.S. Tax Cases
USTC	U.S. Tax Cases

USTR	United States Tax Reporter
UTC	U.S. Tax Cases
WG & L	Warren Gorham & Lamont
W & I	IRS Wage and Investment Operating Division
WL	Westlaw
WTO	World Trade Organization

APPENDIX B. ALTERNATE CITATION FORMS

> This appendix does not cover all possible citation forms. To illustrate the variety of formats in use, I selected several primary source documents and determined how each was cited in citation manuals and in several tax-oriented periodicals. Chapter 9 provides several abbreviation formats for IRS items.

1. Sources Used

ALWD Citation Manual (2000 edition)[*]
The Bluebook: A Uniform System of Citation (17th ed. 2000)
Journal of Taxation (May 2002)
TaxCite (1995 edition)
TAXES–The Tax Magazine (March 2002; May 2002)
The Tax Lawyer (Winter 2002; Spring 2002)
Tax Notes (March 26, 2002; June 17, 2002; June 24, 2002)[**]

2. Citations for Internal Revenue Code section 61

I.R.C. § 61 (year of U.S.C.)	ALWD; TaxCite; The Bluebook
I.R.C. § 61	The Tax Lawyer
Section 61	Journal of Taxation; Tax Notes
Code Sec. 61	TAXES

3. Citations for Treasury Regulation section 1.61-1

Treas. Reg. § 1.61-1 (promulgation/amendment year)	The Bluebook
Reg. § 1.61-1 (promulgation/amendment year)	TaxCite
Reg. § 1.61-1	The Tax Lawyer
Reg. §1.61-1	TAXES
Reg. section 1.61-1; Treas. reg. section 1.61-1; Treasury reg. section 1.61-1	Tax Notes
Reg. 1.61-1	Journal of Taxation

---

[*] ALWD will add tax-oriented citations in 2003; as a result, there are few ALWD citations in this appendix.

[**] Citation format is different in various articles.

4. Citations for Temporary Treasury Regulation section 1.71-1T

Temp. Treas. Reg. § 1.71-1T (promulgation/amendment year)	The Bluebook
Temp. Reg. § 1.71-1T (promulgation/amendment year)	TaxCite
Temp. Reg. § 1.71-1T	The Tax Lawyer
Temporary Reg. §1.71-1T	TAXES
Treas. reg. section 1.71-1T	Tax Notes (varies by article)
Temp. Reg. 1.71-1T	Journal of Taxation

5. Citation for Cumulative Bulletin

C.B.	The Bluebook; TaxCite; The Tax Lawyer; Tax Notes
CB	TAXES; Journal of Taxation

6. Citations for Private Letter Ruling 199929039

Priv. Ltr. Rul. 1999-29-039 (Apr. 12, 1999)	The Bluebook
P.L.R. 1999-29-039 (Apr. 12, 1999)	TaxCite; The Tax Lawyer
LTR 199929039 (Apr. 12, 1999)	TAXES; Tax Notes
Ltr. Rul. 199929039	Journal of Taxation

Appendix C. Potential Research Errors

Statements in this section reflect comments made elsewhere in this text.

Don't assume that a library lacks a source because it is not available in its general print collection or online. Check the CD-ROM, microform, and government documents collections.

Check a service's coverage dates before you begin your research. An electronic service may omit a source's initial years. A print service may not be have been updated recently enough to catch a very recent item.

Before using a service, determine how it treats revoked items. Some services delete these items; others include them but indicate they have been revoked.

If you check research results in a second publication, try to select a source from a different publishing group. Although corporate parents offer several imprints (Appendix F), there is no guarantee they will always use separate editors.

If you find a Code section on point, don't forget to check effective dates and special rules that may not be codified.

Never assume a definition in one section of the Code or regulations applies to all other sections.

Don't forget to compare the issue date of regulations and the decision date for cases against the revision date for relevant statutory amendments. Otherwise you risk citing sources whose authority has been weakened or overruled altogether. Online citators may indicate this information.

Don't confuse an act section number with a Code section number.

Don't assume every relevant provision is actually codified.

Don't assume section numbers in a bill remain unchanged through the enactment process.

Don't confuse enactment date, effective date, and sunset date.

If you use cross-reference tables to trace a statute's history, remember that these tables may not reflect changes in a section's numbering.

Remember to use the designation required by the source you are searching.

342

For example, use H. rather than H.R. on the THOMAS website; don't insert hyphens in IRS documents when searching online; remember that Tax Analysts frequently gives its own names to chief counsel advice documents.

Don't forget to check for pending items (legislation, regulations, appeals from judicial decisions) that may be relevant to your project.

Don't overestimate the degree of deference a court will accord legislative history and IRS documents.

Don't assume the government conceded an issue merely because it didn't appeal after losing a case. Check to see if there is an AOD for the case.

If you find a notice of acquiescence or nonacquiescence, check to make sure the IRS didn't reverse itself in a later Internal Revenue Bulletin.

When searching for cases using the taxpayer's name, remember that early cases are not captioned Taxpayer v. Commissioner or Taxpayer v. United States. Eisner and Helvering are government officials, not taxpayers. Likewise, remember that different services use different caption formats for bankruptcy cases.

Remember that U.S.T.C. is an abbreviation for U.S. Tax Cases; that case reporter service does not include United States Tax Court cases.

Don't confuse page and paragraph numbers. Make sure you know if a service cross-references by page, by paragraph, or by section number. Make sure you know whether new material is located in the same volume or a different volume (and where in the relevant volume it appears).

Don't rely on a service's editor for a holding. Read the document yourself.

Remember that Index to Legal Periodicals doesn't index short articles.

When using electronic materials (CD-ROM or online), make sure you understand the particular service's Boolean search rules and rules for limiting searches to a particular range of dates. From date 1 to date 2 is not the same as after date 1 and before date 2.

Make sure that s means sentence (and p means paragraph) in an electronic service. Some services define sentence and paragraph by a maximum number of words rather than by grammatical rules.

If a URL no longer yields the desired website, assume the site changed its URL but still exists. Try using your service provider's search function (or a search engine) to search for the new URL.

APPENDIX D. BIBLIOGRAPHY

CHAPTER 1. OVERVIEW

J. MYRON JACOBSTEIN, ROY M. MERSKY & DONALD J. DUNN, FUNDAMENTALS OF LEGAL RESEARCH (8th ed. 2002).

Gail Levin Richmond, *Federal Tax Locator: Basic Tax Library*, COMMUNITY TAX L. REP., Fall/Winter 2001, at 11.

ALWD CITATION MANUAL: A PROFESSIONAL SYSTEM OF CITATION (2000).

Robert C. Berring, *Legal Information and the Search for Cognitive Authority*, 88 CAL. L. REV. 1673 (2000).

THE BLUEBOOK: A UNIFORM SYSTEM OF CITATION (17th ed. 2000).

Katherine T. Pratt, *Federal Tax Sources Recommended for Law School Libraries*, 87 LAW LIBR. J. 387 (1995).

TAXCITE: A FEDERAL TAX CITATION AND REFERENCE MANUAL (1995).

Carol A. Roehrenbeck & Gail Levin Richmond, *Three Researchers in Search of an Alcove: A Play in Six Acts*, 84 LAW LIBR. J. 13 (1992).

Louis F. Lobenhofer, *Tax Law Libraries for Small and Medium-Sized Firms*, PRAC. TAX LAW., Fall 1988, at 17, and Winter 1989, at 31.

Gail Levin Richmond, *Research Tools for Federal Taxation*, 2 LEGAL REFERENCE SERVICES Q., Spring 1982, at 25.

CHAPTER 2. SOURCES OF LAW

Franklin L. Green, *Exercising Judgment in the Wonderland Gymnasium*, TAX NOTES, Mar. 19, 2001, at 1691.

Kip Dellinger, *The Substantial Understatement, Negligence and Tax-Return Preparers' Penalties—An Overview*, TAXES, November 1999, at 41.

Office of Tax Policy, Department of the Treasury, Report to the Congress on Penalty and Interest Provisions of the Internal Revenue Code (1999).

344

Shop Talk, *IRS FSA Gives Guidance on Substantial Authority in Penalty Situation*, 91 J. TAX'N 61 (1999).

Staff of the Joint Committee on Taxation, Study of Present-law Penalty and Interest Provisions as Required by Section 3801 of the Internal Revenue Service Restructuring and Reform Act of 1998 (Including Provisions Relating to Corporate Tax Shelters), JCS 3-99 (106th Cong., 1st Sess.) (Jt. Comm. Print 1999).

BERNARD WOLFMAN, JAMES P. HOLDEN, AND KENNETH L. HARRIS, STANDARDS OF TAX PRACTICE (5th ed. 1999).

George R. Goodman, *Tax Return Compliance*, TAX NOTES, Sept. 1, 1997, at 1201.

Shop Talk, *Courts Disagree on Substantial Authority*, 82 J. TAX'N 380 (1995).

CHAPTER 3. RESEARCH PROCESS

John A. Barrick, *The Effect of Code Section Knowledge on Tax Research Performance*, J. AM. TAX. ASS'N, Fall 2001, at 20.

Gitelle Seer, *10 Things You Hate to Hear: Tips from Your Librarian*, LAW PRAC. Q., Aug. 2001, at 20.

Anne M. Magro, *Knowledge, Adaptivity, and Performance in Tax Research* (2000) (http://papers.ssrn.com/sol3/papers.cfm?abstract_id=209788) (SSRN Electronic Paper Collection) (site last visited June 25, 2002).

CHAPTER 4. CONSTITUTION

Bruce Ackerman, *Taxation and the Constitution*, 99 COLUM. L. REV. 1 (1999).

BORIS I. BITTKER & LAWRENCE LOKKEN, FEDERAL TAXATION OF INCOME, ESTATES AND GIFTS ch. 1 (3d ed. 1999 & 2002 Cum. Supp.).

Calvin H. Johnson, *The Constitutional Meaning of 'Apportionment of Direct Taxes,'* TAX NOTES, Aug. 3, 1998, at 591.

Erik M. Jensen, *The Apportionment of "Direct Taxes": Are Consumption Taxes Constitutional?*, 97 COLUM. L. REV. 2334 (1997).

John O. McGinnis & Michael B. Rappaport, *The Rights of Legislators and the Wrongs of Interpretation: A Further Defense of the Constitutionality of Legislative Supermajority Rules*, 47 DUKE L.J. 327 (1997).

Richard Belas, *The Post-Carlton World: Just When Is a Retroactive Tax Unconstitutional?*, TAX NOTES, Oct. 30, 1995, at 633.

CHAPTER 5. STATUTES

WILLIAM D. POPKIN, STATUTES IN COURT: THE HISTORY AND THEORY OF STATUTORY INTERPRETATION (1999).

John F. Coverdale, *Text as Limit: A Plea for a Decent Respect for the Tax Code*, 71 TUL. L. REV. 1501 (1997).

Edward A. Zelinsky, *Text, Purpose, Capacity and* Albertson's*: A Response to Professor Geier*, 2 FLA. TAX REV. 717 (1996).

Jasper L. Cummings, Jr., *Statutory Interpretation and* Albertson's, TAX NOTES, Jan. 23, 1995, at 559.

Myron Grauer, *A Case for Congressional Facilitation of a Collaborative Model of Statutory Interpretation in the Tax Area: Lessons to be Learned from the* Corn Products *and* Arkansas Best *Cases and the Historical Development of the Statutory Definition of "Capital Asset(s),"* 84 KY. L.J. 1 (1995).

Deborah A. Geier, *Commentary: Textualism and Tax Cases*, 66 TEMP. L. REV. 445 (1993).

CHAPTER 6. LEGISLATIVE HISTORIES

See also separate section on deference following Chapter 10.

Tax History Project (http://www.tax.org/THP) (Tax Analysts website for historical research, including such documents as policy papers from presidential libraries, posters, presidential tax returns, *The Federalist Papers*, and a "Tax History Museum").

Michael Livingston, *What's Blue and White and Not Quite As Good As a Committee Report: General Explanations and the Role of "Subsequent" Tax Legislative History*, 11 AM J. TAX POL'Y 91 (1994).

CHAPTER 7. TREATIES

Anthony C. Infanti, *The Proposed Domestic Reverse Hybrid Entity Regulations: Can the Treasury Department Override Treaties?*, 30 TAX MGMT. INT'L

J. 307 (2001).

John A. Townsend, *Tax Treaty Interpretation*, 55 TAX LAW. 221 (2001).

John F. Avery Jones, *The David R. Tillinghast Lecture: Are Tax Treaties Necessary?*, 53 TAX L. REV. 1 (1999).

Philip F. Postlewaite & David S. Makarski, *The A.L.I. Tax Treaty Study—A Critique and a Proposal*, 49 TAX LAW. 731 (1999).

Ernest R. Larkins, *U.S. Income Tax Treaties in Research and Planning: A Primer*, 18 VA. TAX REV. 133 (1998).

Robert Thornton Smith, *Tax Treaty Interpretation by the Judiciary*, 49 TAX LAW. 845 (1996).

CHAPTER 8. REGULATIONS

See also separate section on deference following Chapter 10.

Naftali Z. Dembitzer, *Beyond the IRS Restructuring and Reform Act of 1998: Perceived Abuses of the Treasury Department's Rulemaking Authority*, 52 TAX LAW. 501 (1999).

CHAPTER 9. INTERNAL REVENUE SERVICE DOCUMENTS

See also separate section on deference following Chapter 10.

Marion Marshall, Sheryl Stratton, and Christopher Bergin, *The Changing Landscape of IRS Guidance: A Downward Slope*, TAX NOTES, Jan. 29, 2001, at 673.

Inventory of IRS Guidance Documents—A Draft, TAX NOTES, July 17, 2000, at 305.

CHAPTER 10. JUDICIAL

See also separate section on deference following Chapter 10.

Mark P. Altieri, Jerome E. Apple, Penny Marquette & Charles K. Moore, *Political Affiliation of Appointing President and Outcome of Tax Court Cases*, 84 JUDICATURE 310 (May/June 2001).

Cornish F. Hitchcock, *Public Access to Special Trial Judge Reports*, TAX NOTES, Oct. 15, 2001, at 403.

Robert A. Mead, *"Unpublished" Opinions as the Bulk of the Iceberg: Publication Patterns in the Eighth and Tenth Circuit United States Courts of Appeals*, 93 LAW LIBR. J. 589 (2001).

Daniel M. Schneider, *Empirical Research on Judicial Reasoning: Statutory Interpretation in Federal Tax Cases*, 31 N.M. L. REV. 325 (2001).

Kirk J. Stark, The Unfulfilled Tax Legacy of Justice Robert H. Jackson, 54 TAX L. REV. 171 (2001).

Paul E. Treusch, *What to Consider in Choosing a Forum to Resolve an Ordinary Tax Dispute*, 55 TAX LAW. 83 (2001).

James Edward Maule, *Instant Replay, Weak Teams, and Disputed Calls: An Empirical Study of Alleged Tax Court Bias*, 66 TENN. L. REV. 351 (1999).

Mark F. Sommer & Anne D. Waters, *Tax Court Memorandum Opinions —What Are They Worth?*, TAX NOTES, July 20, 1998, at 384.

CHAPTERS 6-10. DEFERENCE

Mitchell M. Gans, *Deference and the End of Tax Practice*, 36 REAL PROP., PROB. & TR. J. 731 (2002).

Edward J. Schnee & W. Eugene Seago, *Deference Issues in the Tax Law: Mead* Clarifes the Chevron *Rule—Or Does It?*, 96 J. TAX'N 366 (2002).

David F. Shores, *Deferential Review of Tax Court Decisions: Taking Institutional Choice Seriously*, 55 TAX LAW. 667 (2002).

Irving Salem & Richard Bress, *Agency Deference Under the Judicial Microscope of the Supreme Court*, TAX NOTES, Sept. 4, 2000, at 1257.

David F. Shores, *Rethinking Deferential Review of Tax Court Decisions*, 53 TAX LAW. 35 (1999).

Benjamin J. Cohen & Catherine A. Harrington, *Is the Internal Revenue Service Bound by Its Own Regulations and Rulings?*, 51 TAX LAW. 675 (1998).

Steve R. Johnson, *The Phoenix and the Perils of the Second Best: Why Heightened Appellate Deference to Tax Court Decisions Is Undesirable*, 77 OR. L. REV. 235 (1998).

David A. Brennen, *Treasury Regulations and Judicial Deference in the*

Post-Chevron *Era*, 13 GA. ST. U. L. REV. 387 (1997).

Ellen P. Aprill, *Muffled* Chevron: *Judicial Review of Tax Regulations*, 3 FLA. TAX REV. 51 (1996).

Paul L. Caron, *Tax Myopia Meets Tax Hyperopia: The Unproven Case of Increased Judicial Deference to Revenue Rulings*, 57 OHIO ST. L.J. 637 (1996).

Beverly I. Moran & Daniel M. Schneider, *The Elephant and the Four Blind Men: The Burger Court and Its Federal Tax Decisions*, 39 HOW. L.J. 841 (1996).

John F. Coverdale, *Court Review of Tax Regulations and Revenue Rulings in the Chevron Era*, 64 GEO. WASH. L. REV. 35 (1995).

Linda Galler, *Judicial Deference to Revenue Rulings: Reconciling Divergent Standards*, 56 OHIO ST. L.J. 1037 (1995).

Paul L. Caron, *Tax Myopia, or Mamas Don't Let Your Babies Grow Up to be Tax Lawyers*, 13 VA. TAX REV. 517 (1994).

CHAPTER 13. LEGAL PERIODICALS

William J. Turnier, *Tax (and Lots of Other) Scholars Need Not Apply: The Changing Venue for Scholarship*, 50 J. LEGAL EDUC. 189 (2000).

CHAPTER 19. ONLINE LEGAL RESEARCH

Thomas R. Keefe, *The Invisible Web: What You Can't See Might Hurt You*, RES. ADVISOR, May 2002, at 1.

Mary Rumsey, *Runaway Train: Problems of Permanence, Accessibility, and Stability in the Use of Web Sources in Law Review Citations*, 94 LAW LIBR. J. 27 (2002).

Diana Botluk, *Search Engines Comparison 2001*, at http://www.llrx.com/features/engine2001.htm (Aug. 1, 2001).

Gary W. White, *Internet Resources for Taxation: A Selective, Annotated Guide*, LEGAL REFERENCE SERVICES Q., vol. 18(4), at 49 (2001).

Lisa Smith-Butler, *Cost Effective Legal Research*, LEGAL REFERENCE SERVICES Q., vol. 18(2), at 61 (2000).

Appendix E. Publishers of Publications Described in Text

A. Print and CD-ROM—Other than U.S. Government

Acts and Cases by Popular Names (Shepard's)
Akron Tax Journal (University of Akron Law Center)
ALWD Citation Manual (Aspen)
American Federal Tax Reports (Research Institute of America; formerly
  Prentice-Hall)
Authority CD-ROM (Matthew Bender)
Bankruptcy Citations (Shepard's)
Bankruptcy Reporter (West)
Barton's (Federal Tax Press, Inc.)
Bishop & Kleinberger (Warren, Gorham & Lamont)
Bittker, Emory & Streng (Warren, Gorham & Lamont)
Bittker & Eustice (Warren, Gorham & Lamont)
Bittker & Lokken (Warren, Gorham & Lamont)
The Bluebook: A Uniform System of Citation (The Harvard Law Review Association)
B.T.A. Memorandum Decisions (Prentice-Hall)
B.T.A. Reports (Prentice-Hall)
Business Periodicals Index (H. W. Wilson Company)
Casey (Clark Boardman Callahan)
Casner & Pennell (Aspen)
Chief Counsel Advice CD-ROM (Tax Analysts)
Claims Court Reporter (West)
Code of Federal Regulations Citations (Shepard's)
Complete Federal Tax Forms (Research Institute of America)
Congressional Index (Commerce Clearing House)
Corporate Tax Digest (Warren, Gorham & Lamont)
Court Decisions CD-ROM (Tax Analysts)
Court of Federal Claims Reporter (West)
Cumulative Changes (Research Institute of America; formerly Prentice-Hall)
Current Law Index (Gale Group; formerly Information Access)
Current Legal Forms with Tax Analysis (Matthew Bender)
Daily Tax Highlights & Documents (Tax Analysts)
Daily Tax Report (Bureau of National Affairs)
Developments & Highlights (Clark Boardman Callahan)
Divorce Taxation (Warren, Gorham & Lamont)
Eldridge (Hein)
Elections & Compliance Statements CD-ROM (Research Institute of America)
Estate and Gift Tax Digest (Warren, Gorham & Lamont)
Estate Planning (Aspen)
European Legal Journals Index (Legal Information Resources Ltd.)
Exempt Organizations Tax Review (Tax Analysts)
Federal Citations (Shepard's)

350

Federal Courts Collection CD-ROM (Tax Analysts)
Federal Estate and Gift Tax Project (American Law Institute)
Federal Estate and Gift Tax Reporter (Commerce Clearing House)
Federal Excise Tax Reporter (Commerce Clearing House)
Federal Income, Gift and Estate Taxation (Matthew Bender)
Federal Income Taxation of Corporations and Shareholders (Warren, Gorham & Lamont)
Federal Income Taxation of Corporations and Shareholders: Forms (Warren, Gorham & Lamont)
Federal Law Citations in Selected Law Reviews (Shepard's)
Federal Practice Digest (West)
Federal Reporter (West)
Federal Statute Citations (Shepard's)
Federal Supplement (West)
Federal Tax Articles (Commerce Clearing House)
Federal Tax Bulletin (Kleinrock)
Federal Tax Citator (Shepard's)
Federal Tax Coordinator 2d (Research Institute of America)
Federal Tax Forms (Commerce Clearing House)
Federal Tax Laws Correlated (Federal Tax Press, Inc.)
Federal Tax Practice (Clark Boardman Callahan)
Federal Tax Regulations (Clark Boardman Callahan)
Federal Tax Weekly (Commerce Clearing House)
Federal Taxation of Income, Estates and Gifts (Warren, Gorham & Lamont)
Federal Taxation of Inventories (Matthew Bender)
Federal Taxation of Partnerships and Partners (Warren, Gorham & Lamont)
Florida Tax Review (University of Florida College of Law)
Forms Disc CD-ROM (Tax Analysts)
Fundamentals of Legal Research (Foundation Press)
General Digest (West)
Guide Series (PricewaterhouseCoopers)
Hecklerling Institute on Estate Planning (Matthew Bender)
Highlights & Documents (Tax Analysts)
Index to Federal Tax Articles (Warren, Gorham & Lamont)
Index to Foreign Legal Periodicals (American Association of Law Libraries)
Index to Legal Periodicals (H. W. Wilson Company)
Index to Periodical Articles Related to Law (Glanville Publishers, Inc.)
Institute on Estate Planning (Matthew Bender)
Institute on Federal Taxation (NYU) (Matthew Bender)
The Internal Revenue Acts of the United States (Hein)
Internal Revenue Acts—Text and Legislative History (West)
Internal Revenue Code of 1954: Congressional Committee Reports (Hein)
Internal Revenue Manual (Commerce Clearing House)
Internal Revenue Manual CD-ROM (Tax Analysts)
International Microfiche Database (Tax Analysts)
IRS Letter Rulings & Memoranda CD-ROM (Research Institute of America)
IRS Letter Rulings Reporter (Commerce Clearing House)
IRS Practice & Procedure (Warren, Gorham & Lamont)
IRS Practice CD-ROM (Research Institute of America)
IRS Tax Publications (Commerce Clearing House)

Journal of Taxation (Warren, Gorham & Lamont)
Law of Federal Income Taxation (Clark Boardman Callahan)
Law Reprints—Tax Law Series (Law Reprints)
Law Review Citations (Shepard's)
Legal Forms with Tax Analysis (Clark Boardman Callahan)
LegalTrac CD-ROM (Gale Group; formerly Information Access)
Legislative History of Federal Income and Excess Profits Tax Laws (Prentice-Hall)
Legislative History of United States Tax Conventions (Hein)
Limited Liability Companies: Tax & Business Law (Warren, Gorham & Lamont)
Lowell, Tilton, Sheldrick & Donohue (Warren, Gorham & Lamont)
Mancoff & Steinberg (Clark Boardman Callahan)
McGaffey (Clark Boardman Callahan)
McKee, Nelson & Whitmire (Warren, Gorham & Lamont)
Mertens (Clark Boardman Callahan)
Mertens, Federal Tax Regulations (West)
Mertens, Internal Revenue Code (West)
Microfiche Database (Tax Analysts)
Monthly Digest of Tax Articles (Newkirk Products, Inc.)
Murphy's Will Clauses: Annotations and Forms with Tax Effects (Matthew Bender)
NYU Institute on Federal Taxation (Matthew Bender)
O'Connell (Warren, Gorham & Lamont)
OneDisc CD-ROM (Tax Analysts)
OnPoint CD-ROM (Research Institute of America)
Pass-Through Entity Tax Digest (Warren, Gorham & Lamont)
Pending and Enacted Legislation CD-ROM (Research Institute of America)
P-H Citator (Prentice-Hall)
Portfolios Plus Library CD-ROM (Bureau of National Affairs)
Primary Sources (Bureau of National Affairs)
Public Domain Library CD-ROM (Research Institute of America)
Qualified Deferred Compensation Plans—Forms (Clark Boardman Callahan)
Rabkin & Johnson (Matthew Bender)
Real Estate Forms: Tax Analysis & Checklists (Warren, Gorham & Lamont)
Real Estate Tax Digest (Warren, Gorham & Lamont)
Real Estate Taxation (Warren, Gorham & Lamont)
Rhoades & Langer (Matthew Bender)
RIA Citator 2nd (Research Institute of America; formerly Prentice-Hall)
Roberts & Holland Collection (Hein)
Robinson (Warren, Gorham & Lamont)
Saltzman (Warren, Gorham & Lamont)
Schneider (Matthew Bender)
Seidman's (Prentice-Hall)
Social Sciences Index (H. W. Wilson Company)
Standard Federal Tax Reporter (Commerce Clearing House)
Supreme Court Reporter (West)
Tax Advisors Planning System CD-ROM (Research Institute of America)
Tax Court Memorandum Decisions (Commerce Clearing House)
Tax Court Memorandum Decisions (Research Institute of America)
Tax Court Reporter (Commerce Clearing House)
Tax Court Reports (Research Institute of America)
Tax Directory (Tax Analysts)

Tax Law Review (faculty-edited at New York University School of Law)
The Tax Lawyer (ABA Section of Taxation)
Tax Legislative History CD-ROM (Tax Analysts)
Tax Management Memorandum (Bureau of National Affairs)
Tax Management Portfolios (Bureau of National Affairs)
Tax Management Weekly Report (Bureau of National Affairs)
Tax Notes (Tax Analysts)
Tax Policy in the United States (Vanderbilt University Law Library)
Tax Practice Plus Series CD-ROM (Bureau of National Affairs)
Tax Procedure Digest (Warren, Gorham & Lamont)
Tax Treaties (Commerce Clearing House)
Tax Treaties CD-ROM (Commerce Clearing House)
TaxCite (ABA Section of Taxation)
Taxes—The Tax Magazine (Commerce Clearing House)
Taxes on Parade (Commerce Clearing House)
Taxes Today (Matthew Bender)
TaxExpert CD-ROM (Kleinrock)
A Treatise on the Law of Income Taxes (Vernon)
United States Citations (Shepard's)
United States Claims Court Reporter (West)
United States Code Annotated (West)
United States Code Service (LexisNexis)
United States Court of Federal Claims Reporter (West)
The United States Internal Revenue System (Hein)
United States Supreme Court Reports, Lawyers' Edition (Lexis; formerly by Lawyers
    Cooperative Publishing)
United States Tax Reporter (Research Institute of America)
U.S. Code Congressional & Administrative News (West)
U.S. International Taxation: Agreements, Checklists & Commentary (Warren,
    Gorham & Lamont)
U.S. International Taxation and Tax Treaties (Matthew Bender)
U.S. Tax Cases (Commerce Clearing House)
U.S. Tax Treaties CD-ROM (Tax Analysts)
USCA (West)
USCCAN (West)
USCS (Lexis)
Virginia Tax Review (University of Virginia School of Law)
WG & L Journal Digest (Warren, Gorham & Lamont)
Weekly Alert (Research Institute of America)
Weekly Report (Bureau of National Affairs)
Westin, WG&L Tax Dictionary (Warren, Gorham & Lamont)
WilsonDisc CD-ROM (H. W. Wilson Company)
Worldwide Tax Treaties CD-ROM (Tax Analysts)

B. Print and CD-ROM—U.S. Government

Board of Tax Appeals Reports
Bulletin Index-Digest System
Code of Federal Regulations
Congressional Record

Court of Claims Reports
Court of International Trade Reports
Cumulative Bulletin
Derivations of Code Sections of the Internal Revenue Codes of 1939 and 1954
Executive Agreement Series
Federal Register
Internal Revenue Bulletin
Legislative History of the Internal Revenue Code of 1954
Listing of Selected Federal Tax Legislation Reprinted in the IRS Cumulative
  Bulletin, 1913-1990
Listing of Selected International Tax Conventions and Other Agreements Reprinted
  in the IRS Cumulative Bulletin, 1913-1990
Tax Court of the United States Reports
Treasury Decisions—Internal Revenue
Treaties and Other International Acts Series
Treaties Series
United States Code
United States Constitution
United States Reports
United States Statutes at Large
United States Tax Court Reports
United States Treaties and Other International Agreements
Weekly Compilation of Presidential Documents

C. Subscription Websites

BNATAX Management Library (Bureau of National Affairs)
Checkpoint (Research Institute of America)
CIS Congressional Universe (Lexis)
Congressional Universe (Lexis)
Daily Tax Bulletiin (Kleinrock)
Federal Tax Day News and Documents (Commerce Clearing House)
Federal Tax Service (Commerce Clearing House)
Hein-On-Line (Hein)
KeyCite (part of Westlaw)
Legal Resource Index (Gale Group; formerly Information Access)
LexisNexis (Lexis)
Loislaw (Aspen)
Tax Research NetWork (Commerce Clearing House)
Tax Treaties Online (Oceana)
TaxBase (Tax Analysts)
TaxCore (Tax Management/Bureau of National Affairs)
TaxExpert Online (Kleinrock)
Tax Notes Today (Tax Analysts)
U.S. Bilateral Tax Treaties Database (Research Institute of America Checkpoint)
VersusLaw (VersusLaw)
Westlaw (West)
WilsonWeb (H. W. Wilson Company)

D. U.S. Government Websites

Congressional Budget Office (www.cbo.gov)
Congressional Research Service (www.lcweb.loc.gov/crsinfo/)
Council of Economic Advisors (www.whitehouse.gov/cea/)
Federal Judiciary Home Page (www.uscourts.gov)
FirstGov (www.firstgov.gov)
General Accounting Office (www.gao.gov)
General Services Administration (www.gsa.gov)
Government Printing Office—GPO Access (www.access.gpo.gov)
House of Representatives (www.house.gov)
House of Representatives Budget Committee (budget.house.gov)
House of Representatives Ways & Means Committee (waysandmeans.house.gov)
Internal Revenue Service (www.irs.gov)
Internal Revenue Service National Taxpayer Advocate (www.irs.gov/advocate)
Joint Committee on Taxation (www.house.gov/jct/)
Joint Economic Committee (www.house.gov/jec/)
Library of Congress THOMAS (thomas.loc.gov)
National Archives and Records Administration (www.access.gpo.gov/nara/)
Office of Management and Budget (www.whitehouse.gov/omb/)
President/White House (www.whitehouse.gov)
Regulatory Information Service Center (www.gsa.gov)
Senate (www.senate.gov)
Senate Budget Committee (budget.senate.gov/)
Senate Finance Committee (finance.senate.gov/)
Supreme Court (www.supremecourtus.gov)
Tax Court (www.ustaxcourt.gov)
Treasury Department (www.treas.gov)
Treasury Department Office of Tax Analysis (www.treas.gov/ota/)
Treasury Department Office of Tax Policy (www.treas.gov/taxpolicy/)

E. Other Nonsubscription Websites

AltaVista (www.altavista.com)
Cornell Law School Legal Information Institute (www.law.cornell.edu)
Excite (www.excite.com)
Findlaw (www.findlaw.com)
Google (www.google.com)
Hieros Gamos (www.hg.org/)
Hieros Gamos Tax (www.hg.org/tax.html)
HotBot (www.hotbot.lycos.com)
Lycos (www.lycos.com)
MetaCrawler (www.metacrawler.com)
Metor (www.metor.com)
OECD (www.oecd.org)
Villanova University School of Law Tax Master (vls.law.vill.edu/prof/maule/taxmaster/taxhome.htm)
WTO (www.wto.org)

APPENDIX F. COMMONLY OWNED PUBLISHERS

Aspen	WoltersKluwer
Bureau of National Affairs	Bureau of National Affairs
Butterworths	Reed Elsevier
Clark Boardman Callahan	Thomson
Commerce Clearing House	WoltersKluwer
Congressional Information Service	Reed Elsevier
Dialog	Thomson
FindLaw	Thomson
Foundation Press	Thomson
Gale Group	Thomson
Hein	William S. Hein & Co., Inc.
Kleinrock	UCG
Kluwer	WoltersKluwer
Lawyers Cooperative	Thomson
Lexis Publishing	Reed Elsevier
LexisNexis	Reed Elsevier
Little, Brown	*
LoisLaw	WoltersKluwer
Matthew Bender	Reed Elsevier
Michie	Reed Elsevier
Oceana	Oceana
Prentice-Hall	**
Research Institute of America	Thomson
Rothman	William S. Hein & Co., Inc.
Shepard's	Reed Elsevier
Tax Analysts	Tax Analysts
Tax Management	Bureau of National Affairs
Warren Gorham & Lamont	Thomson
West Group	Thomson
Westlaw	Thomson

➔The information available above reflects ownership groups in early 2002.

* Aspen purchased several publications that formerly appeared under the Little, Brown imprint.

** Research Institute of America and Warren Gorham & Lamont purchased several publications that formerly appeared under the Prentice-Hall imprint.

INDEX (REFERENCES TO PAGE NUMBERS)

ABBREVIATIONS
Commonly used, 333-339
Pre-1953 Cumulative Bulletins, in, 138

ACQUIESCENCE
See Internal Revenue Service.

ACTIONS ON DECISIONS
See Internal Revenue Service.

ACTS OF CONGRESS
See Statutes.

ADMINISTRATIVE INTERPRETATIONS
Internal Revenue Service, 135-171
Treasury, 107-134

ADMINISTRATIVE PROCEDURE ACT
See Treasury Regulations.

ADVANCE NOTICE OF PROPOSED
RULEMAKING
See Treasury Regulations.

ADVANCE PRICING AGREEMENTS
See Internal Revenue Service.

ADVANCE SHEETS
See Courts.

AMENDED STATUTES
See Statutes.

AMERICAN FEDERAL TAX REPORTS,
182-183

AMERICAN LAW INSTITUTE
Proposals affecting legislation, 51

ANNOTATED STATUTES
See Statutes.

ANNOUNCEMENTS
See Internal Revenue Service.

APPELLATE REVIEW
See Courts.

ARTICLES, 240-254

AUTHORITY, 7-9

BANKRUPTCY APPELLATE PANEL
See Courts.

BANKRUPTCY COURTS
See Courts.

BARTON'S FEDERAL TAX LAWS
CORRELATED, 276-277

BILLS
See Legislative History; Statutes.

BLUE BOOK
See Legislative History.

BOARD OF TAX APPEALS (BTA)
See Courts.

BRIEFS AND RECORDS
See Courts.

BULLETIN INDEX-DIGEST SYSTEM,
270-272

CCH TAX RESEARCH NETWORK, 317-
319

CD-ROM, 286-301

CHECKPOINT, 322

CHIEF COUNSEL ADVICE
See Internal Revenue Service.

CHIEF COUNSEL BULLETINS
See Internal Revenue Service.

CHIEF COUNSEL NOTICES
See Internal Revenue Service.

CITATION FORMAT, 5

CITATORS, 196-219

CLAIMS COURT
See Courts.

CLOSING AGREEMENTS
See Internal Revenue Service.

CODE OF FEDERAL REGULATIONS
See Treasury Regulations.

CODIFICATIONS
See Statutes.

COLLECTION, BANKRUPTCY AND
SUMMONSES BULLETINS
See Internal Revenue Service.

COMMITTEES, CONGRESSIONAL
See Legislative History.

COMPLIANCE OFFICER MEMORANDA
See Internal Revenue Service.

COMPUTER DATABASES, 302-331
See also CD-ROM.

CONFERENCE COMMITTEE
See Legislative History.

CONGRESSIONAL BUDGET OFFICE
See Legislative History.

CONGRESSIONAL INDEX, 49-50

CONGRESSIONAL INFORMATION
SERVICE, 50, 285

CONGRESSIONAL MATERIAL
See Legislative History.

CONGRESSIONAL RECORD
See Legislative History.

CONGRESSIONAL RESEARCH SERVICE
See Legislative History.

CONSTITUTION, 30-35

CONVENTIONS
See Treaties.

COURT DECISIONS
See Courts.

COURT OF CLAIMS
See Courts.

COURT OF FEDERAL CLAIMS
See Courts.

COURT ORGANIZATION
See Courts.

COURT REPORTS
See Courts.

COURTS, 173-194
See also Citators; Internal Revenue
Service.

COURTS OF APPEALS
See Courts.

CRIMINAL TAX BULLETINS
See Internal Revenue Service.

CROSS REFERENCE TABLES
See Legislative History.

CUMULATIVE BULLETIN, 269-270

CUMULATIVE CHANGES, 274-276

CURRENT LAW INDEX, 242

DAILY TAX BULLETIN, 265

DAILY TAX HIGHLIGHTS &
DOCUMENTS, 262-263

DAILY TAX REPORT, 261

DATABASES
See Computer Databases.

DECISIONS
See Courts.

DEFERENCE
See Courts; Internal Revenue Service;
Legislative History; Treasury Regulations.

DEFINITIONS
See Statutes; Treasury Regulations.

DETERMINATION LETTERS
See Internal Revenue Service.

DEVELOPMENTS & HIGHLIGHTS, 246

DISTRICT COURTS
See Courts.

EFFECTIVE DATE
See Statutes ; Treaties; Treasury
Regulations.

ENACTMENT DATE
See Statutes.

ENCYCLOPEDIAS
See Looseleaf Services.

FEDERAL COURT DECISIONS
See Courts.

FEDERAL DISTRICT COURTS
See Courts.

FEDERAL INCOME, GIFT AND ESTATE
TAXATION, 236-238

FEDERAL REGISTER
See Treasury Regulations.

FEDERAL REPORTER
See Courts.

FEDERAL SUPPLEMENT
See Courts.

FEDERAL TAX ARTICLES, 244

FEDERAL TAX BULLETIN, 265

FEDERAL TAX CITATIONS
See Citators.

FEDERAL TAX COORDINATOR 2D,
231-233

FEDERAL TAX DAY NEWS (CCH), 264

FEDERAL TAX LAWS CORRELATED,
276-277

FEDERAL TAX WEEKLY, 264

FEDERAL TAXATION OF INCOME,
ESTATES AND GIFTS, 33, 239

FIELD SERVICE ADVICE
See Internal Revenue Service.

FILING DATE
See Treasury Regulations.

FINAL REGULATIONS
See Treasury Regulations.

FINANCE COMMITTEE, SENATE
See Legislative History.

FOREIGN LAW
See Treaties.

FORM BOOKS
See Forms.

FORMS, 255-258

FREEDOM OF INFORMATION ACT
See Internal Revenue Service.

GENERAL ACCOUNTING OFFICE
See Legislative History.

GENERAL COUNSEL MEMORANDA
See Internal Revenue Service.

GENERAL EXPLANATION (BLUE BOOK)
See Legislative History.

HEADNOTES
See Citators; Courts.

HEARINGS
See Legislative History; Treasury
Regulations.

HEIN-ON-LINE, 249

HIGHLIGHTS & DOCUMENTS, 262-263

HOUSE MATERIALS
See Legislative History.

INDEX TO FEDERAL TAX ARTICLES,
245

INDEX TO LEGAL PERIODICALS, 243

INDEXES
See Articles.

INDUSTRY SPECIALIZATION PROGRAM
See Internal Revenue Service.

INFORMATION LETTERS
See Internal Revenue Service.

INSTITUTES
See Articles.

INSTRUMENTS OF RATIFICATION
See Treaties.

INTERNAL REVENUE ACTS OF THE
UNITED STATES, 280-281

INTERNAL REVENUE ACTS—TEXT AND LEGISLATIVE HISTORY, 273-274

INTERNAL REVENUE BULLETIN, 268-269

INTERNAL REVENUE CODE
See Statutes.

INTERNAL REVENUE CODE OF 1954: CONGRESSIONAL COMMITTEE REPORTS, 71

INTERNAL REVENUE MANUAL
See Internal Revenue Service.

INTERNAL REVENUE SERVICE, 135-171

INTERNATIONAL MATERIALS
See Treaties.

INTERNET
See Online Legal Research.

INTERPRETATIVE REGULATIONS
See Treasury Regulations.

INTERPRETING STATUTES, 52-56
See also Legislative History; Treasury Regulations.

JOINT COMMITTEE ON TAXATION
See Legislative History.

JUDICIAL DECISIONS
See Courts.

JUDICIAL REPORTS
See Courts.

KEYCITE
See Citators.

LAW OF FEDERAL INCOME TAXATION (MERTENS), 234-236

LAW REPORTS
See Courts.

LAW REPRINTS, 185

LAW REVIEWS
See Articles.

LAWYERS' EDITION
See Courts.

LEGAL ENCYCLOPEDIAS
See Looseleaf Services.

LEGAL FORMS
See Forms.

LEGAL MEMORANDA
See Internal Revenue Service.

LEGAL PERIODICALS
See Articles.

LEGAL RESOURCE INDEX, 242

LEGALTRAC, 242

LEGISLATION
See Statutes.

LEGISLATIVE HISTORY, 61-83
See also Statutes.

LEGISLATIVE HISTORY OF THE INTERNAL REVENUE CODE OF 1954, 281-282

LEGISLATIVE HISTORY OF UNITED STATES TAX CONVENTIONS, 98

LEGISLATIVE PROCESS
See Legislative History.

LEGISLATIVE REGULATIONS
See Treasury Regulations.

LETTER OF SUBMITTAL
See Treaties.

LETTER OF TRANSMITTAL
See Treaties.

LETTER RULINGS
See Internal Revenue Service.

LEXISNEXIS, 304-307

LITIGATION GUIDELINE MEMORANDA
See Internal Revenue Service.

LOISLAW, 311-313

LOOSELEAF SERVICES, 220-239

MARKET SEGMENT SPECIALIZATION PAPER
See Internal Revenue Service.

MARKET SEGMENT UNDERSTANDING
See Internal Revenue Service.

MEMORANDUM DECISIONS
See Courts.

MERTENS, LAW OF FEDERAL INCOME TAXATION, 234-236

MICROFORMS, 284-285

MONTHLY DIGEST OF TAX ARTICLES, 247

NATIONAL TAXPAYER ADVOCATE
See Legislative History.

NEWSLETTERS, 259-266

NONACQUIESCENCE
See Internal Revenue Service.

NONDOCKETED SERVICE ADVICE REVIEWS
See Internal Revenue Service.

NOTICE OF PROPOSED RULEMAKING
See Treasury Regulations.

OBSOLETE RULINGS
See Internal Revenue Service.

OECD, 101

OFFICE OF MANAGEMENT AND BUDGET
See Legislative History.

OFFICIAL REPORTS
See Courts.

ONEDISC, 288-289

ONLINE LEGAL RESEARCH, 302-331

ONPOINT, 292-294

OPERATING POLICIES
See Internal Revenue Service.

PARALLEL CITATIONS
See Courts.

PENDING LEGISLATION
See Statutes.

PENDING LITIGATION
See Courts.

PERIODICALS
See Articles.

POLICIES, INTERNAL REVENUE SERVICE
See Internal Revenue Service.

PORTFOLIOS PLUS LIBRARY, 295-296

PREAMBLES
See Treasury Regulations.

PRECEDENT
See Authority; Courts; Internal Revenue Service.

PREFIXES
See Treasury Regulations.

PRIMARY SOURCES (BNA), 274

PRIOR REGULATIONS
See Treasury Regulations.

PRIORITY GUIDANCE PLAN
See Treasury Regulations.

PRIVATE LETTER RULINGS
See Internal Revenue Service.

PROCEDURAL RULES
See Internal Revenue Service.

PROJECT NUMBERS
See Treasury Regulations.

PROPOSED LEGISLATION
See Statutes.

PROPOSED REGULATIONS
See Treasury Regulations.

PROTOCOLS
See Treaties.

PUBLIC DOMAIN LIBRARY, 292-293

PUBLIC LAWS
See Statutes.

PUBLISHED RULINGS
See Internal Revenue Service.

RABKIN & JOHNSON
Current Legal Forms with Tax Analysis, 256
Federal Income, Gift and Estate Taxation, 236-238

RECORDS AND BRIEFS
See Courts.

REGULATIONS
See Treasury Regulations.

REPEALED STATUTES
See Statutes.

REPORTER SERVICES
See Courts; Looseleaf Services.

REVENUE ACTS
See Statutes.

REVENUE PROCEDURES
See Internal Revenue Service.

REVENUE RULINGS
See Internal Revenue Service.

REVOKED RULINGS
See Internal Revenue Service.

RIA CITATOR, 202-204

RULINGS
See Internal Revenue Service.

SECRETARY OF THE TREASURY
See Treasury Regulations.

SECTION 6110
See Internal Revenue Service.

SECTION 6662 PENALTY
See Authority.

SEARCH ENGINES, 327-331

SEIDMAN'S LEGISLATIVE HISTORY OF FEDERAL INCOME AND EXCESS PROFITS TAX LAWS, 279-280

SEMIANNUAL AGENDA
See Treasury Regulations.

SENATE EXECUTIVE REPORTS
See Treaties.

SENATE MATERIALS
See Legislative History.

SERVICE CENTER ADVICE
See Internal Revenue Service.

SESSION LAWS
See Statutes.

SHEPARD'S CITATIONS, 198-202

SHEPARD'S FEDERAL TAX CITATOR, 198-202

SLIP LAWS
See Statutes.

SLIP OPINIONS
See Courts.

STANDARD FEDERAL TAX REPORTER (CCH), 221-227
Citator, 204-205

STATUTES, 36-60
See also Citators; Legislative History.

STRATEGIC ADVICE MEMORANDA
See Internal Revenue Service.

SUBDIVISIONS OF CODE
See Statutes.

SUBDIVISIONS OF REGULATIONS
See Treasury Regulations.

SUBSTANTIAL AUTHORITY
See Authority.

SUBTITLES OF CODE
See Statutes.

SUMMARY OPINIONS
See Courts.

SUNSET DATE
See Statutes; Treasury Regulations.

SUPREME COURT
See Courts.

SYLLABUS
See Citators.

TAX CONVENTIONS
See Treaties.

TAX COURT
See Courts.

TAX COURT MEMORANDUM
DECISIONS
See Courts.

TAX DAY (CCH), 264

TAX INSTITUTES
See Articles.

TAX LITIGATION
See Courts.

TAX LITIGATION BULLETINS
See Internal Revenue Service.

TAX MANAGEMENT MEMORANDUM,
233

TAX MANAGEMENT PORTFOLIOS, 233-
234

TAX MANAGEMENT PRIMARY
SOURCES, 274

TAX MANAGEMENT WEEKLY REPORT,
261-262

TAX NOTES, 263-264

TAX POLICY IN THE UNITED STATES,
247

TAX PRACTICE PLUS, 295-298

TAX RESEARCH NETWORK, 317-319

TAX RETURN INSTRUCTIONS
See Internal Revenue Service.

TAX SERVICES
See Looseleaf Services.

TAX TREATIES
See Treaties.

TAXBASE, 322

TAXCORE, 322

TAXEXPERT CD-ROM 299-300
Online, 320-321

TECHNICAL ADVICE MEMORANDA
See Internal Revenue Service.

TECHNICAL ASSISTANCE
See Internal Revenue Service.

TECHNICAL EXPEDITED ADVICE
MEMORANDA
See Internal Revenue Service.

TECHNICAL MEMORANDA
See Internal Revenue Service.

TEMPORARY REGULATIONS
See Treasury Regulations.

TITLE 26
See Statutes; Treasury Regulations.

TREASURY DECISIONS
See Treasury Regulations.

TREASURY DEPARTMENT
See Legislative History; Treasury
Regulations.

TREASURY/IRS BUSINESS PLAN
See Treasury Regulations.

TREASURY/IRS PRIORITY GUIDANCE
PLAN
See Treasury Regulations.

TREASURY REGULATIONS, 107-134

TREASURY TECHNICAL EXPLANATION
See Treaties.

TREATIES, 84-105

TREATISES, 238-239

TRIAL COURTS
See Courts.

UNCODIFIED PROVISIONS
See Statutes.

UNIFORM ISSUE LIST
See Internal Revenue Service.

UNITED NATIONS
See Treaties.

UNITED STATES CLAIMS COURT
See Courts.

UNITED STATES CODE
See Statutes.

UNITED STATES COURT OF CLAIMS
See Courts.

UNITED STATES COURT OF FEDERAL
CLAIMS
See Courts.

UNITED STATES DISTRICT COURTS
See Courts.

UNITED STATES INTERNAL REVENUE
SYSTEM, 49, 283

UNITED STATES REPORTS
See Courts.

UNITED STATES STATUTES AT LARGE
See Statutes.

UNITED STATES SUPREME COURT
See Courts.

UNITED STATES TAX CASES, 182-183

UNITED STATES TAX REPORTER, 227-
230

UNITED STATES TREATIES AND
OTHER INTERNATIONAL
AGREEMENTS
See Treaties.

UNPUBLISHED DECISIONS
See Courts.

UNPUBLISHED RULINGS
See International Revenue Service.

U.S. INTERNATIONAL TAXATION AND
TAX TREATIES, 98

VERSUSLAW, 314-316

WAYS AND MEANS COMMITTEE,
HOUSE
See Legislative History.

WEBSITES
See Online Legal Research.

WEEKLY ALERT, 228

WEEKLY COMPILATION OF
PRESIDENTIAL DOCUMENTS
See Legislative History; Statutes.

WEEKLY REPORT, 261-262

WESTLAW, 308-310

WEST'S FEDERAL PRACTICE DIGEST
4TH, 178

WG & L TAX JOURNAL DIGEST, 247-248

WILSONDISC, 243

WILSONWEB, 243

WTO, 101